WITHDRAWN

A M A S I A

Erserum

Arsingan

Ascor

Garga

Caisar

Gensui fl.

Tiagna

Malatiah

Majafaraquim

Adena

Nisis

Marasch

A S S Y R

Ainzarba

Samosat
Edessa

Sererak

Layazzo

Cola

Carahemit

M. Ia

Tarse

Alexandrete

Aleppo

Nisib

Giselet

CYPRUS I.

Basilo

Andeb

Orpha

Hochan

S. Andre

Seleucia

Galantza
Sirmin

Bir
Laffra

MESOPOTAMIA

Laodicea

Antiochia

Jabar

Orbs

Chala R.

C. del Græco

Gabala

Damand

Hanal

Racka

Famagusta

Tortosa

SYRIA

Suza

Sukian Seleby
Seccaz et Prelli

Taiba

Seleby
Deer

Sere

Tripoli

Assia

Errachaby Schara

Anfe
C. Laghie

Libanon

Carra

Elher

Ersy

Gebail

PHOENICIA

Carniola

Baruthi

Faid

Chaider

Sydon Bungi
Saphet

Damascus

A

Tyrus

Gi

Naphto

Atre of Acon

Menia

Cair

Reh

Altlit

Nasareth

Dor

Carmel M.

GALILEA

Tsamma

Caesarea

Samaria
Thabor

Jordaan R.

Sumiscasac

Argia

Joppen

CANAAN

Rama

Anatoth Bethel

Mare
Galilea

Lidda

Jerusalem

Scopus Ai
Samuel Jericho

Jabis

Mexat Ocem

Charebeda

Gaza

Cabrar

Sida

M. Abarrin
M. Nebo

Bethlehem

Mare
Mortuum

Busseret

Hebron

M. Seir

TERRA

Sogar

Zoara

Petra

A R A B I A

A

Tabuc

Acraa

Thaulabia

Tschad

Vytgevoerd te LEYDEN door PIETER VAN DER AA met Privilegie.

This map showing Rauwolf's itinerary in the Mesopotamian area
is found in the Dutch edition (1707) of his travels.

LEONHARD RAUWOLF

Harvard Monographs in the History of Science

LEONHARD

SIXTEENTH-CENTURY PHYSICIAN,

BOTANIST, AND TRAVELER

RAUWOLF

BY KARL H. DANNENFELDT

Harvard University Press: Cambridge, Massachusetts: 1968

PREFACE

In 1703 Charles Plumier, the French botanist of the Caribbean area, dedicated a genus of tropical plants to the Renaissance scientist and traveler, Leonhard Rauwolf. Fifty years later the nomenclature of the plant was firmly established by its inclusion in the great *Species plantarum* of Carl Linnaeus, although the genus was spelled *Rauvolfia* at that time. In 1755 what is apparently the first illustration of *Rauwolfia serpentina* (*Radix mustelae*) appeared in the *Auctuarium* of the *Herbarium Amboinense* of Georg Eberhardt Rumpf. The genus, spelled *Rauwolfia* today, is represented by indigenous species of nearly all the tropical lands of the world. The roots and leaves of *Rauwolfia* had been used for centuries in the Ayurvedic medicine of India, but it was only recently that the alkaloids of the *Rauwolfia* root were isolated and the drug introduced into clinical medicine for its calming and hypotensive effects. Today, *Rauwolfia* alkaloids have become a part of the therapy of most countries of the world, but Leonhard Rauwolf, the man honored by those who treat their mental disturbances or hypertensions with *Rauwolfia* alkaloids, is scarcely known.

In 1582 Rauwolf published a detailed account, in his own Swabian German dialect, of his travels and observations in the Near East. Aside from this description of three years of his life, very little biographical information is available. His name and contributions to botany are usually not found in works on Renaissance science or in histories of herbals and herbaria. Yet there are many reasons why this pioneer botanist deserves to be remembered and his contributions to science and to social and economic history noted. His travels in the Near East in the period from 1573 to 1575 form an excellent example of the difficulties, dangers, and hardships experienced in early scientific field trips, especially those carried out in lands not under European control. Seeking to find new plants and to verify those described by classical and medieval authors, Rauwolf was the first modern botanist to penetrate beyond the Levantine coastal areas. It was not until two centuries after his pioneering trip that other botanists identified and described more fully the plants of the regions he traversed.

With the publication of Rauwolf's book, verbal descriptions and some illustrations of the exotic flora of India, America, and western Asia were available to European scientists. Since the interest in plants was still largely medicinal, most of these botanical surveys were written by physicians. What is more unusual is the fact that the descriptions were all written in the vernacular rather than in Latin. The earliest work which contained much botanical information of America was *La historia general de las Indias* (Toledo, 1535), written by Gonzalo Fernandez de Oviedo y Valdes, a Spanish historian. A more detailed description of American flora was made by Nicolas Monardes (1493–1588), a learned Spanish physician. His *Cosas que se traen de las Indias Occidentales* was issued in three parts at Seville between 1565 and 1574. The earliest botanical work on the flora of India was the *Coloquios dos simples e drogas he cousas mediçinais da India,* which the Portuguese physician Garcia da Orta published in Goa in 1563, without illustrations. In 1578 Christoval Acosta, another Portuguese physician, published in Spanish his *Tractado de las drogas y medicinas de las Indias Orientales, con sus plantas debuxadas al bivo* at Burgos. While this work was largely drawn from that of Garcia da Orta, it is important for its forty-six illustrations of Indian plants. Latin abbreviations of the works of Monardes, da Orta, and Acosta were published by Carolus Clusius, and these epitomes were then retranslated into French and Italian.

Rauwolf preceded those travelers of the seventeenth century and after who wrote full accounts of the Near East, and his detailed descriptions of the peoples, places, and customs he observed have great value for the historian of civilization and culture. To be sure, his knowledge of geography was scanty, but, meager as it was, his descriptions of rivers, towns, and mountains were for the time an advance in information. He was at his best in recording the busy trade and the cosmopolitan atmosphere of the large trading centers. He was the first European to describe the preparation and drinking of coffee, the first modern European to travel the newly opened route from Baghdad to Mosul, and apparently even the first to describe in detail the routine of a Turkish bath. While contemporary accounts stressed life in the Turkish capital of Constantinople, Rauwolf described in detail the provincial capitals of Aleppo and Baghdad and the region along the Tigris and Euphrates rivers. He was also an early Protestant pilgrim in Jerusalem.

The personality of Rauwolf does not often emerge from the large accumulation of facts he objectively reported, but two personality traits are evident. One is an insatiable curiosity: a well-educated man's quest for further knowledge whether it be scientific or social and cultural. The other prominent characteristic is his firm religious belief, especially evident during his pilgrimage to Jerusalem. Besides these, several other things may be said of Rauwolf. He was a fearless traveler, who, without complaining, suffered much for the cause of science. He was an educated man of considerable learning, yet he was modest and respectful of others. He was an enlightened man of the Renaissance, yet still medieval in believing in unicorns and griffins.

While a new English translation of Rauwolf's lengthy travel book is needed, I decided to let the author speak for himself through paraphrase and quotation. Except for some obvious errors, little attempt was made to correct the information he conveys. It was hoped that there would thus be presented the observations and comments of a well-adjusted sixteenth-century scientist and traveler. When the account of Rauwolf gives little information, or when contrast is needed, accounts by contemporary or later travelers have been introduced. Modern spelling has been used for the identifiable cities and places named by Rauwolf. As Arabic terms have always varied in time and place, no attempt has been made to change his transliteration of Arabic words and plant names.

Much of the research for this book was made possible by a Grant in Aid-of-Research from the American Council of

Learned Societies (1962) and by a Faculty Research Grant from Arizona State University (1963). Much of Chapter X and a portion of Chapter XII have appeared in the *Archiv für Reformationsgeschichte,* 55 (1964), 18–36. I am grateful to Professor Jerry Stannard of the University of Kansas for valuable assistance in the identification of certain plants. Without the patience and understanding of my wife and daughters, this book could not have been written.

K.H.D.

CONTENTS

ILLUSTRATIONS

FOREWORD

The interest in the history of science is daily growing stronger. Concepts and ideas play such an important role in the models and strategies of every scientist that he must be familiar with the history of these concepts. Concomitantly, science has developed into such an integral component of virtually all human concerns that even the nonscientist has to become acquainted with its conceptual framework. That a study of the history of science and of scientific ideas is a good way to attain this objective has been stated so often that it no longer needs emphasis.

The first volume in this series was devoted to Chinese alchemy. This second volume describes the life and travels of a pioneer Renaissance botanist, Leonhard Rauwolf. As also virtually all other early botanists, up to the nineteenth century, Rauwolf was a physician by profession, and plants of medical significance were of special interest to him. Little did he dream that through a plant named for him (*Rauwolfiia*) his name should one day become a household word in modern medicine.

By chance, the first two volumes of this series deal with rather remote history. It is planned to deal in other volumes with the achievement of more recent scientists and with the growth of particular concepts or disciplines. Studies of the science of particular periods or regions will be welcome, and even annotated critical editions of texts. Such a series of volumes should prove of inestimable value to every student of the history of science.

Ernst Mayr

LEONHARD RAUWOLF

1 TRAVELERS IN THE LEVANT

Leonhard Rauwolf, the Augsburg physician whose life and travels are here described, is an important figure in the history of civilization and science because of his contribution to the information and scientific knowledge of the Near East that Europeans possessed in the late sixteenth century. His account of the social, economic, cultural, and scientific aspects of the areas in Syria, Palestine, and Mesopotamia that he visited between 1573 and 1575 is a small but valuable part of the tremendous expansion of the knowledge of non-European lands, peoples, and customs which occurred in the sixteenth century. Beginning with the voyages of Columbus and Vasco da Gama in the late fifteenth century, Europeans traveled farther and in far greater number than ever before. Many of those who traveled described the strange peoples and places they visited, and these books found ready acceptance from a public that was becoming increasingly literate. Mariners, military leaders, merchants, diplomats, and adventurers wrote relations, itineraries, and accounts of travels and voyages in the Americas, the Orient, and to a lesser degree, Africa.[1] Western Asia, including the area of the Ottoman Empire lying between the Mediterranean Sea and Persia—the region of special concern in this work on Rauwolf—was also traversed by a number of Europeans. Of this number, Rauwolf was the first European to describe in detail the cities, peoples, customs, and flora of Syria, Palestine, and Mesopotamia.

That Europeans in the sixteenth century should also travel in and describe the lands bordering the eastern Mediterranean was, of course, not an innovation. Throughout the Middle Ages, Christian pilgrims had gone to the Holy Land, often with a side trip to Egypt, to see and pray at the places associated with the Old and New Testament characters and events. Other thousands, often for reasons not so religious, had joined the various crusades to free the birthplace of Christianity from the Infidel. The travel books written by pilgrims on their return varied greatly in accuracy and coverage. Some, like that of Felix Fabri of Ulm, were exceptional in conveying information and the reactions of a European to the life and customs of the Near East. Others were mere lists of the holy places seen. While the pilgrim literature undoubtedly contributed to the interest in exploration so evident in the Renaissance, the expansion of the Ottoman Empire into Syria, Palestine, and Egypt in 1516–17, and the almost simultaneous Reformation of Luther led to a sharp decrease in the already declining number of pilgrims. This decrease in pilgrim traffic was somewhat offset, for our purposes, by the fact that a number of pilgrims during the Renaissance were humanists and well-educated observers, and some of them wrote reports of merit. Among the Renaissance humanists who visited Syria, Palestine, or Egypt were Petrarch, Cyriacus of Ancona, Sebastian Brandt, Johann von Lobkowitz, Peter Martyr, Johannes Dantiscus, Sebastianus a Rotenhan, Peter Falk, Matthieu Beroaldus, Pierre du Chastel, and Guillaume Postel.

Since the number of pilgrims in the sixteenth century was small, special pilgrim ships were a thing of the past. The pilgrims who did go to the Holy Land went on the commercial ships now readily available because of the trade between Europe and the Near East. Only eight years after the fall of Acre (1291) and the loss of the Syrian ports, Venice made a monopolistic and profitable treaty with the Mameluke rulers of the Levant. The trade in spices and luxury items, brought overland from India and China or produced locally, was considerable. This led to the development of regular systems of shipping in the Mediterranean and to systems of credit and banking to meet the needs of the overseas trade. Commerce with the Syrian ports and with Alexandria also became more competitive, although Venice was to maintain her supremacy until late in the sixteenth century. Besides the Italian cities, the French city of Marseilles entered into the eastern trade in the fifteenth century, especially under the stimulus of the enterprising Jacques Coeur. All of these trading cities and nations established their *fondacos,* or warehouses, at the Syrian centers of Aleppo, Damascus, and Tripoli.

After the discovery of the all-water route to India and the Far East, various European nations sought to find ways to supplant the Moslem middlemen of Syria and to establish direct overland trade contacts with Persia and India. Generally this called for exploration of the Mesopotamian area and the use of river and caravan routes for the movement of trade items. While this was the shortest route to India, it was hazardous and complicated by the various modes of transportation that were required.[2] The first traveler to explore the Mesopotamian route was a Portuguese named Antonio Tenreiro (1528).[3] Very few of his countrymen duplicated his trip until the observant Pedro Teixeira took the land route from Basra to Aleppo in 1604. Teixeira's *Relaciones* is so detailed that it has been used in this work as a supplement to the descriptions of Rauwolf, although the observations of the Portuguese traveler were made over a quarter of a century later.

Although the French were very active in the Syrian trade, few Frenchmen penetrated beyond Aleppo in the sixteenth century or wrote about the land and its peoples.[4] Italian travelers in Syria and Mesopotamia were more numerous, and some of these left valuable accounts of their journeys. As early as 1419, Nicolo Conti left Venice for a journey that was to last until 1444. On his way to India he stayed at Damascus long enough to learn Arabic, and then crossed the desert to Baghdad and from there descended the Tigris to Basra. More pertinent as a supplement to Rauwolf's account are the reports made by the Venetian merchants Cesare Federici and Gasparo Balbi. Both of these traveled through Tripoli, Aleppo, and Bir, and then floated down the Euphrates to visit Baghdad and Basra on their way to India and Burma. Since the trip of Federici (1563) was only ten years before and that of Balbi (1579) only five years after that of Rauwolf, the accounts of these observant Venetians are important supplements to Rauwolf's narrative. Richard Hakluyt considered the descriptions of Federici so important for English traders with the same interests that it was printed in 1588 in the translation of Thomas Hickocke.[5]

In the sixteenth century, England, too, saw the economic possibilities of the Levantine trade, especially for the sale of English cloth. In 1553 Sultan Suleiman the Magnificent granted the English merchant Anthony Jenkinson privileges of trade, and in 1580 William Harborne was able to obtain trade privileges for all Englishmen from Sultan Murad III.[6] Soon after, English factors were located in the principal Levantine trading centers, including Tripoli and Aleppo in Syria. From these outposts, English merchants explored the Mesopotamian route to India and beyond. Rauwolf had already been back in Augsburg for five years when John Newberry, the first Englishman to travel in Mesopotamia, left Aleppo in 1581 to go to Baghdad and Basra on his way to Ormuz, the Portuguese station in the Persian Gulf. When he returned to England after traveling through Persia and Constantinople, he organized a group of adventurers, and in 1583 Newberry, John Eldred, William Shales, Ralph Fitch, William Leeds, and John Story traveled down the Euphrates and reached Baghdad and then Basra. Eldred and Shales remained there to trade while Newberry and the others went to Ormuz, where they were imprisoned at the instigation of the Venetian merchants. Sent to Goa, India, for trial, they were released on bail but, with the exception of Story, they then fled into the interior. Newberry died somewhere in Asia, but Fitch eventually returned to England along the Mesopotamian route. The accounts of Newberry, Eldred, and Fitch give us the reactions of Englishmen to the Syrian and Mesopotamian areas within the decade after Rauwolf's passage through the area.[7]

The accounts of pilgrims and merchants who traveled in the Near East informed a curious Europe of many new things, but much more accurate and more lasting in value were the reports of the scientists who sought scientific knowledge in the Levant area. The scientific writings of the ancient classical authors, readily available in manuscript and in books printed in Greek, Latin, and the vernacular, excited the interest of Renaissance scholars in the lands, peoples, plants, and animals of the Near East. In the works of Aristotle, Theophrastus, Dioscorides, Aelian, Pliny, and others they found descriptions of eastern flora and fauna that called for verification and identification. This, together with the growing awareness of the difference between these and the European varieties and the attempts at classification and comparison, produced a new kind of scholar, the traveling scientist. Looking at the natural and social world of the Near East from trained scientific and scholarly viewpoints, these travelers presented accounts that far surpassed the usual pilgrim and merchant literature. Their works also made clear the spirit of adventure, the dangers, hardships, personal losses, and the difficulties of financing that were a part of such early scientific and scholarly expeditions. While some of the scientists whose travels and works are described in the following paragraphs were not botanists or did not do their investigations in the area of Syria, Palestine, and Mesopotamia as Rauwolf did, they are included here as indicative of the growing scientific interest in the Levantine countries.

Perhaps the first of the scientific books of the Renaissance to show the influence of travel in the Near East was the well-illustrated German herbal, *Gart der Gesundheit,* first printed by Peter Schoeffer in Mainz in March, 1485. Just who was the compiler and who the artist involved in this fine folio volume is a matter of dispute.[8] It may have been the printer himself who was responsible, while Erhard Rewich of Utrecht did the drawings for 65 of the 379 woodcuts (368 of plants and 11 of animals). The role of Johann von Cube, who is mentioned in the text, is unknown. As town physician of Frankfurt am Main, he may have prepared the medical sections of the book. Whoever the compiler and artist may have been, the introduction to the *Gart der Gesundheit* is important because it shows clearly both the older religious motivation and the new scientific purpose for travel in the Levant area.

Since, then, man can have no greater nor nobler treasure on earth than bodily health, I came to the conclusion that I could not perform any more honourable, useful or holy work or labour than to compile a book in which should be contained the virtue and nature of many herbs and other created things, together with their true colours and form, for the help of all the world and the common good. Thereupon I caused this praiseworthy work to be begun by a Master learned in physic, who, at my request, gathered into a book the virtue and nature of many herbs out of the acknowledged masters of physic, Galen, Avicenna, Serapio, Dioscorides, Pandectarius, Platearius and others. But when, in the process of the work, I turned to the drawing and depicting of the herbs, I marked that there are many precious herbs which do not grow here in these German lands, so that I could not draw them with their true colours and form, except from hearsay. Therefore I left unfinished the work which I had begun, and laid aside my pen, until such time as I had received grace and dispensation to visit the Holy Sepulchre, and also Mount Sinai . . . Then in order that the noble work I had begun and left incomplete should not come to nought, and also that my journey should benefit not my soul alone, but the whole world, I took with me a painter ready of wit, and cunning and subtle of hand. And so we journeyed from Germany through Italy . . . Candia, Rhodes and Cyprus to the Promised Land and the Holy City, Jerusalem, and thence through Arabia Minor to Mount Sinai, from Mount Sinai towards the Red Sea in the direction of Cairo, Babylonia, and also Alexandria in Egypt, whence I returned to Candia. In wandering through these kingdoms and lands, I diligently sought after the herbs there, and had them depicted and drawn, with their true colour and form.[9]

Unfortunately, the original promise as outlined above was not kept. Although the botanical figures were not to be surpassed until the drawings of Hans Weiditz were included in the *Herbarum vivae eicones* of Otto Brunfels (Strassburg, 1530), most of the llustrations of the *Gart der Gesundheit* were taken from the traditional manuscripts. As has been pointed out, "The figures of plants from Egypt, Syria, and the Levant are disappointingly few in number and poor in quality; with the possible exception of those of senna and ginger, they show no sign of having been made from nature." [10] If Rewich is considered the artist of these botanical pictures, he did better in the drawings he made to illustrate the *Peregrinatio in Terram Sanctam* of Bernard of Breydenbach, a canon of Mainz, which was printed in Mainz in 1486. The woodcuts of this printed travel book, the first to be illustrated, are of historical and scientific interest. They include drawings of cities, Greek and oriental alphabets, Syrians, Saracens, tombs, and animals, including the first known drawing of a giraffe (*seraffa*) made from life.[11]

The interest of Francis I (1515–47) of France in the Turks and the Near East furnished the next occasion for a scientific field trip to the Levantine countries. In December, 1546, a royal embassy under the direction of Gabriel de Luetz, Baron d'Aramon, left France for Constantinople to secure the support and alliance of Suleiman the Magnificent (1520–66) in the wars against Emperor Charles V. The Turkish ruler was hesitant, however, especially after he heard of the death of Francis I. Suleiman decided upon a Persian campaign instead, and d'Aramon was ordered by his government to accompany the Sultan into Persia in March, 1548. While the Turks were in winter quarters later that year, the ambassador extended his travels into Egypt and the Holy Land. He returned to Constantinople in January, 1550, and was back in France a year later.[12]

As Cardinal François de Tournon had proposed that the mission should be concerned with scientific and literary information as well as political matters, a naturalist, Pierre Belon of Mans, and an ichthyologist and humanist, Pierre Gilles of Albi, were attached to the original embassy. Pierre Belon (1517–64) early showed an interest in plants and animals.[13] He studied at Wittenberg and later made an extensive scientific tour of northeastern Germany and of Bohemia in the company of Valerius Cordus, the botanist and humanist, and some students. In 1542 he entered the service of the Cardinal de Tournon, for whom he went on missions to Germany and Switzerland. Later he again joined Cordus who was exploring Provence and Italy. On the death of his friend in Rome in September, 1544, Belon returned to France. He then came to the attention of Francis I who was planning the embassy of d'Aramon.

Belon was at the time planning translations of Theophrastus and Dioscorides into French and was experiencing difficulties in the proper identification of plants and animals mentioned by the Greek scientists. A trip to the East was thus highly desirable, and a gift of money from the Cardinal de Tournon made it possible to attach the naturalist to d'Aramon's embassy. Belon acknowledged his debt to the cardinal in these terms: "After you became acquainted with the desire which I had to gain a knowledge of the things concerning medical matters and plants (which I cannot readily acquire except by wandering to far-away places), it was your pleasure to ask me to go and see them in the distant regions, and to look for them as far away as the places of their origin, something which I had not been able, nor had I dared undertake without your aid, knowing that the difficulty would have been in the charges and expenses."[14]

Belon left the diplomatic mission at Ragusa in March, 1547, but later spent three months exploring and collecting in Constantinople and the Aegean region. He then joined the embassy of Baron de Fumel, an envoy sent to the Turks by the new French monarch, Henry II, on an expedition to Egypt. At Cairo he found several Frenchmen, including the scholar Juste Tenelle who had been sent to the Levant by Francis I to search for Greek manuscripts. From Egypt his travels took him to Sinai, the Holy Land, and Syria, where he rejoined d'Aramon, now with the Persian expedition of Suleiman. Finally he returned overland to Constantinople and was back in France in 1549. Unfortunately, most of the treasured objects he collected had been sent toward France in another ship only to be lost when seized by Moslem corsairs. In France, under the patronage of Cardinal de Tournon, Henry II, and Charles IX, Belon continued his travels and research in Europe until murdered at the age of forty-seven in April, 1564.

Belon's expeditions and research furnished him with material for a number of books, written in the vernacular and in Latin. The first dealt with fishes and was entitled, *L'histoire naturelle des estranges poissons marin avec la vraie peincture et description du Dauphin* (Paris, 1551). Two years later appeared the very popular account of his travels in the East, *Les observations de plusieurs singularitez et choses mémorables trouvées en Grèce, Asie, Judée, Egypte, Arabie et autres pays estranges, rédigées in trois livres* (Paris, 1553).[15] Dedicated to his patron, the Cardinal de Tournon, this work dealt with the history, geography, ethnography, medicine, flora and fauna, ancient and contemporary cities, the antiquities, and the customs and costumes which he observed in the countries he visited. It was illustrated with pictures of native inhabitants, plants, and animals.

Two other works by Belon resulted from his travels in the East. The first of these, *De amirabili operum antiquorum et rerum suspiciendum praestantia* (Paris, 1553), dealt with antiquities, including the Egyptian pyramids, obelisks, tombs, methods of embalming the dead practiced in the ancient Near

East, and the preservatives used.[16] The second work, *Portraits d'oyseaux, animaux, serpens, herbes, arbres, hommes et femmes d'Arabie et d'Egypte* (Paris, 1557), contains descriptions and 217 woodcuts (174 of birds) of the life and vegetation of the areas at the southeastern end of the Mediterranean Sea. It was not until two and one-half centuries later that a similar illustrated ornithological study of the area was made by M. J. C. L. de Savigny in his *Système des oiseaux de l'Egypte et de la Syrie* (Paris, 1810).[17]

While Belon's trip through the Near East preceded Rauwolf's by 25 years, his botanical observations in the area of Syria and Palestine are limited to the major trees and shrubs. In many ways he was the pioneer botanist of these areas, but Kurt Sprengel, the historian of botany, listed no plants of this area as being newly identified by Belon, while 33 new discoveries are credited to Rauwolf.[18] Another botanical historian pointed out that Belon gave "the names of 275 plants of the Orient, but he did not give any descriptions and he did not bring back any seeds from his trip." [19] Some comparison can be gained from the fact that Belon wrote seven pages on Aleppo while Rauwolf described the city and the plants of the region in 66 pages.

Another scholar, Pierre Gilles (Petrus Gillius), was attached to the embassy of d'Aramon in 1546. Gilles was born in Albi (Languedoc) in 1489.[20] Educated as a humanist, his study of Aristotle and other ancient scientists led him to research in the natural sciences and especially in zoology. His chief interest was in ichthyology and he observed minutely the fishes of the Mediterranean Sea and the Adriatic.[21] Gilles obtained the patronage of Georges d'Armagnac, the Bishop of Rodez, and published his first scientific treatise in 1533 at Lyons. This work, *De vi et natura animalum,* was largely composed of Latin translations from Ailianos (Aelian), the Greek naturalist of the third century, and from other Greek authors.[22] In the dedication to Francis I, Gilles points out the honor that would accrue to the king if he would commission scholars to go to the strange lands of the East and obtain accurate descriptions of the curiosities of ancient civilizations described by classical authors. Francis I thereupon was persuaded to commission Gilles to visit all the countries under Turkish control and to collect Greek manuscripts and antiquities. In 1546 he thus became a member of the staff of d'Aramon bound for Constantinople.

Once in Asia Minor, however, Gilles seems to have temporarily lost his position, and having exhausted his funds, he was forced to become a soldier in the army of the sultan, then engaged in the Persian war. In the disorderly passage of the Turkish army through a defile near Bithlis, Gilles lost all his baggage and the books and papers he had already collected. From Tabriz, which Suleiman had taken, he returned to Syria. In one of his letters to his patron, now Cardinal d'Armagnac in Rome, he describes his travels from Constantinople to Tabriz and thence to Aleppo (Beroia) in Syria. The main subject of this letter from Aleppo is his detailed description of a dissection of a young elephant which had died in that city while enroute to Henry II of France as a gift from d'Aramon.[23]

Rejoining the embassy of d'Aramon, Gilles accompanied the ambassador to Damascus, Jerusalem, Cairo, and Alexandria (July to September, 1549). He observed the fishes of the Red Sea and discovered the dugong, the mythical mermaid. Taken prisoner by pirates, Gilles was ransomed by d'Armagnac. From Alexandria he wrote d'Armagnac that he was sending the skins of an elephant and hippopotamus, the skin of a giraffe, the tail of a *bos indicus,* an ichneumon, and locked cages of Arabian and Egyptian rats; all of the objects and animals having been directed by him to traders in Marseilles who were charged with transporting them to France.[24] By the end of January, 1550, he was back in Constantinople, having traveled overland through Jerusalem, Damascus, Tripoli, Antioch, and Nicea. After exploring the ruins at Constantinople and at Chalcedon in Bythinia, he returned to France and then rejoined his patron, Cardinal d'Armagnac, at Rome, where he died in 1555.[25]

The cosmographer and secularized Cordelier, Andre Thévet (1503/04-92) also went to the East in 1549 on money furnished by Cardinal de Lorraine à Plaisance.[26] Arriving at Constantinople from Crete on November 30, he explored the environs there and at Chalcedon in the company of Pierre Gilles. Late in 1550 he traveled through Rhodes to Alexandria where he passed the winter. In the spring of 1551 he left Egypt, visiting Arabia, Palestine, and Syria before returning to France from Tripoli. The

Holy Land, especially, he observed in great detail. In 1554 at Lyons appeared his *Cosmographie de Levant,* a useful work but marked with excessive credulity. A second edition, revised and augmented with many pictures was published at Lyons and Antwerp in 1556. After his return from Brazil in 1556, Thévet published in two volumes his *Cosmographie universelle* (Paris, 1575). Volume I of this work, containing Chapters I–XII and a number of pictures, deals with Africa and Asia, including the Levant.

A German naturalist who visited the Near East was the Prussian physician, Melchior Guilandinus (Wieland) of Koenigsberg.[27] Interested in the therapeutic qualities of plants, Guilandinus traveled to Rome and Venice where Senator Marin Caballo, one of the directors of the University of Padua, became his patron. Caballo financed a trip to Asia and Africa, including Egypt. Later, wishing to go to America to continue his plant research, Guilandinus sailed for Lisbon but was captured and enslaved by Algerian pirates. When ransomed by Gabriele Fallopio, the famous Paduan anatomist, he returned to Italy in 1561 and became a professor of botany. In 1563, Guilandinus succeeded his rescuer as director of the botanical gardens at Padua, where he died at an advanced age in 1589 of too violent a purgative. His library was given to the republic of Venice.

During his lifetime Guilandinus engaged in extensive correspondence and argumentation. Part of his *De stirpibus aliquot, epistolae V.* (Padua, 1558) contains correspondence with Conrad Gesner, the Swiss naturalist, on some obscure Greek and Arabian plant names. For our purposes the most interesting work is his *Papyrus, hoc est commentarius in tria C. Plinij majoris de papyro capita* (Venice, 1572; Lausanne, 1576; Amberg, 1613). In this commentary of the three chapters of Pliny dealing with the Egyptian papyrus Guilandinus enumerated the usages of papyrus, but did not even describe the plant which he saw in Egypt.[28]

Late in the sixteenth century, Prospero Alpino de Maròstico (1553–1617), the Italian physician and botanist, carried on unique and thorough studies in Egypt. He received his medical degree from the University of Padua in 1578 and two years later accompanied the Venetian consul, Giorgio Emo, to Egypt, arriving in Cairo on July 7, 1581. Here he remained until November, 1584, availing himself of a wonderful opportunity to study carefully and at firsthand the civilization of this famed land. He was primarily interested in the medical properties of native plants, and devoted his three years of residence in Egypt to studying and collecting them. He was probably the first European to see and describe the coffee plant, which he saw growing in the garden of a bey in Cairo. Another plant to receive his attention was the balsam-producing tree. On his return to Europe, he was attached as a physician to the Spanish fleet. Later named a professor of botany at the University of Padua, Alpino may have enriched the garden of that city with plants brought from Egypt.[29]

His long stay in Egypt and his studies there resulted in a number of works which were important for their accuracy and details. The first two were *De balsamo dialogus* (Venice, 1591; Patavi, 1640) and *De medicina Aegyptiorum libri IV* (Venice, 1591; Paris, 1646), both in dialogue form. Next he published his monumental *De plantis Aegypti* (Venice, 1592).[30] This work, in the form of a dialogue with Melchior Guilandinus, contains 43 chapters and 49 woodcuts of plants and fruit. Chapter XVI is entitled "De Bon" and describes the plant "illique ipsum vocant Caòua" or coffee (fol. 26r). Alpino mentions in Chapter VII the hand-fertilization of the date palm which he observed. After his death, his son, also a physician at Padua, published *De plantis exoticis libri duo* (Venice, 1627 and 1656) from his father's manuscripts. Finally, over a century after his death, Bartholomaeus Cellari edited some of Alpino's manuscripts under the title, *Rerum Aegyptiarum libri quatuor*. This extensive survey of the antiquities, plants, and animals of Egypt, including many woodcuts, appeared with other of Alpino's works as the *Historiae Aegypti naturalis* (Leyden, 1735).

The travels and literary activities of these scientists are important aspects of the intellectual history of Europe. Their publications, often in numerous editions, added considerable information, in general quite accurate, to serve as a basis for scientific classification and comparison. The clarification of the ancient scientific works was begun. None of these European scientists, however, traveled in the Mesopotamian area. Nor did any describe as many plants of western Asia or collect as large an herbarium of dried specimens as did Rauwolf.

II EARLY LIFE

Very little is known of Leonhard Rauwolf's early life. Even the date of his birth is uncertain, but judging from the known facts of his later life, he was born between 1535 and 1540 in Augsburg, Bavaria.[1] This south German city was an industrial, trading, and banking center, and it is quite possible that his parents were of the merchant class. J. F. Gronovius said he was born *parentibus honestis*.[2] The inhabitants of Augsburg had early accepted Lutheranism, and the city had been the scene of the historic Diet of 1530 at which the Augsburg Confession had been presented. About the time of Rauwolf's birth the city magistrates had joined (1537) the Schmalkaldic League in defense of their Lutheran faith. Since Rauwolf gave continuing evidence of his own Lutheranism throughout his life, his parents must have raised him well in the new dogmas.

After his secondary education had been completed at Augsburg, the young Rauwolf was ready to continue his education at the university level with the intention of becoming a physician. In the dedication to his travel book, Rauwolf stated, without elaboration, that on the advice of his parents and with the consent of his brothers and sisters he went to those German, French, and Italian universities "where the study of medicine was especially strong" and where he could find the plants that were so necessary to a medical education.[3] No record of attendance at an Italian university has been found, but on November 6, 1556, "Leonhardus Rawwolff Augustanus" (Augsburg) registered in the matriculation book of the University of Wittenberg.[4]

The choice was a natural one in view of his religious beliefs, but other physicians who later became famous botanists had also received training at the Lutheran university. Valerius Cordus (1515–44) studied medicine at Wittenberg and stayed on to lecture on Dioscorides and conduct botanical field trips with students; he died at Rome, during one of these trips. Pierre Belon was one of his pupils.[5] Carolus Clusius, later Rauwolf's friend, studied law at Wittenberg (1549–50) before he went to Montpellier.[6] Caspar Ratzenberg, the compiler of a large herbarium, matriculated at Wittenberg on April 24, 1548, and entered Montpellier on November 3, 1560, a few weeks after Rauwolf.[7] When Rauwolf matriculated at Wittenberg in 1556, Paul Eber was the instructor in the sciences, including botany, but shortly thereafter, on the death of Johann Forster, he went fully into theology. The medical faculty at the time consisted of Jakob Milich and Melchior Fendt, but in 1554 Johann Hermann, with his M.D. degree from Bologna, joined the staff and taught medical subjects, including the botanical authors.[8]

In the fall of 1560, Rauwolf entered the medical school at the renowned University of Montpellier in southern France. This choice of schools was excellent, for the medical school of Montpellier was not only venerable but certainly one of the best.[9] Like so many others, the origin of this school is obscure, but medical studies at Montpellier were already important by the middle of the twelfth century. The school may have been an offshoot of the ancient University of Salerno, which it emulated in character and prestige. At Montpellier the influence of Arabic and Jewish medicine and learning became important very early. The first reference to a *universitas medicorum* is in the statutes of 1220. Unlike some universities which were ruled by the students, the University of Montpellier was directed by the masters. In later centuries the students were admitted to limited rights, one of which was the interesting practice of consultation with the doctors on what lectures should be given. In the thirteenth century ecclesiastical control was extended over examining, licensing, and criminal cases involving students or masters. In 1340 the statutes of the university required that the candidate for the baccalaureate, which included the right to give cursory lectures, have completed twenty-four months of actual attendance or about three and one-half years of study. The senior students were also required to use the summer months in practice away from Montpellier. This learning device was also used during the school year when the senior students, accompanied by their own doctors on the staff, visited and practiced medicine on the sick of the city. The coveted doctor's degree was awarded only after five years of study, if the successful candidate already held the master of arts.

From the twelfth century to the middle of the fourteenth, the University of Montpellier was one of the greatest in Europe. Many of its teachers and graduates were justly famous: Gilbert the Englishman, Bernard Gordon, Peter of Spain, Henri de Mondeville, and the great but alchemistic Arnald of Villanova (ca. 1235–1311). Early in the fourteenth century Francesco Petrarca studied law for four years at Montpellier, but after the middle of that century a decline set in, with the school of law especially suffering in reputation and number of students.

In 1340, while the University of Montpellier was still one of the leading universities of Europe, the medical books which were always to be "read" or lectured upon were listed as follows:

1. The first book of Avicenna's *Canon*.

2. Galen's *Liber de morbo et accidenti* and his *De differentiis febrium*.

3. Galen's *Liber de crisi et criticis diebus* and *De malicia complexionis diverse*.

4. Galen's *Liber de simplicibus medicinis* and his *De complexionibus*.

5. Galen's *Liber de iuvamentis membrorum* and his *De interioribus*.

6. Hippocrates's *Liber Amphorismi* with either his *De regimine acutorum* or his *De prognosticis*.

7. Galen's *Liber de ingenio sanitatis* and his *Ad Glauconem*.

8. The first two sections of the fourth book of Avicenna's *Canon* alone or together with Johannitius, *De pulsibus* and the *De Urinis* of Theophilus.

9. Galen's *Tegni* with the *De prognosticis* and *De regimine acutorum* of Hippocrates.

10. Bartholomew the Englishman's *Liber de regimine sanitatis* and his *De virtutibus naturalibus*.

Each of these listings constituted a course, and if there were doctors available, additional lectures could be given on other parts of

Avicenna's *Canon,* on other books of Galen, or on the *De febribus* and the *De dietis universalibus* of Isaac Judaeus. As is readily seen, the main curriculum was heavily Galenic or Pseudo-Galenic in character, but works of Arab and Jewish doctors in Latin translation were included.[10]

The Renaissance was a period of revived activity in the schools of medicine, theology, and arts at the University of Montpellier. In medicine the revival was stimulated by the endowments for instructional salaries given by kings Charles VII (1483–98) and Louis XII (1498–1515). A more important factor was the stimulating leadership of Guillaume Pellicier (1490–1568), the tolerant and learned bishop of Montpellier. As ambassador to Venice for Francis I in 1540–42, the bishop collected so many Greek, Syriac, and Hebrew manuscripts that his admirable library contained 1,104 Greek manuscripts bound in over two hundred volumes at a time when the library of the king of France held only four hundred volumes. The bishop was distinguished both as a *littérateur* and a naturalist. In the preface of his work, *Libri de piscibus marinis,* Guillaume Rondelet praised the bishop for his collaboration and for his knowledge of fish, plants, and many other things.[11] The administration of this scholarly bishop brought to the university a brilliant array of teachers of medicine, and these in turn attracted many students of various lands and faiths.

In Book III, Chapter 34, of his famous *Gargantua and Pantagruel,* François Rabelais, who received his bachelor's degree in 1530 and his doctor's degree at Montpellier in 1537, named as his "antiques amis" Antoine Saporta, Guy Bonguier, Balthasar Noyer, Tollet, Jean Quentin, François Robinet, and Jean Perdier. The "Rondibilis" of the same book is considered to be the great naturalist Rondelet who taught at Montpellier from 1551 to 1566.[12] In 1537 Rabelais himself strengthened the Greek tradition in medicine at Montpellier by giving a course of lectures upon Hippocrates's *De prognosticis* from the original Greek.[13] It was the presence of those just named and others like Jean Schyron, Jean Bocaud, Denis Fontanon, Jean Faucon, Gilbert Griffi, and Honoré De Chastel that attracted students to Montpellier from many lands. Among the almost 4,000 medical students who attended the medical school in the sixteenth century were such outstanding physicians as Alban Thorer (Torinus), Michel Nostradamus, Jean Huber, Symphorien Champier, Gabriel Miron, François Miron, Jean Chapellain, Jacques Dubois, Caspar Wolf, Georges Blandrata, Jean Bauhin, Pierre Pena, Auger Ferrier, Jean Maziles, Jacques Dalechamps, Charles de l'Ecluse (Clusius), Felix Platter, and Matthias Lobelius.[14]

In order that the serious and difficult study of medicine might be better pursued, the entering students were examined to ensure their sufficient knowledge of the liberal arts—grammar, logic, rhetoric, physics, mathematics, and metaphysics.[15] Apparently Rauwolf had been adequately prepared at the University of Wittenberg, for within the required seven days of his arrival and according to the regulations of the University of Medicine, he paid the matriculation fee of three *livres*, ten *sous*.[16] On October 22, 1560 he signed the register as "Leonhartus Rauwolff Augustanus." [17] Actually, in his excitement he signed the date as "November 22," but since the signatures of those before and after his are dated in October, it must have been the earlier month. Rauwolf was one of 54 students who matriculated during the year 1560 and like 21 of these he chose as his chief adviser the dean, Antoine Saporta. Eight yeaars before, Felix Platter had chosen this same friend of Rabelais' "as it was customary that each student choose one from whom he could seek advice." [18] Antoine Saporta was the son of the well-known physician Louis Saporta who had taught at Montpellier from 1506 to 1529.[19] Originally from Lerida, Spain, the Saportas were a distinguished family of Jewish descent who had fled the persecutions in that country. Antoine Saporta received his doctor's degree at Montpellier in 1532, became a professor there in 1540, and in 1551 was named dean. This last position he kept until 1566 when he was chosen chancellor on the death of Rondelet. He died in 1573. His work, *De tumoribus praeter naturam,* was published at Lyons in 1624.[20]

Like all new students, at the time of his matriculation Rauwolf took the following oath:

I, N., swear that I will serve the honor and usefullness of the University of Medicine at Montpellier, and not knowingly go against the laws, either directly nor indirectly; I will help it by advice, assistance, and favor, here and anywhere on earth, and also to whatever station of dignity I shall be able to attain. I also swear that I will be faithful and obedient to the said university, to any one of the teachers. I will honor properly any one of them, and, if I know anything against the honor of anyone, I shall inform the same without delay. Also I swear, that I will not practice in Montpellier, nor in the vicinity, nor permit others to practice; at any rate I shall reveal him to the head procurators of the university, or any of the directors, while and as long as in Montpellier, and not elsewhere, I shall be serving as an officer and I will observe each and all privilege and statute, published and unpublished, and this through my good faith.[21]

The regulations of the University of Medicine, dated October 31, 1550 and under which Rauwolf was a student, prescribed that the chancellor, dean, doctors, and counselors should meet on the Feast of St. Luke (October 18) and decide which books and subject matter should be read and interpreted by the doctors in the coming school year. In the assignments due regard was to be taken of the ability of the various instructors, of the difficulty of the subject matter, and of which courses would be of greatest profit to the students. The theoretical books were to be given to the younger members of the staff while the older and more experienced doctors taught the more practical matters. The authors approved in 1550 were Hippocrates, Galen, Avicenna, Mesue, Rhazes, Paul of Aegina, and Dioscorides.[22] Of the works by these approved authors, some of which Rauwolf must have read and heard interpreted, the statutes of December 16, 1534 list the following:

Hippocrates: *De prognosticis* and the *Liber Amphorismi.*

Galen: *Tegni; De regimine acutorum; Liber de morbo et accidente; De differentiis febrium; De interioribus; De ingenio sanitatis; De alimentis et elementis; De spermate; De malicia complexionis diverse; De juvamentis membrorum;* and *De utilitate particularum.*

Avicenna: The first four books of the *Canon,* the *De viribus cordis,* the *Antidotarium,* and the *Cantica.*

Mesue: *Canones universales.*

Rhazes: *Nonus liber ad Almansorem.*

The statutes of 1534 also limited the medical student to courses on medical subjects, for no lectures on books of grammar, logic, or natural sciences, except the *De animalibus* of Aristotle, were permitted.[23] For Rauwolf's later purposes, it was very fortunate that Avicenna and Rhazes were on the list and that Dioscorides's *De materia medica* was also taught. In his travels in the Near East these authors proved very valuable for plant identification. Four years after Rauwolf's departure from Montpellier, the Arabic authors were stricken from the approved list at the request of the students (1567), and the Greek tradition was firmly established at the medical school.[24]

It is difficult to determine what use Rauwolf made later in his medical practice of the courses and readings acquired during his educational career. However, some idea of the range of his reading is indicated by the classical and Arabic authors he used in his botanical field trip to the Near East in 1573–76. These authors are historians, geographers, philosophers, and physicians who wrote on botany and biology as related to medicine.

The author most frequently cited by Rauwolf in his travel book is Dioscorides Pedacius of Anazarba, Cilicia. Rauwolf had learned his Dioscorides well under Rondelet's tutelage and he cited this author 43 times. Of the 42 plants depicted in the 1583 edition of Rauwolf's book, 13 are identified as Dioscoridean. The name of this Greek physician-botanist of the first century A.D. and that of his *materia medica* were synonymous with botany, for in his work he described 600 plants and their medicinal uses. After a continuous medieval Latin and Arabic manuscript tradition, printed editions in Latin, Greek, Italian, German, French, Bohemian, and Spanish were available by the middle of the sixteenth century.[25] Many of these editions of Dioscorides were illustrated with woodcuts of plants. An iconographic tradition had long been associated with the text of Dioscorides and some of the illustrations of this tradition date back to Cratevas, a Greek botanist of the first century B.C. About 1560, Ogier Ghiselin de Busbecq, a Flemish diplomat in the service of the Hapsburgs, was able to obtain at Constantinople for Emperor Ferdinand a magnificent copy of Dioscorides, written and illustrated in 512 A.D. for the imperial princess Anicia Iuliana.

The interest in Dioscorides in the sixteenth century was widespread, as the many editions and commentaries indicate. However, the most influential Renaissance editor and commentator on Dioscorides was Pier' Andrea Mattioli. This eminent Italian physician and botanist was born in Siena in 1500. His father was a physician in Venice, and Mattioli also studied medicine, receiving his degree from Padova in 1523. He practiced at Siena, Perugia, Rome (to 1527), Trient, and Gorita (now Görz). His great commentary on Dioscorides, published first in Italian, was entitled *Dioscoride libri cinque della historia et materia medicinale tradotti in lingua volgare italiana* (Venice, 1544). Later editions appeared in Venice in 1548, 1549, 1550, 1551, 1559, 1568, 1573, 1581, etc. The Latin edition, *Commentarii in libros sex Dioscoridis de materia medica,* appeared in Venice in 1544 with at least eight more editions in the next thirty years. The commentaries made Mattioli famous and he was appointed physician to the emperors Ferdinand I and Maximilian II at Vienna and Prague. He died of the plague at Trient in 1577.[26] The genus *Matthiola* was named in his honor. Rauwolf used the commentary of Mattioli, probably in the Latin edition, and named the author six times. He called Mattioli "very learned" and, in reference to Bohemian olive trees, noted that they could be found "very naturally sketched in the herbal of the very learned Mattioli." [27]

Another classical author whose works were very useful to Rauwolf was Theophrastus of Eresos (d. 287 B.C.) This Greek philosopher and scientist had studied under Plato and Aristotle and on the death of the latter presided for many years over the Lyceum at Athens. His nine books of the *Enquiry into Plants* (*Historia plantarum*) and the six books of his *Causes of Plants* (*De causis plantarum*) made him famous as a botanist. The medieval manuscript tradition is negligible, but the Greek texts were translated into Latin by Theodore Gaza and printed at Treviso as early as 1483. The *editio princeps* of the Greek text was printed by Aldus Manutius in Venice in 1497 as part of Aristotle's *Opera.* Other editions and commentaries on Theophrastus made his work readily available in the sixteenth century.[28] Rauwolf cited this source, so important for his purposes, a total of 21 times.

Four of the references are in connection with illustrations of plants.

The *Historia naturalis* of Pliny the Elder had always been the botanical reference work used along with Dioscorides and Theophrastus. This encyclopedic work, written in the first century A.D. and largely dependent on Greek authorities, had been very influential in the Middle Ages. Eighteen incunabula, three of them in Italian translation, attest to its popularity in the fifteenth century. Numerous editions in Latin and other languages as well as a number of commentaries had appeared before Rauwolf's trip to the Near East.[29] Rauwolf referred to Pliny as his authority 20 times for names of plants, places, animals, and weather phenomena.

Despite the Galenic character of Rauwolf's medical education, he mentioned the name of Galen only twice.[30] In the dedication to his travel book, he wrote that Galen tells how he too traveled, going to Lemnos, Cyprus, Palestine, and Syria to search for strange plants and ores. Galen is also named as the one medical author that Jewish physicians in the Near East had available in Greek and Arabic. Paul of Aegina, the seventh-century medical writer of Alexandria and one of those authors approved for instruction at Montpellier in 1550, is named by Rauwolf only once. A strange willow (*Salix Safsaf* Forsk.) is considered in the fifteenth woodcut in his book as a plant called *arnabo* by Paul. Editions of this author in Greek, Latin, and French (Book VI on surgery) were available in the sixteenth century.[31]

A variety of other classical writers named by Rauwolf give evidence of his humanistic education at Wittenberg and Montpellier. Strabo (60 B.C.—A.D. 24), the Greek geographer, is cited by Rauwolf as the authority for his statement that Seleucia and Ctesiphon were twin cities once situated on the Tigris below Baghdad. Aristotle (384–322 B.C.) is named once by Rauwolf in connection with the birds he saw on the Euphrates, which were called "pelicans by Aristotle and *onocrotali* by others." Xenophon (445–355 B.C.), the Athenian historian, is mentioned twice by Rauwolf as having called the Kurds of the Assyrian-Armenian area the "carducci." In the dedication to Rauwolf's travel book (i^v), Plutarch, the Greek biographer and philosopher of the first century A.D., is named as the source for Solon's travels through many foreign lands to "learn diverse good arts and customs." In the same place, Diogenes Laertius of the second century A.D. is cited as the authority that Plato traveled to Megara, Cyrene, Italy, and Egypt to learn many things and that he would have also gone to Asia but was hindered by war. Of the ancient geographers, Ptolemy (second century A.D.) is used by Rauwolf nine times in the identification of cities, rivers, and the Kurds. Four of these references concern cities on the Adriatic coast as seen by Rauwolf on his return voyage. Flavius Josephus, the celebrated Jewish historian of the first century A.D., is named a total of thirteen times by Rauwolf. Except for one reference to the Nabateans, all the others deal, quite naturally, with places and events seen by Rauwolf on his Jerusalem pilgrimage. Four of the references name Josephus's "alten geschichte" or *The Antiquities of the Jews*. The *Jewish Wars* of Josephus was used for Rauwolf's comments on Jaffa, and once Josephus is call a "famous historian."

Of the Arabic authors, Rauwolf cited Avicenna twenty-six times; two of these references concern illustrations in the 1583 edition. His use of this medical and botanical authority resulted, of course, from his study of Avicenna's *Canon* and *De viribus cordis* at Montpellier. Avicenna or ibn-Sīna (980–1037) was one of the greatest physicians of all times and his large and famous *Canon* or *Qānūm fial Tibb,* a medical encyclopedia with some 760 drugs in its *materia medica,* was based on the accumulated Greek, Byzantine, and Arabic medical knowledge.[32] Well into the modern period it was to remain pre-eminent in medical literature. The *Canon* was translated into Latin by Gerard of Cremona in the twelfth century and after a long manuscript tradition was repeatedly printed in the fifteenth and sixteenth centuries.[33] A revised translation of the Latin text was made from the Arabic original by Andrea Alpago of Belluna (*ca.* 1440– 1521). This physician had resided for thirty years in Damascus and, fluent in Arabic, used his knowledge and linguistic skill to translate in Latin works of Avicenna, Averroes, Serapion, and other Arabic authors.[34] To his translation of the *Canon* he appended an extensive glossary of Arabic-Latin words. This was edited by his nephew, Paolo Alpago. On one occasion (p. 127) Rauwolf referred to this "Index of Arabic words of Andreae Bellunensis," and he must have used this revised text, which was published in Venice in 1527 and reprinted every few years.

The brilliance of Avicenna barely outshown that of an earlier medical authority, Abu-Bakr Muhammad ibn-Zakariya al-Razi or Rhazes as he was known in European medical circles.[35] This Persian-born physician of the ninth and early tenth centuries was a prolific writer on medical subjects and philosophy. His monumental *Kitāb al Mansūri,* written for his patron Mansūr ibn-Ishāq al Sāmāru, was known as the *Liber Almansoris* in the translation of Gerard of Cremona. It was printed three times before 1501, and the ninth book, or *Liber nonus ad Almansoris,* often printed, was on the 1534 list of courses at Montpellier. The greatest work of Rhazes was his *Kitāb al-Hāwi* or "comprehensive book," a survey done originally in twenty volumes. It was translated by the Sicilian Jewish physician Faradj ben-Sālim in 1279 and printed in 1486 and repeatedly thereafter.[36] Rauwolf named Rhazes 20 times, citing his book for the identification of three illustrated plants. On three occasions the *Liber ad Almansoris* is specifically named and twice the chapter numbers are given. Each time Rhazes is mentioned, his Arabic word for a plant (and once for a vulture) is given.

A third Arabic author cited by Rauwolf was Serapion the Younger, a physician of Iraq who lived late in the eleventh and early in the twelfth centuries.[37] His work on medical simples is a compilation of Dioscorides, Galen, and many other authorities. A poor Latin translation from the Arabic was made by Simon of Genoa and Abraham, a Jew of Tortosa, late in the thirteenth century.[38] The Latin title is *Aggregator* or *De (medicinis) Simplicibus, opus ex Dioscoride et Galeno aggregatum* (Venice, 1497 and 1550; Lyons, 1525; and Strassburg, 1531). The work contained a total of 463 articles with descriptive and therapeutic statements. Rauwolf cited Serapion 18 times. Almost every reference has the name of the plant as given by Serapion, and the chapter number is given six times.

Averroes (ibn-Rushd, 1126–98), the celebrated commentator of Aristotle, is cited only once (p. 74) by Rauwolf and that is in connection with the eggplant which was "eaten more frequently cooked (especially in the manner which Averroes reports) than raw."

Montpellier was apparently the first French institution to use human dissection for medical instruction. The statutes of 1340 ordered the chancellor to have an anatomy performed every two years. Later the frequency of such dissections increased, for in the ten-year period of 1526 through 1535, 31 anatomies were held, averaging more than three a year. The statutes of 1550 prescribed that four anatomies be held annually.[39] Although the procedure at such anatomies was later greatly simplified, the record of payments at a dissection performed in 1527 at Montpellier reveals the complicated procedure then employed in setting up a dissection. The payments included the following:

For the eminent and very wise master Jean Faucon, most learned interpreter of the history of the body, one ecu; for the prosector, twenty sous; for the glass vase destined to receive the intestines, for the material for the fire, and the packing, five sous; for the incense to make the room healthy, eighteen deniers; for the guard of the hospital who kindly released the cadaver, five sous; for the wife of the said guard, who lent the shroud in which he was brought to the school, in order to dispose her to warn us when bodies for dissection will be available, two sous; for the men who brought the cadaver from the hospital to the College of Medicine, two sous; for the wine which served to wash the body and for those who washed the body, two sous; for the pound of candles, necessary for a dissection at night, sixteen deniers; for the shroud for the burial, for the aprons, and the cloth for the dissection, seven sous; for the preparation of the coffin and the grave, the calling of the priest, and the carrying of the tapers required for the funeral, nine deniers; for the trouble of the beadle of the University who agreed to the operation, in opening the doors, in maintaining the fire, in furnishing of his furniture a number of utensils which were needed, five sous; for his wife who later cleaned the room, twelve deniers; for her children, who likewise lent assistance, whether it be by helping those doing the operation, or by running to get what was needed, four deniers; for the priest of Saint Claude and for the grave-digger, six livres; for the priest who accompanied the corpse to the cemetery of Saint Bartholomew, and for the poor who were in the cortege, nine sous; for the priest or prior of the hospital, two sous; for the porters who transferred the corpse to the place of burial, four sous; for the priests of Saint Matthew, three sous, four deniers; for the cemetery of the Church of Saint Bartholomew, twelve deniers; for the funeral couch of the cure of the parish of Saint Firman, four livres; for the coffin, twelve sous; for the cope, the cross, and the priests of Saint Firman, seven sous; and for the mass, said in the name of the deceased, twenty deniers.[40]

While the cadavers might be secured from the morgue of the hospital and from the gallows for official dissections, medical students in the sixteenth century already practiced the honorable custom of body-snatching so well described in Dickens' *Tale of Two Cities*. Rauwolf made no mention of such activity, but Felix Platter of Basle who was at Montpellier from 1552 to 1557 described his own experience in procuring a body for private dissection:

My first expedition of this kind was on December 11, 1554. The night was already dark when [Petrus] Gallotus led us out of the town to the monastery of the Augustinians. There, there was a bold monk who disguised himself with our aid. We furtively entered the cloister where we waited until midnight, whereupon, well-armed, and observing profound silence, we went to the cemetery of Saint Denis. Myconius carried his drawn sword, as the Italians did their rapiers. We disinterred the corpse, using only our hands, for the ground was yet loose. When we discovered the cadaver, we attached a cord and pulled it out with all our force; after we had enveloped it in our mantles, we carried it on two sticks to the city gate. It was about the third hour of the night. We put the corpse in a corner and knocked on the wicket. An old porter, dressed in a nightshirt, came and opened the gate. We begged him to give us a drink, on the pretext that we were dying of thirst. While he was getting the wine, three of us brought in the cadaver and carried it to the house of Gallotus which was not far from the gate. The porter suspected nothing. Thereafter, the monks of Saint Denis were obliged to watch the cemetery, and when students came, they shot crossbow arrows from the cloister.[41]

At the time that Rauwolf was a student at Montpellier, the public anatomies were held in a *theatrum anatomicum*. This new structure had been erected by King Henry II and replaced an earlier amphitheatre in which a stone table, a stone professorial chair, and a bench for the students had been installed in

1527. The new *theatrum,* secured through the efforts of professors Saporta, Jean Schyron, and Jean Bocaud, had been dedicated in 1556, and Felix Platter was there at the time. Traditionally an anatomy was presided over by a professor, with a barber-surgeon doing the demonstration and pointing out the various features of the human body while the professor read the pertinent passages from Galen or other authorities. However, the teaching of anatomy at Montpellier was improved shortly before Rauwolf's time by the introduction of a *dissecteur anatomiste* who regularly carried out the dissection.[42] Felix Platter reported that these dissections, still conducted in the traditional manner in his time, were attended not only by students but by a "great number of lords and bourgeoisie, and also by women when a man was being dissected; many monks likewise came there." [43]

The regular courses taught by the doctors of medicine were given in the period from the feast of Saint Luke (October 18) to the day before Easter. In the spring and summer months from Easter until fall, a period when the regent or reading masters were not lecturing and many of the advanced students were gone from Montpellier, the bachelors could give lectures. The regulations of 1550 also provided that "the chancellor, doctors, and counselors shall select one of the doctors, of the most suitable and adequate, to read to the said students, and to point out visually the medicinal herbs, from the feast of Easter to the feast of Saint Luke, . . . and to search for the said herbs in the said town of Montpellier and in the surrounding area." [44] It was under this regulation that Guillaume Rondelet, in the assembly of April 28, 1558, was chosen to read Dioscorides "and point out to the students the medical herbs" from Easter to the Nativity of Saint John (June 24).[45]

Many a physician of the sixteenth century owed his inspiration and knowledge to this enthusiastic teacher. The son of a druggist, Rondelet was born in 1507 at Montpellier. He studied at Paris and Montpellier (A.B.) and after another period at Paris he returned to Montpellier for his doctor's degree (1537). Along with Symporien Champier, another graduate of Montpellier, he was attached as physician to the Cardinal François de Tournon, the celebrated humanist, diplomat, and patron. In the entourage of the cardinal, he visited France, the Lowlands, and Italy, but in 1551 he returned to Montpellier as an instructor in anatomy. In 1556 he was elected chancellor by the faculty and he held that position until his death in 1566. Rondelet was known primarily for his teaching of anatomy and for his books on ichthyology. On the latter subject he published his famous *Libri de piscibus marinis in quibus verae piscium effigies expressae sunt* (Lyons, 1554) and his *Universae aquatilium historiae pars altera cum veris ipsorum imaginibus* (Lyons, 1555). As an anatomist he was known for the clarity of his demonstrations, and his passion for the subject was so great that he even performed an autopsy on the body of one of his children in order to find the cause of death. Rondelet was a very active and generous man who got along with little sleep, devoting the night hours to study. He was short in stature but very corpulent from eating heavily of fruits and pastry, although he gave up wine because of the gout. He died in 1566 at Realmont (Tarn) of dysentery caused by eating too many figs while on a trip to Toulouse.

In addition to his excellent teaching of anatomy and his work in ichthyology, Rondelet must be remembered as an inspiring teacher of botany. His courses on Dioscorides, his summer field trips, and his generous assistance attracted many students, and not a few of the physicians who graduated from Montpellier became outstanding botanists as well. The impressive list includes such physician-botanists as Carolus Clusius, Felix Platter, Matthias Lobelius, Pierre Pena, Jean Bauhin, Jacques Dalechamps, Jean des Moulins, Laurent Joubert, and Rauwolf. Rondelet wrote little on botany, but he is rightly honored in the genus *Rondeletia* in the *Rubiaceae* family.[46]

Undoubtedly Rauwolf experienced a course with Rondelet during his summers at Montpellier, for in connection with an *Astragalus tragacantha* he later found at Marseilles, he referred to him as "the very learned and famous Doctor Guillaume Rondelet, my faithful preceptor."[47] In the dedication to his travel book, Rauwolf wrote how he explored the flora of the mountains and valleys of the region about Montpellier and from the richness of this South European flora collected hundreds of plants. His botanical field trips took him "to Savoy, Geneva,

Dauphine, Lyon, and Valence, but especially in Provence, in the environs of Avignon, Arles, Marseilles, Chalon de Crau, in the arid and uncultivated lands, and particularly in Languedoc, in the environs of Nimes, Montpellier, on the mount of Cette situated at the edge of the sea, and on the high mountains of Auvergne; and not without much fatigue, danger, and expense to obtain and acquire them." [48] In many of these field trips, Rauwolf was accompanied by his friend Jeremiah Martius (Mertz) of Augsburg who had matriculated at the university two years before Rauwolf.[49] Apparently some exploring and collecting was also done with Jean Bauhin of Basle (1541–1613). In Bauhin's posthumous work, *Historiae plantarum generalis novae et absolutae prodromus,* "the famous Leonhard Rauwolf" is mentioned as a "faithful traveling companion." [50]

Like Felix Platter before him, Rauwolf made his own herbarium of these collected plants by pasting them onto sheets of paper. The credit for beginning this new practice is assigned to Luca Ghini who also established a botanical garden at Pisa as early as 1544. The art became firmly established in the last half of the sixteenth century and a number of herbaria of the period are still extant.[51] That of Felix Platter, begun at Montpellier, contains 813 plants of European and Egyptian origin and is now at the University of Bern. Michel de Montaigne, the essayist, saw and praised his herbarium in 1580.[52] The plants that Rauwolf collected in France at this time number 443 specimens and are found in the first two volumes of his herbarium, which is now in the Rijks Museum of the University of Leyden.[53]

Although Rauwolf makes no mention of it in the dedication to his work, the decades immediately following the middle of the sixteenth century were exciting ones in the city of Montpellier. It was at this time that Protestantism gained the upper-hand in the French city. Already in 1527 it was said that the greater part of Montpellier was "Lutheran" and in the thirties persecution and arrests had taken place.[54] Active in the early propagation of the reformed faith was Guillaume Mauget, the pastor from nearby Nimes.[55] In October, 1553, Felix Platter witnessed the degradation of a converted priest who later, on January 6, 1554, was burned at the stake for his Calvinism. Soon thereafter a Roman Catholic *commissarius* arrived from Toulouse to seek out "Lutherans" and to burn a large number of Bibles and theological works found in a library.[56] Despite such counter-activities, the new faith found many supporters at the University of Montpellier, with the medical faculty being especially zealous as partisans. It was Rondelet, who secretly at first and then openly, espoused Calvinism and found support in Professors Laurent Joubert, Bocaud, Saporta, and Nicolaas Dortoman.[57] When Regent Professor Bocaud died in 1558 his desire to be buried according to Calvinistic rites brought protests and disorders. But even the ecclesiastical supervision of the university by Bishop Pellicier did not prevent three Protestants, Rondelet, Saporta, and Joubert, from successively serving as chancellors in the period from 1556 to 1583. The Protestants in the city of Montpellier took over the church of Notre-Dame-des-Tables and in 1567, five years after Rauwolf's departure, the Protestants destroyed the cathedral of the tolerant bishop who, on suspicion of heresy, had earlier (1552) been arrested and imprisoned on the order of the parliament of Toulouse. From this charge he easily cleared himself, and until his death in 1568 he combatted unsuccessfully the growing strength of Calvinism. Under Henry III (1574–89), a sort of Calvinistic republic was set up in Montpellier; it was to last until royal power was re-established in 1662 by Louis XIII.[58]

Rauwolf remained at Montpellier for about two years and then, in 1562, he transferred to the University of Valence in the French province of Dauphine. Here he received the coveted degree of Doctor of Medicine. The University of Valence had been founded in 1452 by the Dauphin Louis, who later became Louis XI. Papal confirmation was received in 1459. It was intended that the new university should replace that of Grenoble which, although founded in 1339, had never prospered. Valence was primarily a center for law studies. The French jurist Jacques Cujas taught there from 1567 to 1575. François Hotman, an ardent Protestant, taught law at Valence from 1562 to 1568, during which time Rauwolf was there. Among his students were Joseph Justus Scaliger, Jacques Auguste de Thou, and Pierre Pithou—all famous scholars.[59] Just why Rauwolf transferred to Valence is not evident, but Felix Platter recorded the cases of two other Germans who left Montpellier to finish their work for the doctor's degree at Valence.[60]

By 1563 Rauwolf was ready to return to Augsburg and practice his profession. However, before returning home, a field trip through Italy and Switzerland seemed the best way to complete his botanical education. Rauwolf thus visited and collected plants at Padua, Verona, Mantua, Ferrara, Bologna, Florence, Modena, Piacenza, and Parma. He crossed the Alps at Mount St. Gothard, and searched for plants in the fields about Lucerne, in the mountains about Zurich and Basle, and in the Schwarzwald of Germany.[61] The 200 plants he collected are in the third volume of his herbarium. While in Zurich he met the famous Conrad Gesner (1516–65), the encyclopedic compiler and author of the well-known and illustrated *Historia Animalium*.[62]

By the fall of 1563 Rauwolf as back in Augsburg and, no doubt, set up practice. Because of the severe plague that raged in that city that year, on October 12 Rauwolf petitioned the burgomaster, the town council, and the guardians for employment or a position "in these grievous and mortal times."[63] Early in 1564 he was visited by Carolus Clusius (Charles de l'Ecluse, 1529–1609) who had come to Augsburg to take Jacobus Fugger, the young son of Anton Fugger, on an educational tour of Spain. Rauwolf showed Clusius his herbarium of over 600 specimens and modestly accepted the corrections in nomenclature which the older botanist suggested.[64] Rauwolf did not neglect his botanical studies, for he kept a garden of rare plants and exchanged specimens with other botanists. In a letter dated January 7, 1565 and addressed to the Augsburg physician Adolf Occo III (1524–1606), Gesner thanked the "most learned and renowned Dr. Rauwolf" for sending him some unusual seeds and expressed the desire to enter into correspondence with the Augsburg botanist.[65] Gesner, Clusius, and others usually referred to Rauwolf by his humanistic Greek name of "Dasylycus" or "Shaggy Wolf."

On February 26, 1565 Rauwolf married Regina Jung, daughter of the Augsburg patrician, Doctor Ambrosius Jung, the Younger (d. 1559). Among those who sent congratulations was Gesner. After the marriage, Rauwolf removed to Aich in Bavaria and then later to the larger Swabian town of Kempten. At both places he practiced medicine. In 1570, however, he moved back to Augsburg and secured from the city officials the office of "city physician," with an annual salary of one hundred gulden.[66]

III AUGSBURG TO TRIPOLI

Although Rauwolf had a good position and had already acquired a reputation among his scholarly friends and associates, he was restless in Augsburg. In the books he had studied for his medical education he had read of the many useful plants that grew in Greece, Syria, Arabia, and other eastern countries. Thinking about these exotic plants and about the many places, customs, and practices described by various authors and in the Scriptures, he developed an intense desire to travel in the Near East and see these things for himself. As he wrote in 1581:

From my youth I had the strong desire to go to foreign lands, especially those of the Orient, as these were more famous and more fruitful than others, in which the mightiest potentates and monarchs of the world lived and ruled in the past; not only to verify the life, manners, and customs of the inhabitants, but also much more to discover and to learn to know the beautiful plants and herbs described by Theophrastus, Dioscorides, Avicenna, Serapion, etc. in the location and places where they grow; partly that I might more exactly describe them, especially the most strange and rare; partly also, to provoke the apothecaries to try to procure those that are necessary for them to have in their shops.[1]

Most Renaissance scientists interested in traveling to strange lands sought wealthy patrons among the lay or ecclesiastical princes, but Rauwolf was fortunate in obtaining a different kind of patron. His brother-in-law was the important merchant Melchior Manlich of Augsburg, and the Manlich firm was engaged in trade with Levantine ports, shipping out of the French port of Marseille.[2] The head of the firm conceived the idea of sending Rauwolf to the Near East to serve as physician for the agents of the firm residing there and at the same time to study drugs and plants in the land of their origin. The Augsburg botanist was certainly among the first of modern scientists to gain financial support for research in the field from a mercantile firm seeking to profit from the scientific knowledge of an employee. The fact that Georg Rauwolf, the brother of the botanist, was a factor in the firm and residing in Tripoli may have contributed to the choice. Melchior Manlich offered to pay the botanist's expenses and a suitable salary in addition. Rauwolf secured permission to leave from the officials of Augsburg and in the spring of 1573 he was ready to set out on a trip that was to last almost three years.[3]

On Monday morning, May 18, 1573, Rauwolf and a friend, Frederick Rentzen, left Augsburg on horseback for the French port of Marseille.[4] They rode up the Wartach valley and then turned southwest to Mindelheim on the Mindel River. On Tuesday they traveled west to Memmingen and then turned south, crossing the Iller River, to Leutkirch where they stayed the night. On the twentieth the way took them through Wangen, "where they have a very good trade in fine ticking and linen cloth." By noon they arrived at Lindau, a city sometimes called "the German Venice" because of its situation on the Boden See and its trading activity. After dinner they crossed the eastern end of the lake to Fuzach. On the next day, while traveling to Feldkirch on the Ill, Rauwolf recorded the first plants of this expedition: *Chrysoplenium oppositifolium* L., *Geum montanum* L., *Chrysanthemum vulgare*, Bernh., *Rhinanthus crista-galli* L., and *Primula auricula* L. That night, Thursday, was spent at Maienfeld on the upper Rhine River. By the next night they were at the old town of Chur, a trade depot for goods brought across the mountains by pack horses. Thusis was reached on Saturday, the twenty-third. Splügen and the Alpine pass were reached by noon of the next day and Campodolcino, Italy, by nightfall. The trail continued southward the next day through Chiavenna and Riva to Gera Larta on Lake Como. After passing through Como, the party arrived at historic Milan on Tuesday, the twenty-sixth of May.

Rauwolf and his friend did not tarry in Milan, but pushed on the next day through Binasco, where the noted jurist and author Andrea Alciatus had a fine house, to Pavia. On the way they passed the park that had been the scene of the famous battle between Emperor Charles V and Francis I of France in 1525. The next day, the twenty-eighth, they crossed the Po, passed through Voghera to Tortona, depopulated by wars, and then went westward through a wooded area to Alessandria della Paglia and finally arrived at Bellizona. The twelfth day of travel led them through Ast to Poirino, " a pitiful village." The trail then turned southward through the villages of Racconigi and Savigliano to Cueno. On the next day, Sunday, they passed through the vineyard-covered Maritime Alps into France. They spent the night at Sorgo. The next morning, June 1, they arrived at Nice. On Friday, June 5, Marseille was reached after passing through Antibes, le Luc, and Brignoles. The latter place was noted for its prunes, "which would be very useful in burning fevers against the thirst." The journey from Augsburg to Marseille was made in the fast time of nineteen days.

About a week before Rauwolf arrived at Marseille, the new factor of the Manlich firm for Syria had arrived at the French port. His name was Hans Ulrich Krafft (1550–1621), the son of a patrician official of Ulm.[5] He had been carefully trained to be a merchant and had learned his trade by working for various firms in Augsburg, Lyons, and Florence. At Lyons he had been in the employ of the Huguenot merchant Anton Pernig for two years, and from 1569 to 1571 he had worked in Florence for Hieronymous Imhof, the noted Augsburg merchant. While in Italy he had been stirred by the accounts of life in the Near East as told to him by two friends, Jacob Boeckh of Nürnberg and Hans Bayer of Augsburg, who had returned from Alexandria, Egypt. Krafft decided to seek employment with a firm that would offer him an opportunity of service in the Near East. Through the influence of friends, he secured a position with the firm of Melchior Manlich. The agreement of May, 1573, was that Krafft would be assigned as factor in Syria for two years with the possibility of extension. He left Augsburg on May 16, traveling through Ulm and Geneva to Lyons, where he paused briefly at the Manlich headquarters. From Lyons he went southward through Vienne and Avignon and arrived at Marseille on May 30, 1573.

The Manlich firm was the only German company that shipped

out of Marseille. Some indication of the activities of this firm can be gained from Krafft's reports during the summer of 1573, while he and Rauwolf prepared for their departure for Syria. About the middle of July there arrived in Marseille the Manlich ship named "Santa Cristina," which had left Tripoli, Syria, on April 26. The master reported that although pestilence raged in Syria, the three employees of the firm in Syria were well. Several days later news was received that the "Falcon," another Manlich ship, had arrived safely in Constantinople. A third ship, the "Griffon," a great ship built by the firm, had sailed for Lisbon shortly before Krafft arrived at Marseille. Loaded with cannon, priming powder (*Kraut*), lead, and victuals, the ship was to go on to Rouen and England. It was learned that a fourth ship, "la Siropa," had sailed from Venice to Alexandria with a large cargo of quicksilver and other goods. The bark "St. Johann" sailed from Marseille for Alexandria on July 16. On August 20, the firm heard an Italian report that the ship had been plundered by pirates, but later they received information that the ship had arrived safely at its destination. A sixth ship, the small bark "Santa Margareta," sailed early in August from Marseille for Cadiz, Spain. Twenty days later the firm heard that it, too, had arrived safely. The seventh Manlich ship operating out of Marseille was the large "Santa Croce"; this was the craft that was to take Krafft and Rauwolf to Syria.[6]

As the German principalities had no trade agreements with the Ottoman Empire, German ships could not sail under their own flags. After 1569, however, German firms enjoyed the same privileges that had been extended to the French by the Turks. Although Genoa, Venice, and Florence had obtained earlier commercial treaties with the Porte, the Turkish-French treaty which Francis I obtained in February, 1535, from Sultan Suleiman, became the basis for the capitulary regime whereby Western nationals enjoyed exterritorial privileges in Ottoman lands. According to this treaty, French citizens, and later others who resided in Turkish territory were not subject to the local laws but only to the laws of the home government. This treaty of amity and commerce guaranteed the security of Frenchmen traveling or resident in the Near East and thus assured the development of French commerce in the Levant. The first and basic provision provided that "all subjects and tributaries of said sovereigns who wish may freely and safely, with their belongings and men, navigate on armed and unarmed ships, travel on land, reside, remain in and return to the ports, cities, and all other places in their respective countries for their trade, and the like shall be done for their merchandise." The second basic article, assured that "the said subjects and tributaries of the said monarchs shall, respectively, be able to buy, sell, exchange, move, and transport by sea and land from one country to another all kinds of merchandise not prohibited, by paying only the ordinary customs and ancient dues and taxes . . . without being obliged to pay any other new tribute, impost, or storage due." Others of the sixteen articles in this treaty provided for the freeing of slaves and prisoners of war, protection of property, security of lives, freedom of worship, trial by the French consul, and exemption from taxation and forced labor.[7]

On October 18, 1569, a new treaty extended for the first time the privilege of the French to foreign ships flying the French flag. Thus nations not having capitulatory treaties with the Porte could trade in the Levant under French protection and privileges. It was under this principle that the Manlich firm of Augsburg was able to operate its ships out of Marseille.

At Marseille, Rauwolf lodged at the Manlich house and while waiting for the day of embarkation for Tripoli he and Krafft roamed the city and countryside.[8] They talked with the physicians and apothecaries of Marseille, but they were especially befriended by Jacques Raynaudet, "a great lover of plants," who showed the Germans his own botanical garden and his herbarium of dried plants laid between sheets of paper.[9] When the "Santa Croce" had been loaded with over 441 tons (8,000 centners) of iron and brass hardware from Nürnberg, and when the ship had been provisioned, armed, and provided with other necessities for a three-month voyage, Rauwolf and Krafft sent out to the ship their clothes and other items in two chests. On the evening of September 1, and after a farewell party, a group of their friends, singing and jesting, accompanied them in a small boat to the "Santa Croce" which was anchored along with other merchant ships near the Island of Chateau d'If.

In all, 50 persons were to sail on board the "Santa Croce." In charge of all was the captain or patron, Anton Reinhardt. His lieutenant, or *nocchiere,* was in charge of all personnel and the actual sailing. Next in importance was the pilot who was responsible for the right compass bearings and who knew where the hidden shoals lay. Besides these, there was a clerk who kept a written record of everything that was brought aboard the ship or unloaded; a guardian or overseer who was in charge of the overall order of the ship; an *aguzzino* who disciplined the crew members when so ordered by the captain; three master gunners who were in charge of the cannon, priming powder, lead, and all weapons, with the great guns being their special care; two caulkers or carpenters who made repairs and did the work of their craft; a cooper in charge of the casks of water and wine; and a barber-surgeon (*Balbier*) named Johann Nutz, a Lowlander who had been imprisoned in Barbary several years before. There were also a cook and his helper who served two meals a day to all on board; "and although the food was poor, he took trouble and worked hard enough to satisfy everyone." Among the items of food taken on board were supplies of beef, live sheep and hens, eggs, salted fish, biscuits, wine, and water. A purchaser bought all necessary food and dispensed it to the galley. Eight mariners, including the two caulkers, ranged in age from 30 to 40 years old. They centered their activities in the stern or poop where they stood watch and steered the ship with the rudder. The watch was three hours in duration, the period being measured with sand-glass, "which because of the hard labor they eagerly turned."

Also in the crew were sixteen sailors (*fuderini*), eighteen to twenty-four years old, whose station was in the prow and who handled the ropes and sails. The "Santa Croce" also had on board six apprentice sailors or cabin boys (*mozzi*) who were from 10 to 14 years old. For all the hard work and abuse imposed on them, they were paid very little, for as a rule such boys were taken along on the request of their parents to learn the trade. Four passengers concluded the list, for besides Rauwolf and Krafft there were two French merchants aboard. Traveling at their own cost to Tripoli, the Frenchmen paid ten kronen per month. All members of the crew were paid monthly wages by the Manlich firm, which also bore the expense of food and drink for all as long as the ship was gone from Marseille.[10]

If in tonnage the "Santa Croce" was not unusual, it was certainly one of the best armed merchant ships that sailed from Marseille. Its main armament consisted of 13 pieces of ordnance on wheels. These were as follows: one heavy piece, weighing about ten hundredweight and used for scatter-shot and chain-shot; four pieces of nine to eleven hundredweight, a usual piece of ordnance; two falcons of fairly large bore; and six smaller falconets. Each piece had three or four gunners assigned to it so that a rapid rate of fire could be maintained. The ship also carried 1,120 pounds of powder, a large number of balls, and 100 pounds of lead to cast more if necessary. Additional armament consisted of two great double-barreled harquebuses, six ordinary soldier's harquebuses, six shields, twelve long pikes, and the hunting guns which the majority of the men had taken with them. There was also a trumpet and some kettledrums to frighten the enemy with terrible noises.[11]

Before the ship sailed, the captain asked the members of the crew if there were any who did not want to go on this voyage. He also begged all those with quarrels to settle their differences and be at peace. He then requested obedience to himself in fair weather and foul and that all should do their duties with energy. To this all raised two fingers as a sign of obedience. All the preliminaries thus accomplished, about two o'clock on the afternoon of September 2, 1573, two of the sails were unfurled, the small boat was taken aboard, and the trip begun. As soon as the ship began to make headway, it almost collided with another ship lying at anchor. Once the anchorage had been cleared, prayers were said and all commended themselves to God; the crew kneeling and praying three Ave Marias while the two Lutherans, Rauwolf and Krafft, said the Lord's Prayer and the Creed. Now, with all six sails unfurled, the wind blew them southward at about six or seven French miles or two German miles an hour. By nightfall no land was visible and by then all those unaccustomed to the sea became seasick. Rauwolf and Krafft purged themselves that night and were better the next morning, especially when the captain sent them some warm chicken broth.

Some of the others, undoubtedly the apprentice seamen, remained sick for a week.

For two days the northwest wind (*caurus* or *maistral*) remained favorable and about one hundred French miles were covered.[12] However, on September fourth the wind shifted to the southeast and became the *graeco* or *caecias* wind against which little progress could be made even by tacking. By Sunday night and Monday morning (September 6–7) they were in sight of the Barbary coast of Africa. Here about two hundred dolphins played for almost two hours in the sea about them. Not being able to go toward the East and with the coast of Africa before them, the captain found it necessary to put about and head back toward Marseille, three hundred Italian miles to the north. In the evening of the seventh, the wind abated and for a while the ship was becalmed, but the next morning, before dawn, the *maistral* wind again began to blow them eastward so that on the ninth of September they sighted the island of Galite. This mountainous island off the coast of Africa was known as a hideout for pirates, and the armament of the ship was made ready in case of an attack. Filled with weapons as it was, the cabin of Rauwolf and Krafft looked like the ship's armory. Shoals (*leuci*) in the sea called for constant alertness and a careful study of the charts on which such hidden rocks were marked with little crosses.

Later the ship passed to the north of the Spanish-held island of Pantelleria and then coasted the island of Sicily. Buildings and towers on the coast and the high Hyblean range were plainly visible. On Sunday, September 13, they passed near Malta, but the island was so low on the horizon it could be seen only from the crow's nest on the mast. Near Malta they sighted a small ship which they took to be headed for Marseille. In the days that followed the wind shifted from the *maistral* to the *betsch* (*africus;* southwest) and then to the *ponente* (west). September 14 was the festival of the Holy Cross and since this was the name of their ship the crew raised a shout for a celebration. The captain allowed two small falconets and a large one to be fired and at 7:00 A.M. prayers were said in thanksgiving for their safety so far. The two Germans said the Lord's Prayer in silence. Captain Reinhardt then ordered a collation for all. On this day the *betsch* arose with such violence that the ship was tossed and rocked so much that movement on the deck could be made only by creeping on all fours. But that evening the *maistral* rose again and by the morning of September 15 they sighted the western end of Crete and the island of Cerigo (Cythera) to the north. On reaching Crete, the contrary *sirocco* (*vulturnus*) blew from the southeast and since the master would not land on Crete or on the little island of Legosia, the ship was turned south into the high seas. Then a thunderstorm broke upon them and mountainous waves threatened to engulf the ship. On the morning of the seventeenth the wind abated and turned so favorable that they were soon back in sight of Crete and Legosia where they saw two ships, one a bark and the other a great ship. Krafft began writing letters, thinking that if contact was made and the ships were headed for Marseille, the letters could be taken to the officials of his firm. It was soon evident, however, that the ships were headed for Alexandria.

Off the southern coast of Crete the "Santa Croce" was becalmed and, the day being warm, some of those on board jumped overboard for a bath. The mate speared a tunny (*lischa*) about a yard long that proved very good eating. It was hoped that they could land at the port of Calismene (Acts 27.8) to replenish their water supply, down to two full casks, but before they could approach the port, the *sirocco* arose again and they had to turn away. About noon on the nineteenth when they had again turned toward Calismene they sighted an unidentified ship and the guns were again made ready. The ship did not, however, approach them. As the "Santa Croce" neared the port, a strong *tramontana* wind arose from the north and no landing was made. Instead, taking advantage of the favorable wind they continued eastward past the islands of Calderon and Christiana and then the easternmost point of Crete, Cape Solomonis. On the twenty-first, a "sea wonder" that looked like a dog was sighted. By nightfall of this day they were in sight of the island of Scarpanto (Carpathos). There the wind changed to the east and no progress could be made.

At this point, on the twenty-second of September, a ship was sighted bearing down upon them from the east. The "Santa

Croce" raised its French flag and soon the approaching craft was identified as the "Santa Maria de lacura bursa," also of Marseille. The sails were furled on both ships and the captain of the "Santa Croce" and four sailors put out the small boat and rowed to the other ship. After a noon meal there, they returned bringing Captain Johann Monnier and two important merchants along. Those on the "Santa Croce" then learned that the "Santa Maria" had left Tripoli forty-three days before and was badly in need of food. Since the "Santa Croce" had enough supplies, they sold them some biscuits for six ducats. Krafft talked with the merchant about representatives of the Manlich firm in Tripoli, namely Ludwig Lutz of Kaufbeuren, Wilhelm Salvacana of Marseille, and Georg Rauwolf of Augsburg. He received the news that while the first two men were well, Georg Rauwolf had died while on Cyprus. He had been busy loading cotton at Famagusta and in the great heat had drunk too much heavy wine and died. He was buried at the church of St. George there and Krafft later visited his grave there in the corner of the church to the left of the entrance. Rauwolf was not told of the death of his brother at this time. Krafft sent letters back with the merchants, and when the north wind began to blow, thus providing good sailing for both ships, they separated. The "Santa Croce" fired three guns in salute and the other replied with two. The wind held, and early in the afternoon of the twenty fourth they sighted Cyprus. The ship was so far to the south, however, that they had to sail all night and the next day before they arrived at the port of Salina on the eastern coast of the island. From there they could see Mount Lebanon, 150 miles away and above the port of Tripoli, their goal.

The famous port of Salina received its name from the nearby salt deposit. Rauwolf only mentioned that here they find the best bay-salt, but John Locke, an English traveler who visited the area in 1553 while the island of Cyprus was still in Venetian control, reported that the salt pit was "very neere two miles in compasse, very plaine and levell" in which water was allowed to stand from about October until the following July or August. At this time the salt, 6 inches thick, was harvested "without any further art or labour, for it is only done by the great heate of the sunne." Since this deposit and its product was a state monopoly dedicated to Saint Mark, Venetian ships sailing home from Cyprus had to replace their ballast with salt. The valuable pit was carefully guarded against theft.[13] Cyprus was taken from the Venetians by the Turks in 1571, and on March 7, 1573, only six months before the "Santa Croce" arrived, a treaty had been concluded between the Venetians and the Porte in which Venice agreed to pay a heavy war indemnity and renounce all claims to Cyprus.

When the "Santa Croce" arrived safely in port, three guns were discharged in celebration over the safe arrival. A landing party that included Rauwolf, Krafft, and the captain went ashore to get water and to inquire about friends working for the Manlich firm. Soon after the party landed, they were met by three mounted and armed Turks and an Italian interpreter and were ordered to report to the commander of the Turkish garrison. The camp of the Turks was located on a hill which afforded good observation to sea. After an hour's walk they arrived at the cluster of about thirty tents and appeared before the commander. He was short and obese, seated on a rug, and leaning on three beautiful round pillows. He wore a great white turban and a long, red-lined caban, and in his hand was the usual iron backscratcher. He was surrounded by other Turkish gentlemen and by guards armed with guns and scimitars. One of the guards, however, was dressed in a tiger's skin and carried a great iron club.

According to custom, the Europeans approached the commander and with their right hands on their breasts they made low obeisance. The captain of the "Santa Croce" took off his shoes and seated himself before the Turk, but Rauwolf and Krafft sat on seats brought to them. The Turk then began to ask, through the interpreter, whence they had come and how long it had taken, what merchandise they were carrying in the ship, and whether they intended to make any sale of their cargo on Cyprus. When Captain Reinhardt had answered all these questions, the Turk inquired about news from Europe. He wanted to know the strength and location of the Spanish fleet; whether the Spanish ruler had entered into any alliances with others; how the war with the Huguenots was going in France; how strong was the Huguenot city of La Rochelle; and whether the city had been taken by assault or surrender. The conference lasted half an hour and the Europeans were then dismissed with great civility and allowed to go about their business. That evening Rauwolf and Krafft went to the market area of Salina but found only ruins from the Turkish assault of 1570–71.[14] Not finding any friends there, they returned to the "Santa Croce." On this, his first landing off the European mainland, Rauwolf found only a few caper bushes (*Capparis spinosa* L.), some *Rhamnus spina-christi* L., and *Salsola kali* L. When the casks had been filled with water from a well near the harbor, the sails were unfurled and the ship departed during the night.

Soon after the "Santa Croce" left Salina, Rauwolf's two close friends on board, Krafft and the barber-surgeon Nutz, took him aside and told him of the death of his brother Georg, for they knew the physician would be expecting to see his brother at Tripoli. This incident is recorded only by Krafft and he gave no statement of the reaction of Rauwolf to the news.[15] On September 27 and 28, the ship was becalmed. When no progress was made, and with Tripoli only about 30 Italian miles away, Krafft persuaded the captain to release five sailors to row and steer the small boat on board to Tripoli. On arriving at the harbor, Krafft and one mariner rode small asses to the city. There the new factor of the Manlich firm found Ludwig Lutz, Elias Manhofer, and two young Frenchmen at the Manlich firm's residence. Two other employees of the firm were not at Tripoli; Wilhelm Salvacana was in Famagusta on Cyprus and Lazarin de Scallis was in Aleppo. After a good meal, Krafft, attired in borrowed Turkish clothes, was rowed back to the "Santa Croce," still far at sea. Those on board thought they were being visited by a Turkish official and there was considerable speculation and concern until they discovered it was Krafft. Finally, late on the thirtieth of September the ship arrived by moonlight in the roadstead off Tripoli. The passage from Marseille had taken 29 days.

Tripoli had originally consisted of three separate settlements for representatives of the Phoenician cities of Tyre, Sidon, and Aradus, which had merged about 359 B.C. This original city had

been overwhelmed by the sea and Krafft was shown the submerged walls still visible on a calm day. The medieval city was
captured in 1104, during the First Crusade, and became the capital of the fourth Latin state. Tripoli was retaken by the Moslems
in 1289 and the city was leveled to the ground by Sultan Kala'un.
A new city was built on a slope of Mount Lebanon a few miles
from the old site. The Arab sources repeatedly speak of the
abundant supply of water from Mt. Lebanon, the luxurious vegetation, and the merchandise for sale in this port city of Tarabulus, as the city was called in Arabic.[16] By the sixteenth century
Tripoli, in Turkish hands, was more a port of entry and exit
than a market. To Tripoli came the items purchased or produced
in Aleppo and Damascus for shipment to Europe and ships from
Venice, Marseille, and other European ports unloaded their
wares in the harbor for movement into the interior.

Neither Federici, Newberry, or Fitch have much to say about
Tripoli when compared with the account of John Eldred who
arrived at Tripoli on May 1, 1583.[17] On landing, he and his
companions "went on Maying" on the island of St. George
where Christians dying on board ship were usually buried. By
this time the English merchants and their consul had a residence
at Tripoli in a caravansary or *khan* "called Fondeghi Ingles,
builded of stone, square, in maner like a Closter, & every man
hath his several chamber, as it is the use of all other Christians
of severall nations." He reported five small forts with very good
artillery and about a hundred Janissaries protecting the port area.
Between the port and the city, two English miles distant, was a
constantly growing bank of moving sand that, according to an
old prophecy, was destined to overwhelm the city. Despite efforts
to stop the expansion of the sand dune, it was expanding into the
adjacent gardens.[18] Eldred thought that Tripoli was about the
same size as Bristol. It was encircled with walls of no great
strength and the chief defense lay in the citadel within the walls
with its good artillery and a garrison of two hundred Janissaries.
The numerous gardens and mulberry trees were watered by the
stream that flowed through the city. A very white silk cloth was
produced locally from the many silkworms that fed on the mulberry trees. Eldred thought there were more merchants from

Venice, Genoa, Florence, Marseille, Sicily, Ragusa, and England than from the Near East.

Samuel Kiechel of Ulm arrived in the port of Tripoli on December 11, 1587, after a voyage from Venice that took 71 days. On December 31, while he was there, a French ship arrived that had made the trip from Marseille in the remarkable time of 12 days and 11 nights. Kiechel reported that at the harbor there were several large magazines for the temporary storage of goods brought from Europe and a customs house. There were also five well-built towers along the shore. The newest of these had been constructed, he reported, by a Venetian who had been found in bed with a Turkish woman and in order to save his life had to pay for the stone tower. Kiechel was allowed to stay at the French *fondaco* although the vice-consul informed him it was no inn. When four Germans arrived from Jerusalem, where the plague was great, they were not allowed into either the French or Venetian fondacos but found shelter in the house of a German apothecary. Kiechel commented on the poor defenses of Tripoli, the absence of bells, the pleasant situation of the city at the foot of Mount Lebanon, and the many flowers, vegetables, and fruits available at the time when Europe was in the midst of winter. At Christmastime he bought some roses for the table. He found the wine, both red and white, made by the Maronites of Mount Lebanon to be very good a fact also appreciated by the Janissaries and other Moslems. Since the plague at Jerusalem prevented his departure for that city, he brought a horse and rode to Aleppo with a caravan of 150 camels, some bearing the goods brought from Venice on his ship.[19]

In 1596 Fynes Moryson, the English traveler, reported that the harbor of Tripoli was encompassed with a wall with added security being gained from seven towers. He, too, mentioned the "Tower of Love" built by the Venetian. Along the shore were warehouses and shops. He also mentioned the sand dune and noted that the inhabitants of Tripoli had erected on it an enchanted pillar to stop the expanding sand from engulfing the city. North of the city were gardens in which silkworms were bred. He found the streets narrow except for the broad highway that led toward Aleppo. He estimated that in his time the city yielded 400,000 crowns annually to the sultan. Like many other travelers he found the air and water of the city unhealthful.[20] Sanderson, for example, wrote that while he was in Tripoli in the summer of 1587 he himself was sick and that the "Tripoli ayre at that time infected 40 or 50 Inglishmen at least." Five died of the "badd aire." [21]

Rauwolf reported that the harbor of Tripoli, really an open roadstead with several small rocky islands, was defended by five high towers about a musket-shot apart and garrisoned with Janissaries.[22] The non-crew members of the "Santa Croce" landed so late in the day that it was already night when they set out for Tripoli, an hour's walk away. The party consisted of Lutz, Rauwolf, Krafft, an unnamed Frenchman, two men from the "Santa Croce" (the two passengers?), and a pet monkey that Krafft had brought with him from Marseille. They were accompanied by some Turks who bore cudgels as protection against the night-roaming jackals so plentiful in the Near East. Although some jackals were seen, none approached the travelers who, however, found the gates of Tripoli closed on their arrival. Lutz called to friends in the French fondaco, which was just inside the gate and built partly upon the walls, requesting that the French consul get the *sanjak-beg,* or governor, of the city to open the gates for the late arrivals. Food was also requested. The disturbance also aroused a Frenchman who was an enemy of the Manlich representatives and he ran to inform the *subasi,* or constable, and to encourage him to attack the defenseless Europeans with his men. Meanwhile from a window in the wall, the Frenchmen in the fondaco lowered a basket containing a lantern, bread, wine, and a partridge, all wrapped in a cloth to serve as a tablecloth. So Rauwolf and his companions spread the cloth and began to eat while waiting for the gate to be opened.

Just as the gate was being unlocked, a group of ten well-armed men came out of a postern and attacked the party. The subasi in charge ordered the gate kept locked, the light put out, and the seizure of the Europeans. Some of the Moslems drew their scimitars and Rauwolf thought that all would be cut down. Just then the French consul appeared at the gate and earnestly tried to persuade the subasi to release the men into his custody and have the case decided by the sanjak-beg and cadi. It took about half an hour to persuade the subasi that the late arrivals had not intended to burn down the city with the lantern or betray the city to others. Krafft, trying to break away from the Turk who was attempting to pinion his arms behind him, received a heavy blow on the side of the face.

Although the subasi wanted to hold Krafft as security for the present the consul promised him, the consul was able to get the entire party inside the city and into the French fondaco. It was decided that it would be safer for the men of the Manlich firm to remain there overnight than to seek the shelter of their own Manlich house nearby. The next morning the consul called in Krafft and showed his displeasure with the disturbance of the preceding night. He told Krafft that the subasi might report to Constantinople his own version of the picnic at night before the gate. Krafft did not wish the consul to stand any loss for the present he had promised the subasi, so that evening, after the Manlich employees had gone to their own house, Krafft sent the consul 12 ells of damask worth 14 ducats. All the Frenchmen were disturbed at the betrayal of fellow Europeans by one of their number and the consul tried to find out who the culprit was. The identity was almost certainly established when a certain man from Marseille slipped away on a Venetian ship leaving many creditors behind.

In the succeeding days, Krafft was busy packing some newly arrived raisins in the hope of getting them to Europe before others and he did not have time to view the city until after he returned on October 25 from a trip to Famagusta. Rauwolf, however, set out to see the sights and found that Tripoli was a fairly large and populous trading city located in a pleasant region. Nearby was the towering Mount Lebanon and the streams of its slopes watered the many vineyards and fruitful gardens as well as supplying the wants of the citizens. Pleasant and shaded paths led between the gardens, and fruit was so plentiful that if "you want to take some of the fruit, you may either gather some that has fallen or else pull some from the nearest trees without danger and take them home with you." Between the new and the old Tripoli there had been other gardens, but only lately these had been destroyed by the sea and the ever growing sand dune. Rauwolf found the defenses of the city to be poor, with walls that permitted entrance and egress at night. On a rise near the sea and within the city was a citadel garrisoned by a few Janissaries.

Most of the houses were poorly constructed and had flat roofs on which one could walk to visit friends or sleep in the summer heat. The flat roofs, of course, reminded Rauwolf of the paralytic that had been lowered to Christ (Mark 2 and Luke 5). Only a few merchant's houses had large doorways or entries; the other houses usually had only a low door, "sometimes not more than three feet high, so that you cannot go into them without stooping." In many of the houses the entering passageway was so long and dark "that one would think he were going into a cave or cellar." Inside there were great courtyards with cisterns and large paved halls with risers paved in marble, all kept very clean and covered with rugs on which the inhabitants could sit and look out through open arches. The doors of the houses were locked with wooden bolts that were unlatched with primitive wooden keys about 9 inches long and as thick as a thumb, into which were driven a number of short nails that engaged a similar number in the bolt.

The streets of Tripoli were narrow lanes, paved with broad stones. Those streets that were the main thoroughfares had a sunken channel in the middle about 10 inches across in which the laden camels and asses walked in file, leaving just enough room on the sides for pedestrians. Special drains were provided for greater cleanliness and dryness. The only buildings that could be considered noteworthy were the mosques, "into which no Christian must go unless he intends to be circumcised and so become a Mameluke," and the caravansaries or khans with their great courtyards and many shops and chambers. Usually the khans belonged to the sultan or his pashas, having been built in various towns and places to provide revenue "as the Venetians do in Venice out of the German house."

Far exceeding the mosques and khans in sumptuousness and beauty were the bathhouses of Tripoli. In 1355 the Moslem traveler Ibn Batutah had praised the fine baths he found in Tripoli.[23]

Sixteenth-century European travelers did not mention them, but Rauwolf found these institutions "very well worth seeing" and felt it important to record in detail his experiences in this connection. According to the German, the bathhouses were necessary because the Moslems were "bound to bathe themselves often, and especially when they are going to their mosques, to wash themselves clean from their manifold sins which they commit daily." Because of this, the baths were always ready, kept warm day and night with little expense and "with far less wood than one can imagine." The fuel consisted of wood, when available, the dung of camels and goats, or the dried dregs of pressed grapes. The fuel was burned in a great underground vault and the heat thus generated kept the entire building very warm. Like the Greek and Roman baths, the bathhouses at Tripoli were very large and sumptuous. One entered first a large hall, beautifully paved with marble and with a great cupola at the top. Around the sides were broad benches on which the bather laid his clothes and received instead two colored cloths, one for the head and the other to be used as an apron, "like the bakers and millers by us." Next came the passage through several rooms, one hotter than the other, into the great main room. The arches above this room had glass-covered openings which were very decorative and made the room very light. Here the hot water in marble troughs furnished the steam for the bathers. For persons of importance there were several small chambers off this room which gave some privacy. After the sweat-bath, the bather entered another chamber where he could wash himself in a large marble trough. The water came from a number of pipes so that the bather could adjust the temperature of the bath water.

A distinctive part of the bath routine was the "chiropratic treatment" which the bather received soon after entering the bagnio. As Rauwolf recorded the scene, an attendant, generally a Negro, meets you "and lays you backwards down upon the floor and stretches and snaps all your joints in such a manner that they crack; then he kneels down upon your arms, which he puts upon your breasts one over the other, and holds them so for a good while together with his knees, then he bends forward keeping you still like a prisoner under him and stretches with both his hands your head upwards." On one occasion a companion of Rauwolf had his neck sprained in this way and could not turn his head for several days. Next the bather was placed on his stomach and had all his joints stretched again "as if he malixed a plaster." Then the attendant stood on the bather's shoulder blades and rubbed the back of the bather. After all this the bather was helped to his feet.

At some time while in the bath, an attendant would make a depilatory paste of quicklime, a little arsenic, and water and apply this to the hairy parts of the body. After frequent inspections, the paste was washed off before the skin was damaged. Then the entire body was washed with soap, the attendant using a rough, white washcloth made of the same fibers used in rope-making. Lastly, the attendants washed the bather's head, sometimes adding to the water an ash-colored earth called *malun* which besides cleansing the hair was supposed to make the hair grow long. This last mixture was especially used by the women. When the bather was ready to leave the establishment he was sprinkled with sweet water. Rauwolf was especially impressed with the dexterity of the attendants as they washed the various cloths used during the bath, threw them up on lines stretched across the room at a height of twelve to eighteen feet, and then spread them out for more rapid drying with one stroke of a long pole.

These baths were open to Europeans as well as to Moslems, but care had to be taken not to enter the bathhouse when it was occupied by women. The Moslem women, confined to their homes as they were, flocked to the baths in great numbers. When women were in the bath it was customary to hang a cloth over the street entrance as a sign that men should not enter there but seek another bagnio.[24] In the bath, women used to eat an earth called *jusabar,* "as pregnant women in our country used to sometimes eat coals or other things."

French and Italian merchants were most prominent among those trading at Tripoli. While the Venetian consul was resident in Aleppo, the French consul resided at Tripoli. Rauwolf reported that the consuls dressed in the habit of their country, using red satin, velvet, or damask cloth, all richly adorned. The consuls brought with them from Europe their own tailors, shoe-makers, physicians, apothecaries, barber-surgeons, priests, and interpreters who knew both Turkish and Arabic.[25] The Venetian consul had a three-year tour of duty and when the new consul was sent out by the Venetian government, the new consul could not disembark until the departing consul had come aboard the ship and received him. In Tripoli, the French and Venetians had their fondacos beside the two gates that opened on to the sea side of the city. All day long there were dragomans with asses waiting to carry goods to and from the harbor. These fondacos were large and had many vaults and chambers for the merchants and their goods. Each had only one entrance, before which Janissaries kept guard. With the French consul resided merchants from Genoa, Florence, Lucca, Germany, Lowlands, and other places covered by the French treaty with the Porte. With the Venetians dwelt those of Candia (Crete), Corfu, and other places under Venetian control. Whenever a consul went abroad in the city, he was accompanied by numbers of merchants and servants, and with Janissaries armed with great and long clubs forcing people in the streets out of the way.

The European merchants dealt largely through the Jews of Tripoli, who had large houses and a fine synagogue. These Jewish brokers knew the languages, the prices of all merchandise, and were knowledgeable in the intricacies of buying, selling, and the exchange of coins. The silver coins in circulation were *aspers, medines,* and *saijets,* all of which were of good quality and passed throughout the Turkish Empire. When large sums changed hands, it was customary to count out an amount, weigh this, and then arrive at the total by weighing the rest of the coins. Ducats (*altun* or *sultani*) were the only Turkish gold coins in circulation, and these were of fine gold and soft. Besides the Turkish coins there were a great many Venetian gold ducats, French silver *testons,* and silver *Joachimsthalers.* These circulated as good currency or were at times melted down and minted into Turkish coins.

While merchandise could be bought at the khans, most buying and selling was conducted at the bazaars or exchanges. These were wide and long streets, partly arched and covered with timbers, thus providing cover from sun and rain. In the shops on both sides were craftsmen and merchants of all kinds. Here could be found shoemakers, tailors, saddlers, silk-embroiderers, turners, coppersmiths, cutlers, woolen-drapers, grocers, sellers of fruit, cooks, and many others—each craft or group of merchants having its own section of the bazaar. There was great trade in silk, with some merchants dealing in nothing else. The silk cloth was obtained from the spinners and weavers on Mount Lebanon and especially from Damascus. The silkworms were fed on the leaves of the white mulberry trees so abundant about Tripoli and Damascus and the white berries were sold to the lower class of people. In the bazaar there were many silk workers, making all sorts of embroidery on purses, buttons, and sashes. Such work was done seated before the shop and both the embroiderers and the turners used their big toes to hold the cloth or other items of their craft. At certain times of the year great quantities of large raisins (*cibebs*) were brought from Damascus and several ship-loads of these were sent to Europe each year. In the bazaar beautiful rugs could be purchased and costly silks with artistically worked flowers—often roses of several colors, some of which looked like pure gold.

Important as the trade in silk was at Tripoli, the greatest amount of commercial activity centered about the trade in soap and potash. Large amounts of the potash were sent to Venice where it was used in the manufacturing of soap and Venetian glassware. The ashes were obtained by burning the plant *Salsola kali* L. (saltwort) found in great number in the area. The two kinds of this *kali* plant were included in Rauwolf's collection of dried plants. When the plants were burned to ashes, an oily matter settled out and united with the ashes to form a substance as hard as stone when cold. The ashes that remained on top of this mass were considered second rate. Much of the burning of these saponaceous plants and roots was done on the mountains and the ashes were then brought on the backs of camels to Tripoli where there was considerable manufacturing of soap.

Rauwolf gave the following recipe for soap-making as he was informed of it. Take 1,200 pounds of ashes and make this into a good strong lye, using about one-fourth (in the winter) or one-eighth (in the summer) at a time. Pour the lye, one part a day, into a stone cauldron with a thick, copper bottom, containing 1,600 pounds of olive oil. Simmer constantly, adding another part of the lye each day. Before the mixture has simmered for from five to ten days, depending on the season of the year, take 100 pounds of quicklime, mix with ashes, forming lye. Add this to the simmering mixture a few days before the mixture is at the right density. If there is too much lye in the cauldron, remove some through the cock in the copper bottom. When the mixture has reached the proper point, take a copper kettle holding eight to ten pounds and with this scoop off the thick scum floating on top. Pour this on a floor covered with powdered lime or chalk. Let it lie there for one day in winter, or for two days in the summer. When this has hardened sufficiently so that one can walk on it, smooth out the surface, cut the soap into squares and put the firm's identifying mark on it.

IV ALEPPO

Rauwolf remained in Tripoli for several weeks and spent the time observing the people, their customs, and the flora of the pleasant region. But the East beckoned him and on the ninth of November, 1573, Rauwolf, Lutz, and Salvacana set out for the famous trading city of Aleppo.[1] Krafft could not go along at this time and remained in Tripoli until May 10, 1574, when he too left Tripoli for Aleppo.[2] As the journey usually took about a week, bread, cheese, eggs, and other provisions were taken along. It was the beginning of the rainy season and as the travelers met with considerable inclement weather, their progress was slow. It was not until the fourth day that they arrived at Hama (Hamah), about midway to their destination. Rauwolf called the city "Damandt," a term also used by Kiechel fifteen years later.[3] Hama, a fairly large city, was situated on the Orontes River and surrounded by hills so that the city itself was not visible from a distance. A castle on a hill within that portion of the city on the east or right bank of the river was the most prominent feature of the area. Hama had long been celebrated for its huge water-wheels (na'urah) that lifted the water from the river and irri-gated the many orchards and vegetable gardens about the city. Rauwolf found the scene very pleasant and would have liked to have stayed a while longer to examine the plants there; his com-panions, however, were desirous of reaching Aleppo, some 80 miles to the northeast, and so the party remained at Hama only overnight.

At Hama Rauwolf and his friends stayed in a public caravan-sary or khan, a new experience for Rauwolf but one that was to be often repeated. Unlike the inns of Europe, he found there "neither table, chairs, bench, nor bed, but upon the floor was laid a *stromatzo* of twisted reeds, which was to serve us instead of them all." To replenish their supplies, the agents of the Manlich firm purchased food in the bazaar in the city. In 1588 Kiechel described a khan at Hama as being pleasant, well built, with a lead roof, and a mosque or chapel in the court, which also had a spring of good water. At the gate of this khan, eggs, figs, raisins, and other food could be purchased.[4] Rauwolf saw nine or ten of these khans between Tripoli and Aleppo. He described them as open inns, about three German or fifteen English miles apart, in which caravans and travelers could stay overnight free of charge. In these large and stately buildings, usually built square, there were inner courts around which were the rooms, "just like cloisters." Food and drink were generally not available and the weary traveler had to be content to sleep on straw spread on the floor. Some khans had garrisons of from nine to twelve Janissaries, kept there to keep the roads clean and to protect the caravans staying in the khan from molestation by Arabs and local inhabitants. Such precautions were necessary, for in 1563 the small caravan carrying the goods of Cesare Federici between Tripoli and Aleppo was attacked and the Italian lost all his trade items except four cases of glasses, many of which were broken.[5]

From Hama Rauwolf and his friends rode north past vineyards and good fields of grain and cotton, "which is brought from thence and sold to us under the name of the place where it grows." In the area were many wild asses or onagri, the dried skins of which were so tough that they resembled the calcareous inner shell of the cuttlefish. The inhabitants of the region made scabbards and sheaths from the skins for their scimitars and knives. These weapons were praised by Rauwolf as being "made of good metal, well hardened, and so sharp, especially those that are made in Damascus, that you may cut a very strong nail in pieces with them without any damage to the blade." The knives were worn at the rear of their girdles, tied on with finely wrought tapes.

On the way the party passed through a number of villages inhabited by Syrian and Maronite Christians. At times they lodged overnight with these people who treated them very civilly and gave them excellent wine to drink. One of the villages, called "Hanal" by Rauwolf, lay high in a fruitful area. This village, he was told, marked the site of a former great city (Epiphama?), but now only a few ruins could be seen in the fields. Beyond "Hanal" they could see a little town to the east on the mountains and above it the ruins of a crusader's castle overlooking a strategic pass; "but because it is daily haunted by great and frightful spirits, it remains unrepaired and uninhabited." The town was undoubtedly Ma'arrah al-Nu'man.[6] From here the route led on through well-tilled and spacious grain fields. To the west they saw the village of Sarmin, famous for its soap and surrounded by great groves of pistachio trees, the fruit of which was shipped to Europe from Tripoli. The same kind of trees grew along the highway and by the village of "Basilo" where they stayed overnight. On the next day, when the few rough mountains between "Basilo" and Aleppo had been crossed, the great city, "of the size of Strassburg," was reached. Since no Christian was permitted to ride into a Turkish city, the Europeans dismounted before entering Aleppo.[7] Rauwolf went to the French fondaco and lodged there, "as all Germans do that come here."

In the second millennium B.C., Aleppo was known as Khalap and was the center of the contest between the Hittites of Asia Minor and the Egyptian Empire. When Seleucus Nicator (312–280 B.C.) enlarged the city it was renamed Boroea, but with the Arab conquests in the early seventh century A.D., the name Halab was used. Although the crusaders occupied the region about the city, the attempts of Baldwin II to take the city by siege in 1118 and 1124 were unsuccessful. Under Saladin it became the base for his operations against the northern crusading principalities. Later the city was sacked by the Tartars and then plundered for three days by Tamerlane (1400). In 1516 when Selim I, the Ottoman ruler, set out to conquer the Mameluke Empire, the decisive battle for the control of Syria was fought at Marj Dabiq, a day's journey north of Halab.[8]

Moslem geographers and travelers in the Middle Ages left good accounts of this strategic, commercial, and populous city.[9] They stressed the productivity of the region, the great walls about 50 feet high, the large bazaar of the cloth merchants, the beautiful Jami Mosque, and the seven gates that pierced the walls where highways led to the regions from which came the products that made Halab a famous trading center. All these writers had something to say about the citadel, the city's most distinguishing feature. This stood within the walls on a circular and high hill, artificially scarped, in the east-central portion of the city. Of this citadel Jubair wrote in 1185: "A copious spring of water rises in the castle, and they have made two cisterns here to store the water. Round these tanks are double walls. On the city-side of the castle is a deep ditch, into which the surplus water runs. The castle has high walls and towers, and the Sultan's habitation is here."

In the Arabic tradition, the city of Halab was associated with Abraham; indeed, according to this tradition, its very name was derived from the fact that the prophet lived there and gave the milk of his flocks to the poor as alms. The Christian physician, Ibn Butlan, describing Halab about A.D. 1051, wrote that in the citadel "is a cave where he [Abraham] concealed his flocks. When he milked these, the people used to come for their milk, crying, 'Halaba ya la?—Milked yet, or not?'—asking thus one of the other; and hence the city came to be called Halab [milked]." The famous traveler Ibn Batutah visited the city in 1135 and wrote that in the citadel was an oratory (*mash-ad*) called the Oratory of Abraham or the "Halab Ibrahim, that is to say, the Fresh Milk of Abraham, for he lived here and gave the milk of his cattle to the poor." Rauwolf does not mention this tradition, but the story was told to Pedro Teixeira in 1605.[10]

Of the sixteenth-century European visitors to Aleppo, Rauwolf was the earliest of those who described in any detail their visit or residence. Cesare Federici, the Venetian merchant, passed through Aleppo in 1563 on his way to India, but in his account he simply mentioned his seeking companions among the Armenian and Moslem merchants. After Rauwolf's visit, and with the advent of English merchants in the last two decades of the century, reports become more frequent. Newberry was in Aleppo from January 28 to March 19, 1580, but his limited remarks concern the castle "to the southward off the Towne," the banquet he had at the house of the French consul, and the sighting of a meteorite. Eldred, who arrived at Aleppo on May 21, 1583, described the city as "the greatest place of traffique for a dry towne that is in all those parts." The many foreigners enjoyed freedom of conscience. The "goodly castle" in the middle of the city had a garrison of 400 to 500 Janissaries. For a four-mile radius about the populous city lay gardens, vineyards, and orchards. The walls were about three miles in circuit, with the suburbs almost as much more.[11]

Kiechel was in Aleppo from January 12 to February 12, 1588, when he left for Damascus and Jerusalem. Besides the usual remarks about Aleppo as a great trading center for cloth, precious stones, and spices, he gave a number of interesting, if minor, details in his rather full account.[12] He reported that some of the Venetian merchants had wives and children, that the birds using the water of the citadel-moat were protected from being shot, that 500 Janissaries guarded the citadel, that three Franciscan monks served the chapel of the Venetians, that there were many German-made striking clocks in Aleppo with the pictured human figures replaced by flowers to accommodate the Moslems, and that the shoes worn in Aleppo were usually colored red, green, or blue and had nails at the toe and curved irons at the heel. While Kiechel was in Aleppo, a caravan of over 1,000 camels returned from Mecca with many goods, and especially balls of indigo. He described the important role of the Venetian and French consuls and how lavishly they dressed when they went abroad in the city. He found in Aleppo a branch house of the German merchant Albrecht Armbroster. The German observed that, just as the Christian churches in Europe had the choir in the east, so the Moslem mosques and chapels, many of which were beautiful, were oriented to the south, and in that direction the Moslems faced when they prayed. Just like Rauwolf at Tripoli, Kiechel thought the baths of Aleppo well worth seeing, and he briefly described the use of depilatory pastes.

The full account of Aleppo made by Pedro Teixeira in the spring of 1605 may in most details be considered descriptive of the city which Rauwolf saw thirty years earlier.[13] According to the report of this Portuguese traveler, Aleppo stood amid and partly on four hills, with its ancient walls of cut stone nearly round in form and pierced by ten gates. Extensive suburbs lay outside the walls. Of the 45 wards of the city, 20 were within the walls and 25 larger ones outside. In all 26,000 good houses, mostly of stone, made up the city. Of the 300 mosques and chapels, seven mosques were splendid structures. Sheet lead was used for the roofs of most mosques and for the domed roofs of almost all minarets. The streets of Aleppo were paved with marble slabs. Besides the many khans, clean public baths, coffeehouses, and enclosed bazaars, there was an endowed hospital which was not maintained as well as it should have been—"a failure too common in other lands, despite the duty of Christian charity." The citadel, resting on a mound "round as a heap of wheat," was by tradition founded by Joab, King David's general, "though it may be supposed that it must have been somewhat improved in course of time." The position of the fortress was strong by nature, but the walls themselves were not very strong and the one well was salty. Access was over a bridge which crossed the water of the surrounding ditch. The pasha did not reside in the citadel, but in a private house in the city.

Teixeira found most of the people of Aleppo to be fair and well favored. While the women wore veils, one could "judge their beauty by that of their daughters." All were generally well dressed and most men rode horses. But Teixeira also found the inhabitants "of bad character, and of little courtesy." Much silk cloth of a good quality was woven at Aleppo and the hard white soap manufactured in the suburbs was widely exported. While the poor used locally made earthenware utensils, vessels of bright and clean tinned copper were commonly in use. Glass items, locally made but of an inferior quality, were also used. For entertainment there were public places for archery, musketry, and horseback-riding. Sometimes up to a thousand horsemen at a time would assemble to play with the *jarid,* or javelin, a game played every Sabbath evening.

Besides the native inhabitants of Aleppo there were Turks, Jews, Armenians, Greeks, and Europeans. Many of the Moslems engaged in trade spoke European languages in addition to their native Arabic and Turkish. The Jews had about a thousand good houses in their own ward located within the city wall. There they had a large synagogue which they claimed was 1,500 years old. Many of the Jews were wealthy; most were merchants, brokers, or craftsmen. The Armenian, Maronite, Chaldean, and

Greek Christians lived mostly in the suburbs. While each Christian group had its own church, these were poorly built and in need of repair, but restoration was prohibited under pain of death.

The Venetians had 14 merchant houses and a residence for their consul at the time of Teixeira's visit. They had their own chapel in a khan where they met for mass. Teixeira estimated the value of their imports from Venice at from one to one and a half million in gold each year. These imports consisted of 10,000 to 12,000 pieces of woolen, silk, and brocade cloth, much cochineal, and silver coins. In exchange they exported "raw silk, indigo, galls, cotton and cotton yarn, cinnamon, cloves, nutmegs, mace, pistachios, precious stones, seed pearls, good coin, and many other articles." The way of life of these hospitable Venetians was "liberal and noble, and their equipment not only decent but distinguished."

While the Venetian consul was always a noble and had a three-year term of office, the French consul was appointed for life and lived in France, while a deputy resided in Aleppo on a salary of 3,000 ducats. This deputy-consul resided in a khan and had a chaplain who said mass, "which some of them attend." The French had five merchant houses and there was much more of a turnover of personnel than with the Venetians. Teixeira estimated the value of the French trade as 800,000 ducats. Silver bullion made up most of the French imports. In "order, rule, and policy" the French were inferior to the Venetians, but the French consul had the special privilege of being protector of all foreign Christians not trading under a treaty made with the Porte. There were three English merchant houses and the English trade was valued at 300,000 ducats. The English, who were not yet in Aleppo at the time of Rauwolf's visit, imported little coin, but rather kersies, other cloth, lead, tin, copper, and weapons. Besides these Europeans there were some merchants from Lucca and from the Lowlands.

Rauwolf found the fortifications of the city of Aleppo good in some places and so poor in others that, just as at Tripoli, one could enter or leave at any time of the night.[14] Unlike European cities, at the gates there could be found only two or three soldiers, "rather there to take customs than to keep the gates; nor do they have any arms."[15] The ordinary houses of the citizens of this trading center were similar to the flat-roofed structures he had seen in Tripoli. There was one magnificent building, reputed to have cost 120,000 ducats, which had a very low and small entrance, but within there were large halls, high open arches, fountains, orchards, and gardens—a very pleasant and cool place to rest in the hot summer.[16] There were also some fine mosques with high round minarets and balconies, "like a garland," from which the *muezzin* called the Moslems to prayer. Other than these, Rauwolf could find no stately buildings erected to the memory of some great person or ruler.

Outside the city there were some country homes and one of these, four or five miles from the city, had been built for the Turkish emperor. This large building, "not built so stately as so great a monarch deserves," was sometimes used by the sultan when the Ottoman Empire was at war with the Persians. In the great garden of this imperial establishment was a kiosk or pavilion by the river that ran through the estate, and here the sultan had at times held conferences with his officials. Also outside the city were a number of quarries where stones "almost as white and soft as chalk," were quarried for the buildings of Aleppo. In the vicinity of the city there were a number of grottos or caves extending underground to great lengths. As these caves sheltered many people, connecting holes had been dug down from the surface to let in the light. These holes, often near the highways, made night travel in this area hazardous, and there was the additional danger of being attacked by the poor Arabs who lived in the caves. The chalky surface of the area so shriveled the soles of the Arabs who traditionally went barefooted, "that into some of the crevices you may almost put your little finger."

Despite the rocky hills that surrounded the city, the area produced sufficient barley and wheat, which was harvested in April or May. Little oats or hay were grown because of the arid climate, and the cattle were fed barley and straw, the latter being broken into smaller pieces by threshing wagons drawn by oxen. The valley also had many olive trees which annually produced several thousand hundredweight of olive oil for the manufacturing of soap. Other trees included almond, fig, quince, white mulberry, pistachio, orange, citron, lemon, Adam's apple, sebesten, peaches, and pomegranates. A few apples and pears were grown. The myrtles, the berries of which had "white seeds of the shape of jumping cheese-maggots," were much cultivated and used for the decoration of graves. Many sumac trees were cultivated for their seeds, but Rauwolf saw no cherries or amelanchier, and only a few gooseberries, currants, and sour cherries.

Aleppo was the great trading emporium of northern Syria and daily great caravans of pack-horses, asses, and especially camels arrived from far and near. Merchants and caravans from Anatolia, Armenia, Egypt, Persia, India, and other places so crowded the streets of the city that passage was difficult. Each nation had its own caravansary in which the merchants resided while selling their merchandise. Rauwolf gave the names of some as he understood them to be called: Khan *Agemi; Waywoda; Abrac; Sibeli; Mahomets Pasha; Quibir,* the great; *Sougier,* the little; *Gidith,* the new; and *Atich,* the old. In 1574 while Rauwolf was at Aleppo, Ibrahim-khanzadi Mehemet-pasha was building the Khan of the Customs. It contained 52 magazines, 7 chambers, 2 fountains, and a mosque. This may have been the khan Rauwolf referred to as that of *Mahomets Pasha* or his reference may have been to one of the three khans built by Doukagin Mehemet-pasha.[17] Johannes van Cotovico, the Dutch traveler who visited Aleppo at the end of the century, adds one more, khan *Sibene,* to Rauwolf's list.[18] Biddulph (1600) was entertained by Richard Colthust, the English consul, at the khan called *Burgol* at Aleppo.[19] Teixeira (1605) referred to the many khans of Aleppo as places "like cloisters, where the foreign merchants shelter themselves and their goods. The natives also warehouse merchandise in these, because they are strong and safe buildings, all of cut stone, with strong gates and great iron chains to them. In the midst of some, and at the mosque gates, are marble fountains, very clean and well-wrought, with good and abundant water."[20]

The Europeans had their own fondacos in which they resided, although those that married, chiefly Italians, lived in small houses outside the fondacos. The marriages contracted by Europeans resident in the Near East were apparently often of a temporary nature. Biddulph, the English clergyman, remarked in his description of Aleppo that:

> . . . it is no rare matter for Popish Christians of sundry other Countries, to Cut Cabine, (as they call it) that is, to take any women of that Countrey where they sojourne, (Turkish women onely excepted, for it is death for a Christian to meddle with them) and when they have bought them, and enrolled them in the Cadies Booke, to use them as wives so long as they sojourne in that Countrey, and maintayne them gallantly, to the consuming of their wealth, diminishing of their health, and endangering of their owne soules. And when they depart out of that Countrey they shake off these their sweethearts, and leave them to shift for themselves and their children. And this they account no sinne, or at leastwise such a sinne as may be washed away with a little holy water. And these are the vertues which many Christians learne by sojourning long in Heathen Countries." [21]

In the caravansaries, and especially in the one called *Agemi,* all sorts of merchandise could be found. Rauwolf saw handkerchiefs, long fillets, sashes, turbans, and other items of cotton cloth called by the Arabs *mosellini,* from Mosul where it was first made, and muslin by the Europeans. There were also beautiful rugs in many colors and of the kind that were sometimes imported into Europe. The Persian merchants also brought turquoise, a famous indigenous product of which the Persian ruler had a great supply. Earlier, so many of these blue stones had been brought from Persia to Aleppo that the price had been greatly depressed and the king had forbidden exportation of this commodity for seven years. This time period had just expired, so Rauwolf was able to see some of these stones. Great ropes of the pearls found in the Persian Gulf near the island of Bahrain were also offered for sale by Persian merchants. From India came garnets, rubies, balas rubies, sapphires, diamonds, and excellent musk in little bags. To escape high custom fees and robbery, the merchants concealed their precious stones and thus imported them secretly.

Other items brought from India were cinnamon, spikenard, long pepper, turpeth, cardamom, nutmeg, mace, indigo, fine porcelain cups and dishes, China-root, and great quantities of rhubarb. Of these items, the last two are of special interest. China-root, the root of *Smilax pseudo-china* L. and known as Chinese sarsaparilla, was the well-known Eastern medication for syphilis. This new disease had been introduced into India by the sailors of Vasco da Gama and from India it spread to the Far East in the early sixteenth century. Ludvico de Varthema reported a death by "the French disease" in India in 1506 and added that he had seen "this disease three thousand miles beyond Calicut, and it is called *pua,* and they say that it is about seventeen years since it began, and it is worse than ours." [22] Under the medieval concept that remedies for diseases could be found near the place of origin, the Europeans had searched for and found the supposedly curative bark *Guaiacum* in the West Indies. Nicolas Monardes, the Spanish physician who described the botany and therapeutics of the West Indies, stated it thus: "Our Lorde God would from whence the eville of the poxe came, from thence should come the remedy for them." [23]

The East had its China-root by the same fortuitous circumstances, for Garcia da Orta, the Portuguese physician in India, wrote (1563): "As all these lands and China and Japan have the *morbo napolitano,* it pleased a merciful God to provide this root as a remedy with which good doctors can cure it, although the majority fall into error. As it is cured with this medicine, the root was traced to the Chinese, when there was a cure with it in the year 1535." [24] Rauwolf reported that China-root was "more in use among the Arabs than the *Lignum Guaiacum.*" Cesare Federici wrote that to India came "infinite store of the rootes of China" and John Huyghen von Linschoten gave a long description of the use of China-root in India.[25] Francois Pyrard of Laval, who traveled in India in the first decade of the seventeenth century, observed: "Venereal disease is not so common, albeit it is found, and is cured with China-root, without sweating or anything else. This disease they call *farangui baescour* [French piles], from its coming to them from Europe." [26]

The Greeks and Romans had been familiar with the medicinal properties of Iranian rhubarb.[27] Dioscorides (iii.2) had described the black root as growing in "the places beyond the Bosphorus" and as being good for "inflations, ye weakness of ye stomach, all manner of grief, convulsions, splenetical, Hepaticall, Nephriticall, torminaticall, & ye extensions of ye hypochondria, & the affections about ye matrix, Sciaticas, Spittings of blood, Asthmas, the Rickets, dysenteries, coeliacall affections, and courses of fevers, & ye bitings of poysnous beasts." [28] In the tenth century, rhubarb from China (*Rheum officinale* Baill.) became an important item of trade to western Asia, replacing the poorer Iranian rhubarb. The rhubarb "brought by land and by sea" from "India" that Rauwolf found in the bazaar at Aleppo was of Chinese origin, for Garcia da Orta reported that "all the rhubarb that comes from Ormuz to India first comes from China to Ormuz by the province of Uzbeg which is part of Tartary. The fame is that it comes from China by land, but some say that it grows in the same province, at a city called Camarcander. But this is very bad and of little weight. Horses are purged with it in Persia, and I have also seen it so used in Balagate. It seems to me that this is the rhubarb which in Europe we called *ravam turquino* [Turkish rhubarb], not because it is of Turkey but from there." From India, he emphasized, the true Chinese rhubarb was exported through Persia to Aleppo, Tripoli, and from thence to Venice and Spain; some was also shipped to Europe via Alexandria in Egypt. The Chinese rhubarb roots that traveled far by sea were more rubbed and powdered than that carried mostly by land.[29] Federici reported that among the many costly Chinese exports to India, "the Rhubarbe cometh from thence over land, by way of Persia, because that every yeere there goeth a great Carovan from Persia to China, which is in going thither sixe moneths." [30]

A Persian product that Rauwolf saw in great quantity at Aleppo was a strange manna. This sweet and gummy exudate of certain plants was used as a gentle laxative, demulcent, and expectorant. Manna is produced by trees such as the flowering ash, tamarisk, and certain kinds of oaks. Rauwolf described what he saw at Aleppo as "an unknown manna in skins, by the name of *trunschibil,* which is gathered from a prickly shrub called by the Arabs *agul* and *alhagi,* which is the reason that it is mixed with small thorns and reddish chaff. This manna has grains somewhat larger than our coriander seeds, so that to all appearances, it is similar to our manna which we gather from the *Pinus larix*. It might also very well be taken to be the same that the Israelites ate . . . But that it falls upon thorns is also attested by Serapion and Avicenna in those chapters where they treat of manna, which they call *thereniabin* and *trungibin,* and the very learned and experienced botanist Carolus Clusius says the same in his *Epitome* of Indian plants." [31]

The plant *agul* or *alhagi* that Rauwolf named is the *Hedysarum alhagi* Lerch., a widely diffused low shrub with many stems and branches and with sharp axillary spines. In Persia the manna appears on this plant during autumn nights and must be gathered early in the morning. Rauwolf found some of these plants growing about Aleppo. He described them as shrubs "about a cubit high, which shoot out several roundish stalks and divide and spread themselves from the stem into several sprigs like a flower." On the many long thin spines there were "flesh colored reddish flowers that bore small red cods . . . in which are seeds of the same color." The plant had long brown roots and long leaves of an ash color. The Syrians used the herb as a purge; "they take a handful of it and boil it in water." They also had another kind of manna similar to that which was available in Europe "from Calabria by way of Venice." [32]

Europeans first heard of this Persian or Arabic manna from the work of Pierre Belon who wrote (1553) that the Greek priests of Saint Catherine's monastery on Mount Sinai gathered a manna called "tereniabin to differentiate it from the hard kind; because what the Arab authors called tereniabin is kept in earthenware pots like honey and they take it to Cairo to sell. This is that which Hippocrates called 'cedar honey' and the other Greeks called it 'dew of Mount Lebanon.' This is different from the white, dry manna. That which we have in France, brought from Briancon, and gathered above the Meleses at the summit of the highest mountains, is hard and different from the abovementioned. Since it is of two types, one may find both in Cairo for sale in the merchant shops. One is called manna and is hard. The other is tereniabin and is liquid." [33]

Garcia da Orta, whose work Rauwolf mentioned in the Latin

Epitome of Clusius, described several kinds of manna, including the type Rauwolf saw at Aleppo and later at Mosul. This manna Garcia da Orta called *tiriam-jabim* or *trumgibin* (Persian *tärängubin*) and adds: "They say that it is found among the thistles and in small pieces, somewhat of a red color. It is said that they are obtained by shaking the thistle with a stick, and that they are larger than a coriander-seed when dried, the color, as I said, between red and vermilion. The vulgar hold that it is a fruit, but I believe that it is a gum or resin. They think this is more wholesome than the kind we have, and it is much used in Persia and Ormuz." [34]

Among the precious stones Rauwolf saw offered for sale at Aleppo were some bezoar-stones, "which are oblong and roundish, and smooth without, and of a dark green color." These stones, really concretions, were taken by the Persians from the stomachs of certain ruminants, especially goats, and had an international reputation as an antidote against poison. These valuable stones were often counterfeited; "therefore a man must have great care that he is not cheated." A merchant informed Rauwolf of an infallible recipe to detect the false stones: "take quick lime and mix in it a little powder of this stone, and with water make them into a paste, when this is dry grind it, if it then remains white it is considered false, but if it then turns yellow it is good, and brought from Persia." [35]

Garcia da Orta devoted the forty-fifth colloquy of his book on Indian plants to the bezoar-stone and was the first European to give an adequate description of the sources and uses of such stones.[36] Pedro Teixeira reported that besides the Persian variety, many bezoar-stones were produced in India by goats; "and sometimes are as many as thirteen in one goat, and those not very small." The Persians stones were the best; however, and he had seen "many wonders wrought with them in cases of poisoning." He also reported that the "largest perfect pazar stone, of many I saw in Persia, weighed seventeen meticals and a half, or two ounces and a half, a little more or less." [37] Ambroise Paré, the celebrated French physician, made much use of Garcia da Orta's work in writing his own short treatise on bezoar-stones. While serving as physician to King Charles IX (1560–74), he demonstrated to the king the uselessness of the stone as an antidote to poison by conducting an experiment on a condemned criminal, who died a horrible death from the poison administered.[38]

The reputation of the bezoar-stones was such that counterfeit stones were common. Rauwolf gave one recipe for the detection of false stones; Teixeira gave two such recipes, one using lime and thus similar to that of Rauwolf. The other test, "better and surer," was to weigh the stone, then after leaving the stone in water for six or seven hours, weigh it again; "If it keeps its form and weight, it is good, but if it breaks up, or melts, or gains weight, it is counterfeit."[39] Paré, citing Garcia da Orta, wrote that false stones could be identified by the absence of layers similar to those in an onion and also by blowing it up with the breath—"if the wind breake through, and doe not stay in the density thereof, it is accounted counterfeit."[40]

Sometimes the merchants also brought from India solid but flexible reeds, yellow in color.[41] The long reeds were used by the old and lame to assist them in walking; the shorter reeds were excellent for arrows and darts, the latter being wound about with colored silk ribbons and proudly carried by the Turks in processions. In the shops could also be found another type of small and hollow reed, brownish-red in color. Throughout the East, the *Phragmites communis* (L.) Trin. was used in place of goose quills for writing, and Rauwolf identified these reeds as the *syringas,* or *fistularis* of the ancient authors. Pilgrims "that go to see their Mohammed" in Mecca frequently brought back another type of reed that was long, strong, light, and solid.[42] These reeds, tipped at both ends with iron points, were used, especially by the Arabs, as a thrusting or throwing weapon. Very few of these reeds could be seen in Europe for the Christians were forbidden under severe penalty to export them or any other military weapon. Rauwolf heard of a European who, when found with a scimitar in his possession, was accused and fined 70 ducats to be paid in two days. If he had not paid the fine, "they would certainly have circumcised him, and made him a Turk."

Besides the numerous khans where all sorts of merchandise could be purchased, there was the great bazaar in the middle of the city. It alone was "bigger than Friedberg in Bavaria" and had a great many lanes, each divided into areas according to the wares sold. There were grocers, mercers, and sellers of beautiful rugs, woolen cloth, Turkish handkerchiefs, camlet, taffeta, silks, and cotton cloth. Here one could purchase good "Cordovan" leather, expensive marten furs, and furs of wildcats, an animal found in great number in the East. All manner of jewels, precious stones, and pearls could be purchased at the jewelers. Then there were shoemakers, tailors, saddlers, needle and pinmakers, painters, goldsmiths, coppersmiths, locksmiths, and many others —all making their items and selling them in the bazaar. Rauwolf thought the work of the goldsmiths, painters, and locksmiths far inferior to the work of similar European craftsmen.

Rauwolf noticed the absence among all these craftsmen of wheelwrights and cartwrights—not needed in an area where everything was transported by pack-animal. Neither could he find a gunsmith who could make the most simple repairs on a gun. There were bowmakers, however, and turners making arrows and darts. The former had small butts near their shops so the prospective buyer could test the bow before purchasing it. These bows varied in quality and price, for some were plain while others were artistically inlaid with ivory and water buffalo or ibex horn. The archers of the East wore a ring upon their right thumb, like the seal ring of the European merchant, with which to draw the bowstring. These rings were made of wood, horn, or silver and some were set with precious stones. Barbers, carrying their instruments and basins, wandered about seeking customers and when they found one went to work right there in the street, applying lather and shaving the entire head except for a long lock down the back.

It was in the bazaar at Aleppo that Rauwolf observed his first slave markets. He recorded no emotion at the sight, but his friend Krafft, who had arrived at Aleppo May 13, 1574, was moved to tears. It was a pathetic trade for, as Rauwolf explained later in his book, most of the slaves were prisoners captured by Turkish troops. Slave-dealers went along with the armies and bought the prisoners from the soldiers, chained them together with long chains "as if they were cattle," and then sold them at a profit in the chief trading towns. Weekly sales were held in the bazaars of these towns. The slaves, of many nationalities and religions, were "young and old, men and women, some white and others black." Prospective buyers carefully looked the naked slaves over, felt their bodies, trying to discover any unsoundness of limbs or other defects. Krafft reported that the Aleppo slave market was usually held twice a week on Sundays and Thursdays. He gave the following prices for slaves: old men cost between 20 and 30 ducats; old women, the same or less; strong young men cost 60 ducats; young women and beautiful girls cost 50 to 70 ducats; and little children, often purchased as an act of kindness and charity, cost 4 to 10 ducats. Children were generally purchased along with their parents. The young women, the most expensive category, were consigned to heavy housework and got little rest, "except those who were useful as bed companions." When a purchaser was looking for a "bed-companion" he was permitted to remove the face-veil and if he showed real interest in the women, he was permitted to feel the breasts.[43]

The slaves, and especially those that had not learned any trade before their capture, were put to hard labor by their new masters, with the income from such work, of course, going to the master. Since wealth was measured by the number of men and women slaves a man owned, efforts were made to have the slaves increase their own number by begetting children. The children were educated or disposed of at the master's will and pleasure. Christian slaves, "that to their temporal punishment they might not add eternal punishment too," seldom married so as not to produce offspring who would be raised as Moslems. Christians rather planned how to escape their slavery, although escape was extremely difficult in a foreign country without a knowledge of Arabic. Besides the improbable method of flight, deliverance from servitude was possible in a variety of other ways. Contracts could be made before the cadi between master and slave so that liberty could be achieved after a certain period of time or on the payment of a certain sum. Christian slaves who firmly intended to remain in their faith, and especially those who could accumulate some money by their handicrafts, often gained their freedom thus. The manumission of slaves was often denoted in a Moslem's will. Freed slaves were given a pass by the cadi to show officials on the roads as they returned to their native lands. Some slaves were able to buy forged credentials and thus escape, but this method was seldom successful. As Krafft remarked, the lot of the slave was not always bad, but many Christians apostatized to Islam in order to achieve liberty, preferment, and security.

Crowds of many nationalities constantly jammed the narrow lanes of the bazaar and the atmosphere was that of a fair. One could see drunken Turks who arrogantly pushed people out of their way. Christians, especially, distinguished by their apparel or head-covering, were thus frequently abused. Sometimes Turks would squat by the side against the shops and trip a Christian as he passed by. Yet the Christians did not take this abuse without retaliation. Alert to the approaching Turks, they would stiffen themselves and cause the pusher to rebound to one side or into a shop. Instead of being tripped by a squatting Turk they often kicked out from under him the leg upon which he was resting, causing the Turk to fall flat. To show timidity to a Turk would only bring further abuse and laughter, but the Turks admired a Christian who showed courage and "like some dogs that sooner bark than bite" would call such a Christian a brave man, fit to be a warrior.

Rauwolf was frequently impressed by the charity and good works shown by the Moslems. Thus he was pleased to observe in the bazaar some, commonly those who had been to Mecca as pil grims, who went about with skins of water and out of charity gave refreshment to all that desired it, even to thirsty Christians. Sometimes these charitable persons had chalcedonies, jaspers, or fruit in the water-skins "to keep the water fresh, and to recreate the people." All, of course, drank from the same gilded cup. When the drink was offered, the water-carrier also held a mirror before the drinker and reminded him that he was mortal and must die. If the water-carrier, who demanded nothing of those he served, was given a coin he would spurt scented water on the face and beard of the donor. This water was kept in glass bottles carried in a pouch with brass clasps. Other charitable Turks and Arabs kept marble troughs or pots outside their doors from which the thirsty could draw a drink by means of a small vessel kept there. Since these people did not like to see a man drink alone, others would draw a drink even if they were not thirsty; "So you often find a whole crowd about a pot."

Food and drink could also be obtained in shops where the customers sat on the ground or carpets and ate and drank together. In this connection, Rauwolf was the first European to describe the preparation and drinking of coffee. Apparently the drinking of coffee (*Coffea arabica* L.) was begun in the later medieval centuries by the Sufis in Yemen who found the drink aided their religious performances. The drinking of the beverage was discontinued for a time, but later, after continued use, the chief of police at Mecca forbade its use for a brief time (1511). A reaction against the drinking of coffee in Cairo is noted in 1532–1533. Moslem theologians, who varied in their support or disapproval, could not prevent its spread from Egypt into Syria, Persia, and Turkey. The first coffeehouses in Constantinople date from 1544 and were set up by men from Syria.

The coffeehouses which sprang up everywhere in the Moslem Near East became centers for idle conversation and poetry reading.[44] An imperial firman, dated December 2, 1565, pointed out to the cadi of Jerusalem that "whereas from olden times there was no coffee-house in Jerusalem and the local inhabitants were assiduous in (their) divine worship and pious devotion at the five times (of daily prayer), coffee-houses have (now) been newly established at five places. They are the meeting-place of rascals and ungodly people (who) day and night do not cease to act wickedly and mischievously, perniciously and refractorily, (thus) keeping the Muslims from pious devotion and divine worship. (In your opinion) it is (therefore) necessary to remove, eradicate and extirpate the coffee-houses from these venerable places." In 1584, however, a proprietor of one of the three coffee-houses in Gaza came to Constantinople to defend his rights to thus "make his living" and obtained imperial permission to do so.[45]

Rauwolf described coffee as "a very good drink, by them called *chaube* [hot], that is almost as black as ink and very good in illness, chiefly those of the stomach." It was drunk in the morning in open shops and out of porcelain cups, "as hot as they can; they put it often to their lips but drink a little at a time and let it go around the circle as they sit." In the preparation of coffee, they used water and berries, called *bunnu,* in "size, shape, and color almost like a bayberry, surrounded by two thin shells, which . . . are brought from the Indies." Until such time as he would be "better informed by the learned," Rauwolf identified the coffee beans by their "virtue, figure, looks, and name" as being the *buncho* of Avicenna and the *bunca* of Rhazes.[46] Coffee was widely used in Aleppo and there were many coffee shops and merchants selling the coffee beans in the bazaar.

In 1600, William Biddulph wrote that in Aleppo the

most common drinke is Coffa, which is a blacke kinde of drinke, made of a kind of Pulse like Pease, called Coava, which being grownd in the Mill, and boiled in water, they drinke it as hot as they can suffer it; which they finde to agree very well with them against their crudities, and feeding on Herbes and raw meates . . . It is accounted a great curtesie amongst them to give unto their friends when they come to visit them, a Fin-ion or Scudella of Coffa, which is more holesome then toothsome, for it causeth good concoction, and driveth away drowsinesse . . . Their Coffa houses are more common than Ale-houses in England; but they use not so much to sit in the houses, as on Benches on both sides the streets, neere unto a Coffa house, every man with his Fin-ion full; which being smoaking hot, they use to put it to their Noses and Eares, and then sup it off by leasure, being full of idle and Ale-house talke, whiles they are amongst themselves drinking of it; if there be any newes, it is talked off there.[47]

Pedro Teixeira, the Portuguese traveler who made two trips to the Orient late in the sixteenth century and early in the seventeenth century, reported that coffee was "much used in all Turkey, Arabia, Persia, and Syria. It is a seed, very like little dry beans, and is brought from Arabia. It is prepared in houses kept for that purpose." He described the drink as "thick, nearly black, and insipid. If it has any flavour this inclines to bitterness, but very little. All those who want it assemble in those houses, where they are served with it very hot in Chinese porcelain cups, that may hold four to five ounces. These they take into their hands, and sit blowing on it and sipping. Those who are accustomed to drink it say that it is good for the stomach, prevents flatulence and piles, and stimulates the appetite." He noted the new (1604) coffeehouse of Baghdad and reported its product as "black and rather tasteless; and although some good qualities are ascribed to it, none are proven. Only their custom induce them to meet here for conversation, and use this for entertainment; and in order to attract custom there are here pretty boys, richly dressed, who serve the coffee and take the money; with music and other diversions. These places are frequented at night in summer, and by day in winter. This house is near the river, over which it has many windows, and two galleries, making it a very pleasant resort. There are others like it in the cities, and many more throughout Turkey and Persia." The coffeehouses of Aleppo he described as "well built and furnished, adorned with numerous lamps, for that their chief custom is at night, though they have enough by day also." [48]

While the people of the East esteemed coffee as much as the German did his wormwood and herb wine, Rauwolf felt they loved wine better when allowed to drink it. According to Rauwolf, when Sultan Suleiman had given permission for wine to be drunk by the Moslems, the people "met together daily in drinking-houses, and drank to one another, not only two or three glasses of strong wine not mixed with water but four or five of such as came to them from Venice, so quickly one after another and with such eagerness, as I have often seen it, that they would not allow themselves to eat a morsel or two between." The Moslems became so gluttonous as far as wine was concerned that "they excell all other nations in it." On Suleiman's death in 1560, his son and successor, Amurah, immediately forbade the drinking of wine so that anyone who even smelled of wine was fined or punished by bastinadoes. Once the pasha of Aleppo met a drunken servant in his courtyard and beheaded him on the spot. Despite the prohibition and the punishments given, some Moslems continued to drink when they could and the renegades especially were known for their drinking to excess. When wine drinking was prohibited for the Moslems, the Christians fared well, for wine was plentiful and cheap. The oriental wine was "generally red, very good and pleasant." It was kept in skins and brought to Aleppo from various places but especially from Nizip on the border of Armenia, two days travel distant. The use of wineskins reminded Rauwolf, of course, of the story in Matthew 9:17.

The Christians in the Near East, allowed to drink wine, owned whole vineyards and made their own wine. Those Moslems who did grow grapes used them in various ways; some, especially around Damascus where the best grapes grew, made raisins. Others boiled the grape juice until it was the consistency of honey. Those living about Gaziantep, a town west of Bir, made the latter and it was called *pachmatz*. The very thick must was put in little barrels and shipped to other places. The less thick variety was mixed with water and given to the servants to drink instead of a julep; or else it was put into a little cup and bread dipped into it and eaten. Other sweet drinks were prepared from the red berries of the jujubes or from raisins, which when boiled in water and a little honey made a drink called *nassaph*. A kind of mead made from honey and called *tscherbeth* was also drunk. This drink and another made from barley or wheat and called by the ancient names of *zythum* and *curmi* made the Turks "so merry and frivolous, that, as our peasants do when they drink beer, they sing and play on their oboes, cornets, and kettle-drums, which their musicians make use of every morning when the guards are relieved." All of these drinks were sold in the bazaar and were cooled all summer long with ice and snow brought from the mountains. So much ice was put into the drink "that it makes their teeth freeze."

In Aleppo Rauwolf found the bread was nourishing, good, and whiter than could be found anywhere else. The bread was prepared in a variety of shapes and ways; some was made with the yolks of eggs and others had sesame, coriander seeds, or saffron sprinkled on top. Meat was plentiful, because the foothills of the Taurus range to the north afforded pasture for rams, wethers, sheep with broad and fat tails, goats, cattle, and buffalo. The goats were especially plentiful. Daily, numbers of goats were driven through the city and warm goat's milk was sold to any who wanted it. Some of the goats (*Capra mambrica*), although small, had ears up to two feet in length. As these long appendages hindered the grazing of the animal, one ear was usually cut off, causing the animal to graze and walk with the head held sideways. The meat-animals were slaughtered in fields outside the city and the discarded offal attracted a large number of wild dogs which roamed the countryside like the wolves of Germany. The Turks did not kill these wild dogs, but commonly raised the puppies as an act of charity—like the Banians of India who "serve the birds in the same manner as these do dogs and cats." The wolves of the area were like dogs in shape and size; indeed Pliny remarked that the wolves of Egypt were less in size and lazier than the wolves of the northern countries.

As there were no inns in the East where, like in Europe, travelers may lodge and eat, cooked food could be obtained in many of the shops in the bazaar where one could purchase meat, fowls, sauces, broths, soup, rice, "which they boil up to such a stiffness that it crumbles," and thick *bnuhourt* made of cracked barley and wheat boiled with or without milk. This last coarse but nourishing food had been mentioned by Dioscorides, Avicenna, and Rhazes and was prepared in large quantities as a war ration for soldiers and sailors. Another dish, called *trachan,* had the consistency of glue when prepared, but when dried in small portions, it could be boiled and made into a nourishing food in emergencies. For such occasions large quantities were stored in fortifications. Also available was a porridge-like preparation, called pulse in Europe, which Pliny (xviii. 8) said had been used by the ancients. Poultry, snipes, partridges with red bills and feet, and woodcocks were plentiful. Since the adjacent Kuwaid stream was so small and contained a large number of turtles, few fish were available. Some fish were brought from Antioch and from the Euphrates, but these were not considered delicacies by the inhabitants of Aleppo "because most of them [the inhabitants] drink water instead of wine." Little dishes of cole, cauliflower, carrots, turnips, kidney-beans, and fruits could be purchased, as could cheese, raisins, almonds, dried peas, pistachios, and cracked hazelnuts—the last being brought from Europe but seemingly better tasting and more pleasant than Rauwolf remembered eating in Germany. Vendors carried about plates of preserves made with sugar and honey and these were of various colors and shapes and made an attractive arrangement. Despite the abun-

dance of food Rauwolf thought that the inhabitants lived spar-
ingly and inexpensively; "for they do not have such great feasts,
nor so many dishes, nor are they prepared at such great cost as
we do in our country."

Since Rauwolf had taken this distant trip in order to "see those
fine and exotic plants, which the authors so frequently mention,"
he used his long stay in Aleppo for this purpose.[49] In his travel
book he named 130 different plants, trees, fruits, and vegetables,
which he found growing about Aleppo or saw in the bazaar
there. In this search for plants he was often accompanied by his
friends but especially by Krafft. There was some danger involved
in roaming the countryside and collecting plants, for the Turks
and other inhabitants were bound to be suspicious of a European
who was walking about, observing, and recording.

Once when Rauwolf was botanizing outside the city with two
friends, he discovered a strange plant (*Aristolochia maurorum*
L.) called *rhasut* and *rumigi* by the Syrians. Rauwolf did not
have a digging tool along and was having difficulty in uprooting
the plant when an armed Turk came galloping up to see what
the three Europeans were doing. Each of them gave the Turk
some money and he rode away well pleased. However, before
Rauwolf could get the plant out of the ground, the Turk came
back at a full gallop. Rauwolf told his friends to run to the
nearby rows of olive trees while he made one last effort to pull
up the plant. The plant came out, but by this time the Turk was
upon him and Rauwolf had just enough time to gain the nearest
olive tree. Here he found his friends had gone further to other
trees and he was left to face the Turk and his drawn scimitar
alone. Using the tree for protection, Rauwolf dodged from side
to side so the scimitar bit into the tree instead of him. While
doing this Rauwolf decided that if the Turk put up his scimitar
and drew out his bows and arrows, which he also carried, he
would rush the Turk and try to unseat him. The Turk was so
angry that he forgot about his bow and arrows and kept chop-
ping at Rauwolf and the tree for some time. Finally, Rauwolf
decided to play upon the covetous nature of these people and
holding out a silver *saijet,* he offered it to the Turk from behind
the tree. The Turk beckoned him to come out and then took the

coin. But when Rauwolf had pulled the coin from his pocket, he had accidentally dropped his notebook. The Turk now demanded this too and the German refused to part with his precious notes. The Turk became angry, making Rauwolf sorry he had not unseated him when he handed him the money. But as Rauwolf knew that any physical action against a Turk, no matter how justified, would only result in punishment, he gave the notebook to the Turk who then rode away.

V ALEPPO TO RAQQA

For nine months Rauwolf stayed in Aleppo observing the activities of this trading center and its cosmopolitan population. When he had collected "a fine parcel of foreign and undescribed plants," he resolved to go farther eastward to Mesopotamia, Assyria, and Babylonia. As these countries, traditionally known as "the most ancient and fruitful lands where the most ancient peoples and most potent monarchs had lived," could be reached only after difficult and dangerous travel, Rauwolf sought a trusted companion for the trip. He was fortunate in finding in Aleppo an unnamed but experienced Dutchman, a long time resident of that city, who was also desirous of traveling to Baghdad and beyond.[1] Careful plans had to be made, not only how best to overcome the hazards of the journey, but also how to avoid the suspicions of the Turks and the unjust taxes and presents (*avarias*) imposed on foreign travelers. It was decided to travel as merchants and in the company of other merchants so as to be less conspicuous in a land where traders from all over the Near East traveled the trade routes. Krafft, as factor of the Manlich firm, secured for Rauwolf a quantity of appropriate merchandise to take to the great emporium of Baghdad.

To complete the deception and, no doubt, for reasons of comfort, the Europeans put on the garb of the region. First they put on white cotton drawers reaching to the ankles and tied about the waist; then came white cotton shirts without collars. Over this they put long blue cabans, buttoned down the front and cut out about the neck. They thus looked like Armenian merchants. On their heads they wound turbans with blue trim, like those worn by the Christians of the area. Yellow shoes, studded with nails at the toes and with curved irons on the heels, were put on their feet. The colorful costume was completed with a frock of coarse material (*meska*), without sleeves and reaching only to the knees. Material of this kind was usually made of the hair of goats and asses and varied in quality; the best, in black and white stripes, was used for clothing, the poorer kinds were used for tents and provision bags. This outer frock reminded Rauwolf of the sackcloth of the Old Testament: "It is very probable that those were very like these that are still used."

Thus properly attired and equipped with "cloths, merchandise, provisions of biscuits and drink," the travelers awaited an opportunity to join other merchants going to Baghdad. In this connection, another decision had to be made. Would it be more convenient to go by caravan across the desert, a journey of about 50 days, or should they go by water down the Tigris or Euphrates rivers? When they met some Armenian merchants who were enroute to Baghdad and who knew Arabic and Turkish, it was decided to join them and go northeast to Bir and from there float down the Euphrates to Baghdad. The fact that some of the merchants had already made four trips to India was an added attraction. The Europeans put their goods with that of the merchants, secured passes from the pasha and cadi of Aleppo with the assistance of one of the translators with the Venetians, and were ready for the three-day trip to Bir.

Their caravan of many camels left Aleppo on the thirteenth of August, 1574, and headed north.[2] On the first day, the rough route led them through uninhabited desert, and when a little village was reached by night, the caravan was halted and camp made.[3] As a precaution against a surprise night attack, the goods were placed in a circle about the tents and the beasts outside this circle. Shortly after midnight a great caravan of many camels and asses was heard passing nearby, and it was decided to break camp and follow close behind them. The region through which the caravan passed on the second day was more fertile, and plowed fields could be seen. At some places they observed encampments of Arabs, with the tents neatly arranged in streets. The hurried rate of travel, the heavy loads, and the heat of midday brought the caravan to a halt beside a small building for a two-hour rest. During this rest period, some Arab women came down from the hills to gather the dung of the camels, valuable fuel in this treeless land.

When the great heat had abated, the caravan resumed its march and that evening they reached a small village in the valley, above which on a hill was a large camp of Arabs. When the caravan had encamped in the valley near the Arabs, these soon came down to view and speak with the merchants. Although the conversation was friendly enough and the women even brought water and milk, because the Arabs were "hungry and in their appearance like our gypsies," it was decided to keep a sharp watch during the night. Rauwolf remarked that these nomads, living in tents and traveling from place to place, were "used to idleness from their infancy and will rather endure hunger, heat, and cold, than get anything by their handiwork, till the fields, or plant food garden-herbs for their maintenance, although they might do it in several fruitful places in their own possession."

On the next day, the fifteenth of August, the caravan broke camp two hours before daybreak with the hope of reaching Bir before night. However, the poor condition of their camels, oppressed by heavy burdens and the excessive heat, forced them to seek rest for the night near a small village. Supper consisted of some gourds and biscuits. The march was resumed again two hours before daybreak and it was yet early morning when they arrived at the Euphrates River. To reach Bir on the eastern bank, the river, here a mile wide and deep enough to make bridging difficult, was safely crossed by means of boats. To the north could be seen the Taurus mountains, and Rauwolf compared the situation of the city to that of Tripoli and Mount Lebanon or Lausanne and the Alps. While the city itself was neither large nor strong, it did have a citadel on an isolated and inaccessible hill (172 feet high) that dominated the city. The area about Bir was very pleasant and fertile, especially the region about the western bank of the river, which was well tilled and planted with grain. It was harvest time when Rauwolf arrived and the peasants were threshing the grain with little carts drawn by oxen. Eastward of the river, the land was rough and bare, but it did support sheep and goats, which were daily brought to Bir for trans-shipment to Aleppo and other places.

Bir (Al-Birah), the walled port city of the upper Euphrates, had long been a fortress protecting a river-crossing. In the Assyrian inscriptions it is known as Til-Barsip. The Moslem city occupied the site of the Greek city of Apamia founded by Seleucus Nicator; just opposite to Apamia had been the city of Zeugma (bridge), the two cities being connected by a bridge of boats. Bir was known to the Romans as Birtha and to the crusaders it was Bile.[4] Cesare Federici, the Venetian merchant who visited the city in 1563, reported Bir to be "a small city very scarce of all manner of victuals," but a trading city where "the marchants divide themselves into companies, according to their merchandise that they have." Twenty years later, in 1583, Ralph Fitch wrote that the city was "a little town, but very plentiful of victuals," a fact supported by his friend, John Eldred. John Newberry (1581) noted that at Bir "is great store of Linnen cloth made, and great store of Waxe: here is also great store of Corne and Fish, and Cordovan skins, and Hony." John Cartwright (1603) gave the Turkish name as "Biarbech." [5]

John Eldred (1583) found the Euphrates at Bir to be "about the breadth of the Thames at Lambeth, and in some places narrower, in some broader; it runneth very swiftly, almost as fast as the river Trent: It hath divers sorts of fish in it, but all are scaled, some as big as salmons, like barbills." He also pointed out that at Bir the Euphrates "beginneth first to take his name, being here gathered into one chanell, whereas before it cometh downe in manifolde branches, and therefore is called by the people of the countrey by a name which signifieth a thousand heads." [6] Cartwright, who repeated Eldred's description almost word for word, traveled from Aleppo to Bir in a caravan of "a thousand persons, besides Camels, Horses, Mules, and Asses," and an entire day was spent in ferrying this caravan over the Euphrates at Bir.[7]

Bir was the point of embarkation for the river voyage down the Euphrates to Felugia, the port of Baghdad. The boats, generally flatbottomed, were made at Bir or were floated down to Bir from Armenia. Because of the current these boats made only one trip down the river to Felugia, where they were sold cheaply. Federici (1563) said that at Felugia "the marchants pluck their boats in pieces, or sell them for a small price, for that at Bir they cost the marchants forty or fifty chickens [zecchins, ducats] a piece, and they sel them at Feluchia for seven or eight chickens a piece." Fitch also reported that a boat which cost 50 ducats at Bir sold for seven or eight at Felugia. William Barret (1584) gave the cost of a boat of 30 to 35 camel-loads (about 10 tons) as 60 ducats or 2,400 medines. Because of the dangers inherent in traveling down a meandering and shifting stream, Fitch wrote that it was "not good that one boate goe alone, for if it should chance to breake, you should have much a doe to save your goods from the Arabians, which be always there abouts robbing." Eldred wrote that "when men travell in the moneth of July, August, and September, the water being then at the lowest, they are constrained to carry with them a spare boat or two to lighten their owne boats, if they chance to fall on the sholds." [8]

The number of days required for the passage to Felugia varied with the amount of water in the stream. Federici reported that if the river was at flood it took 15 to 18 days, or 40 to 50 days if the water was low. He did not give his own passage time. Balbi took 42 days in January and February, 1580, while Newberry made the trip in about 20 days (March 26? to April 14, 1581). Fitch said 16 days were required and Eldred took 28 days in June, 1583. Sir Anthony Sherley spent 30 days on the river in 1599. It was going to take the unfortunate Rauwolf 55 days.[9]

While the Euphrates was not swift and dangerous at Bir, below that city its current, channels, and meandering course confused even the river-men, who often did not know which of the many branches to take. The hazards of the river voyage to Baghdad often deterred merchants, who felt it better to carry their goods northeast to Kara Amid (Diyar Bakr) on the Tigris and from there float down to Baghdad.[10] The water of the Euphrates was very muddy and undrinkable unless it was allowed to stand for two or three hours so that the sand and mud could precipitate to the bottom of the vessel, often to the thickness of an inch. Thus in every house in the river towns could be seen several large settling pots. For immediate use the water was drunk through a towel.

During Rauwolf's stay at Bir, fishermen brought various kinds of fish to the camp for sale. One kind, called *geirigi,* was similar to the European carp, but thinner and longer. Some of these weighed up to three *rotulas,* that is 16 to 18 pounds. These fish were tasty and cheap; one could be purchased for a *medine,* the equivalent of three German kreuzer. The fish were caught by feeding them poisonous pellets made of the berries of *Menispermum cocculus* L. called by the people *doam samec,* which drugged the fish so that they surfaced and could be pulled ashore. Numerous tame vultures, of the same size but more ashen in color than the European variety, perched on the houses and in the streets. Another variety of vulture, bigger and lighter in color with black wing tips, Rauwolf identified as the *gyuni* of Rhazes and the *rachame* of Avicenna.

Rauwolf and his Armenian merchant friends waited several weeks at Bir for boats to be floated down from Armenia to Bir. When several of these craft did arrive, preparations for loading and departure occupied the group. One boat, belonging to a Turkish merchant, was loaded only with grain to be sold at Baghdad, where drought conditions promised early sale. The patron or captain of Rauwolf's boat had space left so there was a further delay while he collected more goods and passengers for the trip. Finally some Armenians and Persians arrived from Aleppo, headed for Baghdad and Basra. Along with these, the captain took aboard four soldiers assigned to strengthen the garrison at Baghdad. In addition, he took on some Jews, "which are worse than ours, and so we were warned to have a care of them." The passenger list was completed with the addition of some Moslem religious men or dervishes. Rauwolf, like most Europeans, had a very low opinion of these privileged fellows who lived by begging and "pretend to great holiness and devotion, pray often, and persuade the vulgar sort of people that God hears their prayers before any others and grants their desires." For provisions, they stored aboard fruit, raisins, watermelons, garlic, onions, ground grain, honey, and other items.[11] Ample provisions were necessary for there were "no inns upon this river, as upon the Rhine or Danube, where food was prepared for the traveller."

When the three boats had been loaded and provisioned, the river voyage began in "the name of God" on the evening of August 30, 1574.[12] It was intended that about fifteen miles of travel could be made before stopping for the night, but two of the boats entered a wrong channel soon after starting and since it was important that the flotilla stay together, the whole party was delayed while the boats were brought back to the main channel. Thus the party landed for the night at Caffra (*kafar,* "village"), a market town on a hill only five miles from Bir. Camp was broken at the break of day and initially good progress was made. The river here flowed almost due south and the Taurus range to the north began to recede from view while the terrain through which they passed became more desert-like and sandy. Then the river branched into several good broad channels so the pilots did not know which branch was the best. The Turkish boat, leading the way, safely negotiated the passage, but the second boat, through a pilot error, ran aground on a shoal near the right bank. Rauwolf was in the third boat following closely behind, and since the grounded boat turned sideways and blocked the channel, his boat crashed into it. While the force of the collision did not damage Rauwolf's boat, the two uppermost boards of the other were stove in and water poured into the boat. After some of the sand had been cleared from the left bank, Rauwolf's boat now attempted to skirt the damaged ship, but the force of the current again drove the boats together and this time Rauwolf's boat sustained damage, but not enough to ship water. However, Rauwolf's boat cleared the stranded one and landed below it. All helped unload both boats for redistribution of cargo and for the making of repairs. With much effort the grounded boat was pulled free and drawn up on shore for repairs.

While the crews were thus engaged, a large number of Arabs appeared among the shrubs and tamarisks of the shore. Some were on horseback and others afoot. When some of the Arabs tried to steal from the items on the shore, the guards fired several times into the air and since the Arabs were unfamiliar with firearms, the noise frightened them away.[13] The cargo of the grounded boat had sustained considerable loss, especially in silk, damask, soap, sugar, roots of *zarneb melchi* (*Seseli* sp.), "which is good for the pain in the back," figs, and grain.

While the crews and passengers of both boats made repairs and spread the wet goods out to dry, some Jews in the group falsely accused Rauwolf and one of his comrades of drinking wine with the master of the ship. This accusation incensed the Moslem dervishes in the group so much that they took the container of wine, threw it into the river, then pulled it ashore and let the wine run out on the sand. This caused some of the soldiers to come to the aid of the Europeans and the Jews were severely reprimanded for starting the affair. The dervishes did not forget the incident, however, and further trouble was experienced the next day. It was evening and Rauwolf was on guard duty when he saw a dervish with a mug of water. Rauwolf asked for a drink, but in reaching for the mug, he stepped upon and broke a fiddle belonging to one of the Turks. The owner was angry, of course, but was pacified by Rauwolf's offer to repair the instrument with some glue he carried. The next morning, while Rauwolf and the Turk sat mending the fiddle, a dervish complained that they should be helping with the work and taking the fiddle, he broke it, and threw it into the river. The Turk thereupon beat the dervish about the head and arms and would have killed him with his scimitar had not the others intervened. Thus, "no good deed remains unrewarded, and no ill one unpunished."

In all, four days were required to dry out the merchandise, and repair and reload the boats. Travel was not resumed until noon on Friday, September 3. All that day nothing was seen except some wild boars among the bushes that lined the shores. That night a landing was made near a small village, which could be seen on a rise about two or three miles distant to the east. On the shore, Rauwolf "found nothing but a bastard camel's hay, which was like the true one but without any virtue in it." On the next day good progress was made. At noon, the boats passed a ruined but strong citadel called Galantza (Kala'at-an-Najm) on the right side of the river.[14] Here, Rauwolf was informed, the eldest son of the king of the Arabs had foolishly decided to make a stand in 1570 in the wars with the Turks. Usually the Arabs simply melted away into the desert wastes and avoided battle, but here the sultan's forces assaulted the citadel, breached the wall in three places, and captured it. The king's son was taken captive, carried to Constantinople, and beheaded, "as they say," the following year. That night the boats landed on a small and uninhabited island in the midst of the stream. Here they felt secure from marauding Arabs, but no sooner had they bedded down than some Arabs crept among them "rather to visit our goods than us." They were discovered almost immediately, however, and the stolen items were recovered.

During the morning of the next day, September 5, an increasing number of Arabs were seen on the shore and on the heights in the distance. Some squadrons of horsemen, 40 or 50 strong, were also observed and from this it was concluded that the camp of the king of the Arabs must be near. This surmise proved to be true, for when the boats pulled into shore at noon, the king's son came riding up. He was mounted on a tall, black horse and was accompanied by a retinue of about 100 men, most of whom were armed with bows and long pikes made of reeds. The prince was about 24 or 25 years old, "of a brownish color," and wore a white cotton turban with one end hanging down over the back of his neck. All the Arabs were dressed in ordinary sheep skins, with the wool still on, which hung to their ankles. Their prince's costume was distinguished from the others only in that his robe had long sleeves with escutcheons and gold cloth strips about the neck and sleeves. As the Euphrates flowed here through land claimed by the Arabs, custom fees were due the king. The prince first rode to the Turkish boat but did not stay long when he found it laden only with grain. On coming to Rauwolf's boat, the prince seated himself on a bale of merchandise amidships while his followers inspected the goods of one merchant after another, opening now and then a chest or a bale. In doing this they took various items, "more or less, according as they liked them." While this was going on, a 2-year-old prince, clothed only in a cotton shirt and wearing rings of fine Arabian gold about his neck, wrists, and legs, was brought aboard.

Rauwolf and his companions were in the poop of the boat and eventually the Arabs came to them. However, before they could examine the displayed merchandise, the Arabs saw Rauwolf's gun. The gun, a fine one inlaid with ivory, was immediately taken to the prince by the admiring Arabs. The prince recognized it as of European or "Frankish" make, and Rauwolf and his Dutch friend informed him that they had recently come from Europe with the intention of going to India. The prince was very friendly and ordered his men not to search the goods of the Europeans. In the conversation that ensued, the prince told Rauwolf's companion that he remembered seeing him before. This proved true, for some time before, while the Dutchman, a goldsmith, had been in Aleppo, the Venetian consul had sent him and others with presents of costly and richly wrought clothing to the king of the Arabs who happened to be camped nearby. On that occasion, the king had tried to impress the visitors with his troops and had promised aid to the Venetians if they made war against the Turks. After conversing thus for a while, the prince left the boats and taking some of the merchants along, went to the king's encampment nearby.

Rauwolf would have liked to have presented the king with his gun, but he feared that the Turkish soldiers, dervishes, and Jews in the party would have reported him for supplying arms to the enemy. Rauwolf also remembered that when the king of the Arabs encamped near Aleppo, people were strictly forbidden to sell any arms, bows, or pikes to those who came into the city to buy provisions and other things.[15] The group that went to the tent of the king returned so late that no more travel could be made that day and the boats remained there all night. Those who had visited the king reported that he would not believe that they had come from Aleppo until they showed him letters which indicated their place of origin. The king had insisted that they came from Safad, a place that had recently been seized by the sultan from him. By threatening to arrest the group, the king forced from the merchants some Damascus knives tipped with silver and some damask.

Other European travelers of this period recorded similar encounters with Ahmad Abu Rishah, the ruler of the Arabians. Federici made the river voyage in 1563 and wrote that "as you pass the river Euphrates from Bir to Feluchia, there are certein places which you must passe by, where you pay custome certaine medines upon a bale, which custome is belonging to the sonne of Aborise king of the Arabians and of the desert, who hath certain cities and villages on the river Euphrates." Ralph Fitch

(1583) and John Eldred (1583) both call the king "Aborise," while William Biddulph (1600) reported two kings, "Dandan and Aborisha," one a lawful king, the other a usurper. Sir Anthony Sherley visited the camp of the king in 1599 and "saw a poore King with tenne or twelve thousand beggerly Subjects, living in Tents of blacke Haire-cloath: yet so well governed, that though our cloathes were much better then theirs, & their want might have made them apt enough to have borrowed them from us; we passed notwithstanding through them all in such peace, as we could not have done, being Strangers, amongst civiller bred people." Sherley received no demands during the visit, but on returning to his boat he found the master of the king's house awaiting his return and he was "forced to send his Master three Vestes of cloath of Gold, for beholding his person." William Barret in his list of "charges from Aleppo to Goa" noted "For custome to king Aborissei, Duc.[ats] 20. is med.[ines] 800." [16]

The next day, after an early start, the boats passed through an extensive wilderness. The only sign of life was a large number of wild boars. In the evening, however, they arrived at a village and a fortress, situated in a plain on the right bank at a point only two days caravan travel from the Aleppo they had left 25 days before.[17] The castle, according to Rauwolf, belonged to a wealthy pasha named "John Rolandt," who also owned a fine house in Aleppo. This individual also had 60 sons, six or seven of these were sanjaks and others belonged to the sultan's court. The night was spent on the east bank of the river just below the village. The river here turned eastward and all the next day the wilderness continued. Here and there could be seen little huts consisting only of four upright sticks and a roof of brush. They housed many children, however; so many, in fact, that Rauwolf "often marveled at their number."

All these river-Arabs were great swimmers and they often swam the width of the broad Euphrates. If the boats passed within shouting distance, the Arabs frequently asked if their king was in the vicinity. Rauwolf admired their loyalty and obedience to their king, "as no other nation does to their superiors." At times the boats pulled in to shore so the passengers could purchase the milk the Arab women offered for sale in large flat dishes. The travelers exchanged biscuits for the milk and since the Arabs had little grain, the exchange was most agreeable to both parties. The fresh milk was used in several ways by the travelers. At times they broke biscuits into the milk and thus ate it, and if there was not enough milk, water was added to extend the supply. Sometimes the milk was poured into linen sacks and allowed to hang for two or three days and the curdled milk was then eaten with biscuits and onions. In 1583, John Eldred reported that he brought "milke, butter, eggs, and lambs and gave them in barter, (for they care not for money) glasses, combes, corall, amber, to hang about their arms and necks, and for churned milke we gave them bread and pomgranat peeles, wherewith they used to tanne their goat skinnes which they churne withall." [18]

As was his custom, Rauwolf used every free moment on land to examine the riparian plant life. In this wilderness region, the botanist was impressed by the large number of tamarisks, which here grew as big as the cherry and plum trees of Germany. Just before dark, the boats passed the fortress called Kala'ah Jabar on the left side of the river. [19] Belonging to the king of the Arabs, the citadel was very large and had several towers on the walls. Viewing it from the distance, Rauwolf thought it similar to Aleppo. The night of September 7 was spent on an island near the right bank, and once again the thievish Arabs had to be frightened away by firing the three guns in the party. The same trouble was experienced the next night on another uninhabited island. This time the travelers did not even light fires for cooking in the mistaken hope of remaining undiscovered, but again recourse had to be made to the guns.

On the ninth of September as the boats were nearing Raqqa, Rauwolf's boat, the largest of the three, ran aground during the noon meal of raisins and melons. The efforts of the entire party were of no avail in pulling the boat off the shoal, and in desperation they appealed to the Arabs who had gathered in the expectation of plunder. Since the Arabs would not put away their daggers and cudgels, a small guard had to be left in the boat, thus depleting the labor force. Two attempts did not free the boat and the Arabs stopped helping. Unloading the boat was considered, but this would have created a very difficult problem of guarding. At last a third appeal was made to the Arabs to put away their arms and help for a large reward. When this was agreed to, no guards needed to be left on board, and all assisted in getting the craft again into the main stream. After they had paid the Arabs for their help, the voyage was continued. That night they arrived at Raqqa.

Raqqa (Ar-Rahhak) was the capital of the Diyâr Mudar district, "the habitation of the Mudar tribe," in the southwestern part of the Al Jazîrah (island) province. The city was located on the north bank, just above the point where the Balikh river enters the Euphrates from the north. The Balîkh (Bilechai) rises near Harran, the ancient Carrhae, where Abraham settled after leaving Ur and where Crassus met his death after his defeat by the Parthians in 53 B.C. Raqqa means "morass" and it is on the site of the old Greek city of Callinicus or Nicephorium. To distinguish this city from others using the same descriptive term for swampy land, it was called As-Sawda, "the black." Under the Abbasids, the Caliph Mansur built in 772 a nearby town called Ar-Rafikah (the companion or fellow) and garrisoned it with loyal Kharâsân troops. Like Baghdad, the new town was built on a circular plan and the great Harun ar-Rashid built there a palace in which he resided at times to escape the heat of Baghdad. As the older town of Raqqa declined its name was transferred to the suburb, while the older settlement received the name of Ar-Rakkah-al-Muhtarikah (burnt Raqqa). Moslem authorities praise the luxurious growth of the area, the excellent markets, trade in olive oil, soap, reeds for fans, and the fine mosques, houses, and baths. Here on the southern bank of the Euphrates and just southwest of Raqqa, was the celebrated plain of Siffîn, where on July 26, 657, the battle between the followers of 'Ali and Mu'âwiyah came to a halt when the forces of Mu'âwiyah, almost beaten, raised copies of the Koran on their lances.[20]

John Newberry passed by Raqqa on March 28, 1580 and described it as "an old Towne where is a Castle all ruinated, and lyeth close upon the water to the Eastward." William Barret, the first English consul to Aleppo, recorded in 1584 that the customs at Raqqa were five medines per camel load.[21]

The traveler from Augsburg found the town "pitifully built, not well guarded with walls."[22] There was a resident sanjak-beg with 1,200 *spahis,* or cavalry. The ruins of the old town could still be seen on the nearby height and among the walls, arches, and pillars, there was yet standing the ruins of what must have been a strong and great structure, "so that one may conjecture, that it had perhaps been formerly the seat and habitation of their kings or magistrates." Between the old and new city stood a castle where the Turkish garrison resided. Part of the ruins could be traced to the devastation which the Tartar troops under Hulagu had done when they took Raqqa in 1260. Rauwolf remarked that some authorities consider Raqqa to be the site of old Rhages or Edessa, "but because this [Edessa] lies a day's journey farther from the river Euphrates, therefore it cannot be the same."

As soon as the crafts had pulled in to shore, the receiver of customs came on horseback to collect the fees. He came first to the boat of the Turkish merchant and demanded the deliverance of all arms, lances, and bows. These, the Turkish master refused to surrender, as never before had this been the practice. A hot dispute arose and the two would have drawn on each other had not the others intervened. Rauwolf reasoned that the customs collector was angry because he would have collected more money if traders used the Tigris river and the port of Kara Amid, which he also controlled. Getting nothing from the Turkish boatman and not being interested in the grain he was carrying, the collector turned to the other boats in the hope of making up his loss there. He came into Rauwolf's boat and even stayed the night, lying between the two Europeans, so they would not hide their merchandise from him. He accused the Europeans of being spies and threatened to arrest them, confiscate their goods, and send them to Constantinople as slaves. Not frightened by his blustering manner and threats, Rauwolf and his companion showed him their passes. Thus rebuffed, the customs collector left the two alone and began to make unreasonable demands from the other merchants.

To further enforce his demands, the poles and oars were removed from the boats so that departure was impossible. The merchants would not surrender to the collector's demands but instead sent one of their number with an Arab guide to Kara Amid to complain to the pasha there of "these impositions and extortions." When the toll collector found out about this he and his son immediately followed them. The pasha was not in Kara Amid, however, but at "Giselet," three days further distant. While the merchant continued to Giselet, the toll-taker returned to Raqqa and falsely informed the waiting merchants that he had seen the pasha at Kara Amid who had ordered that they pay ten ducats *per centum*. However, while the collector was gone to Kara Amid, the merchants had removed the best and greatest part of their goods and had hidden some of this in the sand. Thus when the collector and his men carefully searched the boats, he found very little of value. While the search was being conducted, the merchant who had been sent to the pasha returned and reported that "the pasha was very much displeased that the collector dealt so unjustly with us, contrary to the orders and law of his master the Sultan, keeping us long and hindering us in our navigation." To show his displeasure, the pasha had written to the sanjak and ordered him, on pain of death, to take the customs collector prisoner and send him to Constantinople for trial. The pasha feared that the collector "would pay with his life for this misdemeanor."

On September 21, while the travelers were retained at Raqqa, the king of the Arabs broke camp and set out in search of better pastures for his horses, asses, and camels. These nomads, despising farming and trading, were constantly on the move, going from one stand of grass to another and on such moves, everything and everybody was taken along. On this particular occasion, Rauwolf had a chance to see such a mass migration for the multitude came toward Raqqa and the Turkish guards shut the gates of the city for four days as they passed by. Some of the Arabs were on horseback and were armed with darts and bows, but the camel was the most evident beast of burden. Rauwolf was told that at times, especially when the king was on the move, 150,000 camels might be used. He, himself, had seen at one time 3,000 to 4,000 of these "strong and hardy creatures, fit to carry heavy burdens and also to subsist without drinking in the greatest heat for three days together." Rauwolf especially admired the Arabian horses as "very noble, neat, and fit for business." These hardy animals could be ridden hard all day long through the wilderness and were fed only once a day. Commonly, the Arabs cut all the hair from the manes and tails of their horses, so that the tails "remain very naked and look something like the tail of a lion." The women usually rode little asses or rode with the children on the camels, "three or four of them together in boxes, as it is the fashion in these countries." The Arabs were "of a brown color like our gypsies" and about one-fourth of them were black, "which difference of color proceeds from their traveling up and down to places where negroes are, and sometimes leaving their own there and taking negroes in place of them." [23]

The king of the Arabs always encamped in the field, shunning any place that could be enclosed. This was especially so after losing his son, who had sought to make a stand at Kala'at an Najm. In the summer, the king moved northward, and in the winter, he went south. These migrations had frequently led to war with the Turks, but Rauwolf was "credibly informed" that a peace arrangement had been secured between the two whereby the king of the Arabs agreed to assist the sultan in his wars. In exchange, the Arab leader was to receive 60,000 ducats annually from the sultan. Rauwolf also understood that upon the death of the Arab king, the new ruler received congratulatory presents and a standard with his coat of arms on it from the sultan. This alliance, Rauwolf felt, was furthered by the fact that both parties were Moslem and that both nations practice polygamy with all wives receiving equal status despite possible diverse origin. Thus one of the wives of the king of the Arabs was a daughter of a sawmill operator in Raqqa. Her father and brother, who operated their mill by hand labor and not by horses or water as in Europe, had shown sympathy to the stranded travelers.

Rauwolf also made friends with a young Arab gentleman, a near relative of the king. This man frequently came to visit the travelers and always brought along 20 servants, armed with bows and darts. The young man wore a white turban and a long violet caban of wool, but his attendants were poorly dressed, some wearing black caps and long colored shirts with wide sleeves and broad leather belts in which were stuck their curved daggers. Once when Rauwolf and his companions were on the town wall enjoying the pleasant prospect of the valley, this young man joined them. After food had been exchanged, eaten, and washed down with river water, the Arab ordered one of his followers to play some music. The instrument had only one string and that as thick as the cord of the bow. For almost two hours the concert continued and Rauwolf and his friends felt that the program was too long and they were very happy when he finished.

VI RAQQA TO BAGHDAD

On September 27, about noon, the travelers set out once again on their river voyage.[1] Rauwolf found little to record for the next few days as they traveled through desert wastes. But even here there were little brush huts housing Arab families. These poor, miserable, and hungry people often swam out to the boats to beg for bread. The travelers threw whole handfuls into the water, and the swimmers "would snap at it just like hungry fish or ducks and eat it." Others collected the wet bread and putting it into the crown of their turbans, swam ashore with it. As the days passed and as the river turned toward the southeast, the region became more mountainous. Here the inhabitants lived in tents or in caves cut into the bare and rough hills. Rauwolf commented on the good marksmanship of the Arabs with their bows and arrows and darts made of reeds. Citing Josephus, the Old Testament, and Pliny, Rauwolf identified these people as the Ishmaelites, the descendants of Abraham and Hagar, his Egyptian wife, and from whom the Arabs are called Agarens.[2] Repeatedly the master of Rauwolf's boat had to answer the Arabs who, calling from the shore, wanted to know the whereabouts of their much respected ruler.

Traveling down the Euphrates like this was not expensive for there were no towns in which to purchase food and lodging. The diet consisted mostly of curds, cheese, fruits, honey, and bread. The honey was especially good and of a whitish color. Carried in large leather bottles, the honey was served in little cups to which was added some butter and the mixture then eaten with biscuits. This reminded Rauwolf of the food of St. John the Baptist.[3] At times, upon landing on the shore, a pit fire would be built of driftwood and meat, rice, or ground grain boiled. Sometimes they baked bread in large, flat cakes about the thickness of a finger by covering the flour and water paste with hot coals. Rauwolf found bread of this type very savory and good.

On September 30, about noon, the river came out of the mountainous region (Jebel Bishri) and on a high hill on the right bank was a triangular fortress, called Zelebie. Its situation reminded Rauwolf of Baden in Switzerland. The citadel was in ruins and inhabited only by birds and beasts. Rauwolf recognized herons, ducks, pelicans, and black cormorants with their long necks.[4] Six miles beyond was another fortification, this time on the left bank, called Lower Zelebie. Rauwolf would have liked to have found out more about these forts and their history, and also about the government of the king of the Arabs, but he was hindered by his lack of knowledge of Arabic. He also feared that too much curiosity would lead to suspicion and to his being charged as a spy. In the low country through which they were now floating, tilled fields and more habitations were evident, so the master of the boat landed the craft and meat and watermelons were bought. At this landing, about midnight an Arab crept up on one of the Turks and pushed him into the river where he would have drowned had he not been rescued by Rauwolf who was on sentry duty. This act of kindness led to Rauwolf receiving many favors of the Turkish soldiers in the party.

On the first of October, when travel was resumed, six mounted Arabs came to the shore and inquired of the travelers where they might find the king of the Arabs, as they were carrying letters from the sultan to the king. The master of Rauwolf's boat told them what he knew of the movements of the king. Soon thereafter the voyagers could see a town in the distance on a rise on the right bank. The town was called "Seccard" and as it belonged to the king of the Arabs, the Turks in the party said it was inhabited by *harami quibir,* or "great thieves." As they approached Deir ez Zor, their next destination, they came to a very dangerous section of the river. It was here that the Turkish captain, who had left Raqqa ahead of the others, had been shipwrecked and lost much of his load of grain. This was a serious loss, since grain was very scarce in Baghdad where it had not rained for two and a half years. When the crafts bearing Rauwolf and the others came to this place, about three miles from Deir, one of the boats became grounded on a mud bank. The master of Rauwolf's boat landed immediately and sent his crew to help. It took over an hour to empty and thus free the grounded boat. They then hurried on hoping to reach Deir before night, and with the help of local pilots who knew the location of rocks and channels, the travelers arrived safely.

The delay had given Rauwolf an opportunity to examine closely the tamarisks and the willows along the bank. The willows were called *garb* by the Arabs and the botanist observed that these unusual willows did "not grow high but spread very much; the twigs are stronger and not so tough as to make bands and withes as ours will. The bark is of a pale yellow color and so are the leaves, which are long, about two fingers broad, and crenated around the edges, so that they are very different from the rest of this kind." He did not see the flowers and fruit of this tree, but refers the reader to the pertinent chapters in Avicenna. Rauwolf was thus the first European to describe this species of aspen or *Populus euphratica* Oliv.—the "willow" on which the Israelites hung their harps (Ps. 137:2).

The town of Deir, lying on the right bank, was not very large, and its walls and ditches were of little military value. The number of houses was considerable, however, and the population came out to welcome the travelers. They planned that this would only be a brief stop to pay customs, to the sultan this time, but the customs official was not in town and they were forced to wait three days for his return. The delay enabled the visitors to get acquainted with the townsfolk, and Rauwolf found them "handsome, large, well set, white, and more mannerly than the rest." When the official arrived, he, too, treated them civilly and in turn was presented with a large dish filled with raisins and several kinds of confection, "laid about with soap-balls as is the fashion in those countries." Rauwolf distributed some sheets of white paper to the official and his assistants, which pleased the recipients a great deal. Around Deir were fertile fields with grain, Indian millet, cotton and other crops. In the gardens, Rauwolf found cauliflowers, colocynths, pumpkins, cucumbers, watermelons, and muskmelons, as well as date, lemon, and citron trees. The watermelons were so plentiful that one could "buy forty large ones for one *asper,* of which three makes one *medine,* about the value of two Kreutzers."

After the customs had been paid to the friendly official at Deir, preparations were made to resume the voyage.[5] Because the landing area was very muddy and the water low, the half-loaded boats were pulled into deeper water and the rest of the goods and newly purchased necessities were carried out in small crafts. On the evening of October 4, the party left Deir, and that night they pulled ashore only a little below the town. The next morning the voyage was resumed and no trouble was experienced until noon. At this time the river was very broad and shallow and the pilot of Rauwolf's boat, leading the way, did not know the best channel. Just then some Arabs appeared on the shore and directed the boat captains to take a certain course. A trap was immediately suspected, for the travelers had heard before that the Arabs had sunk some large stones in the river bed in the hope of causing a shipwreck. In this they had been earlier successful, for only a month before the Arabs had given directions to a pilot that caused the boat to crash into the submerged rocks, split, and sink. The master of Rauwolf's boat managed to bring his flat-bottomed craft into deeper water, but the boat following, having a rounded and thus deeper bottom, experienced considerable difficulty in getting through the shallow areas. Early in the evening, they saw to the east the distant and demolished castle of Buseria along the Khābūr River, which here flowed into the Euphrates. They had hoped to reach "Errachaby" that night, but having been delayed by the difficult navigation of the shallows, the night-landing was made a little above this town.[6]

Early the next morning the travelers came to this town, which was quite large and situated about half a mile from the shore in a very fruitful land. Two of the merchants went to the town to bring back some of the local merchants for trading purposes. The entire day was spent in trading, but early the next morning, October 7, the voyagers left to reach the little village of "Sehara," lying half a mile from the right shore on a height. Here the usual customs were paid the king of the Arabs. Rauwolf had to stay on board although the many bushes and trees on the shore invited examination. For the next several days the boats passed through a desolate and sandy desert area as the river turned eastward again. Rauwolf understood that this was a region of great sandstorms through which the pilots ("caliphi") of the caravans must find their way by compass, just as if at sea. These caravans generally loaded a third of the camels with food and water to sustain the men and beasts in their passage of the desert. No springs were available and the few cisterns were frequently dry. At Aleppo, Rauwolf had been told that the Turkish sultan had ordered 30,000 cisterns dug to furnish water for the Turkish armies fighting the Persians and Arabs. Rauwolf found little to record during these days, but on the ninth of October he saw some ancient turrets on a point called "Ersy," where, "as some say, had been formerly a famous town." Here the river made such a wide sweep that the boats were half a day in passing the site.

That night, while the boats were in shore, they received the usual pilfering visits by Arabs. Rauwolf took his turn as sentinel and, as was usual, took his post in the stern of the boat after providing himself with a strong cudgel. As the night was cold and damp, he wrapped himself in a large coat with long sleeves. After a long period of watching, Rauwolf became drowsy and fell asleep. While he slept, an Arab came swimming in the river and, reaching over the side of the boat, grabbed one of the hanging sleeves and sought to pull it over the side, not knowing that Rauwolf was wrapped up the coat. The tugging aroused the sleeping sentinel, who grabbed his cudgel and tried to hit the head of the swimmer; the Arab was too swift and escaped unharmed. The commotion awakened the others, who, "not knowing the particulars," thanked Rauwolf for his "great care and diligent watching."

The same Arabs who tried to pilfer at night were eager to trade during the day, and frequently the master of the boat would put in to shore so the merchants in the party could trade with the Arabian men and women on the shore. The merchants traded soap-balls, "pater nosters" of crystal and yellow agate beads, bracelets of red, yellow, green, and blue glass set in false gold, and high shoes with leather straps at the top. In exchange they received sheepskins, buckskins, cheese curds, and other things, including money. These Arabs, darker than the gypsies Ruwolf knew, did "not care much for work." The men shaved their heads except for a long lock which, like the Turks, hung down in back. Like Rauwolf himself, they wore long, sleeveless outer coats of coarse cloth, black and white striped, over their long, blue shirts which were girded with a broad, leather belt in which was stuck the usual curved dagger. Those that could not buy shoes, wrapped undressed skins, with the hair outward, about their feet. The men wore "no breeches, but the women do, and these are generally blue and come down to their ankles." Unlike the Turkish women, the Arab women did not wear veils but covered their heads with a broad scarf, usually blue, which hung down the back in a great knot. When displaying their finery, the women wore beads of marble, amber and glass of various colors on laces hanging down over their temples. These weighted strands, some a span long, "fly about from face to neck, so that in bending or moving their head, they often hurt their face, and do not a little hinder them in their actions." The more wealthy women wore silver and gold rings set with garnets, turquoise, rubies, and pearls in one of their nostrils. Some wore a number of rings or bracelets on their legs and arms, "which in their stepping and working, slip up and down about their hands and feet and so make an agreeable sound."

Several European travelers in this period commented on the finery of the Arab women. Eldred noted that the women "all without exception weare a great round ring in one of their nostrels, of golde, silver, or yron, according to their ability, and about their armes and smalles of their legs they have hoops of golde, silver, or yron." William Biddulph wrote: "Their wives wear Rings in their Noses, either silver or brasse, fastened to the middle gristle of their Nose, and colour their Lips blue with Indico, and goe alwayes bare-legged and bare-footed, with Plates or Rings of brasse above their ankles, and bracelets of brasse about their hands." Fitch reported the Arabs as having "large blew gownes, their wives eares and noses are ringed very full of rings of copper and silver, and they weare rings of copper about their legs." [7]

As the boats approached the town of 'Anah the swift current
and rocks in the channel made navigation difficult, and the master of Rauwolf's boat thought it best to land in the evening about
a mile and a half above the town. Rauwolf and the others went
on shore to walk among the very pleasant orchards and groves of
olive, orange, citron, lemon, pomegranate, and date trees. The
dates especially were very plentiful, and Rauwolf found here red
and yellow varieties that differed from those usually sent to Europe. The yellow ones he considered to be the *hayron* mentioned
by Serapion in his sixty-ninth chapter. He found them very tasty.
The next morning, Rauwolf and some others decided to walk
the short distance into 'Anah while the master of the boat
brought his craft into harbor there. The walk through the fruitful fields of cotton, ripe grain, and fruit orchards was very
pleasant.

Rauwolf saw only two unusual plants. One, called *moluchi* by
the Arabs, he considered to be the *Corchorus olitorius* L. of Pliny
(xxi. 52.82 and 106.183). The other plant was called *lubie
endigi* (Indian kidney-beans) by the Arabs, but Rauwolf took it
to be the *Trionum* (*Hibiscus sabdariffa* L.) "which Theophrastus [*sic*] mentioned several times." Since Sprengel cited this plant
as a new discovery by Rauwolf, his full description is here given
as a good example of the difficulties a sixteenth century botanist
encountered in verbally delineating a new plant.

There was also another plant, which because of its height is easily
seen. This was very similar to *Sesamum,* except that the stalk is
longer and fatter. The leaves are also rougher and the uppermost ones
are split into three different lobes, which is not to be seen in the uppermost leaves of *Sesamum* (the leaves of which are more like willow leaves both in length and color). Between the leaves, which
stand singly about the stalk and one above the other, crowd fine, large
flowers, which are yellow on the outside and streaked with red veins,
but of a purple-brown color inside with a long style in the middle.
When these fall off, long pods, about a finger long and thick, grow
out. These are rough on the outside, pointed at the top, and have five
distinct cells inside in which the seeds are contained (which are very
similar to the sort of mallow that is called *Abutilon* by some) and
the seeds are placed in good order one above the other.[8]

The town of 'Anah (Anatho, Bethauna) was very ancient. It is repeatedly mentioned in the records of the Assyrians as Anat which "lies in the midst of the Euphrates."[9] By the sixteenth century the town had spread from the original island to both the right and left banks of the river. The large island, surrounded with old but well-built walls, was about a mile in circumference with a citadel at the upstream end. This island was under Turkish control and had a garrison of troops. Newberry (1583) mentioned the fortified island, one of about fifteen such islands in the river, and the great quantity of fruit, grain, and mutton available.[10]

Pedro Teixeira, the Portuguese traveler, spent several weeks at 'Anah in the winter of 1604-05 and left a full description on which is based the following.[11] The Euphrates at 'Anah ran through rugged and high hills, leaving only narrow strips of level land for town development on both shores. Teixeira estimated these banks to be only 100 to 200 paces wide on the left or Mesopotamian side and 200 to 500 paces wide on the right bank. In these narrow spaces there was room for one street only—the eastern street being about two miles long while the western one was twice as long (two leagues). The left bank was not thickly populated, its inhabitants being mostly workers. On both sides of the western street were small, square houses, each having a garden with palms and trees growing oranges, quinces, figs, pomegranates, and other fruit. The salubrious air, the availability of water, and the alluvial soil made the area very productive. A large drainage ditch at the foot of the hills prevented flooding by winter rains and the same ditch was used for irrigation in the summer, being filled with water drawn from the river by waterwheels. Wood was scarce, but there was plenty of white salt brought from a mine two days travel eastward in Mesopotamia. Dates, the staple food of most of the inhabitants, were plentiful and cheap, but rice, imported from Baghdad, was expensive. Large fish were also available, but these were not highly regarded by the 'Anahlis. Some wheat and barley was also grown.

Teixeira estimated that 'Anah had about 4,000 houses, these being constructed of stone, plaster, mortar, and mud. All the houses, some being two stories high, had flat roofs. The mosque had an unusual tiled roof which sloped to one side. About 120 houses were owned by Jews, who lived decently, if not richly, and were friends of the Arab ruler—for the usual fee, of course. Teixeira found the Moslem inhabitants fair in color and rather well dressed, although the usual cloak was of sheepskin worn with the wool outside when it rained and reversed when it was cold and windy. Among the Moslems were a number of the descendants of the ancient population, who seemed to Teixeira to be Moslems in name only and who really worshipped the sun. As the Christian Portuguese put it, they rated the doctrines of Mohammed "at their true value."

'Anah was a great trading depot, situated as it was on the river trade route and on the land trail from Baghdad to Aleppo. The local rich date harvest was carried to Aleppo, Damascus, Tripoli, and elsewhere. At 'Anah flocks of sheep were moved across the river from Mesopotamia, where the pasturage was better than in the eastern desert area, to be driven to the populous cities of the west. The customs fee, which also covered the cost of ferrying, was 20 ducats per 1,000 head. Oak galls, important for tannic acid, were carried through 'Anah for markets in the large cities. Some of the galls were shipped to India and China by way of Baghdad and Basra. Most of these galls came from the Mosul and upper Tigris area where, according to Teixeira's estimate, 12,000 camel loads were exported annually. Silk and woolen cloth, much of the latter being made in 'Anah, were also much in evidence. Transit dues on all these items were paid to Ahmad Abu Rishah, the ruler of the Arabs who controlled the right bank of the Euphrates here. A small amount of the dues collected was paid to the Turkish officials on the island. These dues were levied by the camel load, each load of silk, cloth, indigo, spices and other valuable commodities costing about five ducats, while for galls, dates, and other less expensive items the customs duty was one ducat per camel load. Extortions by the officials usually doubled these fees. Oddly enough and much to the annoyance of travelers and merchants, by Arab prohibition there were no public markets in 'Anah except for an occasionally held market for mutton. Food and other necessities had to be purchased in the private houses. About 30 market boats traded up and down the river, stopping especially at the many islands.

Rauwolf walked for an hour through the street of the town on the right bank in order to reach the place where the boat had landed. He found the houses themselves to be well built of brick and stone and most had gardens with date, lemon, citron, and pomegranate trees. Along the shore across the river a few summer homes could be seen on the hills. As Rauwolf and his friends walked through the town, some of the party hurried ahead to the master of the boat, who had been born in 'Anah, to contrive to get a third person to accuse Rauwolf of being a spy who "observed all towns and places accurately, and intended to betray them." They convinced the subasi to send one of his men with iron chains and fetters to arrest the European. Rauwolf was allowed to board his boat but was ordered to stay there while they decided his fate. After the accusers had consulted together, they told Rauwolf he could have his liberty if he paid the subasi 500 ducats. Rauwolf, alone in the boat, considered this demand exorbitant and being reluctant to pay, sought another way out. He remembered that there was another official, a Turkish one, in the island town. Securing the pass he had obtained in Aleppo, he took off his outer clothing and prepared to make an attempt to swim over to the Turkish town should the accusers try to seize him. He then informed them what he intended to do and this frightened them so that they reduced their demand from 500 ducats to one—and that to pay the servant of the subasi for his troubles.

After being rescued from such a serious charge "by the power of the Almighty," Rauwolf and the others left 'Anah on the fifteenth of October.[12] The river here flowed through a fruitful and well cultivated land—the alluvial plain or Sawad. Along the shores were a number of fine houses with orchards and gardens. Not only was the region pleasant to pass through, but the danger from the Arab nomads was lessened. Navigation, however, was complicated by the presence of large stones in the stream which had been placed there in such a way as to direct the water to the large and high waterwheels used for irrigation. If two such wheels stood across from each other there was hardly enough space in the middle of the river for the boat to pass. These waterwheels, often three or four in a row, ran night and day, raising the river water up into the irrigation canals. If the bank was too high to make a waterwheel practical, the water was raised by means of "bridges and peculiar engines that are turned by a couple of bullocks, to bring the water up with great leathern buckets which are wide at top and narrow at bottom where the water comes out." The fruit produced in this region was plentiful and inexpensive. The Indian muskmelons were especially tasty. Most of the cultivated fields had been sown with Indian millet (*Holcus sorghum* L.), rather than with wheat and barley, and the harvest was in progress. The millet was used for making ashen-colored bread in which the dough "was rolled very thin, and folded together like a letter, so that they are about four fingers broad, six long, and two thick." The ancient Arabic name of *dora* was still used for the plant, as one would find in Rhazes and Serapion; "He that will, may read more of it in the authors."

As the progress of the boat was good and the danger less, the merchants relaxed by playing games. Some played a game called "eighteenth" and others played chess (*scack*). Others used the leisure time for reading and singing, and Rauwolf took special pleasure in hearing a merchant of Basra sing out of the Koran. Throughout the journey, the Moslems observed the times for prayer, being summoned to their devotions by the religious leaders in the party. Rauwolf found greater religious devotion among the Persian Shiites than among the Turks and Arabs. The Persians were not "hindered, by the darkness of the night, danger of the place, inconveniency of the time," but would pray with such earnestness that tears would roll down their faces.

Early on the eighteenth of October the boats arrived at Hadithah, a fairly large town and caravan station about 35 miles below 'Anah and belonging to the king of the Arabians. Like 'Anah, the river divided the town, which occupied both sides of the stream with the larger settlement on the western shore. Only a brief stop was made to pay two *saijets* for customs and then the crew was encouraged to take as much speed as possible for it was hoped to reach Jibbah that night.[13] They arrived at this Turkish-controlled town late in the day. Jibbah, too was a divided town with a fortress situated on an island in the middle of the river and the larger settlement on the left bank. It was a pleasant town with many fine orchards, and the merchants spent half a day here buying dates, almonds, and figs. On the twentieth the boat arrived at night at Hit, a Turkish castle and town on the west bank on high ground. Here the merchants of the party traded with the inhabitants, giving soap-balls, knives, and paper in exchange for local items. The sheets of white paper were especially prized as a trade item.

Rauwolf made no mention of the nearby bitumen springs, the important source of pitch. Moslem writers commented on the great quantities of fruit raised at Hit and on the unpleasant stench.[14] Balbi (1580) mentioned the "boiling Fountaine of Pitch, wherewith the Inhabitants build their houses, daubing it on boughes cut from trees, so that they seeme rather of Pitch then Wood, every one taking what pleaseth him freely; and if the overflowing Euphrates should not carrie away the Pitch throwne into the field where it ariseth, they say there would be hills raised by it." Eldred (1583) described the scene as a "valley wherein are many springs throwing out abundantly at great mouths, a kind of blacke substance like unto tarre, which serveth all the countrey to make stanch their barkes and boates: every one of these springs maketh a noise like unto a Smiths forge in the blowing & puffing out of this matter, which never ceaseth night nor day, and the noise may be heard a mile off continually. This vale swaloweth up all heavie things that come upon it. The people of the countrey cal it in their language Babil gehenham, that is to say, Hell doore." [15]

After the usual customs had been paid at Hit for the two boats, the group left about noon of October 21. That evening they sighted a mill on the western side of the river and another on the following day. Rauwolf was informed that these were gunpowder mills, which produced powder of poor quality, not from saltpeter, but from the kind of willow trees previously described. The twigs and leaves of this *Populus euphratica* Oliv. were burned and the salt then separated from the ashes by a water process. Rauwolf was reminded of the fact that Pliny (xxxi. 46.107) remarked that niter was made in ancient times of burnt oakwood. Rauwolf also noticed innumerable colocynths growing on the high banks. The inhabitants of the area still used the ancient Arabic name of *handhel* for *Colocynthis vulgaris* Schrad.

After several days of good progress on the broad river, the boats arrived at night on October 24 at Felugia, their river destination. As Rauwolf's party floated down the river at its lowest level the voyage had taken the unusual time of 55 days, 17 of which had been spent at Raqqa.

The party landed in the river harbor, a quarter of a mile from the village. Taking this to be the site of old Babylon, Rauwolf was surprised to find that now there was "not a house to be seen into which we could go with our goods and stay until our departure." They were forced to unload their goods on the open shore and "pay toll under the open sky" to the Turkish officials. As the region was so dry, barren, and incapable of cultivation, Rauwolf would have doubted that here had stood the great and powerful capital of Babylon but he was convinced by "its situation, and several ancient and delicate antiquities that still are standing hereabout in great desolation." [16] One of these "antiquities" that helped assure the traveler that this was the site of Babylon was the remains of an old bridge, the ruins of which could still be seen. The bridge had been built of burnt bricks and the strong and admirable arches could still be seen a short distance up the river from where the boats landed.[17] From Bir to Felugia there had been no bridge and here, where the river was at least half a mile wide and very deep, there were the arches of what had obviously been a great bridge—so this must be the site of ancient Babylon, he reasoned. Near the ruined bridge were heaps of pitch, in some places hard but in others so soft "that you may see every step you make in it."

Near Felugia stood the ruins of a castle on a hill, and near it some other ruins that Rauwolf identified with the Tower of Babel. These last ruins were half a mile in diameter, "but it is so greatly ruined and low, and so full of vermin that have bored holes through it, that one may not come within half a mile of it, but only in two months in the winter, when they do not come out of their holes." Among these insects there were some called *elgo* in the Persian language which were very poisonous and were, as others told Rauwolf, "bigger than lizards, and have three heads, and on their backs spots of several colors." [18]

Rauwolf thought he saw the Tower of Babel in the ruins near Felugia. Other European travelers usually identified the biblical site with the ruins of a large structure lying near and to the west of Baghdad. These ruins are of the ancient Babylonian ziggurat of Dur-Kurigalgu and are associated with the tyrant Nimrod in the Arab tradition. In this tradition the ruins are called the Hill of 'Akarkuf or *Nisr Nimrod*.[19] Federici was at Baghdad in 1563 and described the scene:

The Tower of Nimrod or Babel is situate on that side of Tygris that Arabia is, and in a very great plaine distant from Babylon [Baghdad] seven or eight miles: which tower is ruinated on every side, and with the falling of it there is made a great mountaine: so that it hath no forme at all, yet there is a great part of it standing, which is compassed and almost covered with the aforesayd fallings: this Tower was builded and made of fouresquare Brickes, which Brickes were made of earth, and dried in the Sunne in maner and forme following: first they layed a lay of Brickes, then a Mat made of Canes, square as the Brickes, and in stead of lime, they daubed it with earth: these Mats of Canes are at this time so strong, that it is a thing woonderfull to beholde, being of such great antiquity: I have gone round about it, and have not found any place where there hath bene any doore or entrance: it may be in my judgment in circuit about a mile, and rather lesse than more.[20]

Fitch (1583) also placed the tower about seven or eight miles from Baghdad and commented on the unique combination of sun-dried bricks and "canes and leaves of the palme tree layed betwixt the brickes." Eldred (1583), who visited the ruins several times, "found the remnants yet standing above a quarter of a mile in compasse, and almost as high as the stoneworke of Pauls steeple in London, but it sheweth much bigger." He described the bricks as "halfe a yard thicke, and three quarters of a yard long." [21]

Both Eldred and Federici commented on the optical illusion created by the solitary ruins. Federici noted: "This Tower in effect is contrary to all other things which are seene afar off, for they seeme small, & the more nere a man commeth to them the bigger they be: but this tower afar off seemeth a very great thing, and the nerer you come to it the lesser. My judgement & reason of this is, that because the Tower is set in a very great plaine, and hath nothing more about to make any shew saving the ruines of it which it hath made round about, and for this respect descrying it a farre off, that piece of the Tower which yet standeth with the mountaine that is made of the substance that hath fallen from it, maketh a greater shew then you shall finde comming neere to it." [22]

Rauwolf and his group spent the twenty-fifth of October securing camels and asses to transport their goods to Baghdad.[23] Early the next morning the caravan left Felugia, traveling eastward on a very rough and stony road. After they had passed the castle and the town of "Daniel," the desert was such that even the guide found it difficult to keep the caravan headed in the right direction. All along the way ruins of once stately and ancient buildings could be seen; "some to look upon were quite entire, very strong, and adorned with artificial works so that they were well worth being more closely looked into." Only the "steeple of Daniel," built of black stones and inhabited, relieved the scene of complete desolation. This structure reminded Rauwolf of the steeple of Holy Cross church or of St. Maurice church in Augsburg, and it offered a good view of the surrounding region and the ruins.

Most European travelers of this period do not describe their passage from Felugia to Baghdad, but Balbi (1579) gives at least a few sentences. After leaving Felugia he crossed a bridge over what had once been a canal and came to the ruins of "Sendia." Shortly thereafter began the ruins of old "Babylon" (Baghdad). The night was spent at the mid-way point of "Nareisa," (*Nahr 'Isa,* the 'Isa canal), a place known for its robbers and lions. All the next day the ruins continued on the left, with "pieces of great walls ruined, and one piece of the great Tower of Babylon." Although the soil seemed good, "yet neither is there Tree or greene Grasse, House or Castle: but Mushromes so good that the Moores eate them raw." [24]

After 12 hours of difficult travel in this desolate area, Rauwolf's caravan rested with the hope of breaking camp in the middle of the night and arriving at Baghdad before sunrise. During the rest the curious Rauwolf left the caravan and climbed a nearby rise. The view from the top convinced him that he stood on the very walls of ancient Babylon itself. He found that there were really two long mounds with a ditch between and with open places that must have been the gates.[25] Pliny had said that there were 100 iron gates in the walls that were 200 feet high and 50 feet broad. Rauwolf could only gaze with astonishment as he remembered that this great city, the capital of kings like Nimrod, Belus, Merodach, and Balthazar, was now "reduced to such a desolation and wilderness, that the very shepherds cannot stand to place their tents there to inhabit it." Surely this was a "most terrible example to all impious and haughty tyrants." If such men did not "leave their tyranny and cease to persecute the innocent with war, sword, prison, and all other cruel and inhuman plagues," God would certainly punish them, like he had those of Babylon.

At nightfall, the caravan started on again, the reloading taking only a quarter of an hour. Western Baghdad was reached about two hours before dawn. Here, on the morning of October 27, Rauwolf and his comrade were kindly received into the house of an eminent merchant of Aleppo who had recently returned from India. For four days they remained there and then went across the Tigris into the walled city of eastern Baghdad.

VII BAGHDAD

The Baghdad that Rauwolf saw was far different from the wonderful round city that Caliph Mansur started to erect in A.D. 762 between the Tigris and Euphrates rivers.[1] Time and warfare had reduced the fertile and populous region to desolation and ruin. The four great irrigation canals that drained the Euphrates water into the Tigris and watered the area were dry and their courses obliterated. Early in the thirteenth century the region between the rivers was already deserted, the new Baghdad on the eastern shore of the Tigris housing those who remained. The new suburbs in this area had been surrounded by a wall in the early eleventh century and a single bridge of boats sufficed for the greatly diminished traffic across the Tigris.

It was this already ruined Baghdad that the Mongols sacked in A.D. 1285. An anonymous Moslem author, writing about 1300, graphically described the ruined Baghdad:

Hence nothing now remains of Western Baghdad, but some few isolated quarters of which the best inhabited is Karkh; while in Eastern Baghdad, all having long ago gone to ruin in the Shammasiyah Quarter and the Mukharrim, they did build a wall round such of the city as remained, this same lying along the bank of the Tigris. Thus matters continued until the Tatars (under Hûlâgû) came, when the major part of this remnant also was laid in ruin, and its inhabitants were all put to death, hardly one surviving to recall the excellence of the past. And then there came in people from the countryside, who settled in Baghdad, seeing that its own citizens had all perished; so the city now is indeed other than it was, its population in our time being wholly changed from its former state—but Allah, be He exalted, ordaineth all.[2]

Baghdad became a provincial town ruled by the descendants of Hulagu and then by the Jalayrs. In 1393 Timur occupied the town and ordered it rebuilt. While the Jalayrs regained possession for a short time, after 1411 Turkoman tribes occupied Baghdad. In 1508, Persian troops seized the city, and in 1534 Suleiman the Magnificent, sultan of the Ottoman Turks, conquered the city and region.

In 1563 Federici described Baghdad as "no great city, but it is very populous, and of great trade of strangers because it is a great thorowfare for Persia, Turkia, and Arabia: and very often times there goe out from thence Carovans into divers countreys: and the city is very copious of victuals . . . This river Tygris doeth wash the walles of the city . . . This city of Babylon is situated in the kingdome of Persia, but now governed by the Turks. On the other side of the river toward Arabia, over against the city, there is a faire place or towne, and in it a faire Bazarro for marchants, with very many lodgings, where the greatest part of the marchants strangers which come to Babylon to lie with their merchandize." Fitch in 1583 copies Federici in his brief description. Eldred (1583) is a little more original and describes Baghdad as "a place of very great traffique, and a very great thorowfare from the East Indies to Aleppo . . . The building here is most of bricke dried in the Sun, and very little or no stone is to be found: their houses are all flat-roofed and low." Newberry dismisses the city with a few lines: "The seventeenth day [of April, 1581], we passed through Bagdet. One Castle standeth to the South-east of the Towne, upon the South side of the Water, and another to the North-west of the Water upon the North side, where the Bassa doth keepe his Court, whose name is Hassan Bassa." [3]

Sir Anthony Sherley, like the rest confusing Babylon and Baghdad, wrote that "all the ground on which Babylon was spred, is left now desolate, nothing standing in that Peninsula, betweene the Euphrates and the Tigris, but onely part, and that a small part of the great Tower. The Towne, which is now called Bagdat, and is on the other side of Tigris, toward Persia (onely a small Suburbe in the Peninsula) but removed from any stirpe of the first [Babylon]; to which men passe ordinarily by a Bridge of Boats . . . The buildings are after the Morisco fashion, low, without stories; and the Castle, where the Bassa is resident, is a great vast place, without beautie or strength, either by Art, or

Nature; the people somewhat more abstinent from offending Christians, then in other parts, through the necessitie of the Trade of Ormus: upon which standeth both the particular and publike wealth of the State. Victuals are most abundant, and excellent good of all sorts, and very cheape." [4]

Early in the next century, Cartwright adds nothing new except in his estimate that the wall surrounding new Baghdad "contaynes in circuit but three English miles" and his belief that trade through Baghdad was declining, for "this Towne was once a place of great trade and profit by reason of the huge Caravans, which were wont to come from Persia, and Balsara: but since the Portugals, Englishmen, and Hollanders have by their traffique into the East Indies, cut off almost all the trade of Marchandize into the Gulfs of Arabia, and Persia, both Grand Cairo in Egypt and Bagdat in Assyria, are now not of that benefit as they have beene, either to the Merchant, or Great Turke; his Tributes both in Egypt, and his Customes in this place being much hindred thereby." [5]

Teixeira gave a rather full description of Baghdad as he found it in the fall of 1604.[6] Except for the larger garrison there because of the war with Persia, we can assume that little else had changed since Rauwolf saw the city in 1574. Teixeira compared the city with Seville and Triana on the Gualdalquivir in that, like Baghdad, these cities were located on a stream. He found the Tigris low when he was there but he estimated it to be 230 paces wide. The river was crossed by means of a single bridge of 28 boats, placed four paces apart and overlaid with timbers. Each night, at times of high wind or flood, and at the time of the Friday prayers, the chains that held the bridge in place were separated in the middle and the two halves allowed to pivot to the shores. Teixeira found the water of the Tigris clearer and sweeter than that of the Euphrates, and the fish in the river were plentiful and good. A charge of one medine was made for each load crossing the bridge from either direction.

The part of Baghdad that lay west of the river had been surrounded in 1601 by a deep and wide but dry ditch, with the excavated earth serving as a rampart on the inside. Two wooden bridges enabled people to enter this western suburb, which may have contained 3,000 inhabited houses. There were also markets, caravansaries, public baths, and workshops of all sorts. All necessities were just as plentiful in the western quarter as in the walled city across the river; indeed, most of the provisions for the latter came from the western area. Because of the trade coming from Felugia and other western points, this area had one of the three customs houses of Baghdad, the other two being in the walled city. Only a few structures or gateways were constructed of stone, and these were of very recent construction. Stone had to be brought from Mosul as none was present in this alluvial plain. Outside the rampart and ditch could be seen the vast ruins of the medieval Baghdad of the caliphs.

Eastern Baghdad was surrounded by a wall built of burnt bricks. According to Teixeira's estimate, the wall along the river was a good mile in length and had five posterns besides the great gate at the head of the bridge of boats. The wall that formed the outside of the rough semicircle from the river was about a league and a half in length.[7] On this outside wall, toward Persia, there were platforms and bastions with four of these strong enough to bear many good bronze guns. The citadel which housed the pasha and part of his garrison was located at the northern point of the city. This citadel was in the form of a rough quadrangle, "rather spacious than strong," with walls of brick and with guns mounted on bastions. It was surrounded by a ditch some twelve cubits wide and eight deep. In the city wall just east of the citadel a gate opened northward onto the level and fertile land that stretched toward Persia. Two other gates pierced the wall on its eastern and southern sides.

Within the walls were many ruins of what were formerly fine buildings. About one-third of the enclosed area lay waste while other areas were covered with great orchards of palm trees. Within the walls were over 20,000 inhabited houses, "mostly large and roomy, yet poorly built, and seldom well planned." As was usual, these houses had flat roofs and most had only small doors and no windows on the street side. The houses were built of old bricks quarried from the ruins that stretched for four or five miles around the western quarter. Some of the inhabitants made their living by quarrying and selling such bricks from the medieval Baghdad of the Abbasids. There were only a few large and fine buildings to be seen. Of the two mosques of note, one was just to the left of the bridge-gate and judging from its exterior it must have been costly. Of the many fine buildings of the past, there was only the ruined mosque of the caliph, the ruins of the great College of Mustansiriyah, and some minarets which were "wasting away." [8] Many clean baths were available for men and women. Near the river were seven or eight streets with shops offering items for sale and with workshops for the manufacturing of such items. There were also a number of khans and caravansaries, much frequented by merchants but closed at night with iron chains.

In this city, with its temperate and healthy climate, provisions were plentiful and the streets were crowded with great numbers of camels, horses, mules, asses, and pack-bullocks bearing the trade items that came to Baghdad from Persia, India, Aleppo, Tripoli, Damascus, and other points. The inhabitants of Baghdad were Arabs, Turks, Kurds, and Persians. Arabic, Turkish, and Persian were the languages used but Turkish was most frequently spoken. Two to three hundred houses were inhabited by Jews and about a dozen Jews claimed descent from the Babylonian Captivity. Most of the Jews were very poor but a few were wealthy. The Jews had their own quarter for a synagogue. There were also eighty houses of Nestorians and ten of Armenian Christians. Teixeira reported the inhabitants of Baghdad to be fair and of "good appearance, nature and manners." The men dressed richly and well while the women, many of whom were handsome, had fine eyes. The women wore veils of silk or gauze "so that they see all and cannot be seen," but the veils were dropped at times and on purpose. There were more than 4,000 weavers in Baghdad using wool, flax, cotton, and silk in their craft. Teixeria also reported a long street completely occupied by Moslem goldsmiths and silversmiths.

When Rauwolf saw the city of Baghdad he was reminded of the Swiss city of Basel. [9] Both cities were situated on the banks of rivers, located in a large plain, and divided by the rivers into two parts. Yet here the resemblance ended, for Baghdad was not as pleasant as the European city nor so well built. Rauwolf found the streets of Baghdad narrow and most of the houses miserably constructed. Many of the buildings were in ruins. The mosques were black with age and it was difficult to find one that did not need repair. On the mosques Rauwolf saw many old Arabic "or rather Chaldean" [sic] inscriptions, but he could not read them nor find anyone else who could read these Kufic characters.[10] Rauwolf had hoped to find out what the inscriptions said thinking that thereby "many antiquities of the town might have been truly explained."

Among the buildings worth seeing were the khan of the pasha and the great bazaar in the old town west of the Tigris. Even the baths were not worthy of comparison with those of Aleppo and Tripoli, for in Baghdad the baths had the floor and side walls covered with pitch, which made the rooms black and gloomy.[11] That part of Baghdad lying west of the river was open and unprotected and one could come and go as one willed. However, that part that lay east of the Tigris was well protected with walls and ditches. The side along the Tigris itself was especially well guarded with towers, between two of which was a high old wall with an inscription at the top about a foot high with letters of gold coloring. Undoubtedly this was the long inscription which gave the name and titles of Caliph Mustansir with the information that he had completed in A.D. 1232 the famous Madrasah or college on which the inscription ran. Try as he did, Rauwolf could find no one to interpret the letters to him.[12] Near the towers and the wall was a bridge of boats over the Tigris, here "about as broad as the Rhine at Strassburg," but because the waters were rapid and dark it was not pleasant to see. Still confusing Baghdad with the ancient city of Babylon, Rauwolf thought that the two parts of Baghdad represented Seleucia (east) and Ctesiphon (west). He cited Strabo (xvi. 1, 5, 16) and Pliny (vi. 30. 122–126) as evidence that these two cities had been built out of the ruins of ancient Babylon.

In the eastern portion of the divided city stood the residence of the Turkish pasha. Rauwolf reported it to be a poor structure, not "quite finished" and without fortification, although he noted that because of its nature as a border fortress, the Turkish government maintained a considerable garrison at Baghdad. Before the palace lay some pieces of ordnance almost covered with dirt. When the pasha heard that two strangers had arrived, he summoned them into his presence. Rauwolf did not name the pasha. An Armenian whom they had known in Aleppo accompanied Rauwolf and his friend to act as interpreter and to tell the pasha about the Europeans. When they were ushered into the room, which was very ordinary but enhanced with fine rugs, Rauwolf and his companions showed the proper respect to the pasha, who was seated and was clothed in a costly yellow-colored gown. One of his attendants then asked the Europeans in French where they were from, what merchandise they had brought, and where they intended to go. These questions were politely answered, but the pasha was not satisfied and asked the Europeans to withdraw and await his answer. Rauwolf understood that this was only a device to force a present out of them and they would not leave. Instead they showed the pasha their passes signed by both the pasha and cadi of Aleppo. These the pasha took and examined closely paying special attention to the seals made on the paper after the seal had first been dipped in ink. He found the passes authentic enough and not knowing what else to do, he dismissed them.

Rauwolf and his Dutch companion bought their food in the bazaar and cooked it for their meals in the khan, "for in these countries there are no inns to be found into which one may go and find a dinner already prepared for a chance customer." One could, of course, find cooked food in the bazaar, but it was customary for everyone in the khan to prepare his own food, cooking it in the outdoor fireplace in front of his lodging. The food had to be eaten while seated on the floor because there were neither tables nor stools. Since there were no beds, the night was spent sleeping on the floor wrapped in a long cloak. But the winters were not severe in Baghdad; Eldred considered them to be "as warme as our Summer in England in a maner." [13] Rauwolf found narcissus, hyacinths, violets, and other flowers of a European spring blooming in December. There was a scarcity of food in Baghdad because of the protracted drought, and it would have been worse had not the cities in the north, and especially Mosul and Kara Amid, sent food down the rivers to Baghdad. The food brought down the Tigris was carried on "rafts borne upon goat skins blowen up ful of wind in maner of bladders," wrote Eldred, and when unloaded at Baghdad, "they sel the rafts for fire, and let the wind out of their goat skins, and cary them home againe upon their asses by land, to make other voyages downe the river." [14] The rivers afforded the means of transportation not only for food, but also for merchandise, which arrived daily at Baghdad in many shiploads. Baghdad was the depot to which goods from Anatolia, Syria, Armenia, Constantinople, Aleppo, Damascus, and other cities of the north came to be shipped to India, Persia, and other areas. Exchange items also came from southern Asia and even China.

The main port of entry and shipping for the goods that came to and from India was Basra, located almost 300 miles directly south of Baghdad near the Persian Gulf. [15] Federici reported that the boats that traveled on the Tigris between the two trading cities were made "after the maner of Fusts or Galliots with a Speron [beak] and a covered poope." These boats, called *daneck* and *saffin*, were quite seaworthy and required no pumps because they were well covered with 2 or 3 inches of pitch from the area of Hit on the Euphrates. If the Tigris was low, as in late summer, the trip down the meandering river took about 18 days; if there was plenty of water, as in the spring, only 8 or 9 days were required. Federici made the passage from Baghdad to Basra in 14 or 15 days in 1563 or 1564; Fitch reported a trip of 12 days in 1583; Eldred one of 28 days the same year.

According to Newberry, who made the downstream voyage in nine days in April, 1581, the towns and towers between Baghdad and Basra were named Bourac, Menil, Amor, Sekia, Kendege, and Gurna. The last named town, frequently given as Corna (Qurnah), was about 100 miles in a direct line above the coast of the Persian Gulf and was situated just above the confluence of the Tigris and the Euphrates rivers. The combined waters produced a "monstrous great river" according to Federici and in this estuary the tides of the Persian Gulf could be observed. Eldred said the stream below Qurnah was "eight or nine miles broad," while Balbi reported the necessity of tying the boats to the shore when the tide was rising to prevent their being driven upstream again. The cost for a "barke from Babylon to Balsara" was given by Barret as 900 medines.

The dangers of the river voyage from Babylon to Basra were great. Balbi reported lions, noisome air, whirlpools, great heat, and deadly hot winds. All travelers wrote of the ever present Arab, intent on theft. The Arabs, called Zizarii by Federici, lived in the inaccessible swamps and islands formed by the many channels of sea and river water. Fiercely independent, these marsh Arabs were a constant threat to Turkish control of the area and to trade. Basra had been taken by the Turks in 1546 and for 20 years the Arabs had been peaceful. In 1566, however, revolting Arabs almost succeeded in capturing the port city. Only the timely arrival of Turkish troops finally dispersed the rebels.[16] Since its capture, also in 1546, Qurnah had a Turkish garrison to collect customs and to "prevent theeves, which by hundreds in a companie use to robbe." The dangers and the slowness of communications was such that Rauwolf reported the use of pigeon post between Basra and Baghdad.[17]

The port of Basra lay some 50 miles from the gulf. Originally founded in A.D. 638 it had been located some 20 miles west of the estuary (Shatt all 'Arab) to which it was connected by two great artificial canals. The vicissitudes of war and time had led to the destruction of the original site, and by the sixteenth century the town of Basra was located closer to the estuary. This site, its third, had formerly been the village of Ubullah on the southern of the two canals. European travelers described it as being a city with walls about mile and a half in circuit, but with suburbs, fruitful fields, groves, and gardens outside these walls. Teixeira estimated a total of 10,000 houses. The walls and the houses were built of impermanent sun-dried bricks, or as Newberry reported, of bricks which were "made of a certain kind of stuffe, that may be cut with a knife." There were several baths, but besides the citadel there were no buildings of importance. Scorpions were plentiful, many "as big as common crayfish." The inhabitants of this unhealthy and hot city were mostly Arabs but there were also some Turks. Teixeira found the children and women to be well favored, but the latter had the reputation of being "not very chaste." This valuable city, located in the midst of hostile Arabs and not too far away from the Portuguese fort at Hormuz, was protected in 1583 by 500 Janissaries, some other soldiers, and a fleet of 20 to 25 galleys. Teixeira said that it was recognized that the galleys, "of small scantling and ill-built" and costly because of the absence of lumber, were of no use against the better Portuguese ships but were used as river boats against the Arabs. The north gate of the city had ten pieces of ordnance of various size and two basiliscoes. To Basra came boats from Hormuz "laden with all sorts of Indian marchandise as spices, drugs, Indigo and Calecut cloth," while an abundance of grain, rice, pulses, and dates were produced locally. Most of the trading was conducted in the great bazaars outside of the city walls, where amid shops and buildings made of great reeds, lay heaps of grain piled upon mats placed on the ground.

If the voyage down the Tigris to Basra was hazardous, at least it was relatively easy to sail and float downstream. The trip upstream to Baghdad, however, was not only hazardous, it was long and arduous. Since, contrary to the descent, a halt had to be made every night, usually a flotilla of 25 or 30 boats was assembled at Basra to make the trip together. The larger number of merchants and sailors thus provided better defense against the Arabs. Federici cited the need to be "wel provided of armor, for respect & safeguard of our goods, because the number of theeves is great that come to spoile and rob the merchants." In the broad estuary, sails could be used with the tide assisting, but once the confluence of the Tigris and Euphrates was passed, the boats were pulled upstream by men hauling on ropes attached to the boats. Eldred ascended the river in a flotilla of 70 boats, "having every barke 14 men to draw them, like our Westerne bargemen on the Thames." The mode of travel and the nightly stops made the trip from Basra to Baghdad stretch out to around 40 days; Federici took 50 days, and Eldred 44 days. Teixeira reported one flotilla that took three months to get to Baghdad. This Portuguese traveler was in Basra in August of 1604 and took the seldom used and dangerous land route to Baghdad because he was told at Basra that he would have to wait four or five months before a boat trip to Baghdad would be possible. It was not until after Christmas that the rains put enough water in the river to permit passage.

On December 2, 1574, Rauwolf watched the arrival of 25 ships bearing spices and precious drugs from India by way of Hormuz and Basra. Such cargoes of spices were unloaded in the fields around eastern Baghdad and placed under tents until caravans could be assembled and the spices loaded. The area thus looked more like a camp of soldiers than one of merchants, and Rauwolf was fooled in this respect on his first sight of these until he came near enough to smell the spices stored there. Some of the merchants who arrived from Basra in this flotilla resided at the caravansary where Rauwolf was staying. One of these was a jeweler who brought a variety of precious stones with him. He had diamonds, chalcedonies, rubies, topazes, sapphires, and other gems. The chalcedonies especially were used to make beautiful hafts for daggers. The chalcedonies and diamonds were obtained in Camboya, the other gems were mostly from Ceylon. Because of the covetous officials and the high customs, such gems were often smuggled in. To India were sent corals, emeralds (the best came from Egypt), saffron, chermes-berries, raisins, dates so "pliable and soft that you may pack them together in great lumps as they do Tamarinds," figs, almonds, various items of silk, and Turkish handkerchiefs.

Above all, there was a considerable export of Arabian horses. These beautiful animals were sometimes sent to Syria and on to Europe where they were sold or presented to nobles, but the greatest number were sent to India via the island of Hormuz, the Portuguese station in the Persian Gulf. At Hormuz the Portuguese collected 40 ducats on each horse, yet the dealers were glad to pay this, for the profit realized on the sale of horses in India was great. Early in the sixteenth century, Ludovico de Varthema reported that at Narsinga "a horse is worth at least 300, 400, and 500 pardai, and some are purchased for 800 pardai, because horses are not produced there, neither are any mares found there, because those kings who hold the seaports do not allow them to be brought there." Federici wrote that in 1567 at Narsinga horses sold for from 300 to 1,000 ducats apiece.[18]

In order to encourage the shipping of horses and thus increase the revenue of Hormuz, the Portuguese ruler Manuel had ordered that the merchants on all ships sailing from Hormuz to Goa or other Indian ports and carrying at least ten horses would not be charged at Goa for any other merchandise also carried in the same ship; "but if they lade one horse lesse then ten, then the goods are bound to pay the whole custome" of 8 percent. Federici, who sailed from Hormuz to Goa on a ship carrying 80 horses, said that 20 was the minimum number of horses that could be carried and no fee paid by the merchants for their other merchandise. Fitch embarked for Goa on a ship carrying 124 horses. Rauwolf heard at Baghdad that only half of the customs fee had to be paid by merchants using ships transporting horses. Barret reported in 1584 the interesting fact that if any of the horses died en route the tails were kept to show the officials at Goa that the right number of horses had been put on board at Hormuz. Apparently the sea voyage produced its toll of deaths among the horses carried for there were regulations that "if the horses should die before the midst of the voyage, they pay no custome at all [on the horses], and if they die in the mids of the voyage, then they pay halfe custome, but if they die after the mid voiage, they pay custome no lesse than if they arrive safe. Notwithstanding the merchandise (whether the said horses die before in the mid voyage or after the mid voiage) are free from all custome." [19]

In Baghdad, Rauwolf met many Indians whom he described as "lank in body, brown in their color, well shaped and of a very good understanding." The Indians made "faithful, diligent, and careful" servants. Besides the Indians there were in Baghdad a great number of Turks, Arabs, Armenians, Kurds, and Medes. Persians were especially numerous. Once Rauwolf observed the arrival of a caravan of 300 Persians with their camels and horses en route to Mecca "to visit Mohammed." The Persian language was so different from the others of the area that few could understand them and conversation had to be carried on by means of signs, just as Rauwolf himself had to do. Rauwolf observed that the Persians sat well on horseback, wore long white drawers, and were well furnished with scimitars, bows, and darts. Instead of spurs, pointed irons about an inch and a half long were attached to the back of their shoes. The Persians were known as "Red Turks," a term Rauwolf derived from the fact that they had red markings in the rear of their turbans. Another distinguishing feature was their gray woolen coats of knee length and with three pleats in back. Rauwolf praised the Persians as a "strong and valiant people, of noble countenance, very civil, and upright in their dealings." He also noticed that in business dealings the Persians were very wary and took much more time in arriving at a decision than others. He admired greatly their beautiful rugs with many colors "in which they are well skilled." But of gold and silver working they knew little and they took "anything that is glossy for gold." This deficiency in their skills made the Persians admire and respect the Christians, who showed ability along these lines, but they hated the Turks very much.

Rauwolf observed that the traditional state of warfare that existed between the Turks and the Persians was accentuated by the fact that the two races considered each other Moslem heretics. The Persians were Shiites and condemned the Turks because the latter rejected 'Ali and Omar "as the greatest and highest prophets or legates of God." The two caliphs were highly esteemed by the Persians; "nay, they worship them like Gods." The difference in Islamic views was clearly shown by the divergent views on the status of women as believers. The Turks, said Rauwolf, considered their women as unclean, since not circumcised, and thus unable to be saved. Therefore they were excluded from the mosques. On the other hand, the Persians received women as blessed and admitted them to the mosques. Despite the traditional hatred between the two, conditions of peace were observed and trade could safely be conducted. The situation was far different on the Hungarian frontier where attacks and incursions were frequent even in times of peace. Rauwolf observed that it was both cheap and good traveling to go to India through Persia where the customs and duties were very small.

Rauwolf also understood that there were Christians in Persia. Most of them were "of the persuasion of Prester John, whom they call Amma." The conversion of these Persian Christians had been recent. It occurred about 12 years before Rauwolf's visit when the Persian ruler, hard pressed by the Turks, had sought assistance from the Abyssinians (Prester John).[20] The Abyssinian ruler had replied to the request that no league was possible unless the Shah and his subjects would become Christians, then full support would be given. This had been agreed upon, and the Abyssinian ruler sent one of his patriarchs and some of his priests to Persia. The result, according to Rauwolf, was that by 1574 there were more than 20 towns in Persia where the majority of the inhabitants were Christians. The Abyssinian clergy had brought with them copies of their scriptures including some of the epistles of St. Thomas. The Christians had made the Persians less "zealous in their superstitions" and had convinced them that circumcision was not necessary, especially since their enemies the Turks and the Jews, practiced this rite. Besides this the converted Moslems now ate pork and drank wine, "because their adversaries were forbidden their use by law."

The German physician understood that Christianity was increasing daily in strength and the Persians were being baptized with fire, according to the Abyssinian rite, and in the name of the Father, Son, and Holy Ghost, although they considered the Holy Ghost to be a creature who proceeded from the Father only and not from the Son. These new Persian Christians identified themselves as having a blue cross in the inside of their left leg a little above the knee. It must have pleased the Lutheran Rauwolf to hear that the Persian Christians administered the Sacrament of the Altar to young and old, in both kinds, and without prior confession. Before partaking of communion, they had to wash their feet in the rivulets that ran through their churches and in performing this rite some of their important town officials washed the feet of others. There were no images in their churches and the services were enhanced with music from harps, pipes and other instruments.[21] The best music and the most able musicians could be found at the royal court at Samarkand, "which town, as they say, was built by Sem, the son of Noah, and called after his name."

Writing in 1581, Rauwolf mentioned that after his return to Germany he had heard that on the death of Tahmasp, his middle son, Ismael, had been made ruler (1576). While a young man the new ruler had been very strong and athletic, showing great skill in riding the wild, unbroken, and ashen-colored horses which were procured in the eastern areas of Persia. As a young man he had resolved to avenge his ancestors against the Turks and assembled an army for a surprise attack on Baghdad. However, the pasha of Baghdad, warned by traitors from the Persian force, fell upon the Persians, defeating them and taking the prince a prisoner.[22] Only the entreaties of the old monarch and the surrender of the Mesopotamian city of Orbs to the Turks prevented the beheading of the prince.

In March, 1574, while at Aleppo, Rauwolf had heard that the Turks had lost 25,000 men in a battle with the Persians. When and where this battle had been fought he was unable to find out, "for if they suffer any damage, they always keep it very close and secret." When the Turks suffered misfortune, the Christians were more abused. If the Turks had won a victory, Rauwolf felt sure they would not have been so silent, for the proud Turks believed that "there is no other nation that can conquer the world as they." Seeing the sick and lame Turks of Baghdad led Rauwolf to deduce that the only way the Turks conquered was by their great number. The Persians, much better than the Turks in strength and manliness, could not carry on long and distant wars, for the resources of the king of Persia were meager. Also "his subjects are freed from all taxes and impositions, according to their ancient privileges and customs." Persian armies were not maintained in time of peace but were assembled only when their country was invaded.

While Rauwolf was busily examining the country and the people, he was also trying to arrive at a decision as to whether to continue his travels to India and whether he and his traveling companion should go through Persia or take the water route from Basra through Hormuz. In the midst of his preparations, he received a letter informing him to come back to Aleppo immediately. Rauwolf did not reveal the contents of the letter in his memoirs, but Krafft reported that in the fall of 1574 he wrote to the botanist, through friends at Aleppo, informing him of the bankruptcy of the Manlich firm.[23] It was this unfortunate development in Rauwolf's sponsoring company that made the return necessary. It was a cruel disappointment to the botanist, for the wilderness part of his journey was passed and he had "come into the fruitful eastern countries which would have been very well worth seeing." After considering the possibilities, it was decided that his friend would go on and Rauwolf would return to Aleppo. Two days after the receipt of the letter, his friend, having been fitted out with all necessaries, went with a company of merchants down the Tigris to Basra. Shortly thereafter Rauwolf heard that the ship bearing his friend to Hormuz had encountered a great storm in the Persian Gulf near the island of Baharain and that he and other merchants had been drowned.

Judging from the descriptions which contemporary travelers gave of the ships in the Persian Gulf, such disasters must have been frequent. Federici, the Venetian merchant, sailed from Basra to Hormuz some time after 1563 in a small ship "made of boards, bound together with small cords or ropes, and in stead of calking they lay betweene every board certaine straw which they have, and so they sowe board and board together, with the straw betweene, wherethorow there cometh much water, and they are very dangerous." Fitch (after 1583) repeated the description given by Federici, but added that the boards were "sowed together with cayro, which is threede made of the huske of Cocoes." Eldred, who was at Basra for six months (1583–84), wrote that the ships were "usually from forty to threescore tunnes, having their planks sowed together with corde made of the barke of Date trees, and in stead of Occam they use the shiverings of the barke of the sayd trees, and of the same they also make their tackling. They have no kinde of yron worke belonging to these vessels, save only their ankers." [24]

Rauwolf had another decision to make, this time as to the route he would take back to Aleppo. He could join a caravan leaving for Aleppo that would follow the usual desert route northward. Rauwolf heard that this route took about 50 days of travel but for merchants it had the advantage that there were only two places where customs were paid. Federici, who waited at Baghdad for four months in 1581 for a caravan to leave for Aleppo, gave a detailed description of this route through the desert.[25] He bought a horse at Baghdad for the small sum of 11 *akens* and sold the animal later at Aleppo for 30 ducats. Six European merchants, five Venetians, and a Portuguese, made the trip in 40 days, and so desolate was the area through which they passed that villages were seen only on the first two and the last two days. For the remaining 36 days they traversed a wilderness in which "they neither see house, trees, nor people that inhabite it, but onely a plaine, and no signe of any way in the world." The six merchants carried their own merchandise on 32 camels for which they paid two ducats a load. Three servants gave them good service for "when the camels cried out to rest" their tent was the first to be erected. The caravan traveled about 20 miles a day, with the march lasting from two hours before daybreak until two hours after noon.

The caravan was fortunate enough to experience rain en route and water was not scarce, but as a precaution the European merchants had one camel laden only with water. Although food was carried, fresh mutton was plentiful for every member of the caravan had purchased live sheep in Baghdad and these animals were driven along by shepherds who also butchered the sheep when needed. The six European merchants brought with them 20 sheep, properly marked for identification, and paid the shepherd a medine, which amount was supplemented by the head, skins, and entrails of the sheep butchered. Only 13 of the sheep were consumed en route. An entire animal could not be consumed in one day by any small group, and since it was impossible to carry fresh meat with them, the merchants of the caravan took turns in furnishing mutton to each other. Each caravan crossing the desert was led by a "pilot" who knew the locations of the wells. A "captain" was also always a member of a caravan; he dispensed justice and supervised the guards at night.

In 1584, John Eldred returned from Basra to Baghdad where he and his companion, William Shales, joined other merchants in securing camels and drivers for the trip to Aleppo through the desert.[26] Food in the form of rice, butter, biscuits, honey made from dates, onions, dates, and live sheep were procured. The camels were expected to feed "on thistles, wormewood, magdalene, and other strong weeds which they finde upon the way." [27] The Englishmen also bought tents for themselves and their goods. When the entire caravan was assembled there were 4,000 camels laden with spices and other rich merchandise. One wealthy merchant, "whose honesty they conceived best," was placed in command for the "deciding of all quarrels and dueties to be paid." Forty days were required for the passage with daily rests from two in the afternoon until three in the morning. The daily rate of travel was about 20 to 24 miles. The first eight days were spent in traveling from Baghdad up the left bank of the Euphrates to Hit, where the river was crossed by means of boats. In the desert the travelers saw white, wild asses, roebucks, wolves, leopards, and foxes. Also, many hares were chased and killed. Abu Rishah (Aborise), "the king of the wandering Arabians in these deserts," collected a duty of 40 s. sterling on every camel load and in exchange his officers conducted and protected the caravan. Aleppo was reached on June 11, 1584. Later Eldred made two more trips to Baghdad and returned each time through the desert.

Rauwolf decided against the desert route and chose instead to take a route which, though less direct, would take him through more fruitful places and to famous towns where he could see and learn more. Companions for the route by land to Mosul, his choice, were difficult to find, so Rauwolf stayed a while longer in the khan at Baghdad searching for merchants going this way. Meanwhile he became well acquainted with a merchant from Aleppo who had been on several trips to India. One can imagine how Rauwolf questioned the merchants about the land he was now unable to see himself. This merchant told him that the Jesuits had set up a severe inquisition in India, especially at Goa, where they watched for Europeans who did not doff their hats to the images they had set up on several streets. Such persons, obviously non-Roman Catholics, were imprisoned. The Aleppo merchant expressed great disapproval of such enforced idolatory and when he and Rauwolf discussed the articles of the Christian faith, the German was astonished to find that his friend was a Christian and apparently in sympathy with the Protestant view of Rauwolf. His new companion offered the hospitality of his house and promised to treat Rauwolf like his own son if he would accompany him on his next trip to India. Furthermore, when the merchant found that Rauwolf was a physician, he offered to recommend him to his friend the pasha, who was ill. Rauwolf may have been tempted, but he declined the offers with thanks. He knew of others who had received little reward for their efforts in curing such wealthy Turkish patients. Besides fearing the loss of his liberty, Rauwolf knew that the preparation of drugs for medicinal purposes would be difficult in a region where there were no apothecary shops and where medicinal plants had to be sought out in one shop after another.

While waiting at the khan, Rauwolf also became acquainted with a Persian. This man informed Rauwolf that the Shah of Persia had several unicorns in captivity at Samarkand. Also, on two islands called Alc and Tylos, nine days travel east of Samarkand, the Shah and some griffins. These animals, called *alcra* in Persian, had been sent to the Shah from Africa by Prester John. The Persian described these griffins as being "a good deal bigger and higher than lions, having a red colored head, a curved beak, a feathered neck, a thick body, black wings like an eagle, feet like a dragon, and a long tail like a lion." These carnivorous animals, while young, had often accompanied the Shah, but as they became older and stronger, they had to be fettered and chained by the neck. Apparently Rauwolf had few doubts about this, and he believed his informant the sooner "because he also knew enough to talk about the trees and fruit that grow there, especially those mentioned by Theophrastus, and from him Pliny." No one who could describe Persian mangos, bananas, persea, and peaches could be wrong about unicorns and griffins.

VIII BAGHDAD TO ALEPPO

Forced to forego his planned trip to India, Rauwolf reluctantly prepared to return to Aleppo. With the help of his Christian friend he disposed of the wares he had brought from Aleppo and fitted himself for the perilous journey. As indicated before, instead of taking the route across the desert to Aleppo, Rauwolf chose to go northward to Mosul through the area east of the Tigris River. This route, although ancient, had only recently been re-opened to travelers because in May, 1555, the Porte had made peace with the Shah Tahmasp, the Persian ruler, in the treaty of Amasia. Rauwolf was apparently the first European in modern times to travel this route.[1] As his companions, he chose three Jewish merchants who knew the languages of the area. One of these had come down the Euphrates with him; the other two had come to Baghdad from Hormuz in the Persian Gulf. On the sixteenth of December, 1574, they set out on horseback for "Carcuck" (Kirkuk).[2]

The way, at first north along the Tigris, led through fertile fields and the prospect for a pleasant trip was good. But before the day was done, the wilderness closed about them and camp was made in the open that night. The next morning they could see Persian villages far to the east, but the route they were taking was only desert. In this uncharted wilderness they lost their way and in the evening they found themselves floundering in a swamp. At this point the Sabbath came upon them and since the Jewish religious laws forbade travel and work on that day, they spent the night and the next day in the bog. Great showers of rain added to their discomfort. As it was too early in the growing season, there were not even enough plants to interest Rauwolf. He only found some wild galenga (*Cyperus rotundus* L.), called *soëdt* by the Arabs.

It was not until the nineteenth of December that they left the troublesome mire, only to find more desert before them. Rauwolf was reminded how in the fourth century the Emperor Julian the Apostate had been decoyed into these trackless wastes and then routed by the Persians.[3] On the twentieth, the travelers came to the village of "Scherb," inhabited by Persians and on the border of fruitful fields. No trouble was encountered the next day and the night of the twenty-first was spent at "Schilb." The route now led through freshly ploughed fields and several villages where they could purchase provisions. In the village where they spent the night of December 23, they bought nearly 200 eggs for what amounted only to two German kreuzer.

Rising early the next morning, they could see in the distance the snow-covered Kurdistan mountains, the southeastern extension of the Taurus range. After an easy trip they arrived early at Tauq (Daquq), before the Sabbath began. They camped outside the village, and Rauwolf even had to light the candle for his Jewish companions, forbidden by Mosaic law (Exodus 35:3) to light fires. While these Jews bragged about Moses and the laws, Rauwolf found that they knew nothing of the Ten Commandments. To their amazement, the German repeated the Commandments to his companions in Portuguese as well as he could; "which language is much spoken in India." But when he talked to them of Christ, their mockery led Rauwolf to drop the matter. Although Rauwolf does not mention the fact that it was Christmas Day, that event must have prompted the discussion.

Not far from Tauq they saw a very strong castle, guarded by Turkish troops. The guards were necessary, for this area was the borderland between the Turkish and Persian domains, and now they were entering the territory inhabited by the warlike Kurds, the *Carduchi* and *Cardueni* of Xenophon (*Anabasis* iii. 5. 15, 17; iv. 1. 8–11). Even the Jews could not converse with these people, who spoke neither Turkish or Persian. The Sabbath over, travel was resumed and on December 26 they arrived at Kirkuk, "a glorious, fine city lying in a plain, in a very fertile country." As the Jews had business to attend to in Kirkuk and in the neighboring suburb four miles away, they spent two days there.[4]

The party moved on again on December 29, and that night

was spent in the tents of some people "that were white Moors, or like the gypsies in their appearance." Other travelers joined them in the hair-cloth tent so that they "hardly had room in which to lie down." Their hosts treated the travelers kindly, bringing them firewood, milk, eggs, and dough for cakes that were baked in ashes and which were very good and savory. Rauwolf remembered that the Romans called such cakes *panes subcinericiei* and such bread Sarah had baked in haste when the three men came to see Abraham (Gen. 18:6).

On the thirtieth they came to the well-fortified town of "Presta," situated on the Lesser Zab River, which Rauwolf incorrectly identified as the "Gorgus" of Ptolemy.[5] The inhabitants of this area (modern Altun Keupri?) were known for the rafts they constructed of wood and inflated skin and on which they floated merchandise such as figs, almonds, raisins, nuts, grain, wine, and soap down to Baghdad and beyond. On the last day of the year, their route led through well-tilled fields to "Harpel" (Arbela, Irbil), a large but poorly built city with a wall that would never withstand assault.[6] Here they rested on New Year's Day, which was also the Sabbath.

At Irbil Rauwolf was told that the Turkish sanjak-beg there had condemned and executed eight murderers and highway robbers a few days before. The relatives and friends of those executed had sworn revenge on the sanjak-beg, who had slipped away in disguise to Constantinople to complain to the sultan of the conditions that threatened his life. To pay for his trip to the Turkish capital, the official had forced a rich Armenian merchant who was in the city buying the galls which produce tannic acid to give him 300 ducats. This, when known, brought danger to the merchant, who thought it advisable to join forces with Rauwolf and his party. On January 5, 1575, the caravan left Irbil. It was a large group, for the Armenian merchant had about 50 camels and asses loaded with galls destined for Kara Amid, whence they were to be shipped to Aleppo, where European merchants sent them to Europe. It was a forced march, for they did not stop to eat or drink until about midnight. Then, after refreshing themselves and their beasts, travel was resumed before daybreak. In the morning they crossed the Great Zab River, incorrectly identified by Rauwolf as the "Caprus" of Ptolemy.[7] The river was not wide, but very deep, and the crossing was difficult. Rauwolf suffered some loss to the plants he carried with him.

In the early afternoon they could see "Carcuschey" in the distance, and it was night when they arrived at this market town and camped before it. The Armenian inhabitants treated them well, but camp was soon broken and a night march begun. The night was so dark that while they met several caravans they could only hear and not see them. At daybreak they were at another river, called Kling by the inhabitants of the area.[8] The stream was about a mile broad and the ford difficult to locate, but some in the caravan were found who knew the ford and they all got safely across, except for one ass that was drowned.

Very early on the seventh of January the caravan arrived at the Tigris, where, crossing on a bridge of boats, they came to Mosul. This city, quite large, had some fine buildings and streets but its defensive walls and ditches were poor. Mosul was in Turkish control and was inhabited mostly by Nestorians, who "pretend to be Christians, but in reality they are worse than any other nations whatsoever, for they do almost nothing else, but rob on the highways and fall upon travelers and kill them." Mosul was a depot for trade, some of the items being shipped down the Tigris to Baghdad. Rauwolf saw an abundance of terebinth nuts. Also much in evidence was a variety of manna, "as big as a double fist," brought to Mosul from Armenia. This sweet exudate, brown in color, was very good to eat and the inhabitants consumed quantities of it in the morning despite its laxative character, "as the mountain people of Allgau eat cheese." Rauwolf thought it to be the *manna alhagiezi* of Avicenna.

Across the river from Mosul was the site of ancient Nineveh, the Assyrian metropolis. In Rauwolf's mind, Nineveh was associated not only with Sennacherib but with the dire prophecies of Jonah, Nahum, Zephaniah, and Tobias. Rauwolf saw no antiquities, although the site was occupied by several villages and vegetation grew there in the form of beans and *Colocasia antiquorum* Schott.

As the path from Mosul eastward through Nuseybin (Nisibin)

and beyond to Aleppo led through a dangerous wilderness, Rauwolf's party remained in Mosul several days in order to accumulate a really strong group of travelers going in that direction. Even with such strength, the caravan did not take time out the first day for eating and rests until sunset, when they encamped on a rise near a small village.[9] All night long patrols of three guards circled the camp. The next day, another forced march finally brought them late at night to a source of precious water. Here they encamped. While supper was being eaten some Kurds came into the camp and spoke kindly and offered assistance. It was soon recognized, however, that they were spies sent to estimate the strength of the caravan. The spies soon left and the camp settled down with a strong watch.

After midnight, these guards discerned a large group of Kurds approaching the camp. The shouts of the guards aroused the sleeping men and defense was prepared. When the attackers saw the defense arrangements and heard the defending archers and gunners shouting to them *"tabal, tabal, harami"* that is "Come on, come on, you thieves," the Kurds decided not to attack. Some time later, hoping the guard had been relaxed, the Kurds came again, this time crouching behind a camel and some horses, hoping thus to induce the caravan to believe that another caravan was approaching. But the members of the caravan were not deceived and drew up in defense array. Rauwolf, with his scimitar drawn, was again the left-hand man in the first rank. As an additional precaution he had armed his breast with several sheets of paper he normally used to dry his plants. The Kurds, "fearing their skins as much as we did ours," again hesitated to attack, although one of the caravan members did shoot the camel. After a little while, the attackers withdrew.

Those in the caravan stayed awake and alert the rest of the night, and camp was broken at daybreak. After traveling all morning through dry heaths and seeing neither men nor beasts, a noon halt was made in a large area enclosed with walls and surrounded by ditches. Several of these fortresses could be found in this dangerous area. While encamped here, two Kurds came into the fortress and demanded toll of the merchants. Enraged when the toll was refused, the Kurds drew their swords, but they were soon disarmed, beaten, and thrown out of camp. The caravan members then ate food and fed their beasts, although usually only one meal was taken per day and that at night. This one-meal-a-day practice proved a problem to Rauwolf, accustomed to eating more frequently. He, therefore, usually provided himself with bread and during the day would ride ahead or drop behind the group to eat as he rode. This procedure was necessary as nobody ate "openly by the way in the sight of others, unless he intends to experience danger, because most of them are very hungry and so eager for food that they will assault one another for it and take it away from their very mouths."

After refreshing themselves and the animals, camp was broken and the march resumed. To the west mountains could be seen and as they approached these in the evening, some Kurds were discovered on one of the foothills. It was assumed that an ambush could be expected somewhere in these hills. The assumption was correct for as they came to the first hill, a large troop of horsemen rode out from behind it. The Kurds were drawn up in two squadrons, in ranks of three and it was soon seen that they numbered about 300 and thus were in number equal to those in the caravan. The squadrons wheeled about in the plain on their lank and swift horses; to those in the caravan "a pleasant but very dangerous sight." By the time the attackers were within bow-shot, the caravan had halted, hobbled and tied the beasts together, and made ready for the attack. The drivers and those without horses stood behind the beasts with their bows ready and prepared to sally out for an attack with scimitars. Those in the caravan who had horses drew up in formation and waited for the attack. The two forces faced each other for an hour and at last the caravan sent out two of their number to meet with two of the Kurds. Some sort of agreement was reached—Rauwolf did not know just what—and the Kurds withdrew. The caravan then proceeded "in far better order than we had done before" until they reached a small village where they settled for the night. No wood could be found in this barren place so the evening meal had to be only bread.

While the caravan was encamped here, the inhabitants of the village came to collect the dung of the beasts. This act led Rauwolf to describe the way of cooking used in the area. First a hole was dug in the floor of the tent or house and in the center was placed the covered pot with the food. The rest of the hole was then filled with stones to about the three-quarters level. The last fourth of the hole was filled with dried dung and, when available, twigs and straw. When these combustibles were ignited, the pot and its contents got very hot, "so that they boil their meal with a little fire, quicker than we do ours with a great one on our hearths."

That night, like the previous ones, was "passed more with watching than sleeping." The long hours were spent in contemplating the stars, a usual nighttime activity in the Near East where the nomadic Arabs in particular could tell the hour of the night and when it was time to break camp by the position of the stars. Beds were unknown to these people, who, wrapped in their cloaks or rugs kept warm so that "no frost nor rain, nor dew can hurt them." To avoid the dangers of night travel, the caravan did not move until daylight. This day, January 14, brought no dangers from the Kurds but the way was at first mountainous and rough. The following day they passed through a desert area where the deep sand hindered their advance. By nightfall the beasts were ready to drop, although the city of Nuseybin was visible about four miles away. These last few miles were easier because they came into green meadows with clear springs of irrigating water. It was very late when they arrived at the large khan at Nuseybin. This historic city had been conquered by Trajan in A.D. 115, and in A.D. 217 the Parthian ruler Artabanus had defeated the Roman Emperor Macrinus near Nuseybin. The Arab geographers commented on the roses, scorpions, and gnats of the city.[10]

Nuseybin, under Turkish rule, was not very large and lay on a rise in a region well watered by springs and conduits. The khan where the caravan rested five days while waiting for more company was especially favored in its supply of water. The inhabitants of Nuseybin were mostly Armenians, a good sign because it indicated that they had left the dangerous passage through Kurdish territory. The city was a crossroads for various caravan trails, including an important one which led northwest to Kara

Amid on the upper Tigris. The Armenian merchant who had joined Rauwolf's party at Irbil and several Turks of the caravan who had been friendly to Rauwolf requested that he come with them to Kara Amid. They had heard from his Jewish companions that Rauwolf was a physician, and they promised him good treatment and income if he would come and cure some of their ailing relatives. They also promised to recommend him to the ill son of the important Mahomet Pasha. The possibility of such good business was tempting to Rauwolf, who would have been pleased to serve the Armenians for his kindness, but he had been told by his employer to report to Aleppo with all haste and thus he felt it necessary to decline the offer.

On the twentieth of January, toward night, those going westward to Aleppo broke camp. The route led them through plowed fields and villages where they could communicate with the inhabitants who spoke Armenian, Turkish, and Arabic. Late on the twenty-first, they reached the town of "Hochan," where the Jews rested and observed the Sabbath. It was there that they heard the news that Sultan Selim II had died (December 13, 1574). From Hochan, five days of travel were needed to bring them to Urfa and the route grew more mountainous as they neared the Taurus range. Snow, which Rauwolf experienced only twice in the Near East, added to their troubles. Then occurred one of those incidents that happen when bodies are tired and nerves on edge. A horse belonging to one of the Jews was frightened by something and jumped about. The owner, seeing Rauwolf standing near the horse, thought the European had done something to it and began to finger his bow and arrows as if he intended to shoot the physician. Rauwolf, to save himself, seized the Jew by the leg and unseated him from his horse. The fighting continued in the snow until the other two Jews separated the pair and made peace between them.

That night they came to a village in a narrow valley at the bottom of a long ascent. Near this village they found a large stable cut out of rock and there they lodged the night, protected from the winter cold. The stable was 25 paces long and 20 broad. Here, about midnight, they were awakened by the arrival of an imperial *cha'ush* who had come from Baghdad in the remarkable time of six days. He was seeking fresh horses to replace those he had tired in his rapid riding. With the full authority of the sultan behind him, he took three pack horses from one driver and two more from the Jew who had threatened Rauwolf that day. Generally, such official messengers excluded merchants and strangers from their demands in order to encourage trade, but it was necessary to comply immediately with such requests or suffer punishment.[11] The *cha'ush* soon found that he had picked some poor horses, for those belonging to the Jew had galled backs. He returned these to the Jew who gave him a "child's coat made of delicate Indian stuff." The whole incident and the search for replacement horses by the driver who had lost his to the *cha'ush* meant the loss of a day's time.

Early on the twenty-sixth they left and traveled all day through high mountains and narrow valleys. That night they came to a village inhabited by Christian Armenians, who showed their Christianity by entertaining and befriending strangers. Here one of the Armenians took Rauwolf and the three Jews to his houses where he entreated them to remain the following day also, which they did. Rauwolf would have liked to have conferred with the Armenian about their common faith, but as the only communication could be through the Jews who alone understood Armenian and who, in this case, could hardly be expected to interpret correctly, they were "forced to have patience and to look at one another in silence." It was the Armenian Lent and strict dietary laws kept the Armenians from eating anything "but leguminous food and bread and water." When their host offered them some boiled eggs, the hungry Rauwolf ate them. This caused the host to ask through one of the Jews whether Rauwolf did not know that Christians did not eat eggs during Lent. The Lutheran Rauwolf would have liked to have replied that "it becomes Christians to keep Lent with soberness and abstinency, rather than with distinctions and differences of foods," but he answered the Armenian through the interpreter that according to the European church calendar Lent would not begin for three more weeks.

On the twenty-eighth, travel was resumed through the rough mountains. That night they stopped at a small village on a plain and remained there over the Sabbath, the next day. The mountainous route over, better time was made through fruitful valleys with scattered villages. Early in the evening of the thirtieth of January they arrived at Urfa, a city which has at various times in its long history been known as Edessa, Antiochia, Callirrhoe, and Ar-Runa (corrupted by the Turks into Orfah or Urfa).[12] Baldwin had founded there the first principality of the crusaders in 1098. In 1144 the Moslems retook the city from Jocelin II. In the thirteenth century, Edessa was sacked by the Tartars, and in the fifteenth century the city suffered a similar fate at the hands of Tamerlane. In 1534 it was taken by the Ottoman Turks. The city itself is situated on the eastern slope of a hill and is surrounded by a wall in the form of an irregular triangle. Within the city are numerous bazaars and mosques. One of the outstanding features of Urfa is the beautiful and clear lake known as *Birket el Ibrahm el Khaleel,* "the Lake of Abraham, the friend of God." Urfa was seldom visited by Europeans in the sixteenth century. In 1590 Fitch passed through the city and described it as a "very faire towne" with a fountain full of fish where the Moslems held ceremonies commemorating Abraham.[13] In 1603 Cartwright stopped at Urfa on his way to Kara Amid, five days travel further east. He found there some Latin inscriptions of the crusader Baldwin. The walls of the city were strongly built and three miles in circuit, with the western end resting on the slope of a mountain. Eastward stretched a spacious and fertile valley. The fountain of "Jacob's Well" was full of fish so tame they could be fed by hand.[14]

Rauwolf and his companions stayed at the large and well-built khan for three or four days. He considered Urfa to be "very pleasant, pretty large, and well provided with fortifications." A trading center for merchandise brought by land from Aleppo, Damascus, Constantinople, and other places, Urfa was the point of trans-shipment to Kara Amid and the region beyond. Noteworthy in this trade were the rugs, many of which were made in Urfa. Rauwolf mentioned the belief held by some that this was the town called Harran or Charras of old, but this town is located about 20 miles to the south. The association of Urfa with Abraham seemed confirmed by the presence of Abraham's well.

By tradition it was at this well that the servant of Abraham first saw Rebecca (Gen. 24); here Jacob had made himself known to Rachel (Gen. 29); and to this well came the son of Tobias.[15] Rauwolf noted the whitish color of the water in the well and found it pleasant and sweet to the taste when he drank from the conduit that came into the khan from the well.

When the Jews had finished their business at Urfa with great success, the party continued their journey westward through high and rough mountains. At length they reached the city of Bir, from which Rauwolf had begun his descent of the Euphrates six months earlier. Rauwolf was impatient to go on to Aleppo, only two and a half days away, but his Jewish companions had business to do in the nearby towns of Nisib (Nizip) and 'Ain Tab (Gaziantep) due west of Bir. On the sixth of February, after the Sabbath, they left Bir and after traveling through fruitful fields they arrived at 'Ain Tab that evening.[16] This was a quite large town situated on two small hills and from a distance it presented a pleasant picture that changed when the pitiful buildings were seen close at hand. Once a Persian city, it had been taken by the Roman Emperor Gallienus Odenathus Palmyrenus, husband of the beautiful and ambitious Zenobia, shortly after the defeat of Emperor Valerian in A.D. 260. It was now in Turkish hands. Very little trading was done here but the region was noted for its vineyards and orchards of pomegranates and figs. The raisins of this place were sent to the east in great caravans.

After they had spent one day here, they headed southward for Aleppo. At first they passed through rough hilly country but then they came through vineyards and fields of grain so fruitful that in all of his journey Rauwolf had seen nothing like it. On the tenth of February, Aleppo was reached "with the help of the Almighty God." No representative of the Manlich firm was there to receive him, but some French merchants whom Rauwolf had cured of illness before his departure kindly took him in. With a great deal of satisfaction he removed the torn clothing that had not been off his back for half a year's time.

That no one from the Manlich firm was in Aleppo to meet the returning Rauwolf was due, of course, to the bankruptcy of the

Augsburg merchant company. Krafft, Lutz, and Salvacana had returned to Tripoli from Aleppo early in August, 1574. There they learned about the bankruptcy, news of which the Venetians had received from Crete. Later, when a ship arrived from Marseilles, the bad news was confirmed. Warfare and bad business practices had brought about the fall of the great company. In 1572, the Manlich firm had lost 50,000 Dutch gulden in pepper alone at Flushing, due to the activities of the Dutch Sea-beggars. By 1574 the debt of the company amounted to the great sum of 700,000 gulden. Already on June 20, 1574, the head of the firm, Melchior Manlich, Senior, had foreseen the coming calamity and had fled to Duke Albrecht of Bavaria. Later he went to the Tyrol, where he died in 1576. Melchior Manlich, the Younger, went first to Marseilles, but then he returned to Germany and remained in hiding near Augsburg.[17]

When the news was spread abroad in Tripoli, creditors of the firm demanded payment and when this was not forthcoming, they secured as part payment the wares and personal possessions of the Manlich employees at Tripoli. Then on August 24, Krafft, on the complaints of the creditors, was imprisoned to prevent escape. Krafft was also accused by the sanjak-beg of Tripoli for illegally possessing a horse.[18] It was at this time that Krafft wrote to two Venetian friends at Aleppo who then sent the letter which Rauwolf received in Baghdad. Lutz, too ill to be imprisoned, was placed under house-arrest. He died on February 10, 1575, and was buried in a Greek chapel on a hill outside Tripoli. Krafft was to remain in prison until August 24, 1577—exactly three years.[19]

Rauwolf was detained for a while in Aleppo and while there he learned that during his absence of half a year, the French and Italian residents had not been receiving adequate medical attention from the physicians of Aleppo.[20] It did not take long for Rauwolf to resume his medical practice among the Europeans and as his reputation spread he had difficulty in refusing the continuous demands of the Turks for assistance. He well knew that he, being an outsider, could never please these haughty lords. Under pressure from his friends, Rauwolf did undertake the cure of two persons of importance; one was the sanjak-beg of Jerusalem, a Georgian, who was pleased with his physician's services and paid him well. It was customary in Aleppo for the physician to agree with the patient on the cost of the cure and the money was deposited with a third person who did not pay the physician until the patient was well again.

While there were many physicians, most were unskilled. The medical practice of the Turkish doctors suffered from the fact that the Turks knew only Turkish and thus could not read the medical texts in other languages as the Jewish physicians could. On the other hand, the Jews were known for their covetousness and their endeavor "to promote their own interest rather than that of their patients." It all meant that the Turkish population received very little medical attention "and therefore rather die like flies." The Jewish doctors were little respected by the Turks, as these doctors had a reputation of deserting their patients in time of plague, "which certainly happens once in seven years, if not in five or sooner." In the plague of 1572, the son of a Turkish *defterdar,* or treasurer, and the son of another eminent Turk died of neglect by their physicians, even though the fathers had deposited with a third person 3,000 and 10,000 ducats respectively. A local "remedy" in time of illness was for a friend to grasp the ill one, lift him up and set him down and then shake him several times, "just as they use to do sacks of grain, to make them lie closer, and to hold more."

If the physicians left much to be desired, the apothecaries were disappointing in that they offered little by way of drugs. This disturbed Rauwolf not a little, for he knew that the best ingredients came to Europe from the Near East and yet if a physician needed any drugs in Aleppo he had to go out himself and collect the herbs and roots from the field or from the shopkeepers. One of the drugs Rauwolf did find in great quantities in the shops was *rob ribes* (*Rheum ribes* L.), with its pleasant but sour taste. It was an item of export, with large quantities being sent to the Turkish emperor. Rauwolf saw several stacks of these rhubarb roots, "which are hairy, almost two feet long, and of the thickness of an inch, of a greenish color, and underneath, as also Serapion mentions, reddish," which had been brought from

Mount Lebanon to the cadi. Rauwolf tasted some and was also given some roots for his collection.

In Aleppo Rauwolf saw several strange birds and among these was a kind of jay "of a delicate green and blue color, which were about the size of our nut-crackers, by them called *sucuruck* and *alsecrach* by others." Another bird, called the *alhabari,* was like the peacock, although not as big, and did not fly much. He also saw some civet cats, brought to Aleppo from India, and in the fondaco of the Venetian consul he saw a large and fierce cat, "like our lynx," that frightened even its keeper. Once this cat got loose and ran into a shop whose owner had set up a great many glasses just received from Venice. Before the animal could be again captured, it had broken more than half of these glasses. While Rauwolf was in Aleppo, a young rhinocerous was brought to the city on its way to Constantinople. It was claimed that the animal had killed 20 men before it was finally captured. Daily some tame lions were led about the town. These lions, "which have small bells, that everybody may take notice of them sooner," were so harmless that their keepers sometimes wrestled with them—no doubt to the great amazement of the spectators. The only thing that disturbed these lions was the sight of sheep. In the fields and bushes could be found chameleons, "which are somewhat bigger than our green lizards, but a great deal leaner and higher upon their legs. They walk very slowly and lazily. They live a great while without food like the serpents and are very ugly creatures." When Rauwolf put one on red, yellow, and black, colored cloths, "it changed by degrees its natural green color into the same color as the cloth."

IX MOUNT LEBANON

While in Aleppo, Rauwolf received a letter from Krafft, his imprisoned friend in Tripoli, requesting his presence in that Syrian port. On May 5, 1575, he arrived at Tripoli, having left Aleppo apparently just in time.[1] A few days later a caravan arrived from Aleppo and the chief carrier swore on his faith and reputation that soon after Rauwolf's departure, the subasi of Aleppo had sent his bailiffs to seize the German and put him in prison. The charge was that Rauwolf was a spy who under pretense of collecting plants on the hills about Aleppo had observed the defences of the city and could tell the enemy the best way to take the city. Such accusations were almost routine and were made in the attempt to demand bribes in exchange for release. The carrier had even heard that the price for freedom was going to be 200 ducats. On hearing this, Rauwolf thanked God who had delivered him "from their unjust accusations and contrivances."

Although he had just escaped imprisonment in Aleppo, Rauwolf was by no means out of danger in Tripoli. The same Turkish creditors who had brought about the imprisonment of Krafft now sought to take him also. However, the French consul, Andrew Bianchi, came to Rauwolf's assistance and secured for him a license which permitted him to walk freely about the city and its environs and even to visit his friend in jail. Entrance to the prison was through three small and low doors which were opened for Rauwolf by the jailer "without any grumbling." At times he even stayed overnight in prison with his friend. In general the Turks showed compassion for their prisoners, frequently giving them alms. One man came in daily after the afternoon lecture at the mosque and distributed bread, boiled meat, rice, and other food. If a prisoner had the money, food could be purchased; others had to earn their food by labor. Rauwolf was impressed by the spirit of generosity exhibited by the Moslems, who believed that "God is better pleased with that which they give freely, than that which is begged of them." He noticed that there were almost no beggars in Moslem towns imploring alms, "as they do in our country."

While in Tripoli, Rauwolf stayed at the fondaco of the French consul, and in return for the many courtesies he received he used his knowledge of medicine to cure merchants and seamen who became ill. There were plenty of these in the French fondaco. In the three months he was there he cured over 40 men "of all sorts of maladies, that is, malignant fevers, violent gripings of the intestines, and other severe illnesses which generally befell those that were lately arrived and were not yet accustomed to the air of the country." In addition to the Europeans, Rauwolf also treated others who needed medical help. One of these was the eminent and aged patriarch of the Maronites who was carried down from his monastery on Mount Lebanon to Tripoli, a day's journey away. The patriarch was afflicted with a very painful case of gout (*arthritide*) but the skilled physician of Augsburg soon relieved his pain. On preparing to leave, the patriarch invited some at the fondaco to accompany him to his place of residence. Rauwolf saw in this a wonderful opportunity to visit the famous mountain "of which the holy Scripture makes mention several times, speaking of its great height and famous rivers (of which the Jordan is one), of its sweet-smelling plants, and pleasant tasting fruit; and also because there are a great many strange plants to be found." [2] Rauwolf and some others rode southeast out of Tripoli with the patriarch, watchful lest they be attacked by the Turks. The way toward the mountain led first through pleasant fields of barley, white Indian millet, and other crops, and through fruitful vineyards. At the foot of the mountain were several small villages and near one of these they stopped to eat the lunch they carried with them. The patriarch brought out some of his own wine, in Venetian bottles, which was as pleasant a wine as Rauwolf had ever tasted, and they "drank a great deal."

Lunch over, they pressed on, for they wanted to reach the patriarch's monastery before night. The monastery was called the

Coenobium Santae Mariae or *Kanobeen Kadischa Mir-iam* and was attributed to Theodosius Magnus (d. 395). The ascending path now led through the narrow valley of the Qadisha river. The valley had very steep sides of great height, and near the top of the cliffs were a number of caves in which Maronite Christians lived and kept watch against an attack by the Turks, under whose jurisdiction they had never come. After a while, the party came out of the narrow valley into a level place of wide meadows, pastures, fields, and vineyards. The respite was brief, however, for the path again entered a rough and rocky valley. A rest was taken under large, spreading maple trees, but travel was soon resumed. Then they were met by some of the inhabitants who presented them, the patriarch first, with mugs of wine. Rauwolf, heated by the climb, drank only a little, for he preferred under such circumstances to have "spring water with bread dipped into it." Later other Maronites presented the patriarch with chickens, pullets, and other gifts.

At length, half way to the top of the mountain, they arrived at the monastery, which was so situated that it could not be seen until one came upon it. Before the unpretentious building was a copious spring with excellent water. The monastery itself was located under a great overhanging rock which afforded protection from above. The monks, of which there were not more than ten, came out to meet the travelers. Krafft had visited the monastery in April, 1574, and saw only five old monks and four old nuns. He did not see the patriarch but reported that the head of the Maronites was over 91 years old.[3] Biddulph visited the monastery in 1600 and reported that "one side of the Patriarkes houses is a naturall Rocke, the other of hewen stones and squared Timber: a very strong House, but not very large, nor specious to behold."[4]

As there was no room for the visitors in the monastery itself, the guests were lodged in an arched chapel. Krafft had written his name behind the altar of this chapel at the time of his earlier visit, but Rauwolf could not find it; later Krafft concluded from this that it had been erased, since it was generally known that he was a Lutheran.[5] Rauwolf's party spent most of their time on the roof of the monastery where an excellent panoramic view could be had of the snow-capped peak toward the east above the ce-

dars, the surrounding hills with browsing cattle, and the deep
and dark valley which they had ascended. It was there on the
roof that the evening meal was served at a long table. At this
meal, the white wine, served in Venetian glasses, was excellent,
but the food was simple, consisting of beans, kidney beans and
other legumes. At night the guests were conducted back to the
chapel where they found straw mats and rugs spread for them.
Very early the next morning, the monks came to the chapel and
began to ring the two bells. The peals reverberated off the overhanging rock and thoroughly roused the still sleepy guests, some
of whom had not heard bells rung for two years. Later Rauwolf
looked at their Syriac religious books, which he thought were
written in Arabic characters.

At daybreak Rauwolf and his friends left the monastery to ascend to the place where the famous cedars of Lebanon (*Cedrus
libani* Barr.) grew. Two monks served as guides, for the way
was very difficult. At a small village, probably Bisharri, near the
snow and cedars, the monks quickly collected an armed guard of
12 men. Ostensibly this was for protection against the Druzes,
but Rauwolf learned later that the Maronites were in league with
the Druzes and had no need to fear them. Rather this was simply
a pretext for making a little money. At length the party reached
a barren and rough plain which was the highest part of the
mountain except for a small, snow-covered hill. At the bottom of
this hill grew the famous cedars. Although these cedars had once
been plentiful, Rauwolf was able to count only 24 "that stood in
a circle, and two others, the branches of which are quite decayed
with age." [6] He saw no young trees, although he searched for
them. These cedars, green all winter and with their branches and
cones "in so nice and pleasant order and evenness as if they were
trimmed," presented a majestic sight. The group rested a while
under the cedars, but the cold wind soon forced them to leave
the top of this mountain which was so high (10,060 ft.) that it
might be seen from Cyprus. Its height made daylight come late
in Tripoli and the perpetual snow was brought down by the inhabitants of the region "into the bazaars and exchanges to sell in
order to cool their drinks with, especially in the dog-days, and
they fling it in by the handfulls." Krafft reported that the snow

was dug out in cakes 3 or 4 feet long and 1 or 2 feet wide and transported, well-covered, on camelback to Tripoli where it sold at high prices.[7]

On the way down to the monastery, they stopped at the village of their guards and in a pleasant garden they were served food and wine. Conversation was in Arabic and sign language. Then thanking their hosts for the good cheer, they departed and returned to the monastery at nightfall. After supper, they retired early. Daybreak found them on the route back to Tripoli. The descent was interrupted by a brief stop to have wine with some Maronites and by the collecting of plants by Rauwolf. Among the many plants he observed, seven are considered new discoveries: *Artedia squamata* L., *Michauxia campanuloides* L'Herit., *Acanthus spinosus* L., ?*Astragalus coluteoides* (L.) Willd., *Helichrysum sanguineum* (L.) Kostel., *Centaurea Behen* L., and *Poterium spinosum* L.[8] After passing a Moslem cemetery and thick groves of wild fig trees, they arrived in Tripoli.

Shortly thereafter Rauwolf obtained the aid of "an honest and skillful botanist," an Arab that Krafft knew. Through a Jewish interpreter, Rauwolf asked the Arab botanist for the names of his dried plants. The Arab was astonished that the German knew the old names for the plants, information gained, no doubt, from Avicenna and Rhazes. He then supplied Rauwolf with the current names.[9] Although Rauwolf collected some more plants about Tripoli and heard of many others, time was short and he "was forced to leave them behind, to be hereafter found by such that shall undertake similar journeys."

Rauwolf repeatedly expressed the hope that other botanists would continue the work he had begun on the flora of the Near East. It was not, however, until two centuries later that the Swedish naturalist Pehr Forskal (1736–63), the disciple of the great Linnaeus, accompanied Carsten Niebuhr and others on a scientific expedition to Egypt and Arabia. Since Forskal died in Jerim, Arabia, his *Flora Aegyptiaco-Arabica* was edited and published in 1775 by Niebuhr. The flora of Syria and Mount Lebanon was studied by Christoph Jakob Trew (1695–1769) who published the two volumes of his *Cedrorum Libani historia earumque character botanicus . . .* in 1757–67. Another student of Linnaeus, Frederick Hasselquist, explored Egypt, Arabia, and Palestine but died at Smyrna in 1752. The two volumes of his valuable journal, observations, and descriptions were published in 1757 by Linnaeus in Swedish under the title *Iter Palaestinum*. In 1756, B. J. Strand compiled with the help of Linnaeus a *Flora Palaestina* which was based among other items on the itineraries of Hasselquist and the herbarium of Rauwolf.

In 1574 the Druzes and the Maronites of Lebanon clashed with the Turks in open warfare.[10] Ever since Selim had conquered the rest of Syria in 1516, these peoples had retained a large degree of autonomy, with the Lebanese emirs acting like petty princes. Both groups, the Moslem Druzes and the Christian Maronites, were in effect well-armed feudal nations who welcomed refugees from Turkish rule. The Druzes, more warlike than the Maronites, alone held some forty sanjaks, with considerable potential for making war against the hated Turks. It was only this hatred for the Turks that provided any real unity to the conglomeration of independent tribes, political factions, and religious groups.[11]

As Rauwolf pointed out, there were two main factions among the Arab tribes that made up the Druzes. These were the Whites, or people of the White Banner, and the Reds, or people of the Red Banner.[12] The Whites were more numerous and lived in the easily defended mountains of Lebanon. They were well armed with muskets and their abundance of grain, oil, wine, good meat, and delicious fruit made them independent of outside assistance. Their income was derived largely from the silk trade. About 100 *rotulas,* or about 45,000 pounds, of this commodity were annually produced for export. The people of the Red Banner lived in a hilly region along the sea about Beirut and Sidon, a less defensible region. These Reds were led by an energetic emir, "Macksur," who lived in a castle near Beirut. Although the confusing feudal character of Ottoman Lebanon and the absence of other contemporary accounts makes identification difficult, "Macksur" was undoubtedly Korkmaz ibn Ma'n, the leading chieftain from 1544 to 1585 and called Maanoghli by the Turks.

In a government where only the standing or feudal army

could have firearms, the possession by the Druzes of muskets in considerable number was a cause of constant and serious trouble. Their guns were illegally obtained from the Janissaries of Damascus, from captains of ships coming to Syria, from Christian merchants, and from the gun-runners who brought these weapons from the recently conquered island of Cyprus. An Ottoman firman of 1565 already complained that the Druze insurgents were using muskets which "fire bullets [weighing] 7-8 dirhems; they are extremely long muskets, superior to the muskets [used by the government forces] in this region, since they can fire from places beyond the range [of the latter]." [13] Rauwolf reported that once, before the fall of Cyprus in 1571, the Anti-Turkish Druzes had raised 7,000 armed men to assist some Italian galleys they had been informed were about to raid the coast of Syria and attack Tripoli. The ships failed to arrive, however, and the disappointed Druzes returned to their homes. [14]

The attempt of the Turks to subdue the independent inhabitants of Lebanon began before Rauwolf left Aleppo for Baghdad. As he was informed at that time, the sultan felt that the time had come to curb the growing strength of these rebels. As a step in that direction, he first seized, imprisoned, and unjustly executed the leader of the Reds, who lived in Damascus. [15] The dismay and terror which the sultan had hoped to thus instill in the Druzes and Maronites was not achieved. Rather the Lebanese united under Emir "Macksur," determined to fight for "their ancient liberties." They began to fortify their villages and the mountain passes and to collect guns, bows, and arrows.

At this point Rauwolf left Aleppo for Baghdad, but on his return the rest of the story was told him by the imprisoned Krafft. The sultan, it seemed, attempted to split the Reds from the Whites by negotiating with the emir, whose region was less defensible. The emir agreed to live in peace and even to pay the annual tribute if the sultan would let him alone; otherwise he would come to the assistance of the other Druzes and Maronites. The sultan consented to this and confirmed the emir as lord of Beirut and Sidon with a large annual revenue from these lands. By this device the sultan hoped to make the leader of the Reds obliged to attack the White in conjunction with the Turkish forces. However, the emir would only agree to cut off any Druzes fleeing to his region from the mountains to the north when the attack came. Even this was a deception, for, as Rauwolf wrote, "no Druze ever killed another Druze."

The sultan placed the pasha of Damascus in charge of the campaign. This pasha, with 6 other pashas and 17 sanjak-begs, led "about 200,000 well-armed cavalry and foot soldiers" against 60,000 Druzes. Two days out of Damascus the paths up the mountains became so steep and narrow that the horsemen had to dismount and proceed on foot. Some initial success was achieved, for the Turks burned 6 or 7 villages of the reputed 27, and "cut to pieces" the women, children, and the few men they found there. Guerilla warfare now began, and as the Turks pressed forward they were fired upon from all sides. When the Turks tried to pursue the agile mountaineers, the Druzes only mocked them and thumbed their noses. To the hidden marksmen, the Turks were "like a great flock of pigeons." Once, the Druzes let 8,000 to 10,000 Turks ascend a good road only to block retreat with 6,000 troops while other Druzes "received them so warmly, few survived." The enfilade fire, the lack of provisions, and the rugged terrain all contributed to a Turkish withdrawal. After two months of humiliating reverses and with winter approaching, the pasha of Damascus ordered an ignominious retreat and an end to the campaign.[16]

In the summer of 1575, while Rauwolf was in Tripoli, an attempt to free Krafft from prison proved not only unsuccessful but also tragic. On July 11, Johann Nutz, the barber-surgeon of the "Santa Croce" trip, brought to Krafft a letter from Georg Bronnenmayer, former factor of the Manlich firm in Marseilles. This letter informed Krafft that Pierre Arvie, the captain of the ship "Lion" of Marseilles, had been given 600 ducats which he was to present to the governor of Tripoli and thus secure the release of Krafft. However, before Arvie could accomplish his purpose, he and five Italians set out for Aleppo with the caravan that was carrying the goods brought to Syria in the "Lion." The Europeans rode well ahead of the slower caravan and were resting in the shade outside a khan when they were approached by a well-dressed and armed rider. This man requested that the Europeans come with him into the khan where a subasi wished to speak to them. The unsuspecting Europeans entered the khan where they were fallen upon by a band of robbers who murdered them and buried their bodies. The robbers then rode off with the horses. One of the murderers was seized when a carrier of the caravan recognized his blood-stained horse as one which the Europeans had been riding. Under torture the murderer confessed the crime and was executed at Aleppo. By the time Rauwolf left Tripoli for Europe, none of the other murderers, reputedly Arabs, had been apprehended.[17]

Despite this incident, Rauwolf thought the Turkish officials did take precautions that the roads were kept safe from highwaymen; yet one had to take care when traveling. It was not only the Europeans who were subject to hostile action. Rauwolf heard in Tripoli of two naval engagements between Christian and Turkish vessels in which the latter suffered losses. In an action which took place in July, 1575, six Christian galleys had captured four great Turkish vessels, three fly-boats, and two other craft. These attacks caused the Turks to send out a large number of galleys on patrol. Most of these vessels were based at Rhodes, but on occasion some came into the harbor at Tripoli. The European merchants and ship captains at Tripoli did not care for their arrival, for the Turks always had to be given some cloth, money, or other gifts to keep them peaceable.[18]

X PILGRIMAGE TO JERUSALEM

While in Tripoli in the summer of 1575, Rauwolf considered how near he was to the Land of Canaan, the Promised Land, the home of the prophets, and the scene of the drama of salvation. He desired to see the holy places of biblical history, in order, as he said, "to exercise my outward senses in the contemplation thereof, that I might the more fervently consider with my inward ones his bitter passion, death, resurrection, and ascension, and to apprehend the better and make my own, by faith and firm confidence, Christ our Lord himself together with his heavenly gifts and treasures, as he has manifested himself in the Holy Scriptures." [1] With these religious motives in mind, Rauwolf sought other travelers to accompany him on a pilgrimage to Jerusalem. The quest was short, for he soon met four pilgrims from the Lowlands and a Grecian Carmelite monk whose master Rauwolf had previously cured of illness. This party hired one of the many small coastal boats that lay in the harbor ready to transport travelers and goods to Levantine ports or even to Cyprus and Egypt. The high-pooped vessel, of the type called a "caramusala," was provisioned with a variety of food that included biscuits, raisins, eggs, cheese, melons, oranges, and good wine.[2] In all, enough food was taken to last for eight days, since the master of the boat feared to land along the coast on the way to Jaffa and thus subject his Christian passengers to dangers and unjust demands.

On the seventh of September, 1575, the party set sail and with a good wind they arrived off the Theuprosopon Promontory before dark. All that night the vessel coasted along the rugged shore and the early morning light revealed the Beirut promontory and the famous city that gave it its name. This port, once known for its commercial activity, was still well fortified with strong towers by the sea and surrounded by fruitful orchards and vineyards. Here and in the neighboring towns and villages dwelt the Druzes, called "Trusci" by Rauwolf. Like many of his time, Rauwolf thought that the Druzes were descendants of Frenchmen of the First Crusade.[3]

Once the boat had cleared the extensive Beirut promontory, the Turkish master of the vessel pointed out to Rauwolf a village which he called "Burgi" and explained that it was inhabited by *"harami quibir,"* that is, robbers and murderers.[4] Rauwolf recognized this as an appelation commonly given by the Turks to Christians, and he silently prayed that God would soon free the poor slaves then in hard servitude under the Turks. Rauwolf also observed some towers along the shore, especially two that had been rebuilt and now served as watchtowers from which the Druzes kept watch for pirates. He understood that these towers had originally been built by the Byzantine emperors and were a part of a chain of such towers, about a league apart, that once extended to Constantinople. By the use of fire at night and smoke by day, the watchmen had been able to quickly relay the message to the capital that a rebellion had started.[5]

On the afternoon of the second day of travel the vessel was becalmed, and only a little progress could be made by means of eight oars. It was night when they approached Sidon, which was not a large city but well built and defended by two crusading castles, one on a high rock to the north of the city and the other on a hill to the south. Contrary winds delayed their progress through the night, but morning found them approaching the city of Tyre (Sur). This famous city was of good size and situated on a rock in the sea about 500 paces from the shore. The sight of this historic but ruined city reminded Rauwolf of the seven months' siege by Alexander the Great, who had reduced the city to ashes after building a causeway out from the land. Thus had the city received the punishment decreed for it by the prophet Isaiah 400 years before (Isa. 23). It was also, Rauwolf reminded himself, in the confines of Tyre and Sidon that Christ had healed the daughter of the Canaanite woman (Matt. 15). Near the city, even though out to sea, Rauwolf could hear the sound of large running springs "which rise within the country with so great a vehemency, that they drive several mills." [6]

Below Tyre was the large village called Achib (ez Zib). Here, amid the banks and rocks offshore, the pilgrims' ship waited for a more favorable wind. The time was spent in collecting oysters, catching fish, and filling a large sack with the seasalt found upon the rocks. To the south was the great peninsula of Mount Carmel, and on the high rocky shore about halfway between their resting-place and the promontory lay the famous city of Acre (Ptolemais) of crusading history. Good fields of fertile soil lay about that city, now "(to the great grief of the Christians) subjected to the yoke and slavery of the Turkish Emperor." The next morning the wind was more favorable until noon when a contrary wind blew the ship back to the shelter of the rocks again. That night, two hours before daybreak, the wind having first abated and then turned from the north, they set sail again. In the evening, as they neared the port town of Haifa (Caypha, Porphyria), beyond Acre, several frigates came from shore intending to surround the caramusala, but the master of Rauwolf's boat let fall his sail and with heavy rowing the vessel escaped the pursuers.

For a brief time that night the party landed at the foot of Mount Carmel and Rauwolf was reminded of the contest between the prophet Elijah and the priests of Baal (I Kings 18). Here, too, was the original home of the order of Carmelite monks, endowed in 1205 with special privileges by Innocent III and Albert, the patriarch of Jerusalem. These monks had once been numerous in the area of Mount Carmel, but Rauwolf saw only ruined and uninhabited cloisters and churches. Crusading warfare had also meant ruin for Haifa, which was "pretty large but very ill built, and the houses are so decayed, that half of it is not fit to be inhabited." [7] Despite the danger, Rauwolf's vessel lay at anchor before Haifa until after midnight, when, in the hope of picking up a favorable wind, the caramusala was rowed out to sea. Toward morning the wind freshened from the north and drove them around the tip of the promontory and later past Athlith (Chateau Pelerin), once a mighty fortress of the Templars but now much demolished.[8] Here, two small boats pursued them but the strong wind caused the pilgrim's ship to outdistance the pursuers and arrive off Dora (Tanturah, Merla), a town "so decayed that there is nothing more extant than a large and high tower."

Beyond Dora lay the ancient and famous city of Caesarea.[9] Here, Rauwolf reminded himself, Peter had baptized the centurian Cornelius and the apostle Paul had visited the house of Philip the evangelist (Acts 21:8). That the city had once been great could be surmised from the "important and stately antiquities" still standing, but its walls and buildings were in ruins and the city stood defenseless and almost uninhabited: "We could hardly see anybody in the large and broad streets thereof as we passed by." Beyond the city, Rauwolf saw only a mosque on the hilly shore, and despite the fact that he had lived in Moslem lands for many months, he still retained the erroneous view that there "they meet to worship Mohammed."[10] With the favorable wind holding, the boat arrived at its destination, Jaffa, two hours after sunset on the sixth day after leaving Tripoli.

Early the next morning, September 13, the party landed and immediately sent messengers to the inland town of Ramle to secure passes from the resident sanjak-beg and to bring back asses and drivers for the trip to Jerusalem.[11] While awaiting their return, the pilgrims surveyed the region from the high rocky shore. Rauwolf remembered that here Jonah had taken the ship for the voyage that was to lead to his three days in the belly of the great fish; here the apostle Peter had tarried in the house of Simon the Tanner and had raised Tabitha from the dead (Acts 9); here, as Josephus related, the Romans had killed 12,600 Jews in A.D. 70; and here the Moslems had taken the city by storm from the crusaders in 1196.[12] The last two events had been so destructive that there were "no antiquities at all to be seen." Only some large sections of the ancient walls remained close to the sea to indicate that a city had once stood in the place. Jaffa thus had no houses which could be used as shelter by the pilgrims who throughout the centuries had come into its shallow roadstead. Even the three great subterranean vaults near the shore which had sheltered, among others, Friar Felix Faber and his companions in 1483 were not available to Rauwolf and his friends; the vaults, known to many a pilgrim as *cellaria S. Petri,* were being filled with grain for shipment to Constantinople.[13]

Near the shore Rauwolf found some *Hemerocallis,* a plant he had also found about Montpellier and Aigemort in southern France, and in a marshy meadow he located a delicate kind of *Statice sinuata* L. with blue and purple flowers that were used by the natives in salads. After dinner, the messengers returned with passes and carriers and the party set off to Jerusalem. On approaching the pleasant village of Yazur, they came upon the camp of the Turkish official in charge of the grain collection in the region. Summoned before him, Rauwolf and his fellow pilgrims made the customary obeisance and paid the eunuch nine ducats each, except the Grecian, who, as a Christian subject of the sultan, paid only five.[14] At the request of the Turks they spent the night in the camp, but long before dawn they again set out for Ramle, now with a Janissary along as escort. Ramle, situated on a sandy plain, was reached early in the morning and the party entered the pilgrim house that had been purchased there by Philip, duke of Burgundy, in 1420.[15] This caravansary was very large, had a great many arched chambers, and a fine well. Rauwolf found the inner court all overgrown with green *Aloe perfoliata* L., a plant whose juice was imported into Europe for medicinal purposes. The setting was nice and comfortable, but the three days spent there were consumed in arguing with all sorts of Turkish officials about their pilgrim passes; "so unjust, malicious, and infidel a people are they, that one would hardly believe it."

Ramle was an open and ruined village in the midst of fruitful fields of wheat, cotton and Indian millet.[16] In the area were also grown great quantities of watermelons, and Rauwolf decided he had never tasted such excellent fruit, especially "those that are red within." The town of Lydda (Diaspolis), where Peter cured the palsied Aeneas (Acts 9:32–35), could be seen nearby. The only building there that Rauwolf thought worth mentioning was the church, now a mosque, of St. George, whom the Moslems honored as a knight and hero.

After coming to an agreement with the officials at Ramle, the pilgrims left for Jerusalem. Upon reaching the mountainous ascent to their destination, they were besieged by a number of hostile Arabs whose action forced the accompanying Janissary to come to the aid of the group. Only after giving the Arabs something to drink could they resume their march. Other demanding groups were met so that the pilgrims felt "just like boys that have lost their game and run the gauntlet." [17] At the small village identified as "Anatoth," the birthplace of Jeremiah, they rested and watered their beasts. A little before it, on a height, there was pointed out to them the grave of Samuel the prophet. After passing the village erroneously but traditionally called Emmaus (Nicopolis, el-Khubeibeh), the rough road led them past many olive trees and some vineyards over the last rise where they saw Jerusalem. Rauwolf made no mention of the emotions that usually possessed pilgrims at the first sight of the Holy City.

Before the Hebron or Jaffa gate on the west side of Jerusalem the pilgrims dismounted, for the Moslems would not permit a Christian to ride into one of their cities. Once inside, they dispatched one of the carriers to notify the Father Guardian of the nearby Franciscan monastery of their arrival and to request that he secure the necessary permission of the Turkish officials. While they waited, some friars came from the monastery to welcome them. When the emir and his clerk arrived, the pilgrims were asked whence they came and how many were in the group. When their names had been recorded and the fee paid, the emir promised them safe conduct to visit the holy places. The friars then conducted them through several small lanes to the monastery located to the north of the gate and just within the northwest corner of the city wall. At the handsome and strongly built monastery, the pilgrims were greeted by Father Jeremy of Brixen, who had been head of the institution for 18 years.[18] The monks here were few in number and of several nationalities, but Rauwolf found no Germans among them. These Franciscans acted as guides and, accompanied by an interpreter who knew Arabic and Turkish, led pilgrims to the holy places within and without the city.

Before Rauwolf and his friends left the monastery for their

first tour, the Father Guardian admonished the pilgrims not to go near any Moslem cemeteries, usually located outside the cities, because Christians were considered unclean and besides one usually found women at the graves; "and where women are present, every one had best come away, to avoid danger." [19] The Father Guardian also warned that all who had come to Jerusalem from Europe without the proof that they had received absolution from the pope himself were excommunicated and could not visit the holy places, much less obtain the indulgences offered at such sites. Rauwolf had earlier heard of this usual warning from other pilgrims and he also knew that the monks were glad to see pilgrims with or without papal recommendation and would show them the sights in hope of securing compensation on their departure. Rauwolf "did not much mind this excommunication," but his comrades, two of whom were priests, were astonished and much troubled at the thought of their excommunication. They excused themselves by protesting that they had not known of the need for prior papal approval and by saying that they would certainly go to Rome on their return and obtain belated permission. The guardian played upon their fears for a time, but finally he announced that he had also received full power from the pope to absolve all without certificates. This was then done in the name of the Trinity and the pilgrims were ready for the tours.

In his travel book, Rauwolf devoted an introductory chapter (Part III, Chapter III) to a general description of Jerusalem and its environs. His observations are liberally supported by quotations from the Scriptures and Josephus. His general remarks included comments on the broad-tailed sheep, the dusty streets, the new walls, and the gates, but the one thing that impressed him most was the widespread desolation of what was once a fruitful and populous land. To Rauwolf this desolation was, of course, the evidence of punishment from God for the rejection of the Saviour by the Jews, but he also viewed it as a warning to European Christians that God visits his wrath upon the evil-doer. The desolation in and about Jerusalem was widespread, for the Moslems did "not love to till or cultivate the ground, but will rather starve than take pains to get a livelihood by their hand-labor."

Instead, the Turks overran the country "like grasshoppers" and made no effort to improve the land or houses; "All of which shows, that the Turks destroy or ruin more than they build; wherefore they are deservedly called Turks, that is to say, destroyers." [20]

In his detailed account of the places of Jerusalem, Rauwolf described first his visit to Mount Zion, south of the city.[21] In traveling south from the monastery the party passed the newly rebuilt Jaffa Gate by which they had entered Jerusalem.[22] This gate opened on the north edge of the Tower of David, the Turkish citadel, which was also rebuilt and surrounded with walls and ditches. Several cannon dominated the gate area "to frighten the Christians that come thither in great flocks." [23] Continuing southward on a long street bordering the west wall of the city, they soon came to the Church of St. James and St. John where the Armenian custodians showed them the place where John was beheaded (Acts 12). The nearby house of Annas, the high priest, was briefly visited, but only a large court and an old chapel, called the Angels, were observed here. After passing through the New or Zion Gate in the South Wall, the pilgrims were shown the site of the house of Caiaphas, the high priest, a place also under Armenian care. An orange tree marked the spot where Peter warmed himself at the time of his denial of Christ. A chapel, called St. Salvator, indicated the place where Christ was accused by Caiaphas and mocked and beaten by his servants. Here, under the altar, was the great stone that had blocked the entrance to the Saviour's tomb.

Further to the south and on the top of the desolate and rocky Mount Zion was a large church, the medieval Church of Zion or the Coenaculum, which the Turks in the fifteenth century had converted into a mosque to mark the graves of David, Solomon, and others. The Franciscans had occupied the church and the adjacent monastery since 1313, and had lost the convent area only 14 years before Rauwolf's visit.[24] It was at this time, 1561, that they moved to the monastery in the northwest corner of the walled city. Because no Christians were allowed to enter the mosque, the pilgrims missed seeing the room in which by tradition the disciples of Jesus hid for fear of the Jews, the room where Jesus and his disciples ate the Passover meal, and other items of interest.[25] From Mount Zion a panoramic view could be had of the adjacent valleys, brooks, and hills—all of which brought biblical references flooding into Rauwolf's mind.

In each of the holy places visited on Mount Zion, the monk-guides informed the pilgrims of the number of years of pardon associated with the place. Generally the indulgence was for seven years, but at the more important sites full indulgence and absolution could be obtained. At each place the monks would exhort the pilgrims to kneel and pray the Lord's Prayer and the Ave Maria devoutly and with the knowledge that they would receive the absolution given to the place by the pope. Rauwolf observed that when some of the company had prayed in several places, they "rejoiced mightily and confessed that after it they were holy and so innocent, that if they should die then, they were secure that their soul should go immediately out of their mouth into heaven and eternal life." To all of this Rauwolf asserted that he "expected remission of sin no other ways but only in the name and for the merits of our Lord Jesus Christ." He had not come on this pilgrimage to obtain indulgences, "because all these things are directly contrary to Scriptures." Since Christ is present with those that believe in him, he has no need "of any Vice-gerent, that should on earth usurp such power and take honor and glory to himself, as to give indulgence at his pleasure; be-cause all these things belong only to God." Rauwolf's confession of faith made no impression on his fellows, so he "let them alone in their opinions."

The pilgrims in Rauwolf's company acted like the thousands of others who had visited the Holy Land. Before each holy place, they prayed and then, after gazing at the site, they fell down and kissed the object or place with great devotion. This done they touched the place with beads or rosaries made of the wood of trees of the Mount of Olives, or perhaps with bundles of lace and other items, to make them prized possessions for all time. Wher-ever they could, the pilgrims knocked off chips of stone to take back and distribute among their less fortunate friends at home. While his comrades were thus engaged, Rauwolf stood behind them remembering "what our Lord and Saviour Jesus Christ had suffered for us in these places, how he had humbled himself, and came down to us miserable sinners, to help us and to extol us that were fallen, and to make us free of the heavy burden of our sins." Rauwolf's Lutheran faith becomes evident when he records that he thought about Christ's death and how before his passion "he did institute his holy Supper upon the mount, in the large upper room wherein he doth not only communicate them to us, but giveth us also (if we received the holy broken bread, and the blessed cup with true faith according to the institution) his real body and blood, to feed us to eternal life."

To the north of Mount Zion and within the walls of the sixteenth-century city lay Mount Moria.[26] This height, traditionally the scene of Abraham's near-sacrifice of Isaac and the site of the temple of Solomon, was now occupied by two Moslem mosques, the Dome of the Rock and the Aqsa Mosque. Rauwolf considered the Dome of the Rock neither "very large nor high, but fine and covered with lead." [27] The great courtyard of this area, the Haram esh-Sherif, was paved with white marble and had orange and date trees planted in it, creating a scene which the botanist found very pleasant.[28] Since admission was forbidden, the Franciscans showed the pilgrims the big gate (Bab Dâûd) on the west side, which Rauwolf described as being very old, high, and having good workmanship in it. Through this gate the pilgrims had a glimpse of the interior. Rauwolf would have willingly gone in to see the rock, the fountain, and the buildings, but he realized that "if anyone is caught within, he is in danger of his life, or else he must deny his faith, and be made a Mameluke or renegade.[29] The famous Golden Gate, on the east side of the court, with its ancient arches, looked "more like a church than a town gate" and was walled up in the new city wall.[30]

On the south side of the Haram enclosure stood the great Aqsa Mosque built by 'Abd-la-Malik in the seventh century and modified by others later. This structure was traditionally accepted as the Christian church built by Justinian in honor of the Virgin Mary.[31] Rauwolf, too, accepted this identification and associated it with the porch of Solomon "where Christ did preach, and drove out the buyers and sellers." Underneath this mosque was a great cave or vault, "so wide that some hundred horses may with ease be drawn up in battalia therein." [32] The fact that entrance to the mosque and vault was restricted to Moslems, reminded Rauwolf that the Moslems had "taken many ceremonies and laws from the Jews, and according to their depraved understanding and mind, transcribed them into their Koran."

On Mount Bethzeda, north of the Haram area, the pilgrims were shown the House of Judicature, where Pontius Pilate had sentenced Jesus.[33] As this area was surrounded by high walls, the pilgrims could only look in at the gate. Here in the court stood a very high and old arch, black with age, and surmounted by two other smaller arches. This was identified as the High Place before the Judgment Hall where under one of the smaller arches "stood Christ with his crown of thorns on, and Pontius Pilate in the other, when he said to the people, 'Behold the man.'" Beyond the arches, the pilgrims could see the marble building that stood on the site of Herod's palace. These dwellings were occupied by the Turkish officials and here the magistrates held court, severely punishing the guilty with fines and bastinadoes. In this area of the city the pilgrims were also shown other sites, such as the iron gate through which Peter was led out of prison by the angel, but Rauwolf dismissed these ruins with a mere mention.

The highlight of any pilgrim's visit to Jerusalem was the night spent in the Church of the Holy Sepulcher, and this Rauwolf experienced on September 27, 1575.[34] Admission to the church provided considerable income for the Turks, who were in control of the building, and the entrance fee varied with the distance the pilgrim was from home, and whether or not the pilgrim was from a country under Turkish rule.[35] Rauwolf reported that some paid two or three ducats, others four or five. Apparently the Turks considered European pilgrims to be as wealthy as Europeans now consider American tourists for Rauwolf had to pay nine ducats, and these had to be Turkish or Venetian coins.[36] Rauwolf estimated that even in his time the fees thus secured amounted to several thousand ducats annually. This great figure was, of course, nothing compared with earlier centuries "when all was under popish darkness and the pilgrims used to flock thither in great numbers." In the sixteenth century, the revenues had materially decreased since "by the Grace of God, the Holy Gospel has been brought to light again, and began to be preached (which shows us a far nearer and better way to find Christ, and to have true and full pardon and remission of our sins), so that daily more come to the knowledge of the truth, and return to the Lord."

Rauwolf and his companions paid their fees and waited a long time at the gate for others to gather. The group finally numbered about sixty persons and included some Eastern Christians —Greeks, Jacobites, Armenians, and others. By convenient tradition the gray marble edifice, now only half its original size, contained most of the sites associated with Christ's suffering, crucifixion, death, burial, and resurrection. A wealth of scriptural associations awaited the pilgrims in the various chapels and areas that filled the dimly lit building. Among others there was the dark Grecian chapel where Christ was detained while the cross was being prepared; the place where the soldiers cast lots for the robe of Christ; the great chapel of Helena underneath Mount Calvary, reached by a flight of 29 steps, and the still lower cistern in which Helena found the cross of Christ; the deep cracks in the rocks caused by the earthquake on that fateful day; the ascending gallery of 19 steps that led to two chapels with beautiful inlaid floors where the pilgrims removed their shoes to walk about and see the place where Christ was nailed to the cross and the socket which held his cross; and the fine marble slab, surrounded with iron gratings, on which the body of Christ was prepared for burial. The guided tour ended at the tomb of Christ, lined within and without with gray marble and directly underneath the opening in the leaded dome of the church. Within the tomb, the altar, and indeed the whole scene, was brilliantly lighted by some twenty lamps endowed by various nobles, including the kings of Spain and France.

At each of the sites the guides explained the indulgences available to the pilgrims. Even the Protestant Rauwolf was deeply moved by the experience within the church, for as he said, "it can not be otherwise, but that every true Christian that is upon this mount of Calvary, and thinks there of the cross of Christ, and in the Sepulcher of his glorious resurrection, must find great passion within his breast." For Christ had died "to bring us miserable sinful men to rights again, and to deliver us clearly from all debts and punishment, and so to procure us the only and true indulgence."

After supper was eaten in the vestry, the pilgrims retired to the gallery under the cupola. Here they sought to rest, but Rauwolf slept little, being more interested in the Eastern Christians who spent the night hours singing in the church below and playing their "sweet-sounding cymbals" about the size of a large walnut shell. The next morning Rauwolf's comrades confessed and then persuaded the Protestant in their midst to make another circuit of the sites before the Turkish guards drove them out.

Rauwolf's tour of the holy places included also the Mount of Olives, situated across the brook Cedron to the east of the city.[37] On this rough and stony hill, the botanist from Augsburg observed, besides the olive trees that gave the place its name, fig, lemon, orange, citron, terebinth, palm, and carob trees. Among the herbs were *Origanum creticum* L., ? *Thymus mastichina* L., *Satureia capitata* L., *Andropogon nardus* L., and a peculiar sort of *Conyza*. The pilgrims were first shown the church in the valley that marked the tomb of Mary, the sepulcher-chapel being reached by descending 44 steps. After leaving this place, the pilgrims passed "an old square building like unto a steeple" which was held by Christians and Moslems alike to be the tomb of Absalom. Rauwolf did not say whether he followed the custom he described of throwing stones at the resting place of this disobedient son of David.[38] Beyond this structure, the path began a steep ascent. At the place where Christ looked over toward the temple and foretold its destruction, Rauwolf looked across the valley into the paved court of the Haram esh-Sherif. Farther up the hillside was a large plain from which Christ had ascended into heaven; on the plain were some ancient ruins and a recently built chapel. From the top of the mountain, Rauwolf could see the hills of Galilee to the north and the distant plain in the east that extended southward to the Dead Sea.[39]

The pilgrim party then descended the other side of the mountain to the site of Bethpage, now marked by only a few foundation stones. Farther to the east, along the road to Jericho, lay Bethany. On the way to this village, the pilgrims were shown the rock where Mary met Jesus and reported the death of her brother Lazarus. In the village itself, the Franciscan guides showed the group the small chapel and the cave out of which Jesus called Lazarus. When the villagers found out there were pilgrims in the tomb, they would not let them out until paid. On the return trip the pilgrims were shown the old building where Simon the Leper had lived and also several fig trees cursed by Christ because they had no fruit when he was hungry (Matt. 21:19).

The last excursion was to Bethlehem, about six miles to the south of Jerusalem in the hill country of Judea.[40] Once out of the Hebron Gate, the path led the pilgrims past a cistern where the Star had appeared to the Wise Men to lead them to Bethlehem. Near the cistern grew a terebinthus tree larger than any Rauwolf had seen elsewhere.[41] They passed the so-called Cicerfield with the small pea-like pebbles and an appropriate legend about a miracle of Christ, the old ruins that marked the place where Abraham had pitched his tent (Gen. 7:8), and the two great holes which contained the bodies of 185,000 soldiers of Sennacherib who were slain by the angel of the Lord (II Kings 19:35). Near Bethlehem and to the right of the road could be seen the grave of Rachel and the nearby cistern of David (Gen. 35: 16, 19; II Sam. 23).

Just before the ruined houses of Bethlehem and to the east of the path stood the Church of the Nativity. Rauwolf thought this edifice had been built by Helena, the mother of Constantine, but the delapidated building he saw had in reality been erected under Justinian. Even in its ruined condition, Rauwolf though it "so glorious a building, that one shall hardly find a better anywhere." [42] He commented on the white marble pavement, the large and high marble pillars, "about fifty of them," and the fine and colorful mosaics. The Father Guardian conducted the pilgrims, after they had removed their shoes, to the grotto where the manger stood, now of fine marble. The stable-cave was lined with gray marble, inlaid with blue. Chapels in the church marked the place where Jerome had lived while translating the

Bible and where the pious Paula (d. A.D. 404) and her daughter
Eustachia lay buried. The Father Guardian pointed out to the
pilgrims where colored veins in the marble altar seemed to depict
the aged Simeon holding the infant Jesus in his arms and a simi-
larly made picture of Jerome in the marble of the manger itself.[43] The Franciscan then commented: "That from hence we
may see, conclude and learn, that it is not culpable at all to have
images, seeing that nature itself alloweth so much unto stones,
that images may grow in them. Wherefore they are not only not
forbidden, but rather to be honored." Rauwolf reacted to this
logic with the following: "What every Christian ought to think
of this, being quite contrary to the holy Scripture, every child
that hath but begun to learn the Catechism, can easily and sufficiently decide."

The large and pleasant monastery of the Franciscans at Bethlehem lay higher than the church and was surrounded by a high
wall as protection against the daily incursions of the Arabs. The
large garden within was "rich of fine plants and good fruit."
From the monastery a good view could be had of the hills of
Judea, the area about Jericho and the Dead Sea, and beyond, the
mountains of Arabia. The most prominent feature of the land-
scape was the high hill to the southeast which Rauwolf associated with the castle of Tekoa (Jer. 6:1 and Amos 1:1). He reported that this hill, undoubtedly the Herodium, was held by the
crusaders for 30 years after the fall of Jerusalem and the loss of
the Holy Land to the Moslems. The Christians, on leaving this
stronghold, went to Mount Lebanon and became the Druzes—or
at least so Rauwolf thought.[44] In the fruitful valley that ran eastward toward the Jordan, the shepherds had heard the "good tid-
ings of great joy." Rauwolf cited Nicephorous as authority that
Helena had built a church, now ruined, on the place. In another
valley, not far from Bethlehem, the pilgrims were shown the
large orchards of citron, lemon, orange, pomegranate, and fig
trees that King Solomon had originally planted (Eccles. 2:5 and
Josephus *Antiquities* viii.7).

The pilgrims returned to Jerusalem by a long circuitous route
along which they were shown a spring that was the source of the
water with which the apostle Philip baptised the steward of the

Queen of Ethiopia (Acts 8:27–39).[45] In the rough hills they stopped by a spring to eat supper. The road, lined at some places with carob (St. John's Bread) trees, led to the house of Zacharias where Mary had visited Elizabeth, to the ancient Church of St. John the Baptist, and to the nearby cave where by tradition Elizabeth had hidden with the infant John to escape the soldiers of Herod.[46] Here Zacharias had been killed by the same soldiers.[47] The last site visited was the old yet well-built Church of the Holy Cross where the custodians, Greek friars, "pretend that in that place the tree did stand, that was made use of for the cross of Christ." Soon after leaving this church the pilgrims, undoubtedly weary, entered Jerusalem through the Hebron Gate and that night prepared to leave the next day for Jaffa and the waiting ship.

Rauwolf was not only one of the few early Protestants who went to Jerusalem, he was also about the last Protestant who went as a true pilgrim.[48] Most of those European non-Roman Catholics who came later were more curious travelers than sincere pilgrims. In 1587 John Eldred went to Jerusalem "as one desirous to see other parts of the country . . ." and in 1600, William Biddulph, the English clergyman, was careful to note that he and his companions went from Aleppo to Jerusalem, "not moved as Pilgrims with any superstitious devotion to see Relikes, or worship such places as they account holy; but as Travellers, and Merchants . . ." [49] There can be no doubt of Rauwolf's religious motivation for the trip to the Holy Land, and his continual use of biblical quotations emphasizes this fact. How different from Rauwolf's is the unemotional narrative of the Englishman George Sandys, who in the Church of the Holy Sepulcher was content "with an Historicall Relation." Even the guide at that time (1611) felt it necessary to demand of those in the group "if devotion or curiositie has possest" them with the desire to view the places in the church.[50]

As a pilgrim, Rauwolf was quite uncritical of the traditional locations assigned to biblical events and characters. He did question Absalom's "tomb," but he used the word "pretend" only in connection with the claim of the Greeks that their church stood at the site where the tree used for the Cross had grown. The only other shade of doubt occurred in his description of the pea-field on the road to Bethlehem where it "is said" Christ changed the peas a man was sowing into stones because the sower made an insolent reply to Christ's question as to what he was sowing.[51] In this connection Rauwolf wrote: "Now whether there be any thing of truth or no I cannot affirm; but this I must say, that there are to this day, such stones found in this field." He even collected some of the pea-stones. How different is this from the frequently repeated parenthetical expression "as they say" of the narrative of Sandys.

The sincerity of Rauwolf's religious pilgrimage was apparently such that he suffered no abuse from the Franciscans who sheltered and guided him. This conduct seems to have changed in the last decades of the sixteenth century. In 1600 William Biddulph admitted that he had been well received by the Franciscans, but "this kindnesse and liberties of conscience, which wee found amonst them wee imputed not so much to the men, as to our owne money . . ." He felt it necessary to "admonish those who have a desire to travell to Jerusalem hereafter, to take heed to themselves, that they make not shipwrecke of conscience; for if they come not well recommended, or well moneyed, or both, there is no being for them, except they partake with them in their idolatrous services." [52]

In the description of his Jerusalem experience, Rauwolf showed a high degree of biblical literacy. Undoubtedly, he had been well instructed in his faith through the use of Luther's catechism, as his remark about the "images" in the marble at Bethlehem indicated. Besides the Bible, Rauwolf made frequent use of Josephus' *Antiquities of the Jews* and the *Jewish War*. Once he mentioned Eusebius. On a number of occasions he cited the thirtieth chapter of the eighth book of the *Ecclesiastical History* of Nicephorus Callistus, the Byzantine historian of the fourteenth century. This work, though written in an excellent style, ascribes to the Empress Helena the erection of a large number of churches in Palestine. In all probability her work in Palestine is limited to the Church of the Nativity at Bethlehem and the church on the Mount of Olives. The use of the *Proto-Evangelium of St. James* and the *History of the Martyrs* by Rabus have been indicated earlier. Although he made no mention of his sources, Rauwolf showed considerable knowledge of crusading history. This is seen especially in Chapter IX of his travel book where he described the tombs of Godfrey of Bouillon, Baldwin, and others in the Church of the Holy Sepulcher. Despite the weaknesses of some of the sources, their use shows a serious attempt by Rauwolf to verify or amplify the oral traditions with literary ones.

Before they left Jerusalem, the pilgrims rewarded, "to their full content and satisfaction," the Father Guardian, the interpreter, and all who had served as guides.[53] The Father Guardian thereupon gave them certificates that named all the holy places they had seen. On the return journey, the pilgrims stopped overnight at Ramle. The trip from Jaffa to Tripoli took five days and Rauwolf arrived "in very good health and condition." [54] For this he appropriately gave "eternal thanks, glory and praise unto Almighty God the Father, Son, and Holy Ghost. Amen."

On his return to Tripoli from Jaffa, Rauwolf renewed his attempts to secure the release of his friend Krafft. But his efforts were to no avail; in fact, he jeopardized his own freedom. Since that nothing could be done by his remaining in Tripoli, Rauwolf prepared to leave for the home he left so long ago. His preparations completed, he said a last farewell to Krafft, and on November 6, 1575 he boarded the "St. Matthew," which sailed for Venice the next day.[55] The ship was so laden with goods, to the amount of 600 tons (12,000 centners), that the passengers had to find what shelter they could on the deck. This fact was to contribute greatly to their discomfort later in the rough and lengthy passage that lay ahead.

The voyage proceeded without difficulty until they approached Cyprus on the morning of the third day. Then a sudden windstorm tore off the main sail and wrapped it around the mast. As suddenly as the wind, called *vertex* or *vortex* by Pliny, had arisen, it ended and with the sail replaced they steered for Capo del Graeco and the harbor of Famagusta. But the weather was to decree otherwise, for again a wind arose which blew them out to sea and westward past the island. The weather became increasingly foul and the ship drew near to Asia Minor and the island of Rhodes. Then a northerly wind arose which blew the ship past the mountainous island of Carpathos and then Cape Salomon at the eastern coast of Crete.

The fresh wind would have blown them over to Africa if they had not sought shelter in the lee of the coastal mountains of Crete, where except for the quick action of the pilot and the crew they would have been shipwrecked. It was considered safer in the open sea, but the foul weather caused them to head for shelter at the uninhabited island of Calderon, about five miles from the coast of Crete. Here they landed to await better weather. On the island Rauwolf found a kind of mandrake (*Mandragora officinarum* L.) and many junipers (*Juniperus lycia* L.). While they were there they sighted several water-spouts "in the shape of a pillar that came down from the skies to the next mountain and extended themselves sloping down to the sea." [56] Pliny had mentioned phenomena such as these columns that sucked up the water and disturbed the sea. Rauwolf reasoned that such rotating winds sometimes sucked up "worms, frogs, fungi, snails, mussles, etc.," which then fell with the rain "especially in those places near to the sea." He had personally experienced such rain-brought debris in traveling through the mountains between Bologna and Florence in Italy (1563).

When the wind changed for the better, and when they had provided the ship with wood and fresh water, they sailed on westward. One of the seamen caught a large fish, "some hundred weight in bulk," on a hook baited with meat. When it was cut up, Rauwolf was interested to find that the fish "had very small bones that were more like cartilage." The fish was served at meals, but Rauwolf found it too salty to be edible. Soon after, the Augsburg physician was called upon to cure a pilgrim, a priest from Lille in Flanders, who was violently ill with dysentery.

As they neared the Venetian-held island of Cythera, another hurricane arose at nightfall. The ship was tossed about with great violence and the cargo and loose items tumbled about the ship in the dark night. To make matters worse, the cabinet that held the cannon balls burst open and the balls lurched about the deck as the ship rolled with the waves. Then, with a noise that could be heard about the howling wind, the waves tore off the railing on the stern leaving exposed some nails "about a finger thick" that formerly held it secure. Everyone thought the ship was surely lost when the wind ripped off the main sail and left the vessel entirely at the mercy of the waves "that flung her and tossed her about like a ball from place to place." The captain, stationed at the main mast, often found himself completely under water. The crew and the passengers worked together, as well as they could amid the confusion, to raise a spare sail, but only when the frightening scene was illuminated by flashes of lightning could they see what they were doing.

When the sail had been raised "with great labor, difficulty and danger," and the worst seemed to be over, a scene ensued which reminds one of the colloquy *Naufragium* of Erasmus. The seamen fell upon their knees and began to pray to the patron saint of their choice. Some prayed to St. Peter, others to St. Paul, others to Virgin Mary, but most asked St. Nicholas to intercede for their safety. The last named saint had "in similar imminent dangers, necessities, and calamities, most often above all the rest showed himself by various signs, according to their opinion, ready to assist and help, so that they might be sure of his help and comfort themselves with certain deliverance." After praying thus, some of the seamen assured Rauwolf that they had seen three burning candles on the top of the main mast, a sight which caused some of them to vow solemnly that they would go on a pilgrimage or would give money to one of their churches. The storm continued all night long and the greater part of the next day, causing the seamen to pray to their saints on several occasions. All of this amazed the Lutheran Rauwolf who could not honestly tell whether he "was more astonished at their prayers or at the tempestuousness of the sea." No one had sought the assistance of Christ, but instead all had appealed to saints who knew nothing of them and who, if they had been alive, would have directed them to "the true and only Mediator Jesus Christ." When the waves had covered the ship, Rauwolf had turned to Christ, just as the disciples had once wakened Him during a storm (Mark 4 and Luke 8).

The storm had blown the ship northwestward on its course at

a greatly accelerated rate and the seamen did not know where they were until they sighted the Venetian-held island of Sante. After passing to the west of this island, on the fourteenth day of passage, they sailed into the fine harbor of Argostolion on the island of Cephalonia, another Venetian possession. A grim reminder of their recent peril was seen to the left of the habor entrance where a ship under full sail in a stiff wind had missed the entrance and crashed on the shore. The "St. Matthew" remained in the security of this harbor for several days while the crew and passengers refreshed themselves. Being on the island reminded Rauwolf of the recent naval victory of the Christian fleet over the Turks off Lepanto (1570), for it was in the sea to the east of this island that the Christian armada assembled for the attack.

The crew and passengers of the "St. Matthew" hoped that they could buy some bread in the city to replace the old, black and worm-eaten biscuits that had been originally loaded on the ship in Spain a long time ago; but no provisions could be secured. The inhabitants, living in constant fear of an attack by the Turkish fleet, had moved all their supplies to the strong fortress that lay above the harbor on a height. Even by going from house to house, they could not secure enough bread for one meal. Of good red wine, there was plenty and the merchants of the party bought much of this to take to Venice. While in the port, the pilot who had brought them from Tripoli fell ill. As they would soon enter the dangerous waters of the Adriatic, the captain searched for and finally secured the services of a Greek pilot. When the weather cleared, they continued their voyage toward Venice.

The good weather did not continue long, however, and contrary winds so delayed their progress that it was many days before they arrived off Corfu. They could hardly see the island through the fog and mist. Later, high winds threatened to blow them over to Apulia, but the pilot sought shelter in the channel between the island of Melita and another island. There they anchored for the night. Early in the morning a galley was sighted coming toward them and fearing that it was a Turkish ship, the defences were readied. When the galley came nearer, they could see by its flag that it was a friendly craft and as she went by the

"St. Matthew" discharged "three great guns to salute her according to the usual custom of the sea." Continuing their voyage towards Venice, the pilot hugged the coast and passed to the east of the island called Corcyra Nigra.

On Christmas Eve they came into the harbor at Lesina (Hvar), "called Pharia by Ptolemy." The next morning, Christmas Day, the townsmen joyfully discharged their cannon in celebration. The cannon in the fortress were then discharged, followed by those on the six galleys that had arrived in the harbor after Rauwolf's ship; finally the sixteen great guns of the "St. Matthew" boomed out; "it made such a noise in the harbor that one would have thought all the buildings fell over one another." The smoke was so thick that visibility was limited. After dinner, a landing party brought good new bread to replace the old biscuits. At this harbor the priest whom Rauwolf had cured left the ship with some companions in order to cross over to Ancona and to go from there to Rome. Because of continuing bad weather, the "St. Matthew" lay at Lesina for four days.

At length they weighed anchor and departed for Zara. The area through which they passed was dangerous, for the numerous small islands enroute sheltered many pirates, called "Scacki," who slept during the day and preyed upon the passing ships at night. These bold pirates were known to have even attacked ships at anchor in harbors. The entire company on the "St. Matthew" took turns keeping watch at night and several times they were approached by small innocent-looking crafts that were suspected of holding 40 to 60 hidden men. As soon as any of these boats approached the ship as if to board her, the watch would cry out, *"Fuoco, fuoco,"* that is, "fire," and threaten to shoot at the boats. Aware that the ship could not be taken by surprise, the pirates in the small boats would shout *"amici, amici"* and leave.

Once this danger was past, they were confronted with another. The Greek pilot, whose services had not been satisfactory, feared he would be discharged if he brought the ship into the harbor at Zara. Instead of going to this port, he steered for the island of Vergetes, although the waters, while deep enough for the galleys he had previously piloted thither, were too shallow for a loaded merchant ship. The ship struck a shoal with a great cracking noise, but fortunately the wind carried them over the hidden rocks. In this they were aided by the fact that the rudder, which extended at least 30 inches below the keelline, remained in one piece and by riding up the rock pushed the prow and then the whole ship into deeper water. The captain ordered the ship into the harbor of a nearby island and a sloop was immediately dispatched to Zara for a new pilot.

When the new pilot arrived, they sailed for Venice. But their troubles were not yet over, for as they drew abreast of the castle of St. Michael, the fortress in the sea guarding Zara, a strong north wind arose which threatened to blow them over to the Italian coast. The new pilot, "who knew the shores and the landings of ships better than the former," brought them safely in an unnamed harbor. The wind was so strong that of the six galleys that had been met at Lesina, only two were able to make the harbor. The other four had to go back and find shelter among the islands as best they could. In this harbor they found a small yacht that had also sought refuge there, with its crew of 11 men. The crew was pumping out the water from the boat and drying the sails on the land. Upon inquiry, it was learned that this was a messenger boat carrying letters concerning a peace treaty from the sultan. The letters had been sent overland from Constantinople by the Venetian ambassador to the Adriatic port of Cattaro to be brought by this yacht to Venice.

When the storm was over, the voyage was resumed with stops being made at night at various places along the coast. When they arrived off the village of Segna, the ship entered the narrower part of the Adriatic. At the town of Rovigno, they stopped to pick up an experienced Venetian pilot. As this last passage to Venice was too dangerous to negotiate in a loaded merchant vessel except in the best weather, Rauwolf and the other passengers left the ship there and made the passage to Venice in a bark. Rauwolf arrived in this famous cosmopolitan city about noon on the fifteenth of January. The voyage from Tripoli had taken 70 days.

Rauwolf stayed several days with some friends in Venice and rested and refreshed himself after his difficult voyage. But he was anxious to get back to Augsburg, and despite the winter season he left with the Venetian post for home. His route took him through the cities of Treviso, Trent, Bolzano, and then through the Brenner Pass to Innsbruck and Ammergau. In the latter city he met Hans Widholtz, his cousin, and George Hindermayer. On February 12, 1576, he arrived at Augsburg to be greeted by his parents and friends; no mention is made of his wife. Thirty-three months had elapsed since he had bidden them farewell. Appropriately, he concluded his description of his travels with a prayer in which he thanked God for the many mercies he had received in all of his "great dangers and necessities, both by sea and land."

XI ISLAM

With the fall of Constantinople to the Ottoman Turks in 1453, Western Europe inherited as never before the Christian polemic with Islam. This religious strife was accentuated and its urgency increased by the Turkish military threat to Europe's political life and freedom in the sixteenth century. In many ways there was little new in the form, variety, and content of the polemic, but by Rauwolf's time considerably more information about Islam was available for use. The Koran had been printed at Zurich (1543 and 1550) in the inadequate translation made in 1143 by Robert of Ketton for Peter the Venerable. Travelers, pilgrims, diplomats, and others trained in Renaissance schools made serious efforts to understand and describe more fully and accurately the religion of Islam with which they came in contact in the many cities and areas of the Near East. Yet the medieval concept of Islam, with all its misapprehensions, continued, and to a remarkable degree those who knew Islam by first-hand experience repeated the same criticism and viewed Islam with the same prejudices. Independent judgment was little in evidence especially when the dogma and theory of Islam were discussed.[1]

Although Rauwolf entitled one chapter (Part III, Chapter 6) of his book "Of the Saracen and Turkish religion, their ceremonies, and hypocritical life, with a short hint how long their reign shall stand and last after their Mohammed's death," almost all the chapters in which he described his life in the Near East contain reference to what he called the "hypocritical and superstitious life and beliefs" of Islam. Rauwolf had much to say about "their outward ceremonies and good works, with which they think to fulfill the laws, to cleanse themselves from their committed sins and manifold transgressions, and to obtain God's grace and mercy." Their good works he listed as alms, pilgrimages, fasts, offerings, abstention from certain foods and drinks, washings, and prayers. According to the promises of their prophet Mohammed, the last two good works were most important in freeing and absolving them from their sins.[2] As such works were similar to those of the Jews of the Old Testament, Mohammed must have gotten them from his mother, who was an Ishmaelite.[3] Rauwolf felt that the Moslems had taken many ceremonies and laws from the Jews and "according to their depraved understanding and mind, transcribed them into their Koran." The similarities could be seen in such things as circumcision, offerings, washings, fasts at certain times of the year, polygamy, the prohibition of eating pork or anything unclean, the absence of bells, and the prohibition of wine-drinking, which had been denied the Levitical priests.[4]

Since the Moslems felt that from their ceremonies and good works, absolution and satisfaction for sins and thus eternal life could be obtained, they missed the "only mediator and Saviour, Christ our Lord." Rauwolf cited three Bible passages to show that God the Father could be honored and adored only through his Son. And this true God the Moslems did not know, even though Mohammed had insisted that there was only one God. Mohammed, Rauwolf felt, just could not accept the fact that God did have a Son and that Jesus Christ was the true God. Rather, Mohammed, "in his blasphemous and diabolical mind and thoughts," had reasoned that if God had a Son, such a Son might become disobedient—as happened frequently among the Moslem rulers—and thus all creatures in heaven and earth would be in great danger. Thus Mohammed denied the divinity of Christ, and like Arius, thought him to be no more than a mere man, although a great saint. Mohammed, like the Macedonians, had a similar opinion about the Holy Ghost and sometimes made the Holy Ghost and Christ but one person. So the Moslems, as instructed by their "cursed Prophet," knew no more of the true living God, one in essence and three in person, than when they formerly adored fire, water and other elements—or heaven and earth, like the Persians did before they accepted Islam. Besides they had no more comfort in Christ than did the Jews, for the Moslems did not believe that Jesus, the son of the

Virgin Mary, was crucified, died, and was buried. Rather they believed that another, very similar to Jesus, suffered in his place, for Christ was seated in heaven and was not killed by the Jews, "that impious people." The Moslems could not understand, therefore, why so many Christians devoutly came to see the grave of Christ in Jerusalem since it was not his.

Since Mohammed is preferred above Christ, all Moslem worship, even when performed with devotion, is null and in vain. However, Rauwolf was willing to admit that the Moslems did praise and esteem Christ very highly, and extolled him above any other man "as one that was conceived by the Holy Ghost, born of the Virgin Mary," and that he here on earth carried out his doctrines and confirmed them with powerful miracles. Also they esteemed the five books of Moses and the writings of the other prophets, together with those of the four evangelists, as true and godly. Sometimes the Moslems presented their views so convincingly that it was no wonder that an ordinary man who was not well instructed in the chief articles of Christianity might be easily taken in and misled, despite the great differences. Besides, the Turks would not allow Jews, Moslems, or Christians to say anything ill of Christ or to curse him, and the punishment for such acts was a severe bastinado and a heavy fine.

Rauwolf felt that if the Moslems would only study the Christian Scriptures as their Koran said they should, they might easily be brought back "to the right way." But Mohammed had contradicted himself and having early commended the reading of the Scriptures, he later said that the Scriptures, too difficult to keep, had become superannuated when such things as being good to our enemies, leaving all for Christ's sake, and loving God with all our heart and our neighbor as ourselves were commanded. It was for these reasons that the Moslems claimed that Mohammed was chosen by God to communicate the koranic injunctions to a world steeped in lust, sin, and vice, and thus to bring about a reformation. Besides this, Rauwolf thought that Mohammed was clever enough to so deceive the people by his tricks and conduct that he was received as a messenger and a prophet of God. As he met with initial success, he planned further conquests and in this he and his followers were able, "to our grief in these times," to secure a great part of the world with "his erroneous and pernicious doctrines." In Rauwolf's Christian view, the Moslems, in their blindness, knew not that they sinned when they took property and goods by force, destroyed houses and land, committed all sorts of sexual offenses, did not keep their oaths, and that in their vengeance they were guilty of hatred, anger, contention, and murder. The lands that bordered on the Turkish Empire had daily witness to the above sins, but even among the Moslems themselves, the bearing of false witness was very common.

As a Lutheran, Rauwolf was perturbed at their concept of work-righteousness, for when the Moslems wished to be absolved of their sins, "they go after their own invented devotions and do good works, alms, prayers, fasts, redeeming of captives, etc., to make satisfaction for their sins committed against God, as their Koran teaches them." This concept of justification made the Moslems diligent in their devotions and prayers, especially at the customary five times of the day, "when they leave their work and go to church." Since there were no clocks or watches in the cities, the "priests" (muezzin) cried aloud that "you may hear them throughout the whole town, as far almost as the ringing of a bell." Rauwolf gave the five times of prayer as an hour and a half before daylight, about noon, three o'clock in the afternoon, sunset, and "when the sun is down, the whiteness of the sky is gone, and the stars appear clearly." At times and especially in the larger towns, two "priests" sang, "as with us they sing a fugue." When Rauwolf first heard the early morning call, he thought it was intended to get the people up and working. He admitted that the muezzins sang "very well," but when he understood that the evening call, often extended in length, was to cheer the sick and dying, he condemned their clergy, "who are not more learned than the other laymen," for not knowing the true comfort that comes with a knowledge of God's forgiving mercy.[5]

Like the medieval observers of Moslem religious practices, Rauwolf was more interested in the use of ritual ablution than in the actual prayers performed. Also, the latter were often difficult for Christians to observe because they were prohibited from entering the mosques. Erroneously equating the ritual ablution

with the sacrament of Christian baptism, Rauwolf referred to the
final washing of the dead in preparation for burial as being de-
signed to "cleanse them completely from sins, according to the
law of their Mohammed, which they highly esteem." The service
which washing thus performed for the dead could also be obtained for the living, for Rauwolf reported that the Moslems
washed themselves daily with care and diligence, especially when
they went to the "churches" at the hours of prayer. He, like the
medieval commentators, completely confused the *ghusl,* or major
ritual washing of the whole body, and the *wudū',* or the minor
ritual cleansing of certain parts usually performed before
prayer.[6]

Rauwolf reported that the Moslems washed their hands, privy
members, head, neck, feet, indeed the whole body, "according as
they are contaminated or become unclean." He distinguished between three types of ablution. The washing of the whole body
was performed by bachelors who had contaminated themselves
with concubines. It was for such cleansing, he thought, that the
hot baths of the towns were kept heated and ready day and night
"that those who have occasion to wash their whole body, may
not be hindered in their devotion but soon go to church again."
The second kind of cleansing was performed on the organs of
the five senses and the head "to cleanse them from all spots and
blemishes which are contracted by evil thoughts and indecent
talk and deeds." It was for this kind of ablution that running
fountains were readily available, especially in the mosques and
chapels. In this washing, performed to make their prayers ac-
ceptable to God, the hands were washed first with the water
being allowed to run down their upraised arms to the elbows.
Then they washed the mouth, nose, eyes, ears, head, neck, and
feet, "and speak some peculiar words with it." If water was not
available, as in the desert, the cleansing could be done with sand.
Rauwolf thought that it was because of this kind of ablution that
their clothes had wide sleeves, no collar about the neck, and
drawstrings about their drawers. The third sort of washing was
performed, according to Rauwolf, after bodily elimination with
the washing being performed "publicly without shame . . . in
the sight of everybody" at the fountains. Erroneously assuming

that ritual ablution was for the remission of sins, Rauwolf, like his medieval predecessors, condemned this attention to the outward cleansing, and also to circumcision, while the Moslems "ought, according to God's commands, to cleanse their inward leprosy, by the bath of regeneration, and to circumcise their hearts by the inward spiritual circumcision, of which they know nothing." [7]

Although Rauwolf could not go into the mosques, he did observe the Moslems at prayer in the chapels of the larger caravansaries. He reported that after the worshippers had removed their shoes, they went to the place of prayer without speaking or looking about. Throughout the service they followed the action and words of their "priest," and although Rauwolf does not compare their conduct with the Europeans while at worship, he does admit that while the Moslem worshippers are in their holy places, "you hear none of them sneeze, cough, clear the throat, or spit." He also had to admit that if the Christians "would truly consider and reflect on the fervor and earnestness of the heathen and superstitious in their prayers, each would see what reason he had to awake from his laziness and inactivity and pray with earnestness." Rauwolf understood that in their prayers, the Moslems prayed for good fortune, victories for the sultan, and that "God may send great division among us Christians, that so they may better attack us and the easier do great damage." Not being permitted to have images in their mosques and chapel, "for they wished that man pray only to the one God, creator of heaven and earth," the Moslems decorated their places of worship with pictures of plants and flowers and with the sayings of Mohammed.[8]

When the prayers were over, the Moslems talked with one another and then went back to their various jobs. Even on Friday, the day corresponding to the Christian Sunday, shops could be opened again after prayers, "because idleness may the easier draw them into sin." Rauwolf observed that you could tell whether the proprietor of a shop was a Moslem, Jew, or Christian by noting on which of the three holy days (Friday, Saturday, or Sunday) the shops were closed. Then he added the remark that "none of these forces one to observe the other's holy days, and so they live peaceably and quietly together." Rauwolf also saw the ceremony of the lighting of the lamps on each Thursday evening and on each night during the month of Ramadan, "their Lent." In this striking custom, three rows of lighted lamps, "like a triple garland," were hung about the minarets at nightfall where they remained until they went out one by one.[9]

The mention of Ramadan led Rauwolf to describe briefly the Moslem calendar. Since a lunar calendar of 12 months of 29 or 30 days was used, this calendar did not agree with the Julian calendar then used in Europe. The lunar month meant that their year was ten or eleven days shorter than the European calendar year and that the important ninth month, Ramadan, moved through the seasons. In Rauwolf's time this month began in December and ended in January. The month of Ramadan was a period of special devotion in which the daylight hours must be spent in fasting. At nightfall everyone went home to eat or purchased some food in the shops of the bazaar. It meant that the streets were crowded with noisy throngs all night long; it was "enough to make one mad and deaf." [10]

When the time of Ramadan was ended, "their Easter feast" of three days was spent in solemnity, but with feasting, the exchange of wishes for health and happiness, the distribution of food to the poor, and with games. On these days, the Janissaries would erect swings, "almost like the children and boys by us," and swing people for a small gratuity. Other Moslems went about sprinkling people in the streets with sweet smelling water. As these, too, expected something in return, especially from Christians, it was best for the Christians to stay at home on these days. Besides the "little festival" (*'Id al-fitr*) which ended the fasts of Ramadan, there was a second canonical feast, the "major festival" (*'Id al-adha*) on the tenth to fourteenth days of the twelfth month. Rauwolf observed that on this latter festival the Moslems offered sacrificial animals in honor of Abraham and his son Isaac. It was also the month for pilgrimages to Medina, Mecca, and Jerusalem, and Rauwolf remarked that among such as assembled for the pilgrimage were those who had vowed such a journey in exchange for deliverance from illness or danger.[11]

While he was in Jerusalem as a pilgrim, Rauwolf observed

some of the Moslem pilgrims, for the Dome of the Rock was the goal of great caravans of pilgrims twice a year. Especially those Moslems returning from Medina and Mecca included Jerusalem on their route. Observing these pilgrims of another faith, Rauwolf felt that many Moslems, with little devotion, accompanied pilgrims to Mecca in order to sell merchandise and make greater profits by taking advantage of the free caravansaries and hospitals. Sometimes Christian merchants also accompanied the pilgrims to Mecca to sell items, especially those obtained in Cairo, even though they could not come near the holy places. Such practices, Rauwolf said, could also be found among pilgrims of the Roman Church, who "pretent to be good Christians," and go to Rome, Compostella, and Jerusalem not only to get indulgences, "but rather to make a great profit of goods they buy for that purpose." Other Christian pilgrims made great profit by leasing out their estates to others during their absence. All pilgrims, whether Christian or Moslem, desired to be held in esteem for their action and whereas the Christian who had been to the shrine of St. James at Compostella displayed his scallop shells, the Moslem who had been to Mecca wore a green turban and hung a small chain about the foreleg of his camel for each visit.[12]

Rauwolf noted that among the Moslem pilgrims were many renegade Christians who went on pilgrimage to Mecca "to get by their devotions into greater preferment and wealth." Such renegade pilgrims were esteemed by other Moslems as "holy and creditable men, although they are full of knavery and roguery." Wearing green turbans like descendents of the Prophet, these renegades were much sought after and bribed to serve as extra-reliable witnesses before the Turkish magistrates, "even in causes of which they have not the slightest knowledge." Perjury, cheating, robbing, and breaking faith were common enough among the Turks, but Rauwolf felt that the renegades were far worse "because they have lost all remembrance of confession, penitance, or mending of their lives." These renegades were well known for attempts to deceive and hurt Christians; indeed, Rauwolf felt the renegades would not hesitate to murder Christians if they thought they could escape the punishment of the Turkish authorities. Rauwolf even compared them with the Assassins who had lived on the south slopes of Mt. Lebanon under the Mamelukes of Egypt and who had been sent out "to murder and kill secretly all those who had opposed their Moslem law and religion." The Turks had ended the terror of these Assassins and now murder was severely punished.

The problem of the renegade had always been a serious one to the Christians. Why would a Christian apostatize and become a follower of Islam? Force and despair were obvious answers but not very correct ones, for the Moslems had always been quite tolerant of the "people of the book" (*ahl al-ḳitāb*), as Mohammed called the Christians, Jews, and a few others. Rauwolf had introduced the problem when he mentioned that the Moslems presented their doctrines so convincingly that the uninformed Christian could not see the difference between the two religions. He became more specific in his discussion of the Christians held as slaves by the Moslems. Although ways of escape or release were possible, only a few Christians returned to their homes again. Rather, many of them became Moslems. Rauwolf admitted that this was not because their Moslem masters forced them to change their religion, "as many think." To be sure, the slaves were sometimes threatened or treated more harshly than usual, "which happens often among the Christians also," but rather it was the secure and impenitent life that the easier religion of Islam offered to a Christian that caused him to forget his God and the Holy Word. Rauwolf felt that if these Christians really understood the differences between these two widely divergent religions, they would rather die than be seduced from Christ and "precipitate the soul with the body into damnation." But lacking this knowledge and with their faith almost extinguished, "they daily voluntarily fall from their religion like worm-eaten fruit." They sought a way to find compensation for their suffering and saw how the Moslems got money by robbing and burning and as privileged persons lived according to their own pleasure. At last, they believed the chief good of this world consisted in voluptuousness and became renegades.

When a Christian desired to become apostate, he indicated his decision by raising his forefinger over his head in the presence of

Moslems. Such an indication of apostasy occasioned great joy among the Moslems, for the many apostasies seemed to indicate confirmation of Islam. Preparations were soon made for the three-day ceremony of transference. It was customary to lay a cross before the ex-Christian on which he trampled three times, then spat upon it, and repeated "some words" out of the Koran. Undoubtedly these "words" were the verbal profession of faith through the famous formula *la ilaha illa-l-lah muhammadan rasūlu-l-lah* (No God but Allah; Mohammed is the messenger of Allah), for a person is nominally a Moslem once the formula is uttered. Rauwolf himself recognized the formula as a "summation of their religion, confession, belief, and law." Three arrows were then shot into the air and before they fell a Turkish name was given the new Moslem.

If the apostate was a man, he was dressed in rich robes, placed upon a horse, and led through the streets of the town for two days so all could see and recognize the new Moslem, now free to associate with others of his new religion on an equal footing. If the apostate was a man of some prominence, he was accompanied by well-dressed Turkish gentlemen with a Janissary escort. These soldiers would fire their guns for joy to attract attention, especially if they saw Christians in the streets. It was a festive and noisy occasion, with the pounding of kettle-drums, other large and small drums, "which they beat at the same time both above and below," with oboes sounding, and other musical instruments being played. The noisy crowds of the street ran in front and behind the cavalcade, some of whose members carried aloft long poles with streamers attached. On the third day circumcision took place and the apostate was now a true Moslem. As such he could go into the mosques and buy and read their religious books which could not be sold to an unclean non-Moslem.

For a variety of reasons, Christians had always had difficulty in converting Moslems and also in explaining the successes of Islam. One reason, Rauwolf felt, was that Moslems defended Mohammed's "false doctrines" with the sword rather than on rational grounds. Mohammed, "prompted by the devil," had insured the preservation of his views among his followers by issuing a number of strong prohibitions. No Moslem was to engage in discussion or disputation with anyone of another group or sect, believe their statements, or read their religious books, which were not true anyway. What was good and true in the Old and New Testaments could be found in the Koran, which must be believed and held as God's word without any criticism or investigation. Anyone who spoke against the Koran must be killed and eternally damned. Thus everyone could see how this "accursed" Mohammed had insured that all who had gotten entangled in his snares or fallen into his net must remain there and be damned forever. Mohammed made his religion attractive by promising "privileges, pay, and permission for sodomy, robbing, burning, perjury, etc." These sins were considered minor by the Moslems because Mohammed had promised his followers that "if they pray and wash themselves often" they would be "cleaner than we Christians became from our sins in the bath of regeneration."

Even if a Moslem might have his own opinions regarding his religion, he would be afraid to say anything or could not give a rational answer. Thus if a Moslem was asked why he did not eat pork or drink wine, he would answer that he was but following his parents who did not eat and drink these unclean and forbidden items. Or else he would answer that he was afraid that he might over-eat and over-drink and then vomit and contaminate his clothes. The nature of Mohammed's "cruel and tyrannical" law was indicated by the fact that a naked scimitar was carried through the streets before a nobleman's son who was to be circumcised, and that the priests on occasion showed themselves on the minarets after prayer with a burning torch in one hand and an unsheathed scimitar in the other. So the followers of Mohammed were encouraged to conquer all by the sword unless they became Moslems or paid a yearly tribute as obedient subjects. The inhabitants of Asia, Syria, Palestine, Egypt, Thrace, Greece, and other lands knew how well the Moslems followed Mohammed's injunctions in this respect. So successful had the Moslems been in their use of force that few Christians could still be found in most conquered lands. God had thus punished these Christians for their manifold sins and for their ingratitude to God for his holy Word. Since the Europeans, too, were guilty of the same sins and vices, it cannot be a source of amazement that a just God should send the Turkish tyrants against them. Unless there was amendment of life, the Europeans could be expected to be conquered also.[13]

Early in the ninth century there developed in Mesopotamian Islam the mystics or Sufi. Sufism, in emphasizing the mystical elements already in Islam and by stressing feeling and religious experience, was a reaction against the intellectual formalism of early Islam. Basically, the Sufi sought a more intense and direct approach to God and religious truth. As the centuries passed, Sufism assimilated Christian, Neo-Platonic, Gnostic, and other elements. Ascetism was regarded by many as one way to achieve a mystical union with God; others held that true knowledge of God could be gained only by ecstasy (*wajd*). In the twelfth century, the individual basis of Sufism gave way to religious brotherhoods with the founder of such a corporation generally becoming a saint (*wali*). The members of such fraternities were commonly called dervishes (*darwish*) and each order had its own dress and ritual. This ritual (*dhikr*) took various forms, such as an interminable repetition of a phrase accompanied by certain breathing exercises, by dancing or ritual movements, or by gashing the body with knives—all done to achieve a state of ecstasy in which communion and union with God was possible. While most of the orthodox mystics remained in their monasteries, some became itinerant mystics who roamed about in cities, highways, and deserts. Often these wandering mystics became charlatans who by their tricks (miracles), crimes, misconduct, and extravagant methods brought disrepute on the better mystical orders. In the sixteenth century, Sufism reached its climax, and monastic and itinerant dervishes could be found everywhere in the Ottoman Empire.[14]

Rauwolf had an opportunity to closely observe some of the itinerant dervishes, for the master of the boat in which he made his voyage down the Euphrates took aboard some of these religious men at Bir. Rauwolf had observed that these men lived by begging (*faqir,* mendicant), desiring that "you give them something *Allah hitsi,* that is for God's sake." Yet despite their religious utterances, they were known to rob people when the opportunity came. These "hideous, useless, but hardy men" roamed everywhere doing a great deal of damage, so that "one must have a special care of them, especially on the roads." Rauwolf could not understand how such men, with their abuses so obvious, could be considered such privileged persons who by pretense of great holiness and devotion could persuade the common people that God heard the prayers of a dervish before those of others. Even Rauwolf recognized that their many misdeeds were catching up with them and the people did not believe them as readily as in the past. The dervishes, too, had to keep moving from place to place so that their roguery would not be so evident.[15]

Rauwolf had some personal trouble with one of the dervishes on the trip down the Euphrates. He described this fellow as having long, black, and unkempt hair with scars on his head, breast, and arms where he had cut or burnt himself. Apparently Rauwolf witnessed such self-inflicted torment, for he said that the dervishes put burning or glowing embers on their flesh or else took tightly twisted rags, about an inch thick and shaped like a pyramid, and burned these on their bodies "with a great deal of patience." The burn was then bound up with cotton cloth. Rauwolf had seen a number of dervishes with at least 20 scars, mostly on the arms, besides wounds and scratches. He could not imagine where the dervishes had learned such an inhuman way of tormenting themselves, unless the practices had come from the ancient priests of Baal who wounded themselves with knives (I Kings 18:28). The scars were very evident on the particular man in Rauwolf's party, for like the members of his order, this dervish wore no clothes, winter or summer, except a little breech cloth. Only a sheepskin was used for cover at night. The nakedness, Rauwolf felt, was a part of the whole pretense of holiness and virtue, as if these dervishes "were dead to the world." [16]

Rauwolf also observed a variety of religious men of other orders, including a strong young man of the order of *Geomaliers,* which was a secular rather than a clerical order.[17] Persons like this young man were called *tschelebys,* "that is gentlemen or rich men," who took great delight in traveling in their youth, "under the pretense of holiness and at other people's cost," to see things and gain experience. This young man had on only a blue coat, tied with a sash, and shoes of sheepskin. Another man had a great ring, about the thickness of a finger, in each ear. The weight of the rings was such that the ear lobe was stretched down to the shoulder. He was of the order known as the *Calendiers*.[18] Members of this order led a sober and abstemious life, separated themselves from people whenever they could, and walked about in the desert like hermits, praying ardently. Repeatedly this man left the boat when he could, "that the beasts could rather see and hear him than we that were in the boat." When he returned, he looked so devoutly as if he had been in a rapture or trance.[19]

Often, and especially after sunset, another dervish would assemble about himself two or three others, including at times some of the merchants of the party. Standing in a circle they would pray certain formulas, very slowly and softly at first, then louder and more rapidly. As they repeated the phrases, they turned their heads from one side to the other. Finally, the phrases were abbreviated to *lahu huhu* and the men became giddy and weary, while cold sweat ran down their bodies. The dervish no longer pronounced the words with the rest but beat his breast with his fist in rhythmical thumpings that made a noise such as that of an angry turkey-cock ("Indianischer Han"). The dervish, looking more like an apparition than a man, at last fainted and fell down, and, the ritual over, his companions covered him and left. Such extravagant acts, Rauwolf felt, were intended to move the common people to accept the dervishes as devout and privileged persons, in order that, "under pretence of piety, they may go on in their hoggishness, uncleanness, and robberies, as they do, without any control." But, Rauwolf repeated, their misdeeds had been such that the dervishes were no longer held in the same esteem as formerly. Moslems had told the German traveler that because such rituals changed the dervishes' God-given voices into unnatural voices, such persons ought to be accounted beasts rather than be esteemed as divine.[20]

Although Rauwolf did not consider the Druzes as a Moslem sect, his views of these people should be presented here. The

Druzes had seceded from the Ismaili sect in 1021 when they refused to believe that the cruel Fatimid Caliph al-Hākim had really died. Rather they believed that Hākim was the last incarnation of God and organizing their own sect, they adopted their own secret precepts, moral rules, and a doctrine of metempsychosis. Their first great missionary was al-Darazi; hence the name Druzes. Their strongest center was in southern Lebanon and it was there that Rauwolf heard about and saw them.[21]

As he coasted the shore of Syria on his pilgrimage from Tripoli to Jerusalem in 1575, Rauwolf found two Druzes among the crew of his boat. These informed him of their people. Rauwolf called them "Trusci" and said that they "pretend to be Christians" and descendants of the crusaders. He agreed, however, that they were "neither Christians, Turks, nor Jews." Yet, while the Druzes hated the Moslems and the Jews, they had a strong liking for Christians and were very hospitable to European Christians, although they did not differentiate between German, Frenchman, or Italian. They showed this kindness especially to the Christian merchants who came to them to buy their silk cloth, and to their Christian neighbors, the Maronites. Yet they did not go "to mass" or hold any sort of public worship but on occasion called out to heaven that God should protect them.[22]

Rauwolf found their views very strange. Following the view of Pythagoras, the Druzes believed that the souls of the dead transmigrated into another body; the souls of those who had been pious went into the bodies of newborn infants, while those of evil persons went into the bodies of dogs or some wild animals. Their marriages, according to Rauwolf, were definitely incestuous for they would not marry into a strange family. To explain this conduct, Rauwolf reported that they had a number of expressions like "God has given me this child as a seed, why should I carelessly throw it away upon a stranger" or "I have a garden and God gives me flowers or fruit in it, is it not reasonable that I should enjoy them?" The Druzes also had an annual feast at which they exchanged wives. Yet, Rauwolf admitted, they did not steal, or murder, or commit other crimes. He explained this by the fact that the Druzes had all the food and other things they needed and by the fact that anyone found guilty of a crime was immediately executed.[23]

Beyond the conventional and traditional condemnation of Mohammed, Rauwolf did not include in his work the attacks on the person of the Prophet so common in the Middle Ages. Nowhere does he give the supposed sordid details of Mohammed's life, but while in Jerusalem, the sight of the Dome of the Rock led him to recount several stories of Mohammed. The Dome of the Rock was in Moslem eyes next in holiness after Mecca and Medina because the Prophet had made his famous night-journey (*mi'raj*) from Mecca to Jerusalem on the swift beast called "Elmparac" (*al Burak*, the lightning). At Jerusalem he had been met by the angel Gabriel who helped him off the beast, tied it up (at the modern Wailing Wall), and then led the Prophet into the sanctuary. Here Mohammed found a circle of many prophets, resurrected from the dead by God, waiting to receive Mohammed and tell him what God had prepared for him. To this last Rauwolf sarcastically added "namely ever burning flames of fire." There was Moses, who presented Mohammed with a cask of wine; Abraham, who gave the Prophet a cask of milk; and Jesus, who offered a cask of water. A voice from heaven then told Mohammed "If you choose the cask of wine, you and your people shall perish; if you choose the cask of milk, you shall also perish, but if you choose the cask of water, you and your people shall be saved eternally." Rauwolf did not say which cask Mohammed chose, but later he pointed out that, despite the prohibition against wine, the Moslems drink "more than any nation." In this connection, he considered it true that Mohammed's followers had chosen the cask of wine offered by Moses "to their own ruin and destruction, wherefore I pray that God may fulfill their prophecy, Amen." [24]

Rauwolf said this story and many other "stupid lies and fables" about Mohammed were believed by the Moslems to be as true as the Gospel. He recounted another story he heard in Jerusalem, where it was commonly believed that on the Day of Judgment, Mohammed will be seated on Mount Moriah and Christ on the Mount of Olives across the Valley of Jehosaphet. When

God had assembled all the people of the earth there, all those who had served Mohammed faithfully will be led into Paradise and eternal happiness. Like the Christians of the Middle Ages, Rauwolf held that this Moslem Paradise consisted in "gratifying fleshly lusts and desires, in eating and drinking, fine clothes, costly jewels, gold, silver, pearls, etc., pleasant gardens, and beautiful, cleanly women." [25]

Rauwolf's views of the dogma and practice of Islam were well within the Christian medieval tradition. To him Islam fell short of Christianity, particularly in connection with the position and role of Christ in the Trinity. While there was interest in and even some admiration for the religious practices of Islam, these were considered vain and false. These practices were, of course, equated with the Christian acts of worship and found wanting. Rauwolf did not understand the communal side of Islam and like his medieval predecessors he tried to find in Islam, a heresy, the ecclesiastical structure of Christianity. Since Rauwolf was one of the early Protestants to write about Islam from first-hand experience, he viewed what he thought was "work-righteousness" in Islam from a Lutheran position. This may be considered a new approach to Islam, but the condemnation of the practices was the same as that of Roman Catholic writers. Some independence in judgment may be found in the little emphasis Rauwolf placed on the supposed sexual laxity of the Moslems; nor does he dwell on the assumed lecherous character of Mohammed, points much emphasized in medieval literature. As a Christian, Rauwolf hoped for and prognosticated the end of Islam's power.

With their lunar calendar, the Moslems were very much concerned with the phases of the moon, especially the appearance of the new moon. Rauwolf understood that the moon's light was the basis for prognostications. He had also been informed by some Moslems that they had a secret and closely kept book in which was written what was to happen to them each year. The dates in this book began with the Hegira and continued for one thousand years. The emphasis on the thousand years led some Moslems to think that then the period of Islamic strength would soon be over and the Christians would conquer. Rauwolf interpreted the closing of the gates of towns and caravansaries about nine o'clock in the mornings of their feast days as indicative of their fear of being attacked by the Christians at this time.[26]

The prognostications of the Moslems led Rauwolf to see if he, too, could not predict an early end to the reign of the Moslems. While he was in the Near East it was the year 1575, or 982 A.H. Deducting 982 from 1,000 Moslem years left only 18 years. The figure of one thousand years was supported with references to Revelations 20:7 and to Ezekiel 38 and 39. Also in Revelations 13:18 could be found the figure 666, which corresponded very closely with the date of the Hegira (A.D. 622). Writing in 1581 as he was, Rauwolf thought that "it looks in these miserable times (when it seems as if everything would turn over and over) that these days are passed and that Satan is loosed, as if our dear Lord God would make an end of this wicked malicious world." There was also the fact that "some learned mathematicians" had prognosticated that great alterations would soon be made in all parts of the world and especially in the year 1588. Further numbers are brought to bear on the matter when it is remembered that in Daniel 12:11–13 and also in Revelations 11:2 there was the figure of 42 months (1,260 days or three and one-half years); "the eighteen years that are still wanting of the one thousand years of their Mohammed (as is above said) will be completed, so that these two year's numbers agree again very well together." Rauwolf closed his chapter with a prayer: "God Almighty preserve us in all adversities with the acknowledged truth of his Holy Gospel, and send us penitent hearts, that we may be sensible of his merciful visitations, and also overcome with patience the last two misfortunes that are not quite over. Amen." [27]

XII EASTERN CHRISTIANS AND JEWS

Rauwolf found a great variety of Christians residing in the parts of the Ottoman Empire he visited.[1] Generally, these Eastern Christians were concentrated in the great trading centers where they usually had their own sections in the suburbs. They worshipped in their own small churches, but when these deteriorated with age, were burned with fire, or were destroyed by war, permission had to be obtained from the Turkish magistrates before any construction or repair could be made. Consent could be obtained only by paying a good sum of money as a bribe. To the German Protestant, long familiar with the role of the church bells in regulating daily life in Europe, the absence of all bells was especially noteworthy. As the Moslem authorities permitted no bells or striking clocks in either their own or the Christian churches, different systems were used to indicate the time for worship. The Moslem muezzin called aloud, with his ears stopped, from the minaret or in the market place the five times of prayer, repeating twice "Alla Haickbar" and "leila hillalla, Mahammet rasur alla" (as Rauwolf understood the Arabic). The Christians, on the other hand, had servants who at the appointed time of worship went about striking certain thick doors with a cudgel they carried for that purpose. The reverberations from the blows could be heard throughout the streets. When the Christians and Jews prayed, they observed the same ceremonies as the Moslems in that they faced toward Jerusalem, generally south, prayed softly at first, raised up their arms, bent their heads and whole bodies forward, fell upon their knees, and then kissed the earth several times. Their devotion while doing this impressed the German scientist.

In the Ottoman Empire Rauwolf found a situation quite different from that in Europe, for, in general, the Eastern Christians were not molested or interfered with because of their religion. The Turkish officials tolerated their presence as long as the annual tribute was paid promptly when due. However, all Christians residing in Turkish territory had to pay the government one-fourth of their revenue; "if one has four olive, almond, or quince trees, the fourth one belongs to the Turks." Besides this every male Christian had to pay a head-tax of one ducat a year. Sometimes, especially when the sultan was planning an attack on the Christian states of Europe, this tax was doubled. Those Christians who could not pay were forced to sell one of their children into slavery to obtain the necessary tax money. Also, every fourth or fifth year, Turkish emissaries took the best son of Balkan Christian families with three boys. These boys, called "Azamoglans" ('Acemi-oglanis or recruits) were given to the Janissaries as servants and to be trained as soldiers. Rauwolf sympathized with the poor Christian parents who thus lost their children "to such a shameful cattle-like existence."

The Turks found it easy to convert these young Christians to Islam. Other Christians, taken prisoners in war and made slaves, often became Moslems, but this was not so much due to pressure as to the desire of the slave to better his position. Some individual Christian slaves who had been important officials or nobles before capture were subjected to pressure, for their conversion would impress other Christians of the desirability of becoming Moslems. Such important converts were not trusted; however, for the Moslems reasoned that "anyone who would deny his religion, would also betray his land and people." Rauwolf knew several Christian slaves whose masters did not press them further when the slaves pledged themselves to loyal service but would not submit to conversion. But if a Christian was found in a mosque, spoke ill of Mohammed and Islam, or said aloud in Arabic the words of confession found inscribed everywhere, he had to become a Moslem or lose his life.

In general, Rauwolf thought that the Eastern Christians were sufficiently numerous in the Ottoman Empire that, "to speak according to all human probability," they could overthrow the Turks without assistance. However, God had placed the Turks in the position of master as punishment for the sins of all Christians. Besides, the strength of the Turkish government, "where small crimes are vigorously punished," was such that the officials feared no revolt from the unarmed Christians. On the other hand, these same Christian subjects, through taxes and recruits, contributed greatly to the strength of the empire and to the size and ability of its armed forces.

In the Church of the Holy Sepulcher and elsewhere in Jerusalem Rauwolf had observed a variety of Christians and their different rites and ceremonies. These Christians, each with their own chapel, were "of so different opinions in many articles of faith . . . that many of them might sooner be reckoned amongst the superstitious and heretics than Christians." As Rauwolf was certainly one of the early Protestants to observe these non-European Christians closely, he felt compelled to explain the chief characteristics of each group from a Protestant viewpoint, being careful to point out any similarities with Potestantism.[2]

The Greeks, though coming from a land once known for its learning and wisdom, he found unlearned and delighting in idle discourses. While they did know how to write in Greek, the humanistically trained Rauwolf found their writing "as corrupt and different from the ancient as the Italian is from the Latin." The Turks despised the Greeks for their laziness and cowardice, but admired the Germans, French, and Italians, all labeled Franks, as courageous soldiers. Rauwolf seemed pleased to report that the Greeks sang the mass in their own language so that all could understand, that they did not believe in purgatory or "that praying, fasting, or offering for the dead can do them any good," and that they were displeased that the Roman priests did not marry, "nor give the Lord's Holy Supper in both kinds, as our Lord himself did institute it." Like all the Christian groups in Jerusalem, the Greeks were jealous of their prerogatives and when, shortly before Rauwolf's arrival, a Roman priest profaned one of their altars by saying mass on it, the Greeks accused him before the Turkish cadi, who fined the offender 500 ducats.

The Syrian Christians, or Surians, held the Church of St. Mark in Jerusalem and said their masses in Arabic. Rauwolf described them as "a sort of poor, naked, covetous, and helpless people" whose black and white striped gowns of goat's hair reached only to their knees. Having lived for so long under the Moslems, their religion differed little from that of Islam. To Rauwolf they seemed "to mind their trade more than their religion" and if a Christian wanted to buy from them drugs like opium or scammony, "which they commonly falsify, he must look to himself as if he had to deal with Jews."

In the Church of the Holy Sepulcher, the Georgians held the place where by tradition the newly risen Christ had appeared to Mary Magdalen. The Georgians were described by Rauwolf as "very civil and simple people, but yet strong and brave warriors," who esteem St. George as their patron. For the most part their priests followed "the doctrines and errors of the Grecians," and use the same writings and offices. Their priests were allowed to marry.

Rauwolf had met the Armenians before in his travels through the regions at the headwaters of the Tigris and Euphrates rivers. He found them a "pious and honest people, innocent, but very zealous in their religion." Like the Georgians, they were great merchants who traveled widely in the Near East. In their religious practices, Rauwolf felt that they "agree in very many points and articles exactly with those of the reformed religion," but he also said they had some errors and scandalous customs that must be rejected. In Jerusalem they possessed the beautiful Church of St. James the Greater and another chapel. In these places the priests were separated from the people by large hangings before the chancels. The German Protestant could not understand the animated mourning practices in their cemeteries and the fact that after expressing great sorrow, they sat down together among the graves to "eat, drink and be merry." The Armenians did not esteem the pope in Rome, but had their own respected prelates. They did not believe in purgatory or indulgences, their priests were permitted to marry, and the vulgar language was used in their services. They baptized in the name of the Trinity, and young and old were admitted to communion. Their Lent, which began after Easter, was observed with strict dietary laws.

In his travels Rauwolf had met many Nestorians, especially among the Kurds, a "strong and warlike people, but full of vices, and from their infancy given to robbing." The Nestorians were respected by the Turks not only because of the danger of giving an occasion for insurrection, but also because, by tradition, Mohammed was tutored by Sergius, a Nestorian friar. This last would account for the fact that the Nestorians "agree more than any other sect with the Saracens." They saw in Christ two distinct persons and rejected Mary as the mother of God.

In the chapel behind the Sepulcher, Rauwolf had seen some Jacobites "that boast to be Christians." The Jacobites "pretend to have been first converted to the Christian religion by the holy Evangelist and Apostle Matthew" but afterwards fell into many errors and divisions. Some Jacobites were monophysites, some followed St. Anthony, some use circumcision, but most "have their children baptized with fire, and have crosses made on their foreheads or temples."

In the Church of the Holy Sepulcher, just to the left of the entrance door, was the area assigned to the Abyssinians who, by special permission of the Turks, had the right of free egress and regress. To Rauwolf, who spoke to them through an interpreter, the "dark brown" Abyssinians showed themselves kind and friendly, "and always did give with a great deal of discretion such answers to our questions, that one might easily conclude that they were of good understanding and well instructed and grounded in their religion." They claimed their royalty was derived from David and Solomon through the Queen of Sheba. Thus, like the Jews, they kept the Sabbath and did not eat unclean flesh. These and other Jewish customs they were allowed to retain when Philip baptized Candace, the steward of the Queen of Ethiopia. Circumcision was not considered necessary, but baptism was. This rite was done with fire and in the name of the Trinity, but the Holy Ghost was held to "proceed only from the Father, and not from the Son . . ." In the rite of baptism, they "take the oil of Achalcinte, dip a stick into it, and lay frankincense upon it, and set it on fire; and so they let some drops fall down, which do not hurt the children, being mixed with the oil; and at last they make a cross with it upon the left side of the forehead near unto the temple." Like the Armenians, their Lent began about Easter and was observed with dietary laws. Their priests married "according to the words of St. Paul, that a Priest shall be a husband of one wife; they give the Lord's Supper to young and old alike in leavened bread in both kinds; and they confess their sins like unto the Jacobites, to nobody but only God."

The Maronites had been closely observed by Rauwolf in their homeland of Mount Lebanon, but since they too made pilgrimages to Jerusalem, Rauwolf thought best to describe them along with the other Christians he saw in the Church of the Holy Sepulcher. These Christians were followers of the heretic Maron, who was a disciple of Marcarius. They once believed that there was "but one nature, understanding, and work in Christ," but in the sixteenth century they were under the pope in Rome. Despite this, they administered the Sacrament of the Altar in both kinds to the laymen "as almost all other nations do, according to the words of institution of our Lord Christ." In other doctrines they followed the Roman Church. Their patriarchs, housed in a monastery on Mount Lebanon, were much respected and were chosen by the people and confirmed by the pope. Rauwolf had found them very courteous and hospitable.

The chief proprietors of the Church of the Holy Sepulcher were the Franciscan Minors, and Rauwolf felt they kept the church "in very good order." Besides their establishment in Jerusalem, the Franciscans held also the birthplace of Jesus at Bethlehem, the Church of St. John the Baptist in the hills of Judea, the tomb of Lazarus in Bethany, and other places. Their head, of course, was the pope in Rome, "who pretends to be the Vicegerent of Christ, and taketh upon himself so much power, as to prescribe to all men laws according to his own pleasure, which Christendom finds every day to its great grief." The Franciscans themselves had "grown into so many divisions, idolatry, and ceremonies, that they quite out-do all the before-named nations." Rauwolf felt he need not describe these friars in detail, since, as he sarcastically added, "thank be God, they are very well known to everybody." The twenty or so European Franciscans in the Holy Land were distributed among the various places under their jurisdiction. Two friars were always in the Church of the Holy Sepulcher, the tour there being fourteen days. Since the

Moslems locked the church during the day, food was passed to them through the three holes of various sizes in the door.[3] Inside the church, the time was spent in singing, praying, reading, and tending the lamps in the Sepulcher. The Franciscans in Jerusalem were entirely dependent on gifts received from the pilgrims, and this source of revenue was much less than it had formerly been. To add to their troubles, armed groups of Bedouins frequently demanded food and other things of them, as Rauwolf saw happen in Bethlehem. Any show of wealth would lead to a false accusation before the Turkish magistrate and a fine.

Among the Christian groups Rouwolf associated with the Church of the Holy Sepulcher were the Knights of St. John. Apparently he did not personally observe the ceremony of knighting, which under certain circumstances took place in the church, but he described the process in detail—again from a Protestant viewpoint. He reported that the candidate is admonished that once knighted he "must be in all things subject and obedient to the Roman Chruch; that he might fight and resist the Turks and Lutherans as enemies and heretics, so long as his blood and heart are warm." When taking the oath, the knight must swear that he will "always defend and protect the Roman church against the Lutherans, and their adherents, with words and deeds . . . ; and that he will never be in a place where any evil is taught, or spoken of his Holiness the Pope." Also that "he will assist those that would willingly turn Roman Catholic, and endeavor to bring them over, but then he will keep none in his service, nor any ways assist them that do not firmly adhere unto it." Whereas formerly admission to the order was restricted to noblemen, now anyone who paid the eleven or twelve ducats was knighted, said Rauwolf, "for his Holiness wants champions, because he taketh upon him the Civil Government as well as the Ecclesiastical, that when they may defend and uphold it by power and strength of arms." [4]

Rauwolf found many Jews in the cities of the Near East and especially in the trading centers of Tripoli and Aleppo. The Moslems called the Jews "Choisfut" or "Chifoutler" and held them in less respect than they did the Christians. The Moslems would not eat meals with the Jews or intermarry with them. A Jew could not be a direct convert to Islam without having first been baptized a Christian, eaten pork, and said prayers in a Christian church for several days. Rauwolf felt that Jews frequently denied their religion in order to make greater profit as a Moslem.[5]

As a sixteenth-century European Christian, Rauwolf believed that the Jews as a nation had killed Christ with "the shameful and cursed death of crucifixion." Because of this, God, who had once given the Israelites a fruitful country, had dispersed them, allowed Jerusalem and the Temple to be destroyed, and caused the land to be made into a desolate desert. All of this served as a warning to the Christians of Europe to turn from their evil ways. God's former people had become "so blind, full of errors, and live such a depraved life, that there is hardly any like them to be found even among the infidels and impious." Therefore the Jewish homeland of Palestine had been turned over to the Turks, Arabs, and other Moslems. The Jews were despised by all men and especially by the Turks, who hated them more than they did any other nation. Rauwolf repeatedly mentioned the need for special care to avoid being cheated while dealing with the Jewish merchants, "who excell ours in cheating and fraud." He reported that the Jewish brokers in Tripoli themselves confessed "that no one could profit in dealing with them unless he was a greater Harami that is thief, than they who sold walnuts for nutmeg or myrobalans were." [6]

Despite his condemnation of the sharp practices of the Jewish merchants, it must be remembered that Rauwolf chose two Jewish merchants with whom to make the long trip from Baghdad to Aleppo. He also repeated a story about toleration he heard at the sultan's summer house outisde Aleppo. According to the gardener of the place, Suleiman had met there with his viziers and was told by them not to tolerate the Jews in the provinces of the empire because of their unbearable usurious practices. When the courtiers recommended that the Jews be destroyed, the sultan showed them the many colorful flowers that grew about the pavilion, pointing out how the colors and varieties complimented each other. The sultan then explained that just like the flowers, there were many nations in the empire and that these combined to give his empire strength and greatness. Therefore the Jews should be tolerated along with all others. This advice the councilors took and followed.[7]

The Eastern Christians and Jews dressed like all the other inhabitants of the area, but the distinguishing item of clothing was the turban. Only Moslems were permitted to wear pure white turbans, although some special Moslem pilgrims who had been to Mecca wore head-coverings of green—Mohammed's color. The Armenian Christians wore blue turbans, the Nestorians flesh-colored, and the Grecians, Maronites, Syrians, and others wore white with blue beading. The Jews had yellow turbans, "like they wear yellow skull-caps with us." While traveling in areas where they were not known, the Jews frequently exchanged this yellow turban for a white one. This was done for greater security and in order to avoid the heavy custom duties imposed by the Turkish authorities. For the same reasons, some Jews pretended to be traveling noblemen or even imperial messengers, a deception that was dangerous but often successful because of their facility with language. Jewish physicians wore high hats of a scarlet color while the less numerous Moslem physicians dressed like their other countrymen. Jewish physicians were generally more able and learned because they could read the books of Galen and Avicenna in the original Greek and Arabic.[8] Very few of the doctors understood Latin, nor were good books in that language available except for those obtained in the fall and sack of Cyprus in 1571.[9]

XIII GOVERNMENT AND SOCIETY

The territory through which Rauwolf traveled in the Near East was governed by an absolute ruler, the sultan of the Ottoman Empire, who resided in Constantinople. Sultan Selim I had conquered Syria and Palestine in 1516 and Suleiman the Magnificent had taken possession of the Mesopotamian region in 1534. The provinces of this vast empire were governed by beglerbegs with several sanjak-begs under each acting as governors of cities and the surrounding districts. Assisting the sanjak-begs were subasis, or captains in charge of the Janissaries and other troops. Cadis or judges worked with the subasis in maintaining law and order. For the highest officers in this administrative system, the honorary title of pasha was used.[1]

Rauwolf had a rather low opinion of the Turkish officials he encountered on his trip. He frequently saw the governing pashas as they walked or rode about the larger cities in their fine clothing and with their retainers. The pashas had their own palaces in imitation of that of the sultan and also had apartments guarded by eunuchs for the concubines they gained in war or "picked up here and there." The pashas delighted in the hunt and often went some distance to do so. Since the Moslems considered wild animals killed in hunting as unclean, the beasts were given to the Christians—a change from Roman days. This was part of the ridicule heaped upon the Christians who were called *chansir quibir,* or "great boars," and "hog-eaters." Although the pashas were powerful enough during their tenure of office, in reality they were but "slaves" to the sultan, doing his bidding and fearing his vengeance. If the sultan transferred them to an inferior position, they had to obey immediately.[2]

The pashas, though rich, seldom built any great commemorative buildings, unless it was a chapel, mosque, or khan. Since on the death of a pasha the sultan took possession of all visible estates and left the children only an annuity, the pashas hid their wealth and secretly gave it to their posterity. They did not spend much money on costly jewelry set with precious stones, being too covetous, and besides, Rauwolf felt they had few artisans who could do such work well. In their greed and desire to accumulate wealth during the brief time in office, they oppressed their subjects. The exactions of the pashas, including the taking of the greatest share of the inheritance of the rich, had an adverse effect on the economy for little attention was paid to improving property or soil when this would only invite attention and extortion.

Foreigners especially were fair prey for the greedy officials, and the situation would have been even worse for them if the consuls had not protected their fellow nationals from extortion. Some of the pashas acted haughtily in their resentment of the privileges of the consuls, and Rauwolf saw evidence of this on March 6, 1575, while in Aleppo. The pasha of that city had died and the new appointee entered Aleppo with much pomp and ceremony on the above date. On his arrival, the Venetian consul, accompanied by a great number of richly dressed merchants, presented the new pasha with fourteen sets of clothing, beautifully wrought with silk. When the consul requested continued protection for his merchants that they might trade in peace, the pasha refused the gifts as inadequate and gave the consul a scornful reply. In such a case there was always the possibility of an appeal to the sultan, a right exercised by even the lowest private person in the empire. If the Venetian consul did take his case to the Porte at Constantinople, and Rauwolf did not say, the pasha might have been punished, for the sultan desired the revenues obtained from foreign trade.

The sanjak-begs were really military governors charged with maintaining public order through the use of the Janissaries and spahis in their control. The sanjak-begs, themselves experienced soldiers, led their troops into the exercise field several times a week. The spahis drilled with their horses while the foot soldiers shot arrows on the run at targets high on poles. The sanjak-begs governed the towns in their districts through a number of subasis. Rauwolf thought these last officials were selected from the local inhabitants to hold the post for only half a year. The subasis brought violators to court, conducted the torture used to exact confessions, and executed the sentences. Rauwolf often saw condemned criminals being escorted to the place of execution. He described one such scene where the poor malefactor was taken on the back of a camel through the streets to the gallows or other place of execution. He had a cross tied to his back and between the cross and his shoulders two burning torches had been placed. These were so prepared with fat that the melted grease ran all over his body, burning him severely. The punishment of criminals varied with the crime; thieves and robbers were hung, traitors impaled, and murderers beheaded. The many attendants of the subasi roamed the streets of the city to seize and bring before the subasi those who were caught breaking the laws by assault, an infrequent occurrence, or by theft, murder, and so on.

For lesser crimes the violators were brought before the cadi who, knowledgeable in the law, heard the charges, examined the witnesses, and gave sentence. If the accused was found guilty of not paying his debts, he was imprisoned until the debt was paid. Severe fines and beatings were given in other cases. Just like the subasi, the cadi had his own attendants and spies to seize those who drank wine, failed to pray frequently, did not keep the fasts, etc. Those found guilty of these violations were fined or bastinadoed on the soles of their feet and charged an asper per blow in addition. Because there were many punished by bastinadoes at Tripoli, the cries of the punished could be heard in the nearby French fondaco.

Although the cadis were busy enough in judging violators of the laws, their notarial duties took most of their time. The matrimonial cases were particularly time-consuming since all contracts for marriage and the agreements that were a part of these had to be made before the cadi and recorded in his books. Those married were given a copy of the contract. If poor, the contract was written on smooth plain paper; the rich had their contracts written on a piece of white satin about a yard long. The contracts were composed of only a few words and were written in eight or ten lines about two inches apart. These were executed by clerks who wrote on their knees rather than on a table.

The Turkish officials wanted to be known for their integrity and excellent performance of duty, but, in reality, in their covetousness they allowed their decisions to be influenced by bribes and gifts. For money, they accepted false depositions brought to them by those who accused innocent persons out of spite and a small present enabled a man to get revenge on his enemy through a false accusation. The rich and strangers were spied upon especially and fined for some trifle. Knowing that their term of office was short, the officials wasted no time in accumulating wealth in this way.[3] Nor did they fear punishment from their superiors, for they were all guilty of the same practices.

The Turkish government sought to prevent some of these injustices and to punish the greedy cadis by having higher judges, called "cadileschiers" (*ḳadi-'askers*), over them. These, generally considered to be the leading authorities in Islamic law, were called upon to make decisions in the more intricate cases and appeals. Often these judges went from place to place to check on the administration of justice by the cadis. Those cadis who were guilty of malfeasance of office feared the arrival of these inspecting judges and often ran away rather than face their accusers before the *ḳadi-'askers*. Rauwolf reported that very frequently the unjust cadis were accused by their victims, and if guilty were deprived of their office and beaten. If their crimes were great, they were beheaded, strangled, burned, or otherwise executed. There was one other recourse against an unjust cadi. Complaints could be sent or taken in person to the Imperial Divan at Constantinople.[4] This court met frequently and justice was quickly obtained. Rauwolf reported that poor petitioners were maintained from the sultan's treasury while awaiting the hearing of their case.

In this connection, Rauwolf cited the case of an interpreter of the Venetian consul of Tripoli. Since the interpreter had wealth, the subasi coveted his money and not being able to find and prove any crime against the interpreter, he decided to make him the victim of a false charge. One of the servants of the subasi secretly hid a prostitute in the house of the interpreter and when the soldiers broke in and found her there, the subasi had his case. Despite his pleas of innocence, the interpreter was found guilty and forced to pay a fine of 900 ducats. The victim of this false accusation was learned in the law, however, and without the knowledge of the official, rode immediately to Constantinople and pleaded his case before the Imperial Divan. He was not only declared innocent, but shortly thereafter the sultan sent an imperial *cha'ush,* or messenger, with a short note ordering that the head of the unjust official should be brought to Constantinople. By special permission the official was permitted to say a few words in farewell to his wife, but then he submitted himself to decapitation. The possibility of such appeals to the Divan often helped insure justice and rectify injustices.

Wherever Rauwolf went in the Near East he encountered Turkish soldiers, generally Janissaries, but also the spahi, or cavalry. These soldiers usually wore blue woolen clothes that were furnished by the government and their pay was four to eight medines per day, depending on their position. The same pay was given in peace and war and was supplemented by booty gained on campaigns. In peacetime the soldiers wore white turbans underneath which they placed painted paper as a talisman against injury. In these turbans they usually had stuck several crane feathers conveying the impression that the soldier was a brave warrior who had served on so many campaigns or killed so many Christians. In time of war, the turban was generally exchanged for a white felt hat, called a *zarcella,* which was used instead of a helmet. In the front of these hats there was usually a gilded ornament, set with inexpensive garnets, rubies, turquoise, and other jewels, in which crane feathers were stuck. Like the rest of the Turks and other Moslems, the head was shaven except for a lock that hung down in the rear. Formerly no beards had been allowed but now beards were common and very long mustaches were in evidence.

In war the soldiers were armed with muskets, but in peace long poles were carried. The soldiers were allowed to marry and also to keep as concubines or sell as slaves those women they captured in war. While the soldiers were known for their ability to eat very little on a campaign, in peacetime they were eager for wine, when they could get it and drink without being seen; "they will drink without mixture more than any nation." Despite their brave appearances, Rauwolf felt that the Turkish soldiers were like all other soldiers in that they were not ready "to take to the field and exchange a good, quiet life to which they have become accustomed over an extended period for a bothersome one or a secure life for a dangerous one, as they have in former times."

In analyzing the reasons for the Turkish success in war, Rauwolf thought the Turkish troops less well armed than the Christians of Europe, who with their muskets and pikes could keep the Turks at a distance. While the Turks thought little of losing large numbers of men, they were also known to flee if their first assault was unsuccessful. But the Christians constantly lost territories to the advancing Turks, and for Rauwolf, the reason was the "manifold transgressions" of the Christians because of which God brought punishment upon them. Turkish success was also attributable to the divisions and quarreling among the Christians. These conditions prevented the Christians from going against the Turks with sufficient forces. This lack of unity encouraged the Turks to wage war and by the use of ambushes and numerically superior forces destroy the Christian armies.

The Turks were well aware that the divisions among the Christians were to their advantage. Rauwolf reported that after a victory, the Turks would pray that the Christian "magistrates may quarrel with their subjects, the clergy with the laity, and that from this, such disorder would arise that the Christians would go on transgressing the laws of God more and more." The Turks also prayed that the Christians would lose their belief in Christ and that the good order and policies dissolved, God might use the Turks as punishment. And when they saw that among the Christians "rich men oppress the poor, that the magistrates do not protect the just and innocent, but that the leaders and heads strive to ruin each other, then they rejoice at our misfortune and misery and do not fear in the least that we can do them any harm (which we might easily do if we were united) but rather threaten what harm they can do us."

The Turkish danger to Europe was increasing constantly, with the areas of Greece, Thrace, Serbia, Bosnia, Hungary, and Wallachia, already reduced to slavery. To facilitate the retention of a conquered territory, the Turks removed all nobles and leaders so that there remained no heirs of hereditary leaders and no inherited estates to furnish the basis for revolt. As a reminder of what happened to the Christian rulers overcome by the Turks, Rauwolf found in Aleppo an elderly queen of Wallachia with her sons, the youngest of whom had been born after the death of the king. This queen was a very intelligent woman who knew Turkish and Arabic well. She and her former subjects still lived in the hope of liberation from Turkish rule.

Rauwolf thought that the same system of disrupted succession was evident also in the Turkish government and Moslem families. The pashas could not bequeath power and wealth to their offspring, and the multiple marriages of the Moslems poduced confusion and disorder among the children. The fact that Mohammed had permitted his followers to have four wives as well as concubines and the facility with which a divorce could be obtained produced such "disorder and uncertainty that very few children know who their parents are"; nor were there any strong family ties or love evident.

Rauwolf found the Turkish women pretty and "well shaped" and very civil in conversation and general behavior. When a woman was married and carried to the bridegroom's house, a noisy crowd of relatives accompanied her through the streets. The weddings of the rich and important people were celebrated with such diversions as dancing, running, acting, singing, and tightrope walking during the daytime and by displays of fireworks at night. Rauwolf found the tightrope walkers especially expert and entertaining as they danced, jumped, walked on stilts, and performed on the three ropes set one higher than the other. He also saw in some houses, especially in the country, the strangely shaped earthen vessels given by relatives at weddings and thereafter displayed but never used. Despite the affection shown at the time of a wedding, the married couple soon forgot their parents and had no desire to see them again for a long while.

The polygamous practices of the Moslems and the fact that divorce could easily be obtained for "little cause" had always shocked and interested the Christians. Rauwolf commented on the little love between husband and wife or wives. He thought that the Moslems esteemed a man with several wives higher than a man with only one wife, for the Moslem with several wives was considered to be the more faithful to Mohammed's injunction and thus was given preference in position and salary. Rauwolf admitted that although the wives may have been of different station and extraction, yet they all received the same power and share in family affairs and were provided with the same food and clothing. Marriages had to be ratified by the cadi and the wives must agree to live peaceably together and not rebel against their husband unless he favored one over the others. In such a case the wife who considered herself abused could complain about her husband before the cadi and if the woman was absolved of blame, they were divorced immediately. Krafft, who also reported this privilege of the wife, commented: "We on the other hand, and especially we Germans, would really beat the backs of our wives for that." [5]

The husband was in the position of real power and privilege, for the woman brought no dowry and had to be purchased from her parents by the husband, often at considerable cost. The husband could even marry and divorce the same women up to three times; if he married her for a fourth time without the woman having been married to another, he was accounted a base fellow. In this connection, Rauwolf told how Sultan Bajazet had scornfully refused to do battle with Tamerlane by saying that he would rather take a wife again after he had divorced her three times than go to war with the Mongols.[6]

The circumcision of boys did not take place on the eighth day after birth, but rather the parents waited until the boy was 8 to 10 years old and could make the profession of faith by himself. Some of the Arabs waited until the thirteenth year in imitation of their patriarch Ishmael. The circumcision was usually done in the home of the parents and was the occasion for festivities. If the parents were wealthy a great feast was prepared and Rauwolf reported the roasting of an entire bullock into which had been placed a wether into whose stomach was placed a chicken and in the chicken an egg. What remained of the feast was given to the poor. The young children were clothed in attractive coats of several colors. Colored caps, embroidered with flowers and readily available in the bazaars, were worn until circumcision when the cap was replaced with a white turban. These turbans were of cotton and nearly 20 yards long. A strange custom used by young and old of both sexes was the painting of the area around the eyes with a paste made of galls and calcined copperas. The users thought it beautiful and it protected the eyes from inflammation. Rauwolf was reminded of such use of cosmetics in Ezekiel 23:40.

The education that Rauwolf observed was limited to teaching boys and girls to read and write the Arabic characters that were common to both Arabic and Turkish, although the languages themselves were quite different. There were also schools for more advanced training of young men who were instructed in the laws of the realm. Those who learned their lessons well could soon be made a cadi or *kadi-'asker*. But there was no instruction in the liberal arts (*freyen Künsten*) as in Europe; nor were any learned men in evidence, "for they consider the learning of these sciences as an impertinence and a waste of time." Rather the inhabitants of the Near East preferred the old rhymes and ballads that told of the deeds of rulers and other champions. Other of these poems ridiculed their enemies. Whether handed down from long ago or of contemporary composition, these poems were recited, with gestures, in parks outside the towns where the people gathered to hear them and also to enjoy singing, dancing, and other diversions. That the Moslems were more pleased with these "useless writings" than with arts and sciences was clear from the fact that they did not value the "noble art" of printing books.

This absence of printing was appreciated by the many scribes found everywhere in the cities who made a great deal of money copying sayings from the Koran and by writing for the people whatever had to be put down on paper. The paper used was smooth and glazed and when a letter or document had been written, with a paucity of words, the paper was folded and re-folded until it was only about an inch wide. The outer fold was then filled with wax or some other glue and the letter thus sealed. Identifying ring-seals, generally made in Damascus "where the best artists live that cut in steel," were covered with ink so that in the impression of the seal only the letters were white. Any paper that had writing on it was not used again for wrapping or other things, and if a scrap of paper was found in the street, it was carefully picked up, folded, and put in the most convenient crevice. This was done in the fear that the paper may have the name of God on it. Instead of paper for wrapping, the grocers used the large leaves of the *Colocasia antiquorum* Schott (elephant's ear), which were plentiful.

The oriental love of display and use of color impressed Rauwolf. He noted that the Turkish officials and their wives went about richly clothed in fine silks of many colors. They seldom bought these expensive clothes; however, "for they do not like to part with their money." Rather, the clothes were generally bribes given to them by those who had law cases pending before the covetous officials; "where honor and gifts are not given first, little is accomplished or gained." When the Turkish officials went abroad in the city they rode beautiful horses that were richly accoutered. The saddles were ornate and the saddle-cloths were of scarlet velvet or other silks. The bridles, stirrups, and collars were garnished with silver or gold. Rauwolf once saw the impressive entry of a newly appointed sanjak-beg into Tripoli. The new governor was received with honor by the inhabitants. His train consisted of horsemen and archers with weapons and shields. The sabers and stirrups were gilded so that they reflected the bright sunlight. They were accompanied by men playing drums, kettledrums, and other musical instruments.

The same love of color was reflected in the common items of clothing, which Rauwolf described in detail. The outer garments were of cotton, generally of blue color, with wide sleeves and no collar. These buttoned down the front and were longer in the rear than in the front. Under this a cotton shirt was worn. Next to the body, spacious drawers were worn that reached to the ankles, about which they narrowed. The fact that these were tied about the waist with strings facilitated the ritual washings of the lower body. Rauwolf commented on the absence of a fly, and the practice of the men to urinate while squatting like a woman and being careful to face north and thus away from the direction of prayer. A Christian was easily recognized by his standing erect while urinating. Since neither the shirts or outer garments had collars, a long neckerchief was wound about the neck as a protection against the hot sun. Their shoes were "similar to those worn by our lackeys and as easy to put on and off as slippers." They were usually yellow or blue in color, pointed in front, and had nails under the toe and curved irons on the heel. These shoes were removed on entering a house so as to preserve the beautiful rugs, serges, and colored mats that covered the floors. Sometimes wooden shoes were worn in the houses and on the streets. These were about four inches high, painted with many colors, and had a deep instep carved out between the sole and the heel. They were readily available in the shops. All of the above items of clothing were worn by men and women alike, although the drawers of the women were laced on the sides and were more colorful and longer. The women, of course, wore black veils made of fine silk or coarse horsehair depending on their wealth. As a headcovering the women wore no turbans but white scarves of cotton that were broad enough to cover also the arms and back. This reminded Rauwolf of the young women of Germany who put a linen cloth or tablecloth over their heads in rainy weather.

The Moslem women were seldom seen in the streets or marketplace. Only a few of the important women prayed at the mosques, and if they did go, which was seldom, they prayed in a screened place separate from the men. So jealous were the Moslem husbands that when another man entered a house the women fled to "secret corners and places." Occasionally one would see three or four women accompanied by their children, all of whom were the offspring of one husband, going to the baths or cemeteries, the two places most frequented by women. When the women went to visit the graves of their parents or relatives, they usually took a picnic lunch of bread, cheese, eggs, and meat along to eat at the graveside. This practice reminded Rauwolf of the *parentalia* of the Romans. At these meals at the grave, the women often left the remnants of the meal for the birds and animals to eat after they had left, for "such a good deed done to the animals is as pleasing to God as when done to man."

When a Moslem died, his body was washed and then dressed in his best clothes. The corpse was laid on a board and covered with sweet-smelling herbs and flowers. The face was left uncovered so that friends and relatives could view the deceased as he was carried to the cemetery. If a dead man was a nobleman, his helmet and ornaments were placed by his head. The funeral procession had no order and the friends and relatives preceded or followed the corpse with joyous shouts. The women followed after and cried with such ever increasing intensity that one could hear them several streets away. The burial places were located out of town along the highways. Thus those who passed by would be reminded of the departed one and pray for them. To facilitate prayer, many chapels were constructed about the cemeteries. The graves were covered with large stones that were in "the form of our bedsteads for children, high at the foot and head, and hollowed out in the middle." The depression in the stone was generally filled with earth and in this fine plants and especially gladioli were planted. Green branches of myrtle were also put into the little air-holes around the grave in the belief that the dead were happy as long as the branch remained green in color. Such myrtle branches could be purchased in the market.

Rauwolf found the use of the Turkish language widespread among the governing class and among those in the garrisons. He thought Turkish a "manly language" and not unlike German in sound. Most of those who spoke Turkish were also expert in Arabic, the language common to the entire Near East and spoken by Moslems, Christians, "and heathen." Rauwolf felt that the Turks had some very fine manners and customs. He noted how affable they were and how they greeted each other politely and with kisses. However, while he praised them for such things he condemned the Turks for their laziness and indolence, their little love for the liberal arts, and their preference for playing music rather than working. He often saw the Turks spend a whole day playing chess and other games or playing on their guitars, or "quinternen" as he called them. These instruments had three, five, seven, or even eleven strings and were plucked with the finger or a quill. The soldiers especially walked all day through the streets playing guitars. But laziness and lechery went together and the Turks often contaminated themselves with all sorts of vice and sodomy. Since such sins were common among both high and low, they were seldom punished.

Perhaps the most usual characteristic of both the Turks and the Syrians was greed. Rauwolf said that they "loved money so much that they would rather spend half a day wrangling and quarreling about a penny than spend one willingly." Anyone traveling in the Near East must keep his purse well hidden so that no one knew how much money was there. Nothing was done without a reward, and if it was suspected that money was carried, every effort would be made to get it. Pilgrims traveling to the Holy Land in poor clothing were less bothered than those whose clothing indicated wealth.

In the houses Rauwolf found no tables, chairs, or benches. Only rugs covered the floors and on these the people sat cross-legged according to their fashion. Instead of the featherbeds of Europe, they used quilts and mattresses which were folded together and hung in a corner when not in use. At night they were again spread out and slept on. Sheets and bed-linen were seldom used and instead of hand-towels they made use of their long neckerchiefs or sashes. In the kitchen one found only a few utensils like pots, pans, and plates, for all food was cooked in one kettle "so that the maids did not have many to clean and put away."

At dinner time, a round piece of leather was spread on the floor and about it were placed rugs and sometimes cushions upon which the diners sat cross-legged. After a prayer had been said, the food was eaten hastily and without much conversation. The rich people used napkins of fine cotton tied about their necks or tucked into their silk girdles. The women did not eat with the men, but remained in their apartments. When the meal was over, the diners arose with a jerk, swinging themselves about, something "which our countrymen cannot easily imitate until after they have been there a long time, for the limbs are half asleep from sitting cross-legged in an unusual position." The round leather "table" was then taken up, drawn together with a string, and hung in the corner until the next meal.

XIV   LATER LIFE

Just as in the early part of his life, little is known of Rauwolf's activities after his return from the Near East. He had obtained a leave of absence from the officials of Augsburg to make his trip, and now that he returned he resumed his practice and his position as "official doctor" of the city of Augsburg. He was associated with the plague hospital and in the last quarter of 1577, his salary was increased from 100 to 250 gulden.[1] Rauwolf also maintained his botanical garden. On July 16, 1577, Clusius wrote Joachim Camerarius the Younger (1534–1598) congratulating him on having seen Rauwolf's garden with its exotic and strange plants.[2] Dr. Johann Aicholtz (1520–1588), "Titularhofmedicus" and professor of anatomy at the University of Vienna, saw the garden some years before 1582.[3] Rauwolf even attempted to grow plants from some of the seeds he brought back with him. One such experiment at acclimatization was conducted with the seeds of *Poterium spinosum* L. from Mount Lebanon. These were planted in the extensive gardens of Hans Heinrich Herwarts (d. 1583). Although the plant grew and almost bloomed, it died the following winter "as the exotic plants are not likely to survive here."[4] He apparently was more successful in raising plants from the seeds of *Tordylium syriacum*. L.[5] Rauwolf also exchanged seeds with other botanists. Clusius recorded in 1584 that he sent Rauwolf some bulbs and seeds.[6] Some seeds of *Gingidium Dioscoridis* (*Artedia squamata* L.), found on Mount Lebanon, were sent by Rauwolf to Camerarius.[7]

On Monday, January 5, 1581, Rauwolf had an unexpected but most welcome visitor—Hans Krafft. This factor of the Manlich firm had finally been released from the prison in Tripoli on August 24, 1577, exactly three years after his incarceration. His release was affected through the efforts of the French vice-consul

Pierre Fabre on the condition that Krafft would pay the creditors of the Manlich firm 1,000 ducats and the cadi of Tripoli 100 ducats. Krafft sailed from Tripoli for Marseilles on August 28. When a furious storm arose en route, the captain of the ship wished to set Krafft ashore as a hated Lutheran and thus gain God's favor and good weather, but he was dissuaded from doing so by others on the ship. Krafft landed at Marseilles on October 19, and after a trip to Genoa and return, he left Marseilles on December 9, 1578, traveling to Germany through Milan and Chur.[8]

When he appeared at Rauwolf's residence in Augsburg, Mrs. Rauwolf admitted him but did not recognize him, thinking he was a traveler who needed medical assistance. When Krafft asked her where the physician was, she replied, "In the study." Krafft went into the study and found Rauwolf seated behind a table reading a book. The physician looked up at Krafft and when the latter began to sing "Christ is arisen," Rauwolf recognized and joyfully embraced his long-lost friend. When the news of Krafft's return spread through Augsburg, many old acquaintances came to greet him. Krafft planned to leave for Ulm on Wednesday, January 7, but he awoke that morning with a severe stomachache. So serious was the illness that Rauwolf called in a consulting physician. Krafft was well again by Saturday, however, and went to see Otto Langinger, burgomaster and chief trustee of the bankrupt Manlich firm. The reception was cool. Krafft felt that the trustee would have preferred that he lay buried among his dead companions at Tripoli, for they had no funds with which to pay him. On Sunday, Krafft and Rauwolf were invited for the noon meal to the house of Hans Heinrich Herwart, who had been town councillor since 1568. Krafft was well received and the company, which included Herwart's two sons, his son-in-law, two doctors, and others carried on a stimulating conversation around the round table from 11:00 A.M. to 4:00 P.M. A few days later, still unable to obtain his back salary for six years, Krafft left for Ulm and home. His stay in Augsburg had lasted two weeks and since Rauwolf was then working on his book there must have been considerable exchange of information and comparing of notes.[9]

In 1582, six years after his return to Augsburg, Rauwolf published his travel book. It was written in Swabian German and the publisher was Leonhart Reinmichel of Laugingen. The dedication, dated September 30, 1581, is addressed to his cousins Hans Widtholtzen, Christoff Christel, and Nicholas Bemer. Here Rauwolf explained how after his return early in 1576, he was urged by a number of good friends to record the experiences and botanical findings of his journey. Rauwolf, always modest, was reluctant at first, but was at last persuaded and in the dedication (iv^r–vi^v) he marshalled, as justification, a variety of reasons for undertaking such an arduous task. Primarily he wished to share his experiences with others who might not have the opportunity to travel as he had. He also hoped "that others may be excited to inquire further into these things and induced, by reading this account, to travel themselves into those parts of which I have writen, to observe more narrowly and exactly the things about which I have been too brief."

To those who might say that he could have spared himself all the trouble and work of writing since many similar travel books were in print, Rauwolf asserted that "what others have written I have not put into my little book, but I have here given an account only of what I have myself seen, experienced, observed, and taken in my hand." His book, he felt, would be worthless to those omniscient persons who believed nothing new could be described. Rather, he wrote, "who is not made aware by daily experiences that the terrible wars, plagues, and epidemics which occur daily are causing great changes in kingdoms, lands, towns, and villages. Places formerly prized and praised as magnificent and beautiful are now devastated and useless. What was formerly despised as undesirable and barren is in our time highly extolled and is adorned and endowed with the best fruit and plants. He who realizes this will admit that our time has yet much to learn and find out what was never accomplished, observed, or recorded by others. The world is such a big book that we can never read through all of it."

Rauwolf also wished his book to be useful in that his description of the ruins of Jerusalem, the desolation of Babylon, and the devastation of the Holy Land would show how the wrath of

God descends on the impenitent and sinful. He also hoped to instruct the reader in the life, customs, practices, laws, and regulations of the Near East and to warn the reader what knavery and tricks were used in war and peace. In his book could also be found descriptions of many sects and religions and of the many kind people who were not far from the true understanding of God and who could easily be brought to the correct Christian faith. Finally, Rauwolf hoped his work would enable apothecaries and physicians to find descriptions of many useful plants.

The task of writing the travel book was facilitated by the careful notes Rauwolf had kept during his field-trip in the Near East. In the dedication (iii^v–iv^r) he referred to the fact that he "consigned all in good order, as it occurred daily, in a pocket-journal, to keep as a memorial of my life." That two editions should appear in 1582 and a third in 1583 suggests the immediate popularity of the work. On September 4, 1582, Clusius wrote to Joachim Camerarius that he would appreciate receiving a copy of the *Hodoeporicum* or travel book of Rauwolf. Not knowing of its contents, Clusius wrote that it would be desirable if Rauwolf would put on paper his observations on exotic plants and that his best friends should implore him to do so. On October 30, Clusius thanked Camerarius for sending a copy of "Dasylycus" (Rauwolf), and on November 21 he reported that Dr. Aicholtz was reading the book aloud at meals, a little each day. Clusius found the book quite worth the trouble, but he hoped that Rauwolf would put his botanical observations into Latin and in detail. He also urged Camerarius to spur Rauwolf on to do this.[10]

In writing his book, Rauwolf identified the plants he had seen in the Near East with those described by the classical, Arabic, and contemporary botanists. The classical and Arabic authors have been named earlier. Of all the contemporary botanists, Rauwolf named his friend and correspondent Carolus Clusius most frequently. On 13 different occasions he referred to him, most frequently using the adjective "most learned" and at times adding the phrase "especially knowledgeable in plants." Clusius (Charles de l'Ecluse) was born in 1526 at Arras in Flanders. His education was gained at Ghent, at Louvain where he studied at the College des Trois Langues, at Marburg where he became a

Lutheran while studying law, and at Wittenberg. In the autumn of 1551 he was at Montpellier, where he was influenced by Rondelet to turn to botany. After receiving his degree at Montpellier in 1554, he devoted most of his long life to writing and to making translations, areas in which he was well qualified. He traveled widely, was director of the imperial botanical gardens at Vienna for 14 years but finally in 1593 he became professor of botany at Leyden, where he died in 1609. Clusius is immortalized by the botanical family *Clusiaceae* and the genera *Clusia*.[11]

Most of Clusius' writings and translations were in the area of botany, although he also edited the letters of Nicolas Clenardus (1495–1542), the Flemish scholar and grammarian, and translated into French two Plutarchian biographies. His long trip to Spain and Portugal with the young Jacob Fugger resulted in his important *Rariorum aliquot stirpium per Hispanias observatarum historia* (Antwerp, 1576) and his observations in Austria and Hungary led to his *Rariorum aliquot stirpium, per Panoniana, Austriam et vicinas quasdam provincias observatarum historia* (Antwerp, 1583). Both of these flora were revised for the complete edition of his works which began to appear in 1610. In a letter to Clusius, dated September 7, 1584, Rauwolf told his friend he was reading with pleasure the recently published work on the plants of Hungary. His enjoyment was derived from the fact that he was acquiring "a more extensive knowledge about the properties of these plants; and this pleasure only grows when, in reading your work, I learn a multitude of things which I did not know. For this work, as well as for all of your other works, we owe you, we who are dedicated to the study of medicine, and our successors will equally owe you, a profound gratitude." [12]

For the purposes of his study of Near Eastern plants, Rauwolf found Clusius' Latin translation and epitome of the flora of India by Garcia da Orta most important. Garcia da Orta was a Portuguese botanist and physician to the viceroy of India. At Goa in 1563 he published his *Coloquios dos simples e drogas he cousas mediçinais da India*. Clusius' Latin epitome of this Portuguese work was published in Antwerp in 1567, with reprints in 1574,

1579, 1593, and 1605 during his lifetime. Rauwolf cited the *Epitome von Indianischen Kreuttern* four times. Clusius also translated into Latin an abbreviation of Christoval Acosta's illustrated Spanish work, *Tractado de las drogas y medicinas de las Indias Orientales, con sus plantas debuxadas al bivo* (Burgos, 1578), but the Latin version appeared too late (Antwerp, 1582) to be used by Rauwolf. The Augsburg botanist would have profited from Clusius' Latin translation (Antwerp, 1579) of Pierre Belon's *Les observations de plusieurs singularitez et choses mémorables trouvées en Grèce, Asie, Judée, Egypte, Arabie et autres pays estranges, rédigées en trois livres* (Paris, 1553, and often thereafter), but he seems not to have been familiar with this popular work.

Another contemporary botanist named by Rauwolf was Rembert Dodoens (Dodonaeus) who was born at Malines, near Antwerp, in 1517.[13] He received his medical degree at Louvain, but then visited a number of French, Italian, and German universities. In 1572 Malines, where Dodoens was city physician, was sacked by Spanish troops and Dodoens lost everything. From 1574 to 1576 he was physician to Emperor Maximilian II and thereafter held the same post under Rudolph II. Later he became professor of medicine at the University of Leyden, where he died in 1585 about five years after his appointment. His main botanical work, an herbal entitled *Cruydt-Boeck*, was written in Flemish and published at Antwerp in 1554. Later many revised editions appeared in French, English, and Latin; Clusius was the translator of the single French edition (1557). The first Latin edition, with 1,309 woodcut illustrations, is entitled *Stirpium historiae pemptades sex sive libri XXX* (Antwerp, 1583, reprinted 1616). In his five references to Dodoens, Rauwolf does not mention which of the non-Latin editions he used; it was probably the French. Three times Rauwolf referred to Dodoens as "very learned" and once he named the *Sisynrichium* of Theophrastus, "which is well and pleasingly sketched in the booklet of the very learned Rembert Dodonaeus on the flowers and fragrant herbs which belong to the coronilla." [14] On Mount Lebanon Rauwolf found a specimen of *Helichrysum sanguineum* (L). Kostel.

which he identified as the "true Baccharis of Dioscorides" and in describing it said that its leaves were similar to those of "Tabaca, or the *Hyosciamus Peruvianus* of Rembertus Dodonaeus." [15]

Matthias Lobelius (L'Obel; 1538–1616) is named three times by Rauwolf. Born in Lille, France, this eminent botanist traveled in Germany and Italy and then became the favorite pupil and disciple of Rondelet at Montpellier.[16] Lobelius inherited the botanical manuscripts of his master when Rondelet died in 1566. Lobelius practiced medicine at Antwerp but the terror of the Duke of Alva's Council of Blood caused him to join other Flemings in flight to England. His book *Stirpium adversaria nova perfacilis vestigatio,* written with the aid of Pierre Pena, another student of Rondelet, was published in London in 1570–71. The work contained well-executed drawings of about 270 plants. Rauwolf named this book of "the excellent Matthias Lobel" in connection with a plant (*Ulex provincialis* Loisel.) he found at Marseilles in the summer of 1573. Lobelius returned to the continent to become the physician of William of Orange at Delft. In 1576 the Plantin press at Antwerp published his *Plantarum seu stirpium historia . . . cui annexum est Adversariorum volumen.* This folio volume was illustrated with almost 1,500 large woodcuts. His Dutch *Kruydtboek* (Antwerp, 1581)) had over 2,000 illustrations, which were also published separately in two volumes as *Icones stirpium seu plantarum . . . cum septem linguarum indicibus* (Antwerp 1591). On the assassination of William of Orange in 1584, Lobelius returned to England where he eventually became physician to James I. The botanical family *Lobeliaceae* (order *Campanules*) and the genus *Lobelia* are named in his honor.

In the dedication (vi^r) to the first edition, Rauwolf expressed regret that because of many problems, no illustrations could be included, but he also evinced the hope that in time this deficiency could be remedied. The value of including pictures of plants along with verbal descriptions had already been recognized by the ancient authorities. In the *Natural History* of Pliny, a work much used by Rauwolf, the Roman author pointed up well the value and also the problems of botanical illustration. Writing in the first century A.D., Pliny wrote that the subject of

botany had been treated by certain Greek writers: "of these, Crateuas, Dionysius and Metrodorus adopted a most attractive method, though one which makes clear little else except the difficulty
of employing it. For they painted likenesses of the plants and
then wrote under them their properties But not only is a picture
misleading when the colours are so many, particularly as the aim
is to copy nature, but besides this, much imperfection arises from
the manifold hazards in the accuracy of copyists. In addition, it
is not enough for each plant to be painted at one period only of
its life, since it alters its appearance with the fourfold changes of
the year." Because of this problem, "the other writers have given
verbal accounts only; some have not even given the shape of the
plants, and for the most part have been content with bare names,
since they thought it sufficient to point out the properties and nature of a plant to those willing to look for it." Later Pliny mentioned a difficulty that Rauwolf often experienced; "an added
difficulty in botany is the variety of names given to the same
plant in different districts." [17]

Some of the drawings originally made by the above-mentioned
Crateuas (first century B.C.) may have survived in the sixth-
century Byzantine *Codex Aniciae Iulianae* of Dioscorides. Written herbaria of the Middle Ages frequently contained some illustrations, often stylized in copying. In the later medieval manuscripts, naturalistic representations of plants increased in number
and accuracy. Even though the verbal descriptions of plants improved, the *Herbal* of Rufinus (*ca.* 1287) being an outstanding
example, the text of many manuscripts on botany bore little relation to the illustrations. Often the text of a classical botanist described Mediterranean and Near Eastern plants while the illustrations were done by a European artist who knew only the native species. The advent of woodcuts in the late fourteenth or
early fifteenth century and the later invention of printing proved
a great advance for science, for now pictorial representations
were disseminated in thousands of copies exactly alike. The first
pictures of recognizable plants in a printed book are those of
Konrad von Megenburg's *Buch der Natur* (Augsburg, 1475).
From this humble beginning botanical illustration improved
gradually in detail and accuracy. The great classical models for

botanical illustration, but not for texts, are the *Herbarum vivae eicones* of Otto Brunfels (Strassburg, 1530) and the *De historia stirpium* of Leonhard Fuchs (Basel, 1542).[18]

In the third edition of Rauwolf's work (Laugingen, 1583), 42 woodcuts of Near Eastern exotic plants were added as a fourth part. The artist who copied these plants from the dried specimens in Rauwolf's herbarium is not known. This fourth part is dedicated to his friends Constantinus Paulus Phrygioni and Oswald Gabelchover, both physicians for Ludwig, the duke of Württemberg. The dedication is accompanied by two Latin encomiums addressed to Rauwolf and written by the physician Johann Posthius (dated July, 1582) and by Tobias Fischerus Silesius, "mathematician and student of medicine." Apparently this fourth part was also printed separately for those who had earlier editions of Rauwolf's travel book. Clusius requested and received from Rauwolf "quarta parte Hodoporici" on September 22, 1584.[19] Alberto von Haller mentioned a Latin manuscript translation of this fourth part by Danty d'Isnard, but no printed edition in Latin was published.[20]

In 1586–87, however, the French botanist Jacques Dalechamps published at Lyons his *Historia generalis plantarum, in libros XVIII per certas classes artificiose digesta*. The two volumes of this work contained 2,751 woodcuts, with some 400 of the illustrations being repeated for different plants. At the conclusion of this work there was placed an appendix with separate pagination, in which 53 exotic plants are described and, with few exceptions, illustrated. The descriptions and illustrations for the first 18 plants were taken mostly from Acosta's work on Indian plants. After a subtitle, *Plantarum Aegyptiarum et Syriacarum eiconicae figurae, cum historiae summa diligentia et cura descripta a Leonardo Rauwolf Medicinae doctore Augustano*, 35 of the original 42 plant illustrations of the 1583 edition of Rauwolf's work are given. These woodcuts are redrawn and reversed, the latter happening, of course, when a printed picture was pasted on a block of wood and recut. The cutter also had a horror of blank spaces, for he added insects and falling leaves around many of the plants. The Latin text accompanying these 35 pictures is so extensive that it might well have been written by Rauwolf himself. The fact that the description of *Terebinthus Indica* (p. 31) contains a sentence beginning "Ego cum manderem . . ." seems to substantiate Rauwolf's authorship.

Through the publication of these two works, Rauwolf's own German travel book and Dalechamps' *Historia,* Rauwolf's name and accomplishments were spread throughout Europe. Perhaps the first botanical study to make extensive use of Rauwolf's *Raisz* was the *Hortus medicus et philosophicus* (Frankfort am Main, 1588) of Joachim Camerarius. Here the author often cited Rauwolf and his book, giving the Arabic nomenclature for the Near Eastern plants and naming the places where the Augsburg botanist observed particular plants. In connection with the plant *Apocynum verum* (*Cynanchum erectum* L.), Camerarius noted that this plant had been found near Tripoli and "later described in his excellent *Hodaeporico Orientali* by Dr. Leonhard Rauwolf, physician of Augsburg, a most learned man, one indefatigable in the study and investigation of nature, and my singular friend." [21] Among the 47 illustrations of plants in Camerarius's *Hortus,* seven have Rauwolf's name associated with them. One illustration, that of *Gingidium* (XVI, p. 67), refers to the picture of this plant in Rauwolf's work (fig. 38), but the illustration of Camerarius is better drawn.

Johann Bauhin's *Historia plantarum universalis,* completed by others and published posthumously in three volumes in 1650, cited Rauwolf's travel book for a number of plants and fruits, including those of the banana, manna, rhubarb, several willows, tragacanths, coffee, and lillies. For a number of plants, Bauhin indicated the discoverer by adding "Rauwolfii" as part of the name, including one, *Ligusticum Rauwolfii* (*Siler trilobum* Crantz.) that is not in Rauwolf's book or herbarium. [22] Leonard Plukenet and John Ray also referred to the travel book of Rauwolf. [23] Dalechamps' monumental work, generally known by the abbreviated title *Historia plantarum lugdunensis,* was widely used by botanists of the sixteenth and seventeenth centuries in both the Latin edition and the French version of Des Moulins (Lyons, 1615 and 1653). This work was probably more responsible for the international reputation of Rauwolf than his own German work. Bauhin, Plukenet, and Robert Morison made repeated mention of the appendix in Dalechamps' work when they wrote of Rauwolf's observations.[24]

After his return from the Near East, Rauwolf also revised and rearranged the earlier portions of his herbarium and set up a fourth volume with the rare plants he had collected in the Orient.[25] All four folio volumes were prepared with title pages written in Gothic characters by an expert calligrapher. The first three volumes contain the 634 plants collected from 1560 to 1563 in southern France, northern Italy, and Switzerland. In these volumes the pages measure 31 by 23 centimeters, and each volume has 106 leaves or 212 pages. Plants are glued on each side of the strong sheets of paper and the pages are framed by borders of marbled cardboard pasted along the margins. When the volumes are closed these frames prevent the adjacent specimens from touching, and they also have prevented damage by mice and insects. At times two or more plants are glued to the same page. Each of the first three volumes has a page listing the plants and the number of the page on which they are found, all in a handwriting judged to be that of Rauwolf.

The fourth volume contained 200 of the plants collected by Rauwolf on his trip during the years 1573 to 1575. These plants are divided into four parts according to the areas where the plants were collected: Piedmont, Nice, and Marseilles; Tripoli and Aleppo; Euphrates; and Mount Lebanon. The fourth volume is larger (49 by 36 centimeters) and originally contained 200 leaves, some of which are now missing. The title page has four drawings in color: Jesus in Gethsemane at the top; the entry of Jesus into Jerusalem at the bottom; a physician (Rauwolf?) holding a flower in his hand on the right; and a peasant spading the earth on the left. Under the figures are baskets of flowers and in the four corners are angels. The cover of this volume is of wood covered with leather with engraved copper corners and latch. Unlike the first three volumes, the plants of the fourth volume are glued on one side only of the numbered pages. Each plant is identified with its Latin name and often, in addition, the

German, French, or Arabic name is given along with the place of origin and, at times, the class name.

The title of the fourth volume is as follows:

Viertes Kreutterbuech—darein vil schoene und frembde Kreutter durch den hochgelehrten Herrn Leonhart Rauwolffen der Artzney Doctorn unnd der Stat Augspurg bestellten Medicum gar fleissig einegelegt unnd aufgemacht worden. Welche er nit allain in Piemont umb Nissa unnd in der Provincia umb Marsiglia sonder auch in Syria an dem Berge Libano unnd Antilibano auch durch Arabiam neben dem Fluesz Euphrate in Chaldea Assyria Armenia Mesopotamien unnd andern Orten in seinen mitt Gottes hilff volbrachten dreyjarigen Raysen, mit groszer muehe arbait gefehrligkhait unnd uncosten bekhuemen hat davon Er auch in seinem Rayszbuech so in dem druckh auszgangen ist meldung thuet. Geschehen nach der geburt unnsers Seligmachers—Ihesu Christi, M.D. LXXIII–LXXIIII—und LXXV jar.

The history of the herbarium is of interest to botanists.[26] Camerarius wrote in the *Hortus medicus* that Rauwolf had kindly permitted him to use the specimen of *Sesamum verum* (*S. indicum* L.) in the herbarium in order for him to make the first illustration of this plant (No. XLIV). Rauwolf also sent him a dried specimen of *Ribes sylvestre* (*Rheum ribes* L.) from his herbarium.[27] In the letter Rauwolf wrote to Clusius on September 7, 1584, he told his friend that he "would gladly offer to some liberal and generous prince who would be pleased to study them," the plants he had acquired "only at the cost of great effort, much difficulty, and danger." The Augsburg botanist wrote Clusius further that if "such an individual were to be found and if you had an opportunity to speak to him about the matter in my name, you would do something for which I would be particularly obliged." [28] Some time before the death of Rauwolf, according to Krafft, the herbarium was acquired by the ruler of Bavaria for 200 gulden and placed in the Kunstkammer in Munich.[29] During the Thirty Years' War it was removed by the Swedish soldiers and taken to Sweden. About 1650 Queen Christiana presented the herbarium to Isaac Vossius, the scholarly Dutch librarian at the Swedish court. In 1655 Vossius brought the herbarium to Holland where Professor Heinrich Meibom of Helmstadt saw it in 1660.[30] Jacob Breyn, a German botanist (1637–97), reported that when he saw Rauwolf's "beautiful and curious" herbarium in 1663, the dried specimens still retained their freshness.[31]

In 1670 Vossius took the herbarium to London. Here, Robert Morison, the eminent Scottish botanist and professor of botany at Oxford, used the "herbario vivo," as he called it, for his *Plantarum historiae universalis oxoniensis.* Another botanist, Leonard Plukenet reported seeing examples of *Aristolochia maurorum,* L., *Campanula (Michauxia campanuloides* L'Hérit), and *Eupatoria conyzoides (Centaurea Behen* L.) in the herbarium. John Ray noted that Jacob Bobart saw an *Acanthus Dioscoridis (A. spinosus* L.) in Rauwolf's collection. On October 25, 1692, Captain Hatton wrote to Ray that "those few plants of Rauwolfus's Collection, published in the Appendix to the *Historia Lugdunensis* [of Dalechamps], got him so great fame amongst the lovers of Botany, that I have heard Isaac Vossius declare, above 400 l. [livres] Sterling had been offer'd for the 4 specious Volumes he had of dried plants collected by Rauwolfius: and to most Strangers, who came to see his deservedly famed Library, he constantly shewd'd those amongst his other most valuable books.[32] On the death of Vossaus in 1688, the University of Leyden purchased his library, including the herbarium, for 32,000 florins. There the herbarium remains today, a prized possession.

In the eighteenth century, the botanist Johann Friedrich Gronovius (1690–1760) used the herbarium of Rauwolf as the basis for his work entitled *Flora orientalis sive Recensio Plantarum quas Botanicorum Coryphaeus Leonhardus Rauwolffus, Medicus Augustanus, annis 1573, 1574, et 1575 in Syria, Arabia, Mesopotamia, Babylonia, Assyria, Armenia et Judaea crescentes observavit, et collegit, earumdemque ducenta Specimina, quae in Bibliotheca publica Lugduno-Batava adservantur, nitidissime exsiccata et chartae adglutinata in volumen retulit. Has Methodo Sexuali disposuit, Synonymis probatioribus illustravit, Nominibusque Specificis insignivit* (Leyden, 1755). He enumerated 338 species, as found in the fourth volume of the herbarium and in Rauwolf's travel book, and, as the long title in-

dicates, classified these according to the new sexual system of
Carolus Linnaeus. For each species he gave the Linnaean nomenclature, the names used by other famous botanists like Morison, Clusius, Belon, and Ray, and then gave the name and place
of origin as given by Rauwolf.

Rauwolf's medical career and his service to the city of Augsburg were suddenly interrupted in the spring of 1588. For this
his Lutheranism was primarily responsible. Since the Augsburg
Interim of 1548, the city had gradually become bi-confessional,
with a considerable restoration of Roman Catholicism, especially
in the ruling circles. When he was writing his description of
Mount Zion in 1581, Rauwolf included a prayer in which the
wording seems to indicate the religious friction in Augsburg. He
prayed God that the Holy Spirit would "keep us in the knowledge of the Holy Word and so strengthen and comfort us in it
that we may freely and without fear confess it before our enemies and adversaries, and that we may overcome with patience
the offenses, all disagreeableness, persecutions, and crosses, that
thy honor may be preserved and our faithfulness perceived." [33]

Much of the religious strife in Augsburg centered on the
intention of the city officials to introduce the new Gregorian
calendar. The disturbances began in 1582 and apparently Rauwolf was a leader in the Protestant opposition. In the dedication
(iii^r–iii^v) to part four of his book, dated May 15, 1583, he mentioned the meeting of the Reichstag in Augsburg in 1582 and
thanked the personal physicians of Ludwig, duke of Württemberg, for having defended his good reputation before their patron against "all the calumnies and evil talk." Despite the efforts
by both sides to seek a peaceful solution, by 1582 the strife was
bitter, with the evangelical preachers declaring that they would
not celebrate religious festivals in their churches according to the
papal calendar. Despite the determined opposition and the plea
for caution from Ludwig of Württemberg, the majority in the
city council was strong enough to introduce the calendar in 1584.[34]

By 1588 the Roman Catholic officials of the city had restored
many priests and since the Protestant burghers did not accept
them, it was considered necessary to move against influential Lutheran individuals. All the city employees were now questioned

either by the privy councillor or the city architect as to whether or not they would thereafter go to the Roman Catholic priests. Among the number of city employees who refused to accommodate themselves to the re-established Catholicism were Rauwolf and another city-physician, Adolf Occo (1524–1606). Occo, a celebrated numismatic and compiler of the important *Pharmocopoiea Augustana,* had been serving as assistant to the dean of the College of Medicine established at Augsburg in 1582. Occo, too, had opposed the introduction of the Gregorian calendar, and, like Rauwolf, had because of his position and reputation influenced many Lutherans to oppose the changes tending toward Roman Catholic control. Both Rauwolf and Occo were deprived of their positions and income. On March 9, 1588, Rauwolf received his last salary from the city treasurer.[35]

Occo stayed in Augsburg and devoted himself to the study of antiquities, especially numismatics, but Rauwolf left his native city on July 28 and removed to Linz, Austria. Here he remained as town physician and *Poliates et Ordinum Archiducatus Austriae Medicus* for eight years.[36] His restless nature, however, caused him to leave Linz on July 13, 1596, and march with the troops from that area into Hungary where the emperor was fighting the Turks. On September 3, 1596, the Christian troops succeeded in taking with much slaughter the Turkish fortress of Hatvan on the Zagiva River. It would have been desirable for the victorious army to stay at Hatvan to rest and recover from the siege, but the news that the sultan had 200,000 troops at Ofen led the Christians to seek a more defensible position. On the ninth of September, the camp was moved to Waitzen (Vacz) on the Raab. Rauwolf had acquired a severe case of dysentery from drinking the polluted water of Hatvan, and after suffering for several days, he died at Waitzen between five and six o'clock on the morning of September 15, 1596. He was buried there on the evening of the same day.[37]

His unmarked grave could well have for an epitaph the words he included in the dedication (i^r-i^v) of his travel book:

So those who make the attainment of skill in the . . . liberal arts their principal end and the study thereof their delight are not deterred from prosecuting this design by any distances of places, by winter or summer, fearing neither rain nor snow, nor the traversing of horrid deserts, or the wild and roaring seas, nor the wasting or weakening of their patrimonies, if at last they can but arrive at those places, where they may gain the acquaintance and familiarity of the eminently learned masters, able to instruct them in those arts and sciences, to the knowledge and comprehension of which they aspire; or where they may inform themselves of the constitutions and customs of famous nations and of other things subservient to their intentions.

APPENDIX I

SELECTIONS FROM RAUWOLF'S TRAVEL BOOK

The following translated sections of Rauwolf's travel book (pp. 53–63; 110–28) are found in the 1738 English edition (pp. 35–42; 73–86). I have revised and somewhat modernized the translation for this appendix. The selections deal with his descriptions of some of the plants he saw or collected in Tripoli and Aleppo. They point up well the difficulty of verbal description in pre-Linnean days and bring out the use Rauwolf made of classical, medieval, and contemporary authorities. Where the botanist used a German term, an English equivalent has been given with the Latin name added. The Latin nomenclature used by Rauwolf has been retained, but if the modern usage is different, the plant name is given in brackets. Plants identified only by an Arabic term have been given the Latin name. The Arabic has been given in the transliteration used by Rauwolf. When Rauwolf used the word "Arabs" he was referring to the medieval authorities; "Moors" refers to the inhabitants of Syria.

PART I, CHAPTER IV

A description of some plants I gathered and acquired at Tripoli in the time of my stay there.

Considering that I undertook this journey into the eastern countries, not only to see these people and to observe their manners, etc., but also, and that principally, diligently to inquire and to search out the plants that were growing there, I cannot but briefly describe those I found about Tripoli during my stay there and I will begin with such as grew on the seashore. These were *medica marina* [*Medicago marina* L.], *Gnaphalium marinum* [*Diotis candissima* Desf., *D. maritima* (L.) Sm.], *Leucoium marinum* [*Matthiola triscupidata* (L.) R. Br.], *Juncus maritimus* [*Scirpus mucronatus* L.,] *Peplis* [*Euphorbia peplis* L.], *Scammonium montpelliense* [*Cynanchum acutum* L.], which the inhabitants call *meudheudi*, but Rhazes, in his book *ad Almansoris*, called it *coriziola*, and seaside bindweed [*Con-*

volvulus soldanella L.], which spreads its roots above the sand for some cubits around and has rather square leaves instead of round ones. A kind of wild white lily is common, which is called *Hemerocallis* [*H.* sp.] by the Latins and Greeks, and it grows not only on the seashore but also in great plenty on the islands in the port, with a great many others which I forebear to mention here.

Behind the customs house near the harbor, I found henbane [*Hyoscyamus albus* L.] in the ruins of the old wall that remain of the old city of Tripoli and near it in the sand, an herb [*Convolvulus cneorum* L.] not unlike the second *Cantabricae* of Carolus Clusius, except that the stalks and leaves are wooly. But the castorbean [*Ricinus communis* L.] grows there above all in such great quantity that you can hardly make your way through it. The inhabitants still call it *ķerua,* its old Arabic name.

If you turn from there to the highway on your right you see the spurge called *Tithymalus paralios* [*Euphorbia paralias* L.] and also a kind of thorn described by Dioscorides [*? Conyza Dioscoridis* Desf.], called *Conyza* by the Latins and Greeks. Out of one root there spring up several stalks, some of which grow upright, but most of them lie on the ground and so shoot out new roots which afterwards put out new stalks. It bears long olive-like leaves which are thick, fattish, somewhat wooly, and have a strong and equally sweet smell. For the rest, like the flowers, it is very similar to the large ones. You find there also the larger and smaller *Medica* [*Medicago sativa* L.], which the Moors to this day call *fasa.* Likewise, so many large *Scilla* [*Urginea maritima* Baker] that the inhabitants weed them up, especially those that grow near their gardens, and throw them in great heaps like stones. Also growing there are *Securidaca minor* [*Astragalus hamosus* L.], *Tribulus terrestris* [L.], called *haseck* by the inhabitants, and a kind of Echium [*E. orientale* L.], which grows by the way as you go to St. James Church . . .

Hereabouts and in other adjacent places grows a great quantity of sugarcane. [*Saccharum officinarum* L.] . . . These are as high and big as our canes and not much different from them, but within and down toward the roots, where they are best, they are full of this pleasant juice. The Turks and Moors buy a great many of them, it being very pleasant for them to chew and eat, for they are very pleased with sweetmeats, of which they have a variety . . .

By the river of Tripoli are also found *Anthyllis marina* [*? A. vulneraria* L.], *Visnaiga* [*Ammi visnaga* (L.) Lam.], the first *Apocynum* [*Marsdenia erecta* (L.) R. Br.], oleander [*Nerium oleander* L.] with purple flowers and called *defte* by the inhabitants, a nice kind of *Scabiosa* [*S. cretica* L.], the *Melissa moluca* [*Molucella laevis* L.], and if you go nearer the gardens you see *Heliotropium maius* [*H. europaeum* L.]. Also in the hedges and brush can be seen the pungent bindweed [*Convolvulus*], *Vitis nigra* [*Tamus communis* L.], *Phaseolus turcicus* [? *Vigna sinensis* (L.) Savi] with yellow flowers, which still retains the old name of *lubie,* yellow loosestrife [*Lysimachia vulgaria* L.], and wild vines called *Labrusca* [*Vitis* sp.], on which nothing grows except the flowers called *Oenanthe*. Also, a shrub similar to the *Polygamus* of Carol Clusius, which climbs up into high trees and hangs down from the twigs; and truly I believe they are the same as the *Ephedra* [*E. distachya* L.] of which Pliny makes mention in the seventh chapter of his twenty-sixth book.

When I went farther with the intention of considering the plants that grew in the country, I first found some sycamores [*Ficus sycomorus* L.], which Dioscorides and Theophrastus in particular mention and tell us of two kinds. When I called these things to mind, I saw one of the second kind of sycamores, which grow abundantly in Cyprus. Therefore these wild fig trees might be called, the one the Cyprus sycamore and the other the Egyptian or Pharaoh sycamore, according to the places where they are most frequent and fruitful. I found a great many of them. The Moors and Arabs call them *mumeitz*. They are as great and high as the white mulberry trees and have almost the same leaves, but they are somewhat rounder and are also complete at or about the sides. They bear fruit similar to our fig trees, only they are sweeter, have no little seeds inside, and are not as good. Therefore they are little esteemed and are mostly bought by the poor . . .

Many thorns also grow here . . . called *hauseit* by the inhabitants and *hausegi* by the Arabs, but the Latins call them *Rhamnus* [*Lycium europaeum* L.]; and also white poplars [*Populus alba* L.] still to this day called *haur* by the old Arabs. A great and high tree also grows here, which bears beautiful leaves and flowers, pleasant to look upon, and called *zenselacht* by the inhabitants, but called *astirgar* or *astergir* and *azardaracht* by Rhazes and Avicenna [*Melia azedarach* L.]. Of these you see some planted in the streets here and there in order to make a pleasant shade in the summer. The fruit remains on the tree all year long until they bloom again. They are harmful and kill dogs if they are given to them to eat.

Near the town upon the highlands (where you see many grain fields and an abundance of pleasant olive trees [*Olea europaea* L.] that reach quite up to Mount Lebanon) are found *Polium montanum* [*Tuecrium polium* L.], *Pecten veneris* [*Scandix pecten-veneris* L.], *Sferra cauallo* [*Hippocrepis unisiliquosa* L.], *Chamaeleon niger* [*Carthamus corymbosus* (L.) Pers.] with its sharp pointed and black roots and leaves, very similar to the leaves of the *Carlina,* of which the stalks are of a reddish color, a span long, and of the thickness of a finger, on which are small prickly heads of a bluish color, similar to those of the little *Erygium.*

Another fine plant [*Satureia capitata* L.] grows thereabouts, called *sathar* in their language, but when I consider its beautiful purple-colored flowers and its small leaves which are long, I rather judge it to be the *hasce* of the Arabs or the *Thymum* of Dioscorides, which we call *Quendel romanum.* It has as pleasant an odor as any spice can have . . . This herb is never found in our apothecary shops. They take another in its place, which has smaller and greener heads and is rather the first kind of *Satureiae* of Dioscorides [*S. thymbra* L.] brought from Crete. There are also two sorts of *Clinopodium,* of which the smaller and more tender (considering its long stalks, leaves, and flowers, which grow in good order and at equal distances one over the other) may very well be taken for the true one of Dioscorides [*Clinopodium vulgare* L.]. There are also *Ilex minor* [*Quercus coccifera* L.], *Sabina baccifera* [*Juniperus sabina* L.], *Terebinthus* [*Pistacia terebinthus* L.], and many others.

In the town are found several strange plants. One is called *musa* [*Musa sapientum* L.], of which the stalks are from 9 to 12 feet high, smooth (and on the outside they are enclosed in their leaves and often quite surrounded like our reeds), and of a fine shining green; at the top of these the leaves spread themselves out and look like a great bush of feathers, for they are very long and so broad that the biggest person may lie upon them very well with his whole body. The leaves have a rib in the middle which keeps them straight and so strong that although the wind breaks them at the sides in several places, yet they remain upright. These trees bear their fruit only once, whereupon they are cut down and the root shoots out several others stalks about a foot distant from the old one, which grow up and bring forth fruit, which grows on a thick stalk in great numbers. They are almost shaped like a gourd, round and bended, only they are smaller, smooth on the outside, and covered with a thick rind which is first yellow, but turns black when kept for a few days; the rinds are easily peeled when new. Within they are whitish, full of seeds, sweet and good to eat; but they fill one easily and are apt to cause colic. Therefore (as Theophrastus mentions [iv. 4.5] in the fifth chapter of his fourth book), Alexander the Great forbad his army to eat them when he went to India. Very little of this fruit grows about Tripoli, but it is brought in large amounts from the neighboring places.

We also find there another tree, not unlike our privet, called *alcanna* or *henne* [*Lawsonia inermis* L.] by the Arabs and *schenna* by the Greeks in their vulgar tongue. These are brought from Egypt, where they grow in abundance, especially in Cairo . . . The Arabs burn their spodium out of the roots of this plant, as Avicenna remarks in his chapter 617. This being so, it appears that there is no small difference between these two, ours and theirs. I am of the opinion that theirs (which is mentioned in the first chapter of the Song of Solomon) is closer to that which Dioscorides described than to our *Ligustrum*.

Within and outside of the gardens, can also be found a peculiar sort of *Malva,* called *chethmie* [*Hibiscus syriacus* L.] by them, which is very large and high, and, like other trees, spreads its woody twigs and soft boughs, which are covered with a brownish bark . . . Nearby, I found another strange flower, which was almost decayed so that it had neither leaves, flowers, nor seeds . . . I made great inquiry, but could obtain no certain information about it. However, it seemed to me to be very similar to the *xabra* and *camarronus* of Rhaszes [*Euphorbia mauritanica* L.], called *tanaghut* and *sabeam* by the Arabs, and may be taken, according to that author's description, for it.

Farther thereabouts, especially in the town at the cisterns and conduits, I found *Adiantum* [*A. capillus-veneris* L.], called *Capillus Veneris* by the apothecaries, and in the old walls the *Apollinaris* [*Hyoscyamus albus* L.]. I also found in the shops in their bazaar two sorts of roots, of which one was more round, which may be the *Dulcigini* [*Cyperus esculentus* L.] of the Venetians, which are called *Thrasi* at Verona where they grow (as the learned Mattioli testifies). Many of these are sent out of Egypt to Tripoli and sold there under the names of *habel assis* and *altzis,* chiefly to be eaten in June. This being true, and since they are very similar both in name and quality to the grains of *altzelem* of the Arabs, they must be the same, although Rhazes reckons them among the fruits. The other, called by them *haķinrig* and *haķeurbi* [*Doronicum plantagineum* L.], is somewhat longer and not unlike our *Doronicum*. There are also a great many of them sold. They are hard, of a sweetish taste, with a piercing bitterness, and in their size and white roots (which spread themselves underground in the garden round about like our *Angelica tragi*) so like the *haronigi* of Serapion and to the *durungi* and *durunegi* of Avicenna, according to their descriptions, and so uniform, that they must be taken for the same. I also found in their shops an abundance of the seeds of *sumac* [*Rhus coriaria* L.], of which they make a red powder to excite the appetite of the stomach. These and more strange and unknown simples I did find at Tripoli. But because it would be too tedious to describe them all, therefore I have only made mention of those that authors have described.

PART I, CHAPTER IX

A short and plain relation of the plants I gathered during my stay at Aleppo, in and round about it, not without great danger and trouble, which I glued on paper very carefully.

Since I undertook this long journey, chiefly, among other reasons, that I might myself see those fine and exotic plants, which the authors so frequently mention, in this area and place and to learn to know them, I was very glad to have an opportunity to stay longer at Aleppo in order that I might more often go out into the fields with several of my friends and comrades to bring in more of such plants, not without great danger from the Turks and Moors. In this, my friend Hans Ulrich Krafft especially, who came into these parts along with me, has very often faithfully and honestly assisted me.

But having previously made mention of the garden herbs and fruits, I will write here only of those which grow abroad outside of the gardens, and I will do that with all possible brevity. I begin with the poplar trees [*Populus alba* L.], as the most common of all, which the inhabitants still call by the old Arabic name of *haur*. They grow very high in these countries and an abundance of them grow about the rivulet near Aleppo, and provide very shady walks in the heat of summer.

There is also a peculiar sort of willow [*Salix Safsaf* Forsk.] called *safsaf*, etc. These willow trees are not all alike in size and height, and in their trunks and twigs, which are long, thin, weak, and of a pale yellow color, they are not unlike the birch tree. They have soft ash-colored leaves, or rather like the leaves of the chaste tree, and on the twigs, here and there, are shoots of a span in length, like those of the Cyprian wild fig trees, which send forth tender and wooly flowers in the spring, like the blossoms of the poplar tree, only they are of a more drying quality, of a pale color, and have a fragrant smell. Because they bear no fruit, the inhabitants pull off great quantities of these and distill an expensive water out of them, very useful in strengthening the heart. The Arabs call these trees *zarneb* and *zarnabum*. Rhazes in his Chapter 353, and Avicenna in his Chapter 749, and in the same manner Serapion in his Chapter 261 make mention of them by the common name of *zurumbeth* and Theophrastus in his fourth book, chapter eleven, where he treats of the *Elaeagnus,* which is very similar and may be taken for the same purpose, although they differ in size, which often and easily happens according to the soil and place where they grow.

Ein außländische Stauden unserm Bain oder
Mundholtz gleichend/welche die farb gibt/mit der die Türc-
ken iren Rossen die Mähninen und Schwäntz rot ferben/
wie auch ihnen selb die Nägel an fingern/ wirt von
Griechen Cyprus, den Arabern Henne
unnd Alcanna genennet.

Nů: 60.

G ij   Ein

Fig. 1—*Lawsonia inermis* L.

Ein vnbekannts gewächs Morgſani genañt/
welches für Andirian Rhaſis vnnd Ardifuigi
Auicennæ.zůhalten.

Nů: 113.

Schöne

Fig. 2—*Zygophyllum jabago* L.

Hereabouts are other small trees [*Elaeagnus angustifolia* L.] which I rather take to be thorny shrubs. These are very similar in leaves to the others and are called *seisefun* by the Moors. They like to grow in moist places and in hedges. From the roots shoot out several stems, clothed with a smooth brown-colored bark. At the top they bear pretty long and strong twigs, which here and there are set with a few prickles on which grow small flowers, white on the outside and yellow in the inside, of which three by three they sprout out between the leaves. I did not see any of the fruit, but yet I do believe that they are like the olives of the Bohemian olive tree, to which the plant is very similar (which is very naturally delineated in the herbal of the learned Mattioli). These trees produce such an odor in the spring that anybody that goes by must be aware of it presently. Therefore the Turks and Moors cut many of their branches and stick them up in their shops.

Within and outside the city grow also many sorts of trees, viz., that which Avicenna calls *azedarack*, but Rhazes calls *astergio* [*Melia azedarach* L.]; white mulberry trees [*Morus alba* L.]; date trees [*Phoenix dactylifera* L.]; cypress trees [*Cupressus sempervirens* L.], called *sarub* by the natives, which here grow very big and high; terebinths [*Pistacia terebinthus* L.]; and others.

About the fences and hedges you will find wild pomegranate trees [*Punica granatum* L.] with fine double flowers, and wild almond trees [*Amygdalus communis* L.], the fruit of which the Moors carry about in great amounts to sell to the poor. Nearby, in old decayed brick walls and stony places, you shall see caper bushes [*Capparis spinosa* L.]. Among the rest there grows a very strange bush, called *morgsani* [*Zygophyllum fabago* L.] by the inhabitants, which is very green and thick, has a long, woody coat, from which sprout several stalks with round leaves, like caper leaves except that four of them stand together all opposite one another like our beans. Between them there appear small flowers, red within and white on the outside, from which grow long pods, similar to those of *Sesamum*. This plant has a very unpleasant scent; therefore the inhabitants frequently use it to destroy worms. What the ancients formerly called it, I do not know, but I am really of the opinion that it must be, according to the description, the *ardifrigi* of Avicenna and the *andirian* of Rhazes; he that pleases may read more thereof in the quoted places.

In these places are also found the thorny acacia [*Mimosa nilotica* L.], called *schack* by the inhabitants and *schamuth* by the Arabs. These are very small and low, especially those that are in the fields, which give as much trouble to the plowman as the ferns and restharrow do ours. The twigs are of an ashen color, crooked, full of prickles like those of the rose bush, and have very small, feathered leaves like the *Tragacantha,* and which are almost divided like our female ferns. The flowers of these I have not seen, but the cods that grow out of them are brownish on the outside, in their shape thicker and rounder than our beans, spongy within, and contain two or three reddish seeds.

Besides these, I have seen in the shops pods of a chestnut brown color, sold under the name of *cardem,* which have two or three distinct cells or bags, in each of which is a reddish seed, in the form of our male balsam. These are brought from Egypt and are by some thought to be the true acacia of Dioscorides, whether it is so or not, I cannot well tell because I never saw the plant. Very near, in untilled places, grow the *Galega* [*G. officinalis* L.], the *Sisynrichium* of Theophrastus [*Ixia bulbocodium* L.], which is very curiously delineated in the booklet of Rembert Dodoens on the flowers and fragrant herbs belonging to the *coronilla.*

There is also found another fine plant, called *tharasalis* [*Sisyrinchium* sp.] by the inhabitants, which has seven or eight waved leaves which stand about a round stalk, almost as it is to be seen in the *Sisyrinchium,* only they are a great deal broader and so long when the stalk, which is not more than a cubit long, is grown through and above them. At the top is a white flower, not very unlike the low, blue lillies which bloom early in the spring. It has a roundish root, like that of the narcissus, and also many long, white fibers. Not far from there, when you get up on the hill, others grow in the rough places, viz., snake or viper's root [*Dracunculus vulgaris* Schott], still called by the old name of *luph* by the inhabitants, a fine sort of mullein [*Phlomis lychnitis* L.], *Scorzonera* [*S. hispanica* L.] with purple flowers, saffron [*Crocus sativus* L.] with small narrow leaves and a pretty yellow flower. Also one finds *Arisarum* [*Arum tenuifolium* L.] or *homaid* in Arabic, and *Arum* [*Calla orientalis* L.], called *carsaami* by them, of which there are four sorts among the rest a strange one with long ears, which they therefore call *ovidae* in their language [*Calla orientalis* L. var.]

About the rivers there are also some anemones [*Anemone* sp.] of several sorts and colors, very beautiful, as red, purple, yellow, etc., all of which they call with a common name *schakaick* and give them an additional name according to the color, viz., *schakaick achmar, schakaick asfar, aserack,* etc., that is to say, red, yellow, violet, etc., which would be too long and tedious to describe here, especially if I should at length relate about the common ones, as the wild rue *Asphodelus albus* [Mill.], the *Rheseda* of Pliny [*Reseda lutea* L.], *Flos solis* [*Helianthemum vulgare* Gaertn.] with little slender leaves like wild thyme, wild onions [*Allium ursinum* L.], and innumerable others.

As you come back down by the other way nearer to the grain fields, you find many other fine herbs, such as the wild rue [*? Ruta graveolens* L.], *Harmala* [*Peganum harmala* L.], a pretty sort of *Astragalus* with leaves of the small *Hedysari* [*Astragalus christianus* L.], and near it another which is very similar to the true *Astragalus* of Dioscorides [*A. syriacus* L.] so that I really believe it to be the same. There are a great many of them on the height. It is a low herb with a long brownish root, as big and long as the root of horseradish, which sends out some strong fibers at the sides, which are almost blacker and harder to cut than the root itself. Some of them go downwards, and other, the greater part, upwards and are curved like horns. They are dry as well as sweet. They shoot out at the top into several branches of the same color, yet not more than the length of a finger, which incline towards the earth, out of which grow nine or ten small leaves, like lentilleaves, not very unlike those of the *Orobus* and distributed in the same manner. Between them sprout out purple-brown flowers, and after them come long, thick, and full bladders, some of which are a big as those of the *Colutea*. All these and several other herbs I have preserved and glued to some papers, with great and particular care, so that they are to be seen in their natural colors, exactly as if they were green.

On a hill by the river, I found a tender and fragrant herb [*Seseli* sp.] with long and white roots, of a pretty acrimonious taste. Its leaves were like our coriander, only somewhat rounder and not so much cut, but only a little about the edges. I found no stalks or flowers for it was early in the year and about Easter, which is the time of their first sprouting. These they called *zarneb melchi,* and the inhabitants dig up so many of these roots that they annually send chests full into Persia where they use them, I am informed, very frequently for pains in the back and all other accidental pains. As far as I can see, when I look at the leaves, I consider it to be the third sort of *Daucus* of Dioscorides.

A little lower, as you come to the plowed fields, I also found a second sort of *Chondrilla* of Dioscorides [*Erigeron tuberosus* L.] with round roots of a smooth and dark yellowish color, at the base perhaps half a finger thick and five or eight fingers long. At the end where it is thinnest, there is another round root of the size of a chestnut, which is so full of milk that it is ready to burst. At the top, where it is divided into three parts, sprout many long and small grass leaves together, which lie flat on the ground. Between them come out yellow flowers like those of the yellow *Auricula muris,* each of which has its own stalk.

Not far from it, but in rougher and stonier ground, grows another *Chondrilla* [*Erigeron tuberosus* L., var.], which is like the former in all parts except that the leaves are broader, more wooly, and of an ash color, very similar to the *Holostium* that grows at Montpellier. As one goes out toward the great sultan's garden (about four miles away), there are a good many plants, viz., the *Draba* of Dioscorides [*Lepidium draba* L.], *Orobanche* [*O. rapum* Reichb.] called *halinu, Spina solstitialis* [*Centaurea solstitialis* L.], a kind of *Carduus Mariae* [*Silybum marianum* (L.) Gaertn.], wild cucumbers [*Ecballium elaterium* (L.) Rich.] called *adiural hamar* by them, *Zyphium* [*Gladiolus communis* L.], *Peplium* [*? Euphorbia Peplus* L.], the *Heliotropium tricoccum* [*Chrozophora tinctoria* (L.) A. Juss.] of Carolus Clusius, his *Paronychia hispanica* [*P. argentea* Lam.], and his third *Lychnis* [*Silene muscipala* L.] with pale and red-purple colored flowers, the *Coris* of Mattioli [*Hypericum coris* L.] with yellow flowers, two pretty kinds of geraniums [*Geranium gruinum* L.], and upon the old walls I found a little *Eruca* [*E. sativa* Mill.] with pale colored flowers, *Umbilicus Veneris* [*Cotyledon umbilicus* L.], and a great many more.

I cannot leave unmentioned those that grow in the nearby fields and arable land; among the many clovers is a *Medica* [*Medicago polymorpha* L.] with dissected trifoliated leaves and many more, of which some have long and straight pods and others many curved pods in a cluster. Farther one finds one with many white and hoary heads [*Trifolium tomentosum* L.], which look like *Lagopodium,* and especially another little one with green-colored pods pressed together [*Medicago radiata* L.], as long and as broad as those of senna, which were a great ornament to the whole plant. Also hereabouts are found many kinds of cornflowers, quite different from ours; as also the horned *Papaver corniculatum* [Pall.] with many stately brown flowers. Also the cornpoppy [*Papaver rhoeas* L.], called *schuck* in their language, of which they make a conserve with sugar and use it for coughs.

One also finds there the little *Eryngium* [*E. tricuspidatum* L.], with bluish tops and starred heads, two kinds of henbane, of which the one that grows in the fields has red-purple colored flowers [*Hyoscyamus reticulatus* L.]; the others which I found in the town upon the old walls had white ones, called *Apollinaris* [*Hyoscyamus albus* L.] by the Latins. In the grain there grow any small *Melampyrum* [*Ceratocephalus falcatus* Pers.], called *paponesch* by them, which bear thick yellow flowers at the top that are very similar to the *Melampyrum tragi;* also the second kind of wild cumin [*Hypecoum procumbens* L.], with yellow flowers and long bended pods; the *Poterion* of Mattioli [*Astragalus poterium* Vahl.], called *megasac* by the inhabitants, which they put up in their rooms and chambers to keep them from being bewitched. Also a pretty sort of sage [*Salvia ceratopylla* L.], with small, wooly, and dissected leaves. Also a garden cypress with gold-colored flowers, *Scabiosa* [*S. cretica* L.], *Anchusa* [*Onosma echioides* L.], and a *Salvia* [*S. acetabulosa* L.], which has many roundish leaves and with purple-colored bells growing about their square stalks. In the bells are black seeds, like that of the *Melissa molucca* [*Moluccella laevis* L.] I found at Tripoli.

In the grain also grows *Leontopetalon* [*Leontice leontopetalum* L.], called *aslab* in their language, with its brown-colored round root and large leaves, which are roundish and very nearly divided as those of our *Paeonia*. The stalk, which is about a foot high and hollow, has more twigs at the top; the point of each twig bears many small purple and yellow flowers, which make roundish bladders that sometimes contain one, two, or more often, three seeds. The children used to play their tricks with them as they do with the flowers of *Papaver rhoeas* in our country. The great root they bruise and rub spots in clothes with it, which, as they say, they remove immediately.

With those in the grain also grows the true *Chrysogonum* of Dioscorides [*Leontice chrysogonum* L.], which is as high as the former and also very similar to it in its flowers, stalk, and roundish root, which is redder inside. Only the stalk is more slender and has more and longer shoots, at the end of which you see stately, yellow flowers, so that it is thicker and more spriggy than the other. Its pennated leaves (of which there are generally four that come from the root with long foot-stalks almost as slender as a thread), lie close to the ground, as you can easily imagine and each have their ribs, two and two leaves growing together, on each side, one after another, so that four of them stand together in a cross. They are darkish green and at the outside, where they are broader, very similar to oakleaves.

Now as these and others that grow in these countries are as yet very little known, so may also the following that grow in ploughed fields be reckoned among the unknown, which is very similar to the *Lycopsis* of Dioscorides [*Echium orientale* L.], for which it ought to be taken. This plant has a red coat and a straight stalk about two feet high, from which many strong and rough leaves spread themselves in a circle round about the root, as if it were from one center, not unlike the red or wild bugloss. They decrease a little by degrees as they grow higher and higher. Out of each of them, close to the stalk, sprout out over 20 side-branches with their own small leaves, as you see in the *Echium*. Between the leaves, very tender purple-colored flowers shoot out, which are whole within and divided into six small, long leaves, almost like those of the *Caryophillus montanus*.

At the beginning of February, I saw several kinds of hyacinths, and the oriental one [*Hyacinthus orientalis* L.] in the greatest quantity, which they call *zumbel* in their language. In April I saw another very pretty one, known to them by the name of *ayur* [*Hyacinthus* sp.], with the long and very small leaves of our *Phalangium*. It grows pretty high and bears four stalky flowers at the top. The leaves are very similar in shape and color to the three leaves that stand up in the little blue lilly. The root, in its color and roundness, is very similar to that of the tulip [*Tulipa gesneriana* L.], of which I have also seen a great number in these fields of purple and yellow colors. I have also found some meadow saffron [*Crocus sativus* L.] like our own and also another kind with nine or ten white saffronflowers, which sprout earlier in the spring in the grain, not as bare as ours, but between the leaves. The leaves are pretty thick, but narrower, longer, and more pointed than the above-mentioned. They also spread more about the ground and come from a white root surrounded with a brown-red skin and divided in the middle. It is called *kusam* in their tongue, but it is still called *surugen* [? *Colchicum illyricum* Stokes] by some others.

These and a great many more strange herbs I have found, but because they were unknown to me, I forbear to mention any more of them. But yet I cannot but describe one more to you in the taking of which I and my two comrades fell into great danger (as we often did, both of the Turks and the Moors), which need not all be related here. This is called *rhasut* and also *rumigi* [*Aristolochia maurorum* L.], by the inhabitants. It has a strong but unpleasant odor and about four stalks of a whitish color. At the root they are as tender and as small as a pack-thread, on which at each side grow seven or eight tender ash-colored leaves one against the other and distributed like those of ferns, except that they have round ears toward the stalk, like the small sage, and between the lowermost, which are a little more distant, are flowers like our *Aristolochia,* yet a great deal larger, of a more brownish color, and hanging on longer stalks. The root strikes very deep and is very similar to our pellitory, of a drying quality, and somewhat hot, as the bitter taste intimates . . .

I found about the river the other *Tragium* of Dioscorides [*Astragalus tragacanthoides* L.] in the ploughed ground and afterwards also in abundance on the hill, but generally in moist places near the spring that runs down the hill. Its root is whitish, pretty long, and slender, and from it some woody stalks spread themselves, not longer than a finger, on which grow many leaves toward the top. The leaves were long and had on each side of their ribs small leaves, one opposite the other, which were divided (just like the red saxifrage called *Trichomanes*) only somewhat longer and about the size of those of the *Asplenium*. They are (as the other) a delicately shaded green color inside, but on the outside and against the ground an ash-color and wooly, especially the small ones that are just sprouting out between the others. Out of these first-mentioned stems come first naked long stalks, upon which violet-brown flowers grow close together at

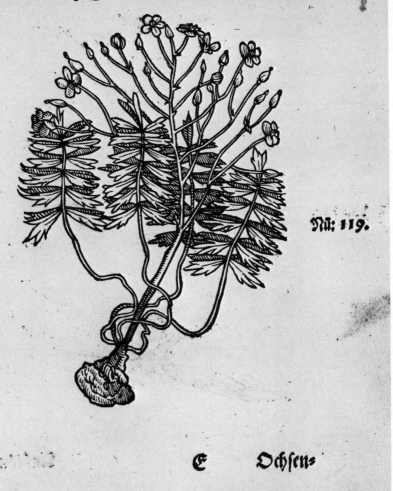

Ein frembds Kraut/welches für das rechte
Chryſogonum Dioſcor: zůhalten.

Nů: 119.

E Ochſen=

Fig. 3—*Leontice chrysogonum* L.

Ein frembds Kraut/ welches für das ander

Tragium Diosc: zůhalten: dessen auch Auic: vnder
dem namen Secudes vnd Sucudus gedencket.

Nů: 123.

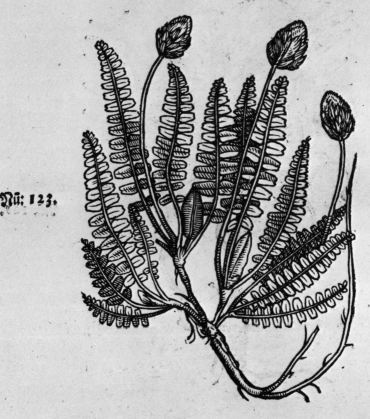

Schön

Fig. 4—*Astragalus tragacanthoides* L.

the top, as if it were an ear of grain. The inhabitants called it *secudes* and so did the ancient Arabs, especially Avicenna in his Chapter 679, where he also attributes the virtue that it is very useful for dysentery.

In their gardens the Turks love to raise all sorts of flowers, in which they take great delight and put them in their turbans, so I could see the fine plants one after another daily, without trouble. In December I saw our violets [*Viola odorata* L.] with dark-brown and white flowers, of which they gave me in that season several nosegays. Then came the tulips, hyacinths, narcissus [*Narcissus tazetta* L.], which they still call by the old name *nergies*.

Before all others, I saw a rare kind of narcissus with double yellow flowers, called *modaph* [*Narcissus* sp.], and a strange *Convolvulus* with leaves like the *Hedera helix* and great purple flowers [*Convolvulus nil* L.], out of which grew seed-vessels, as you see in the rue *Harmala,* with three distinct capsules, in which is kept its black seed, to which they attribute the virtue of evacuating slime. This is found sometimes in the gardens and is called *hasinsea* by the inhabitants, *acafra* by the Persians, *habalnil* by Serapion, Chapter 273, and *Granum Indicum* or *Carthamus Indicus* by the Latins; and he that wishes to know more about it, let him look into the author himself, in the above-mentioned place and in Chapter 306 of Avicenna and Chapter 208 of Rhazes. In their gardens I also found balm [*Melissa officinalis* L.], basil [*Ocimum basilicum* L.], and a fine sort of *Amaranthus* [*A. tricolor* L.], which for its color's sake may be the *Symphoniam* of Pliny and therefore called "parrot's feather."

I cannot forbear, before I conclude, to mention some which I found here and there in the bazaars, and among them a strange sort of white lilly [*Lilium candidum* L., var.] which I am told grows in sunny, moory, mossy, and moist places. On it grows a long stalk of the same color and thickness of ours, only a great deal broader, but broadest of all at the top where it is about three fingers broad, so that it is like a spatula that is pointed at one end. On each side of this stalk grow several tender leaves, which are pretty long, but very small and pointed, and at the top some white flowers like ours. On several occasions when I was thinking about what they were called by the ancients, it came to my mind that I had read of them in Theophrastus, Book 4, Chapter 9, and I really believe it to be the same. However, whereas Theophrastus writes in the quoted place [4.8.6] that they do not touch the ground, I cannot say, for I never saw any of them growing.

They also have some small roots to sell, called *Mamirani tchini* [*Mamira* of China; *Coptis teeta* Wall.], which is good for the eyes, as they say. They are yellowish like *Curcuma,* but a good deal longer, thinner, and knotted, and very similar to our *Poliganatum* and may be considered to be the true *Mamiran* of which Rhazes makes mention in several places. There is also among others a great quantity of the juice of scammony [*Convolvulus scammonia* L.], which is still very soft. It is brought in leather bags from out of the country, and so it is sold to our merchants in their fondacos. However, those that buy it must have great care that they are not cheated, for it is often adulterated.

There is also a good deal of the juice called opium by the apothecaries and *ofium* by the inhabitants, which the Turks, Moors, Persians, and other nations take inwardly not only in war, to make them courageous and valiant at the times when they go to fight their enemies, but also in time of peace to drive away melancholy and care, or at least to ease it. Their religious people also make use if it, and the dervishes above all the rest, and they take so much of it that it soon makes them drowsy and without feeling, so that when in their barbarous and silly way they cut, slash, or burn themselves, they may feel less smart or pain. If anyone has begun to make use of it (they take about the quantity of a large pea at a time), they cannot well leave off again unless they intend to throw themselves into sickness or other inconvenience, for, as they confess themselves, if they stop taking it, they find themselves very ill in their bodies.

Opium is usually taken from the white-poppy heads, called *cascasch* [*Papaver somniferum* L.] in their language, in which they cut (when they are young and tender) a little winding circle round about it, one under the other. Out of these runs some milk which they let remain there until it grows thick, then they gather it and make it into little balls, like our perfumed soap-balls in roundness and size. Because the Turks use this opium so commonly, it sometimes happens that they take so much of it that it is very dangerous. Therefore they have an antidote (as I was informed) in the good root called *aslab* [*Leontice leontopetalum* L.], of which I have made mention before, which they give to them as a special medicine.

I also found in the great bazaar a special sort of seaweed [*Algae* sp.] sold in their shops. This was dark red and therefore very useful for dyers. It had stalks of the thickness of a finger and was surrounded with several thin scales, or rather, it appeared, folded leaves packed together. Therefore it may be taken to be the *saderuam* of Serapion and the herb *alargiuan* of Andreas Bellunensis, of which he makes mention in his *Index,* where he interprets the Arabic words. Similar to this, because it yields a delicate purple color is that alga [*Fucus cartilagineus* L.] that is found in the seas near Crete and which is described by Theophrastus in the seventh chapter of his fourth book [4.6.5].

Lastly, among the rest, I also inquired about the *Amomum* [*A. aromati-*

cum Roxb.], thinking that because they were near the confines of Armenia, they might easily obtain it by means of the caravans which come daily from those parts. However, I was forced to look a great while for it, till at length I got a little stalk of it in one shop (they call it by the name of *hamama*). But of the other, called *Amomis* by Dioscorides [*A. subulatum* Roxb.], which is like it and therefore easily taken for the right one, they had a great deal. These two small shrubs, although they are very similar to each other, may be distinguished by their stalks and different colors. Therefore Dioscorides bids us (if we will not be imposed upon) to pick out the larger and smoother one with its noble seed and to leave the smaller. This stalk, which I found to be about the length of a finger, is almost the color of the bark of the cinnamon tree and also in its sharp odor and good color still very strong, although it was old. At the top had been several woody stalks, close to one another, on which I believe had been the flowers and the seeds. But the twigs of the other sort, which are cracked and bent, are of a brown color and at the top divide themselves into other smaller ones like a tree, on which grow several stalks with little heads, like the *Masaron* or better *Quendel romanum* [*Satureia capitata* L.] from Crete, in which is no great strength or odor.

APPENDIX II

PLANTS NAMED OR DESCRIBED BY RAUWOLF IN HIS TRAVEL BOOK AND IN THE FOURTH VOLUME OF HIS HERBARIUM

The sequence in the identification of plants is as follows:

I. Family name as based on identifications of Gronovius and Saint-Lager, who examined the herbarium, with authorities and modern names or variant readings added where necessary.

II. Rauwolf's term(s) in Latin or German.

III. Local name, if any, according to Rauwolf.

IV. Classical, medieval, or contemporary authority named by Rauwolf and their nomenclature, if given.

V. Place(s) where found and page(s) in Rauwolf's *Raisz*.

VI. Number of illustration in the 1583 edition of the *Raisz*.

VII. Page in Rauwolf's *Herbarium*.

VIII. Page in Appendix of Dalechamps' *Historia generalis plantarum*.

IX. Number in Gronovius' *Flora orientalis*.

Those plants, thirty-four in all, marked with an asterisk are identified as new discoveries by Kurt Sprengel, *Historia rei herbariae*, I, 378–380. Numbers 63, 93, 104, 141, 195, 213, 272, 275, 279, 281, 289, 315 are not found in Gronovius.

PLANTS NAMED OR DESCRIBED BY RAUWOLF

I	II	III	IV	V	VI	VII	VIII	IX
Family name	Rauwolf's term	Local name	Authority named by Rauwolf and nomenclature	Place found and page in *Raisz*	Number of illustrations in 1583 *Raisz*	Page in Herbarium	Page in Dalechamps	Page in Gronovius
EUMYCOPHYTA **Ascomycetes**								
ROCCELLIACEAE—Lichen Family								
1. *Roccella tinctoria* DC; *Fucus cartilagineus* L.	*Alga*		Theophrastus	Aleppo bazaar, 127				332
PHAEOPHYTA								
FUCACEAE—Algae Family								
2. *Algae* sp.	*Alga*		Serapion (saderuam), Avicenna (alargiuan)	Aleppo bazaar, 127				333
TRACHEOPHYTA **Filicinae**								
POLYPODIACEAE—Fern Family								
3. *Adiantum capillus-veneris* L.	*Adiantum, Capillus veneris*			Tripoli, 63				330
4. *Ceterach officinarum* Willd.	*Ceterach*			Mt. Lebanon, 286				331

Gymnospermae

PINACEAE—Pine Family							
5. *Cedrus libani* Barr.	Cederbaum			Mt. Lebanon, 280–281	33		295
6. *Pinus halpensis* Mill.	wilde Feuchtenbaum			Mt. Lebanon, 283		173	294
CUPRESSACEAE—Cyprus Family							
7. *Cupressus* sp.	ein frembdes Gummi	taxa (Persian)		Baghdad bazaar, 230			297
8. *Cupressus sempervirens* L.	Cypressenbaum	sarub, saru		Aleppo, 113		89	296
9. *Juniperus lycia* L.; *J. oxycedrus* L.	Oxicedros			Calderon (isle), 466		66	320
10. *Juniperus sabina* L.	Sabina baccifera			Tripoli, 59			321
EPHEDRACEAE—Ephedra Family							
11. *Ephedra distachya* L.	grösseren Poligino		Pliny (ephedra), Clusius	Tripoli, 56–57			322

Angiospermae (Monocotyledonae)

GRAMINAE—Grass Family							
12. *Andropogon nardus* L.	Spica nardi			Mt. Olives, 439			19
13. *Andropogon schoenanthus* L.	Camelhewes			Raqqa, 153, 160			20
14. *Avena sativa* L.	Habers			Aleppo, 71			21
15. *Arundo donax* L.	Rohr			Aleppo bazaar from India, 97			23
16. *Hordeum distichon* L.; *H. vulgare* L.	Gersten			Aleppo 71; 'Anah, 198; Mt. Lebanon, 274			26
17. *Phalaris arundinacea* L.	Rohrgrass	negil	Dioscorides	Baghdad, 230–231			24
18. *Phragmites communis* (L.) Trin. (*Arundo phragmites* L.)	Rohr		Dioscorides (Syringas, Fistularis)	Aleppo bazaar, 97			22

(continued on next page)

I	II	III	IV	V	VI	VII	VIII	IX
Family name	Rauwolf's term	Local name	Authority named by Rauwolf and nomenclature	Place found and page in *Raiz*	Number of illustrations in 1583 *Raiz*	Page in Herbarium	Page in Dalechamps	Page in Gronovius
19. *Saccharum officinarum* L.	Zuckerrohren			Tripoli, 55–56				18
20. *Sorghum vulgare* Pers.; *Holcus sorghum* L.	Indianischen Hirschen	dora	Rhazes, Serapion	'Anah, 198–199; Mt. Lebanon, 274–275	28	164		325
21. *Triticum vulgare* L.	*Triticum*			Dortona, 6; Mt. Lebanon, 274				25
22. *Zea mays* L.	Türckisches Korn			Bir, 137				287
CYPERACEAE—Sedge Family								
23. *Cyperus esculentus* L.	der Venediger Dulcigini	habel assis, altzis, grannis altzelem	Rhazes, Mattioli	Tripoli bazaar from Egypt, 63				16
24. *Cyperus rotundus* L.	*Cyperus*, wilde Galgand	soëdt		Baghdad, 229, 235	31	166		15
25. *Scirpus mucronatus* L.	*Iuncus maritimus*			Tripoli, 54		45		17
PALMAE—Palm Family								
26. *Phoenix dactylifera* L.	Datteln, Dattelbaumen			Tripoli, 24; 'Anah, 192, 194; Deir, 184; Hadithah, 200		193		334
ARACEAE—Arum Family								
27. *Arum tenuifolium* L.	*Arisarum*	homaidt		Aleppo, 115		99		286
28. *Colocasia antiquorum* Schott	*Colocassia*			Tripoli, 24; Aleppo, 73, 92; Nineveh, 245		35		285
29. *Dracunculus vulgaris* Schott	Schlange, Natterwurtz	luph		Aleppo, 115		94		284

No. & Species	German name	Vernacular	Source	Theoph. p.	Locality & references		
30. Calla orientalis L.	Arum	carsaami			Aleppo, 115	100	282
31. Calla orientalis L., var.	Arum	ovidae			Aleppo, 115	101	283
LILIACEAE—Lily Family							
32. Allium cepa L.	Zwybel	bassal			Tripoli, 24; Aleppo, 73		102
33. Allium sativum L.	Knobloch				Tripoli, 24; Aleppo, 73		101
34. Allium ursinum L.	Allium sylvestre				Aleppo	153	103
35. Aloe perfoliata L.	Aloe				Ramle, 315		119
36. Asparagus acutifolius L.	Aspargen				Marseilles, 10; Tripoli, 24		112
37. Asphodelus albus Mill.	Asphodelus albus	kusam,			Aleppo, 115		108
38. ?Colchicum illyricum Stokes	ein anderen geschlechts Zeitlosen	surugen			Aleppo, 121	150	122
39. Hemerocallis sp.	Hemerocallis				Tripoli, 54; Jaffa, 313		105
40. Hyacinthus orientalis L.	Hyacinthen	zumbel			Aleppo, 120; Baghdad, 213	143	115
41. ?Hyacinthus sp.	andere schöne Hyacinthen	ayur			Aleppo, 120	148	116
42. ?Hyacinthus sp.	Mertzenblumen				Baghdad, 213	146	117
43. ?Hyacinthus sp.	H. minor comosus peregrinus				Baghdad	149	118
44. Lilium bulbiferum L.	purpurfarbe Gilgen		Theophrastus	25	Gera, 5		104
45. Lilium candidum L.	weisse Gilgen			30	Aleppo, 125	159	106
46. Ornithogalum sulphureum Auct.	ornithogalum majus				Aleppo	154	110
47. Ornithogalum umbellatum L.	Feldzwibel				Aleppo, 115		111
48. Ruscus aculeatus L.	Ruscus				Brignola-Marseilles, 9		323

(continued on next page)

I Family name	II Rauwolf's term	III Local name	IV Authority named by Rauwolf and nomenclature	V Place found and page in *Raiz*	VI Number of illustrations in 1583 *Raiz*	VII Page in Herbarium	VIII Page in Dalechamps	IX Page in Gronovius
49. *Smilax aspera* L.	*Smilax aspera*			Brignola-Marseilles, 4; Tripoli, 56; Ramle-Jaffa, 461				316
50. *Smilax pseudo-china* L.	wurtzlen China			Aleppo bazaar from China, 96				317
51. *Tulipa gesneriana* L.	Tuliban			Aleppo, 120, 124; Mt. Lebanon, 282				107
52. *Urginea maritima* Baker	Möhrzwibel			Tripoli, 55				109
AMARYLLIDACEAE—Amaryllis Family								
53. *Narcissus* sp.	schönes geschlecht *Narcissos*	modaph		Aleppo, 124		156		98
54. *Narcissus tazetta* L.	*Narcissos*	nergies		Aleppo, 124; Baghdad, 213		155		99
DIOSCOREACEAE—Yam Family								
55. *Tamus communis* L.	*Vitis nigra*			Tripoli, 56				318
IRIDACEAE—Iris Family								
56. *Crocus sativus* L.	Saffran; blaw kleine Gilgen			Aleppo, 115; Baghdad, 216; Adriatic isle, 478				13
57. *Gladiolus communis* L.	Xyphium, Schwertel			Aleppo, 117; Tripoli, 52		118		14
58. *Ixia bulbocodium* L.	*Sisynrichium Theophrasti*		Theophrastus, Dodoens	Aleppo, 114				100

No. / Name	German	Local name	Classical author	Reference			
59. ?Sisyrinchium sp.	ein and's schöns gewächs	tharasalis		Aleppo, 114–115	93		279
MUSACEAE—Banana Family							
60. Musa sapientum L.	Musa Arabum	musa	Theophrastus, Pliny	Tripoli, 59–60; Baghdad, 232–233	66		324
ZINGIBERACEAE—Ginger Family							
61. Amomum aromaticum Roxb.	Amomum	hamama		Aleppo, 127–128			338
62. Amomum cardamomum L.	Cardamomlein			Aleppo bazaar from India, 96			2
63. Amomum subulatum Roxb.	Amomis		Dioscorides	Aleppo, 128			
64. Costus arabicus L. (C. speciosus Sm.)	Costus Syriacus	chast		Mt. Lebanon, 289			3
CANNACEAE—Canna Family							
65. Canna indica L.	Gummi Benzoin			Aleppo bazaar from India	68		1
(Dicotyledonae)							
PIPERACEAE—Pepper Family							
66. Piper longum L.	langer Pfeffer			Aleppo bazaar from India, 96			11
SALICACEAE—Willow Family							
67. Populus alba L.	weisse Papelbaum	haur		Dortona, 6; Tripoli, 58; Aleppo, 111			319
68. Populus euphratica Oliv.*	frembdes geschlecht der Weyden	garb	Avicenna	Euphrates, 160, 182–183, 201	161	26	307
						30	

(continued on next page)

257

I	II	III	IV	V	VI	VII	VIII	IX
Family name	Rauwolf's term	Local name	Authority named by Rauwolf and nomenclature	Place found and page in *Raiz*	Number of illustrations in 1583 *Raiz*	Page in Herbarium	Page in Dalechamps	Page in Gronovius
69. *Salix aegyptiaca* L; S. *Salsaf* Forsk. *	Weyden	safsaf	Theophrastus (Elaeagnos), Rhazes (zarneb), Avicenna (zarnabum), Serapion (zarumbeth), Paulos of Aegina (Arnabo)	Aleppo, 111–112; Ramle-Jaffa, 460	15	87	25	33
BETULACEAE—Birch Family								
70. *Corylus avellana* L.	Haselnutz			Aleppo, 76, 109				292
FAGACEAE—Beech Family								
71. *Quercus coccifera* L.	*Ilex minor, Ilex coccifera*			Marseilles, 8; Tripoli, 59				291
MORACEAE—Mulberry Family								
72. *Ficus carica* L.	Feygenbaum			Aleppo, 71; Mt. Olives, 439; Bethlehem, 457				328
73. *Ficus sycomorus* L.	wilde Feygenbaum	mumeitz		Tripoli, 57; Mt. Lebanon, 287	5	61	21	329
74. *Morus alba* L.	weisse Maulberbaum	tut		Tripoli, 36; Aleppo, 71–72; Ramle-Jaffa, 460		36		309

SANTALACEAE—Sandalwood Family								
75. Osyris alba L.	Cassia Monspeliensium	mackmudi, muckmisi, habel mickenes	Rhazes (auacsium)	Mt. Lebanon, 288				308
ARISTOLOCHIACEAE—Birthwort Family								
76. Aristolochia maurorum L.*	frembde Kreuter	rhasut, rumigi		Aleppo, 121	23	151	29	280
77. Aristolochia rotunda L.	Osterluccien			Simles (isle off Africa), 13				281
POLYGONACEAE—Buckwheat or Knotweed Family								
78. Rheum rhabarbarum L.; R. officinale Baill.	Rheubarbara			Aleppo bazaar from China through India, 96				129
79. Rheum ribes L.*	Ribes arabum			Aleppo, 266; Mt. Lebanon, 282	32	169, 170	32	130
CHENOPODIACEAE—Goosefoot Family								
80. Anabasis aphylla L.*	Kali Arabum	schinan		Tripoli, 37–38	2	32	20	73
81. Atriplex halimus L.	Portulaca marina			Tripoli		41		326
82. Atriplex laciniata L.	Atriplex marina			Tripoli		42		327
83. Salsola kali L.*	Tragum Dioscoridis, saltskruyt	schinan, usnen	Dioscorides	Tripoli, 37; Raqqa, 173	1	163		72
AMARANTHACEAE—Amaranth Family								
84. Amaranthus tricolor L.	Amaranthus, Symphonia Plinii		Pliny	Aleppo, 125		158		289
AIZOACEAE—Mesembryanthemum Family								
85. Glinus lotoides L.	Alsine exotica			Euphrates		165		143

(continued on next page)

I	II	III	IV	V	VI	VII	VIII	IX
Family name	Rauwolf's term	Local name	Authority named by Rauwolf and nomenclature	Place found and page in *Raiz*	Number of illustrations in 1583 *Raiz*	Page in Herbarium	Page in Dalechamps	Page in Gronovius
CARYOPHYLLACEAE—Pink Family								
86. *Lychnis viscaria* L.	*Lychnis sylvestris*		Clusius	Aleppo, 117		22		138
87. *Paronychia argentea* Lam.	*Paronychia Hispanica*		Clusius	Aleppo, 117		121		71
88. *Silene muscipula* L.	dritte *Lychnis*			Aleppo, 117		56		139
89. *Spergularia rubra* F. & C. Presl.; *S. media* G. & G.	*Polygonum marinum*			Marseilles, 9		14		140
RANUNCULACEAE—Buttercup Family								
90. *Adonis autumnalis* L.	*Oenanthes*					105		173
91. *Anemone* sp.	*Anemone*	sakai		Aleppo, 115	17		26	172
92. *Ceratocephalus falcatus* Pers.	*Melampyrum*	paponesch		Aleppo, 118		133		174
93. *Coptis teeta* Wall.	*Mamirani tchini*		Rhazes	Aleppo, 126				
BERBERIDACEAE—Barberry Family								
94. *Berberis vulgaris* L.	*Erbsichbeerlein*	berberis		Aleppo, 106; Mt. Lebanon, 281				120
95. *Leontice chrysogonum* L. *	*Chrysogonum Dioscoridis*		Dioscorides	Aleppo, 119	21	144	28	113
96. *Leontice leontopetalum* L.	*Leontopetalon*	aslab		Aleppo, 119, 127		143		114
MENISPERMACEAE—Moonseed Family								
97. *Menispermum cocculus* L.	*Cocculis orientalis*	doam samec		Bir, 140				123
MYRISTICACEAE—Nutmeg Family								
98. *Myristica fragrans* Houtt.	*Muscatnusz*			Aleppo bazaar from India, 96				336

LAURACEAE—Laurel Family

99. *Cinnamomum* spp.	Zimmetröslein				128
100. *Mimusops schimperi* Höchst.	*Persea*	sepha (Persian)	Aleppo bazaar from India, 96; Baghdad, 233	69	148*

PAPAVERACEAE—Poppy Family

101. *Glaucium* sp.	*Papaver corniculatum*		Nice, 8; Aleppo, 118	130	155a
102. *Glaucium* sp.	*Papaver corniculatum*		Nice, 8; Aleppo, 118	131	155b
103. *Papaver argemone* L.	*Anemone*	sakaick	Aleppo, 115	104	158
104. *Papaver corniculatum* Pall.	gehorneten Magsomen		Aleppo, 118		
105. *Papaver rhoeas* L.	Klapperrosen	schuck	Aleppo, 118		157
106. *Papaver somniferum* L.	weisse olnagens	cascasch, ofium	Aleppo bazaar, 126–127		156

CAPPARIDACEAE—Caper Family

107. *Capparis spinosa* L.	Capperen	cappar	Galeta (isle) 12; Cyprus, 20; Aleppo, 75, 113; Baghdad, 230	82	154a
108. *Capparis spinosa* L.	Capparenbaum				154b

CRUCIFERAE—Mustard Family or Crucifers

109. *Anastatica hierochuntia* L.	(Not in Rauwolf's *Raisz* or Herbarium, but attributed to him by Camerarius, *Hortus*, 147 and fig. 42 and by Morison, *Historia*, III, 328.)				193
110. *Anastatica syriaca* L.	(Not in Rauwolf's *Raisz* or Herbarium, but attributed to him by Ray, *Cat. Orient.*)				194
111. *Brassica botrytis* (L.) Mill.	Cauliflori		Tripoli, 24; Aleppo, 73		203b
112. *Brassica oleracea* L.	*Caulorapa*		Aleppo, 73		203c
113. *Brassica oleracea* L.	Cappiskraut		Tripoli, 24		203a

(continued on next page)

I	II	III	IV	V	VI	VII	VIII	IX
Family name	Rauwolf's term	Local name	Authority named by Rauwolf and nomenclature	Place found and page in *Raiz*	Number of illustrations in 1583 *Raiz*	Page in Herbarium	Page in Dalechamps	Page in Gronovius
114. *Brassica rapa* L.	Rüben			Tripoli, 24				204
115. *Cakile maritima* Scop.	*Raphanus marinus*			Tripoli		44		202
116. *Cochlearia armoracia* L.	Kren			Tripoli, 24				198
117. *Eruca sativa* Mill.	kleine Rauckelen			Aleppo, 118		124		206
118. *Farsetia clypeata* R. Br. (*Alyssum clypeatum* L.)	*Alyssum Dioscoridis*		Dioscorides	Mt. Lebanon, 283		175		199
119. *Lepidium draba* L.	*Draba Dioscoridis*		Dioscorides	Aleppo, 117		114		195
120. *Lepidium latifolium* L.	*Tarcon, Tragon*	cozirihan	Rhazes	Aleppo, 73		109		197
121. *Lepidium perfoliatum* L.	*Nasturtium peregrinum*			Aleppo				196
122. *Matthiola tricuspidata* (L.) R. Br.	*Leucoium marinum*			Tripoli, 54		43		200
123. *Nasturtium officinale* R. Br.	*Nasturtium aquaticum*		Pliny			18		205
124. *Raphanus sativus* L.	Rettich			Tripoli, 24; Aleppo, 73				201
RESEDACEAE—Mignonette Family								
125. *Reseda lutea* L.	*Rheseda Plinii*		Pliny	Aleppo, 115				171
CRASSULACEAE—Orpine Family								
126. *Cotyledon umbilicus* L.	*Umbilicus veneris*			Aleppo, 118		5		141
127. *Sedum album* L.	*Vermicularis fruticans*			Marseilles, 10				142

(continued on next page)

No. & Name	German name	Vernacular	Authority	Locality				Ref
SAXIFRAGACEAE—Saxifrage Family								
128. Chrysoplenium oppositifolium L.	Saxifraga aurea			Feldkirch, 3				127
129. Ribes rubrum L.	S. Johanns Treublein			Aleppo, 72				66
130. Ribes uva-crispa L.	Krausselbeer			Aleppo, 72				65
PLATANACEAE—Plane-tree Family								
131. Platanus orientalis L.	Ahornebaum			Mt. Lebanon, 276				293
ROSACEAE—Rose Family								
132. Amygdalus communis L.	Mandelbaum			Tripoli, 24; Haditha, 200; Aleppo, 71				146a
133. Amygdalus communis L.	wilde Mandelbaum	lauzi, laus		Aleppo, 71, 113		90		146b
134. Amygdalus persica L.	Pfersich	hel (Persian)		Aleppo, 72; Baghdad, 233				147
135. Cerasus vulgaris Mill. (Prunus cerasus L.)	Amarellen			Aleppo, 72				148
136. Crataegus oxyacantha L.	Oxyacantha			Tripoli, 23				150
137. Cydonia vulgaris Pers.	Quittenbaum			Tripoli, 71				152
138. Geum montanum L.	Cariophyllata alpina			Feldkirch, 3				153
139. Poterium spinosum L. * (Sanguisorba spinosa Berthol.)	Hippophaes Dioscoridis	bellan	Dioscorides	Mt. Lebanon, 286	39	185	34	290
140. Sorbus aucuparia L.	wilde Speirlingbaum			Mt. Lebanon, 276				151
LEGUMINOSAE—Pea and Pulse Family								
141. ?Anthyllis vulneraria L.	Anthillis marina			Tripoli, 56				222
142. Astragalus christianus L.*	Christiania radix, Cices de montaigne			Aleppo, 116		112		227
143. ?Astragalus coluteoides (L.) Willd. *	Tragacantha		Clusius	Mt. Lebanon, 281	34	174	32	223
144. Astragalus hamostus L.	Securidaca minor			Tripoli, 55				

	I	II	III	IV	V	VI	VII	VIII	IX
	Family name	Rauwolf's term	Local name	Authority named by Rauwolf and nomenclature	Place found and page in *Raiz*	Number of illustrations in 1583 *Raiz*	Page in Herbarium	Page in Dalechamps	Page in Gronovius
145.	*Astragalus poterium* Vahl.	*Poterium Matthioli*	megasec	Dioscorides, Mattioli	Aleppo, 118		135		226
146.	*Astragalus syriacus* L.	*Astragalus Dioscoridis*		Dioscorides	Aleppo, 116		111		214
147.	*Astragalus tragacantha* Pall.; *A. massiliensis* Lmk.	*Tragacantha*		Rondelet	Marseilles, 9	18	12	26	225
148.	*Astragalus tragacanthoides* L. *	das andere *Tragium Dioscoridis*		Dioscorides, Avicenna (secudus, secudes)	Aleppo, 123–124	24	152	29	224
149.	*Calycotome spinosa* Link.	*Aspalatum*, die andere *Acaiam*			Marseilles, 8; Mt. Lebanon, 285–286		184		212
150.	*Ceratonia siliqua* L.	St. Johanns brot, *Keratia, Keratonia, siliqua*	charnubi		Tripoli, 24; Mt. Olives, 439; Jerusalem, 458; Ramle-Jaffa, 460		195		315
151.	*Cercis siliquastrum* L.	Baumlein Iuda, wilde St. Jans brood			Mt. Lebanon, 284		176		131
152.	*Cicer arietinum* L.	Kicheren Erbis, Cicern, Ziserbsen, Eiserbisz, *Cicer arietinum*	cotane, ormos	Avicenna (hamos)	Aleppo, 75, 109; Bethlehem, 449		84		220
153.	*Cytisus nigricans* L.	*Pseudocytisus*							219
154.	*Galega officinalis* L.	*Galega*, Gayszrauten			Aleppo, 114; Bir, 137; Euphrates, 160; Raqqa, 174		7		213

No. Name								
155. *Guilandina moringa* L. (*Moringa pterygosperma* Gaetrn.)	Baumlein	machaleb	Serapion (nahandt)	Baghdad bazaar, 229–230				335
156. *Hedysarum alhagi* Lerch.* (*Alhagi camelorum* Fisch.)	Agul	algul, alhagi	Avicenna	Aleppo, 94; Raqqa, 173; Baghdad, 208	14	85	24	228
157. *Hippocrepis unisiliquosa* L.	Sferra Cauallo			Tripoli, 58–59				229
158. *Indigofera tinctoria* L.	Indich			Aleppo bazaar from India, 96				237
159. *Lens esculenta* Moench	Orobos	ades, hades		Aleppo, 76, 116				221
160. *Medicago marina* L.	Medica marina			Marseilles, 9; Tripoli, 53–54		39		230
161. *Medicago polymorpha* L.	Medica	cot, alfassasa		Aleppo, 118		175		233
162. *Medicago radiata* L.	Kleekreuter			Aleppo, 118		128		231
163. *Medicago sativa* L.	Medica, Foin de Bourgogne			Tripoli		52		232
164. *Mimosa nilotica* L.	*Acatia*	schack, schamuth	Dioscorides	Aleppo, 114; Bir, 138; Raqqa, 173; Felugia-Baghdad, 208		92		159
165. *Phaseolus mungo* L.	unbekandtes gewächs	mas	Serapion (mes), Avicenna (meisce), Clusius	Aleppo, 76				217
166. *Phaseolus vulgaris* L.	Phaseoln			Aleppo, 75				215a
167. ?*Phaseolus vulgaris* L., var.	kleine Phaseoln			Aleppo, 75				215b
168. *Psoralea bituminosa* L.	*Trifolium asphaltites*			Marseilles, 9				236
169. *Spartium junceum* L.	*Spartium*			Ramle-Jaffa, 460				211
170. *Trigonella corniculata* L.	Kleekreuter			Aleppo, 118		126		234
171. *Trifolium tomentosum* L.	Kleekreuter			Aleppo, 118		127		235

(continued on next page)

I	II	III	IV	V	VI	VII	VIII	IX
			Authority named by Rauwolf and nomenclature	Place found and page in *Raiz*	Number of illustrations in 1583 *Raiz*	Page in Herbarium	Page in Dalechamps	Page in Gronovius
Family name	Rauwolf's term	Local name						
172. *Ulex europaeus* L.	*Scorpius*		Clusius	Mt. Lebanon, 281				218a
173. *Ulex provincialis* Loisel.	*Nepa*		Lobelius	Marseilles, 10				218b
174. *?Vigna sinensis* (L.) Savi	Türckische Phaseoln	lubie		Tripoli, 56		60		216
GERANIACEAE—Geranium Family								
175. *Geranium gruinum* L.	Storckenschnabel			Aleppo, 118		123		207
LINACEAE—Flax Family								
176. *Linum maritimum* L.	*Linum sylvestre*	bezercheten				63		97
ZYGOPHYLLACEAE—Caltrop Family								
177. *Peganum harmala* L.	*Harmala*	harmel		Aleppo, 115		108		165
178. *Tribulus terrestris* L.	*Tribulus terrestris*	haseck		Tripoli, 55		53		136
179. *Zygophyllum fabago* L.*	frembde Stauden	morgani	Avicenna (ardifrigi), Rhazes (andirian)	Aleppo, 113–114	16	91	25	132
RUTACEAE—Rue Family								
180. *Citrus aurantium* L.	Pomerantzen			Tripoli, 24, Aleppo, 72; Mt. Olives, 439; Bethlehem, 457				239
181. *Citrus limonium* Risso	Limon			Tripoli, 24; Aleppo, 72; Mt. Olives, 439; Bethlehem, 457				238b
182. *Citrus* sp.	*Poma Adami Mattioli*		Mattioli	Tripoli, 24; Aleppo, 72				238c

#	Species	German name	Arabic name	Authority	Locations				Page
183.	Citrus medica L.	Citron			Tripoli, 24; Aleppo, 72; Mt. Olives, 439; Bethlehem, 457				238a
184.	?Ruta graveolens L.	wilde Rauten	sedah		Marseilles, 9; Aleppo, 115		20		135
185.	Ruta montana Mill.	Ruta sylvestris secunda					21		134
BURSERACEAE—Burseria Family									
186.	Commophora sp.	Bdellium			Tripoli from Arabia, 32				337
MELIACEAE—Mahogany Family									
187.	Melia azedarach L.	hoher Baum	zenzelacht	Avicenna (azadaracht), Rhazes (astirgar, astergir)	Tripoli, 58; Aleppo, 113		63		133
EUPHORBIACEAE—Spurge Family									
188.	Chrozophora tinctoria (L.) A. Juss.	Heliotropium tricoccum		Clusius	Aleppo, 117		120		298
189.	Euphorbia chamaesyce L.	Chamaesycen frembdes doschets blumlein	tanaghut, sabeam	Rhazes (xabra, camarronus)	Raqqa, 173	8	162		161
190.	Euphorbia mauritanica L.				Tripoli, 62		72	22	160
191.	?Euphorbia Peplus L.	Peplium			Aleppo, 117		117		164
192.	Euphorbia paralias L.	Lactuca marina, Tithymalus Paralios			Marseilles, 9; Tripoli, 54				162
193.	Euphorbia Peplis L.	Peplis			Tripoli, 54		46		163
194.	Ricinus communis L.	Wunderbaum	kerua		Tripoli, 54		49		299

(continued on next page)

I	II	III	IV	V	VI	VII	VIII	IX
Family name	Rauwolf's term	Local name	Authority named by Rauwolf and nomenclature	Place found and page in *Raiz*	Number of illustrations in 1583 *Raiz*	Page in Herbarium	Page in Dalechamps	Page in Gronovius
ANACARDIACEAE—Cashew Family								
195. *Mangifera indica* L.	Mangas		Clusius	Baghdad, 232				310
196. *Pistacia lentiscus* L.	*Lentiscus, Lentisios* (mastix)			Brignola-Marseilles, 9; Ramle-Jaffa, 460				
197. *Pistacia narbonensis* L.	frembde Terebinthennuszlein, Indianische Terebinthi	botin, albotin quibir, terbaick (Persian), fael	Theophrastus, Serapion, Avicenna, Rhazes	Baghdad, 228; Mosul, 245; Ramle-Jaffa, 461	29	198	31	313
198. *Pistacia terebinthus* L.	*Terebinthus*			Brignola-Marseilles, 9; Tripoli, 59; Aleppo, 113; Mt. Olives, 439				311
199. *Pistacia vera* L.	*Pistachi* baum	fisluc		Sermin, 67; Aleppo, 72, 109	9	75		312
200. *Pistacia* sp.	frembde Terebinthennuszlein	botn sougier, bel	Serapion, Avicenna, Rhazes	Baghdad, 228; Mosul, 245; Ramle-Jaffa, 461	30	199	31	314
201. *Rhus coriaria* L.	Sumach	sumach		Tripoli, 63; Aleppo, 72; Ramle-Jaffa, 460		74		91
202. *Rhus cotinus* L.	*Cotynus Plinii*		Pliny	Mt. Brothum, 6				92
RHAMNACEAE—Buckthorn Family								
203. *Rhamnus spina-christi* L. (*Paliurus spina-christi* Mill.)	weisse Brustberleinbaum, dritte geschlecht *Rhamni*		Dioscorides, Theophrastus	Tripoli, 23; Ramle-Jaffa, 461		196, 197		58
204. *Zizyphus vulgaris* Lam.	rote Brustberleinbaum	ennab, hanab		Marseilles, 10; Aleppo, 106		28		56

Entry	German name	Vernacular	Ancient source	Places	No.	No.	No.
205. *Zuzyphus vulgaris* Lam.	rottenbrust Beerlen-baum						57
VITACEAE—Vine or Grape Family							
206. *Vitis* sp.	wilden Weinräben, *Labrusca*			Tripoli, 56	29		64a
207. *Vitis vinifera* L.	Weingärten, Cibeben			Tripoli, 23, 37; Aleppo, 76; Mt. Lebanon, 274			64b
TILIACEAE—Linden or Basswood Family							
208. *Corchorus olitorius* L.	*Corchorus Plinii*	moluchi	Pliny, Avicenna	Aleppo, 75; 'Anah, 193	83		170
MALVACEAE—Mallow Family							
209. *Gossypium arboreum* L.	Bomwoll	cotum, bombax		Hama-Aleppo, 65; Bir, 137; 'Anah, 192	191		208
210. *Hibiscus sabdariffa* L.*	*Trionum, Trionos Theophrasti* [sic]	lubie endigi	Theophrastus [sic]	'Anah, 193; Ramle-Jaffa, 461	200	31	210
211. *Hibiscus syriacus* L.	Papelen	chethmie		Tripoli, 62; Aleppo, 69	71		209
GUTTIFERAE—Garcinia Family							
212. *Hypericum coris* L.	*Coris Matthioli*		Mattioli	Aleppo, 117	122		240
213. *Hypericum crispum* L.	S. Johanns kreutlein			Mt. Lebanon-Tripoli, 286			
TAMARICACEAE—Tamarix Family							
214. *Tamarix aegyptiaca* Bertol.	Tamariskenbaum	tharse, athel		Euphrates, 146, 160	19	27	94
215. *Tamarix gallica* L.	Tamarisken			Marseilles, 9			93
CISTACEAE—Rock-rose Family							
216. *Cistus monspeliensis* L.	*Ladanum*			Nice, 8			168
217. *Cistus salvifolius* L.	*Cistus*			Marseilles, 8			167

(continued on next page)

I	II	III	IV	V	VI	VII	VIII	IX
Family name	Rauwolf's term	Local name	Authority named by Rauwolf and nomenclature	Place found and page in *Raiz*	Number of illustrations in 1583 *Raiz*	Page in Herbarium	Page in Dalechamps	Page in Gronovius
218. *Helianthemum hirtum* Pers.	ein geschlecht *Ladani*		Clusius	Marseilles, 8				169
219. *Helianthemum vulgare* Gaertn.	*Flos solis*			Aleppo, 115		102		166
VIOLACEAE—Violet Family								
220. *Viola odorata* L.	Mertzen Violen			Aleppo, 124; Baghdad, 213				278a
221. *Viola odorata* L.	Mertzen Violen			Aleppo, 124				278b
THYMELAEACEAE—Mezereum Family								
223. *Passerina orientalis* Willd.	*Sanamunda*		Clusius	Mt. Lebanon, 281		25		126
223. *Passerina tarton-raira* DC.	Tartenrayre			Marseilles, 10				125
ELAEAGNACEAE—Oleaster Family								
224. *Elaeagnus augustifolia* L.* (*E. hortensis* Bieb.)	*Elaeagnus Matthioli*	seiseūn	Mattioli	Aleppo, 112; Mt. Lebanon, 276		88		34
LYTHRACEAE—Loosestrife Family								
225. *Lawsonia inermis* L.*	Baumlein	alcanna, henne, schenna (Grk.)		Tripoli from Egypt, 60	7	70		124
PUNICACEAE—Pomegranate Family								
226. *Punica granatum* L.	Granatöpffel, Granaten			Tripoli, 23; Aleppo, 72, 113; 'Ain Tab, 261; Bethlehem, 457		33		144
MYRTACEAE—Myrtle Family								
227. *Myrtus communis* L.	Mirtenbeer	ass		Tripoli, 32; Aleppo, 72		38		145

UMBELLIFERAE—Carrot Family

No. & Latin name	Synonym	Other name	Reference	Locality				
228. Ammi visnaga (L.) Lam.	Visnaiga	kelle		Tripoli, 56; Mt. Lebanon, 285		55		83
229. Apium graveolens L.	Eppich			Tripoli, 24; Aleppo, 73				90
230. Artedia squamata L.*	Gingidium		Dioscorides	Mt. Lebanon, 287	38	186	34	81
231. Bupleurum fruticosum L.	Seseli aethiopicum			Marseilles, 10		27		77
232. Coriandrum sativum L.	Römische Coriander			Aleppo, 106				86
233. Daucus carota L.	gelbe und weisse Ruben			Aleppo, 73, 109				82
234. Eryngium campestre L.	Eryngium, Panicault			Marseilles, 9		15		75
235. Eryngium maritimum L.	Eryngium marinum			Aleppo, 118		16		74
236. Eryngium tricuspidatum L.	Brachendistel			Tripoli, 24		76		76
237. Foeniculum vulgare Mill.	Fenchel							89
238. Hypecoum procumbens L.	wilde Kümmichs			Aleppo, 118				36
239. Molospermum cicutarium DC.	Seseli Peloponnesia-cum		Dioscorides	Brignola, 8		134		84
240. Pastinaca secacul Soland.*	Gerelen	secacul		Aleppo, 74	13	80	23–24	79
241. Scandix pecten-veneris L.	Pecten Veneris			Tripoli, 58				87
242. Seseli sp.	Dauci Dioscoridis	zarneb melchi	Dioscorides	Aleppo, 116–117; Raqqa, 146				88
243. Siler trilobum Crantz	(Attributed to Rauwolf by Morison, *Historia*, III, 276)							85
244. Tordylium syriacum L.	Caucalidis			Syria		58		78
245. Turgenia latifolia (L.) Hoffm.	Caucalidis					57		80

ERICACEAE—Heath Family

No. & Latin name	Synonym	Other name	Reference	Locality				
246. Arbutus unedo L.	Arbutus			Ramle-Jaffa, 460				137

PRIMULACEAE—Primula Family

No. & Latin name	Synonym	Other name	Reference	Locality				
247. Coris monspeliensis L.	Coris Monspeliensium			Marseilles, 9				55
248. Lysimachia vulgaris L.	gelbe Weyderich			Tripoli, 56				41
249. Primula auricula L.	Auricula ursi			Feldkirch, 3				40

(continued on next page)

	I	II	III	IV	V	VI	VII	VIII	IX
				Authority named by Rauwolf and nomenclature	Place found and page in *Raiz*	Number of illustrations in 1583 *Raiz*	Page in Herbarium	Page in Dalechamps	Page in Gronovius
	Family name	Rauwolf's term	Local name						
PLUMBAGINACEAE—Plumbago or Leadwort Family									
250. *Plumbago europaea* L.		Dentillaria			Marseilles, 9				42
251. *Statice limonium* L.		Limonium					189		95
252. *Statice sinuata* L.*		Limonium			Jaffa, 313, 314	41	190		96
STYRACACEAE—Storax Family									
253. *Styrax officinale* L.		Styrax	astarach		Mt. Lebanon, 276; Ramle-Jaffa, 460		171		149
OLEACEAE—Olive Family									
254. *Jasminum fruticans* L.		Polemonium Monspeliensium		Dodoens	Brignola-Marseilles, 8				4
255. *Olea europaea* L.		Olea, Oelbäume			Tripoli, 58; Aleppo, 71; 'Anah, 192; Mt. Lebanon, 274; Mt. Olives, 439; Bethlehem, 456; Ramle-Jaffa, 460				6
256. *Phillyrea media* L.		Phillyrea			Tripoli, 23; Mt. Lebanon, 276				5
LOGANICEAE—Logania Family									
257. *Strychnos nux-vomica* L.		Nuces Vomicae	cutschula		Tripoli from Antioch, 289–290				61
APOCYNACEAE—Dogbane Family									
258. *Nerium oleander* L.		Oleander	clefte		Tripoli, 56; Mt. Lebanon, 285				67

ASCLEPIADACEAE—Milkweed Family

259. Cynanchum acutum L.	Scammonium Montpeliense	meudheudi	Rhazes (coriziola)	Tripoli, 54		47		70
260. Marsdenia erecta (L.) R. Br.	Hundsköl, erste Apocynum			Tripoli, 56; Bir, 137				69
261. Periploca graeca L.	Apocynum repens		Pliny	Mt. Lebanon, 285				68

CONVOLVULACEAE—Morning-glory Family

262. Convolvulus cneorum L.	Cantabrica		Clusius, Pliny	Tripoli, 54		50		43
263. Convolvulus nil L.	frembde Winde, Granum Indicum, Carthamus Indicus	hasnisea, acafra (Pers.)	Serapion (hab-alnil), Avicenna, Rhazes	Aleppo, 124–125		157		44
264. Convolvulus scammonia L.	Scammonia			Aleppo bazaar, 126; Bir, 138				46
265. Convolvulus soldanella L.; C. imperati Vahl.*	Möhrköl			Tripoli, 54	4	48	20	47
266. Cuscuta europaea L.	Filtzkraut			Aleppo, 94				35
267. Ipomoea turpethum R. Br.	Turbith			Aleppo bazaar from India, 96				45

BORAGINACEAE—Borage Family

268. Cordia myxa L.	Sebesten	myxa, myxaria, malcita		Tripoli, 24; Aleppo, 72		37		121
269. Echium orientale L.; E. italicum L.*	Lycopsis Dioscoridis		Dioscorides	Aleppo, 120	22	145	28	38
270. Heliotropium europaeum L.	Heliotropium maius			Tripoli		59		37
271. Onosma echioides L.	Anchusa			Aleppo, 119		141		39

VERBENACEAE—Verbena Family

272. Verbena officinalis L.	Sacrum herbam Dioscoridis		Dioscorides Clusius	Raqqa, 173				

(continued on next page)

I	II	III	IV	V	VI	VII	VIII	IX
Family name	Rauwolf's term	Local name	Authority named by Rauwolf and nomenclature	Place found and page in *Raiz*	Number of illustrations in 1583 *Raiz*	Page in Herbarium	Page in Dalechamps	Page in Gronovius
273. *Vitex agnus-castus* L.	*Agnus castus,* kleinere Schaffsmüle	bergerchest		Aleppo, 113; Raqqa, 174		86		191
LABIATAE—Mint Family								
274. *Calamintha officinalis* Moench	*Calamintha montana*			Brignola-Marseilles, 9				185
275. *Clinopodium vulgare* L.	*Clinopodium*		Dioscorides	Tripoli, 59				178
276. *Lavandula stoechas* L.	*Stoechas*			Brignola, 8				179
277. *Marrubium peregrinum* L.	*Marrubium Creticum*		Lobelius	Mt. Lebanon, 283				184
278. *Melissa officinalis* L.	*Melissa*			Aleppo, 125				
279. *Mentha* sp.	ein schönes frembdes [Gewächs]		Dioscorides (Polycnemon)	Raqqa, 173–174				
280. *Molucella laevis* L.	*Melissa moluca*			Tripoli, 56				181
281. *Ocimum basilicum* L.	*Basilien*			Aleppo, 125				
282. *Origanum creticum* L.	*O. onite,* frembde Wolgemut			Mt. Lebanon, 285; Mt. Olives, 439; Ramle-Jaffa, 461		187		186
283. *Phlomis lychnitis* L.	Wullkraut			Aleppo, 115		95		180
284. *Salvia acetabulosa* L.	Salbey			Aleppo, 119		142		10
285. *Salvia ceratophylla* L.	Scharlach			Aleppo, 119		136		9
286. *Salvia horminum* L.	*Orminum sativum*		Dioscorides	Aleppo		137		8
287. *Satureia capitata* L.	*Thymum,* Römische Quendel	sathar, hasce	Dioscorides	Tripoli, 59; Bethlehem, 456; Ramle-Jaffa, 461		65		176
288. *Satureia thymbra* L.	*Satureiae Dioscoridis*		Dioscorides	Tripoli, 59				177
289. *Teucrium chamaedrys* L.	*Chamaedryn*			Mt. Lebanon, 286				

No. & Species	Common name	Other names	Authority	Locality				Page
290. *Teucrium polium* L.	*Polium montanum*			Tripoli, 58; Mt. Lebanon, 283				175
291. ?*Thymus mastichina* L.	*Tragoriganum*			Mt. Olives, 439; Bethlehem, 456				182
292. ?*Thymus tragoriganum* L.	andere *Tragoriganum*		Clusius	Mt. Lebanon, 286				183
SOLANACEAE—Nightshade Family								
293. *Hyoscyamus albus* L.	*Apollinaris*, weisse Bülsen			Tripoli, 63; Aleppo, 118		73		52
294. *Hyoscyamus niger* L.	Dolkraut			Tripoli, 54				50
295. *Hyoscyamus reticulatus* L.	Bülsen Kreuter			Aleppo, 118		132		51
296. *Lycium europaeum* L.	*Rhamnus*	hauseit, hausegi, alhausegi, nausegi	Clusius	Tripoli, 58; Euphrates, 160; Jerusalem, 381		160		59
297. *Lycium* sp.	*Lycium*	zaroa, hadhadh	Dioscorides	Mt. Lebanon, 285; Ramle-Jaffa, 460	36	192		60
298. *Mandragora officinarum* L.	Alrauns			Calderon (isle), 466				53
299. *Solanum insanum* L.; *S. incanum* L.*	schwartze *Melantzana*	bathleschain	Averrhoes	Aleppo, 73	11	79	23	62
300. *Solanum melongena* L.*	*Melantzana*	melongena, bedengian		Aleppo, 73	10	78	23	63
SCROPHULARIACEAE—Figwort Family								
301. *Gratiola officinalis* L.	*Gratiola*			Marseilles, 9				7
302. *Linaria cymbalaria* Mill.	*Cymbalaria*			Gera, 5				188
303. *Rhinanthus crista-galli* L.	Hanenfusz			Feldkirch, 3				187
304. *Verbascum sinuatum* L.	Wullkraut			Marseilles, 9				54
PEDALIACEAE—Pedalium Family								
305. *Sesamum indicum* L.	*Sesamum*	samsaim		Tripoli, 24; Aleppo, 106; Felugia, 137		34		190

(continued on next page)

I	II	III	IV	V	VI	VII	VIII	IX
Family name	Rauwolf's term	Local name	Authority named by Rauwolf and nomenclature	Place found and page in *Raiz*	Number of illustrations in 1583 *Raiz*	Page in Herbarium	Page in Dalechamps	Page in Gronovius
OROBANCHACEAE—Broom-rape Family								
306. *Orobanche rapum* Reichb.	*Orobanche*	halinu		Aleppo, 117				189
GLOBULARIACEAE—Globularia Family								
307. *Globularia alypum* L.	*Alypum*			Mt. Lebanon		177		27
ACANTHACEAE—Acanthus Family								
308. *Acanthus spinosus* L.*	welsche Berenklaw			Mt. Lebanon, 285		182		192
PLANTAGINACEAE—Plantain Family								
309. *Plantago albicans* L.	*Holostium monspeliense*					4		30
310. *Plantago lagopus* L.*	*Catanances Dioscoridis*		Dioscorides	Marseilles, 10	6	31	21	32
311. *Plantago psyllium* L.	*Psyllium*			Marseilles, 10		26		31
RUBIACEAE—Madder Family								
312. *Coffea arabica* L.*	ein gut getranck	chaube	Avicenna (buncho), Rhazes (bunca)	Aleppo, 102–103				49
VALERIANACEAE—Valerian Family								
313. *Rubia tinctorum* L.	Ferberröte			Marseilles, 8				29
314. *Centranthus ruber* DC.	roten Balduam		Dodoens	Marseilles, 10		30		12
315. *Nardostachys jatamansi* DC.	*Spicanardi*			Aleppo from India, 96				
DIPSACACEAE—Teasel Family								
316. *Scabiosa cretica* L.	*Scabiosa*			Tripoli, 56; Aleppo, 119		139		28

Species	German names	Arabic names	Authority	Localities				
CURCURBITACEAE—Gourd Family								
317. *Citrullus vulgaris* Schrad.	Indische Melonen, *anguriae*	baticchas	Serapion (dullaha)	Tripoli, 24, 184; Aleppo, 73; Ramle, 316				305
318. *Colocynthis vulgaris* Schrad.	Colocynthen, Coloquintöpfel, wilde Kürbisöpflen	handhel, handhal		Euphrates, 202; Felugia-Baghdad, 208; Baghdad, 229				304
319. *Cucumis* sp.	Schlang Cucumeren	gette		Aleppo, 73		77		302
320. *Cucumis sativus* L.	Cucumeren			Deir, 184				301
321. *Cucumis Melo* L.	Melones			Tripoli, 24				303
322. *Curcurbita lagenaria* L.	Cürbsen, Kürbsen			Tripoli, 24; Aleppo, 73; Deir, 184				306
333. *Ecballium elaterium* (L.) A. Rich.	wilde Cucumeren	adiural hamar		Aleppo, 117				300
CAMPANULACEAE—Bellflower Family								
324. *Michauxia campanuloides* L'Herit.*	das rechte *Medium Dioscoridis*		Dioscorides (*medium*), Rhazes (mindium)	Mt. Lebanon, 284	35	180	33	48
COMPOSITAE—Composite Family								
325. *Ambrosia maritima* L.	*Ambrosia*		Renaudet	Marseilles, 9				288
326. *Artemisia dracunculus* L.	*Tragon*	tarchon	Rhazes	Tripoli, 24; Aleppo, 73				258
327. *Artemisia judaica* L.*	*Absinthium santonicum*	scheha		Bethlehem, 456	42		36	259
328. *Anthemis valentina* L.	*Buphthalmum, Oculus bovis*	bihaa				54		271
329. *Bidens tripartita* L.	*Cannabina, Eupatorium*					167		255

(continued on next page)

I	II	III	IV	V	VI	VII	VIII	IX
Family name	Rauwolf's term	Local name	Authority named by Rauwolf and nomenclature	Place found and page in Raix	Number of illustrations in 1583 Raix	Page in Herbarium	Page in Dalechamps	Page in Gronovius
330. *Carthamus corymbosus* L.	*Chamaeleon niger,* schwartze Chamaeleonen		Dioscorides	Tripoli, 59; Mt. Lebanon, 285		183		250
331. *Carthamus tinctorius* L.	wilder garten Saffran							254
332. *Centaurea Behen* L.*	frembdes Kraut	behen abiad, behmen abiad		Aleppo, 106; Mt. Lebanon, 288	40	188	35	273
333. *Centaurea calcitrapa* L.	*Carduus stellatus*			Aleppo		115		275
334. *Centaurea solstitialis* L.	*Spina solstitialis*			Aleppo, 117		116		276
335. *Chondrilla juncea* L.	*Chondrilla Viminea*			Marseilles, 10		23		241
336. *Chrysanthemum vulgare* Bernh. (*Tanacetum vulgare* L.)	grössern Maszlieben			Feldkirch, 3				270
337. *Cichorium endiva* L.	Endiuien			Tripoli, 24; Aleppo, 73				248
338. ?*Conyza Dioscoridis* Desf. (*Pluchea Dioscoridis* DC.) *	Dürnwurtzel *Dioscoridis, Conyza*	thaun	Dioscorides	Tripoli, 54	3	51	20	268
339. *Crupina vulgaris* Cass.	*Scabiosa*			Aleppo				274
340. *Cynara scolymus* L.	Artischochi		Serapion (raxos)	Aleppo, 73		140		253
341. *Diotis candissima* Desf.	*Gnaphalium marinum*			Marseilles, 9; Tripoli, 54		40		257
342. *Doronicum plantagineum* L.	Würtzlein	hakinrigi, hakeuribi	Serapion (haronigi), Avicenna (durungi, durunegi)	Aleppo, 63				269

No.	Name	Synonym / German	Vernacular	Source	Location				Ref.
343.	Echinops sphaerocephalus L.	Carduus sphaerocephalus				24			249
344.	Erigeron tuberosus L.*	andere Chondrylla		Dioscorides	Aleppo, 117	113	20	27	266b
345.	?Erigeron tuberosus L.*	Chondrylla altera		Dioscorides	Aleppo, 117	112	19	27	266a
346.	Gundelia Tournefortii L.*	frembde Kreuter	hacub	Dioscorides	Aleppo, 74	81	12		251
347.	Helichrysum sanguineum (L.) Kostel.*	frembdes Kraut		Dioscorides (baccharis)	Mt. Lebanon, 285	18	37	33	262
348.	Helichrysum stoechas (L.) DC.	Stoechas citrina			Mt. Brothum, 6	3			260
349.	?Helichrysum sp.	Gnaphalion			Mt. Lebanon, 284	179			261
350.	Inula viscosa (L.) Ait.	Coniza maior			Marseilles, 10				267
351.	Lactuca sativa L.	Lattich			Tripoli, 24; Aleppo, 73				242
352.	Pallenis spinosa (L.) Cass.; Asteriscus spinosa G. & G.	Aster atticus luteus			Marseilles, 10				272
353.	Picris echioides L.	Sonchus asper				9			243
354.	Santolina chamaecyparissus L.	Pumila cupressus, Garbkraut			Tortona, 6	1			256
355.	Scolymus maculatus L.	Carduus, Scolymos		Theophrastus, Pliny		6			247
356.	Scorzonera hispanica L.	Scorzonera	corton		Aleppo, 115	97			244a
357.	?Scorzonera hispanica L.	Scorzonera			Mt. Lebanon, 282	98			244b
358.	Senecio cineraria DC.	Cineraria			Mt. Brothum, 6	2			277
359.	Silybum marianum (L.) Gaertn.	Mariendistel	bedeguard	Dioscorides	Aleppo, 117	117			252
360.	Sonchus maritimus L.	Hieracium marinum				11			246
361.	Sonchus oleraceus L.	Hasenfohl, Cicerbita				8			245
362.	Xeranthemum sp.	Asteris Attici		Dioscorides		103			263
363.	Xeranthemum sp.	Jacca			Mt. Lebanon, 283	129			264
364.	?Xeranthemum inapertum Mill.	Jacca			Mt. Lebanon, 283	178			265

APPENDIX III

EDITIONS OF RAUWOLF'S WORK

GERMAN

Leonharti Rauwolfen der Artzney Doctorn und bestelten Medici zu Augspurg. Aigentliche beschreibung der Raisz so er vor diser zeit gegen Auffgang inn die Morgenländer fürnemlich Syriam, Iudaeam, Arabiam, Mesopotamiam, Babyloniam, Assyriam, Armeniam, usw. nicht ohne geringe mühe unnd grosse gefahr selbs volbracht; neben vermeldung vil anderer seltzamer und denckwürdiger sachen/ die alle er auff solcher erkundiget/ gesehen und obseruiert hat. Alles in drey underschidliche Thail mit sonderem fleisz abgethailet/ und ein jeder weiter in seine sondere Capitel/ wie dero innhalt in zu end gesetztem Register zufinden. Laugingen: Leonhart Reinmichel, 1582. [CtY, NjP, NN, MB, PPAN]

Beschreibung der Reysz Leonhardi Rauwolffen der Artzney Doctorn/ und bestellten Medici zu Augspurg/ so er vor dieser zeit gegen Auffgang in die Morgenländer/ fürnemlich Syriam/ Judeam/ Arabum/ Mesopotamiam/ Babyloniam/ Assyriam/ Armeniam/ u. nicht ohne geringe Mühe und grosse Gefahr selbst vollbracht: Neben vermeldung viel anderer seltzamer und denckwirdiger Sachen/ die alle er auff solcher erkundiget/ gesehen und obseruiert hat. Alles in drey underschiedliche Theyl mit sonderem fleisz abgetheylet/ und ein jeder weiter in seine sondere Capitel/ wie dero Innhalt in zu end gesetztem Register zu finden. Frankfurt am Main: Christoff Raben, 1582. [ICU, MoSB]

Leonharti Rauwolfen/ der Artzney Doctorn/ und bestelten Medici zu Augspurg. Aigentliche beschreibung der Raisz/ so er vor diser zeit gegen Auffgang inn die Morgenländer/ fürnemlich Syriam, Iudeam, Arabiam, Mesopotamiam, Babyloniam, Assyriam, Armeniam, usw. nicht ohne geringe mühe unnd grosse gefahr selbs volbracht: neben vermeldung etlicher mehr gar schön frembden und auszländischen Gewächsen/ sampt jren mit angehenckten lebendigen contrafacturen/ unnd auch anderer denckwürdiger sachen/ die alle er auff solcher erkundiget/ gesehen und obseruiert hat. Alles in Vier underschidliche Thail mit sonderem fleisz abgethailet/

unnd ein jeder weitter in seine sondere Capitel/ wie dero jnnhalt in zu end gesetztem Register zufinden. Laugingen: Georgen Willers, 1583. [CtY, CU-M, DA, ICN, DLC, NCH, MH-A, MoSB, PHC, PPA in P; BM, BN] Separate title page and dedication for Part IV: *Der Vierte Thail Leonharti Rauwolfen/ der Arzney Doctorn/ etlicher schöner auzländischer Kreuter/ so uns noch unbekandt/ unnd deren doch bey den alten Medicis unnd in seiner Raysz in die Morgenländer gethon/ gedacht wirt/ artliche unnd lebendige contrafactur/ dem germainen nutz zu gutem/ in Truck verfertiget. Getruckt zu Laugingen durch Leonhart Reinmichel/ in verlegung Georgen Willers.* Forty-two woodcut illustrations of plants.
Reyssbuch des heiligen Landes, ed. Sigismund Feyerabend (Parts I–III only). Frankfurt am Main, 1584, 1609, and 1629; Nürnberg, 1659.

ENGLISH

A collection of curious travels and voyages in two tomes: The first containing Dr. Leonhart Rauwolff's Itinerary into the Eastern countries; as Syria, Palestine, or the Holy Land, Armenia, Mesopotamia, Assyria, Chaldea, etc. Translated from the High Dutch by Nicolas Staphorst . . . London: S. Smith and B. Walford, 1693. Edited by John Ray (1627–1705). [CU; BM, BN] Second edition, London: S. Smith and B. Walford, 1705. [CU]
Travels through the Low-countries, Germany, Italy, and France, with curious observations, natural, topographical, moral, physiological, etc. . . . By the Rev. John Ray, F.R.S. Vol. II: *A collection of curious travels and voyages containing Dr. Leonhart Rauwolf's journey into the Eastern countries . . . Translated from the original High Dutch by Nicolas Staphorst . . .* London: J. Walthoe, 1738. [CtY, CU, DLC, MB; BM, BN]

DUTCH

Seer aanmerkelyke reysen, na en door Syrien, 't Joodsche land, Arabien, Mesopotamien, Babylonien, Assyrien, Armenien, etc. In 't jaar 1573 en vervolgens, gedaan en beschreven door Leendert Rouwolff. . . . Nu aldereest uyt het Hoogduytsch vertaald. . . . In *Naaukeurige versameling der gedenkwaardigste reysen na Oost en West-Indien,* edited by Pieter van der Aa, deel 17, No. 2. Leyden: P. van der Aa, 1707. [CU, DLC; BM, BN] Second edition in *De aanmerkenswaardigste en alomberoemde zee-en landreizen,* ed. Pieter van der Aa, vol. 7, no. 16. Leyden: P. van der Aa, 1710. [CtY, CU, DLC] Third edition, Leyden, 1727. [DLC; BM]

EXCERPTS ONLY

Hanns Jacob Breuning von und zu Buochenbach. *Orientalische Reyss in der Turkey, etc. benanntlich in Griechenland, Egypten, Arabien, Palaestina, und Syrien.* Strassburg, 1612. According to E. Robinson and E. Smith, *Biblical Researches in Palestine, Mount Sinai and Arabia Petrae,* III (London, 1841), First Appendix, 14, "The author has occasionally copied Rauwolf."

Leonis Flamininus. *Itinerarium per Palaestinam, das ist eine mit vielen schönen curiositaeten angefüllte Reiss-Beschreibung, darinnen . . . viel merkwürdige und seltzame Begebenheiten von dess Türckischen Keysers Stats-Ration . . .* Rotenberg: N. von Millanau, 1681. The author copied the story of Rauwolf's pilgrimage with some omissions.

Max Pannwitz. *Deutsche Pfadfinder des 16. Jahrhunderts in Afrika, Asien und Südamerika,* pp. 122–138. Stuttgart, 1911.

BIBLIOGRAPHY

Adam, Melchior. *Vitae germanorum medicorum.* Frankfurt am Main, 1705.

Allgemeine deutsche Biographie. 56 vols. Leipzig, 1875–1912.

Andel, M. A. van. "Rembertus Dodonaeus and His Influence on Flemish and Dutch Folk-Medicine," *Janus,* 21 (1917), 163–173.

Arber, Agnes. *Herbals, Their Origin and Evolution: A Chapter in the History of Botany, 1470–1670.* Cambridge, Eng.: Cambridge University Press, 1938.

Astruc, Jean. *Mémoires pour servir à l'histoire de la faculté de médecine de Montpellier.* Paris, 1767.

Atkinson, Geoffroy. *La littérature géographique française de la renaissance. Répertoire bibliographique.* Paris, 1927.

——— *Les nouveaux horizons de la renaissance française.* Paris, 1935.

Avicenna (Ibn Sina). *Libri in re medica omnes.* Venice, 1564.

Babinger, Franz. "Leonhard Rauwolf, ein Augsburger Botaniker und Orientreisender des sechzehnten Jahrhunderts. Mit neuen Beiträgen zu seiner Lebensgeschichte," *Archiv für die Geschichte der Naturwissenschaften und der Technik,* 4 (1913), 148–161.

Bainton, Roland H. *Hunted Heretic: The Life and Death of Michael Servetus.* Boston: Beacon Press, 1953.

Balbi, Gasparo. *Viaggio dell' Indie orientali, di Gasparo Balbi, Gioielliero Venetiano.* Venice, 1590.

Bauhin, Johann. *Historia plantarum universalis.* 3 vols. Ebroduni, 1650–51.

Beckmann, Johann. *Literatur der älteren Reisebeschreibungen.* 2 vols. Goettingen, 1807–09.

Belon, Pierre. *Les observations de plusieurs singularitez et chose mémorables, trouvées en Grèce, Asie, Judée, Egypte, Arabie et autres pays estranges, rédigées en trois livres.* Paris, 1555.

Biographie nationale de Belgique, vols. V, VI (Brussels, 1876, 1878).

Blunt, Wilfrid. *The Art of Botanical Illustration.* London: Collins, 1950.

Boos, Heinrich. *Thomas und Felix Platter. Zur Sittengeschichte des XVI. Jahrhunderts.* Leipzig, 1878.

Bouron, Narcisse. *Les Druzes; histoire du liban et de la montagne haouranaise.* Paris: Berger-Levrault, 1930.

Bouwsma, William J. *Concordia mundi: The Career and Thought of Guillaume Postel, 1510–1581.* Cambridge, Mass.: Harvard University Press, 1957.

Bruneau, André. *Traditions et politique de la France au Levant.* Paris: F. Alcan, 1932.

Bullough, Vern L. "The Development of the Medical University at Montpellier to the end of the Fourteenth Century," *Bulletin of the History of Medicine,* 30 (1956), 508–523.

Camerarius, Joachim. *Hortus medicus et philosophicus.* Frankfurt am Main, 1588.

Campbell, Donald. "The Medical Curriculum of the universities of Europe in the sixteenth century with special reference to the Arabist tradition," *Science, Medicine and History,* 1 (London, 1953), 357–367.

Camus, Jules. "Historique des premiers herbiers," *Malpighia,* 9 (1895), 283–314.

Carruthers, Douglas. "The Great Desert Caravan Route, Aleppo to Basra," *Geographical Journal,* 52 (1918), 157–184.

Cartulaire de l'université de Montpellier. 2 vols. Montpellier, 1890–1912.

The Catholic Encyclopedia. 16 vols. New York, 1907–12.

Charrière, Ernst. *Négociations de la France dans le Levant.* 4 vols. Paris, 1848–60.

Chesneau, Jean. *Le Voyage de Monsieur d'Aramon, ambassadeur du Roy en levant.* Published by Ch. Schefer in *Recueil de voyages et de documents pour servir à l'histoire de la géographie depuis le XIIIᵉ jusqu'à la fin du XVIᵉ siècle,* vol. VIII. Paris, 1887.

Choulant, Ludwig. *Handbuch der Bücherkunde für die ältere Medicin.* Leipzig, 1841.

Corbière, Philippe. *Histoire de l'Église Réformée des Montpellier depuis son origine jusqu'à nos jours.* Montpellier and Paris, 1861.

Cotovico, Johannes van. *Itinerarium Hierosolymitanum et syriam.* Antwerp, 1619.

Crié, Louis. "Les Voyages de P. Belon et l'Egypt au XVIᵉ siècle," *Revue scientifique,* ser. 3, vol. 5 (1883), 197–203.

Dalechamps, Jacques. *Historia generalis plantarum.* Lyon, 1587.

Daniel, Norman. *Islam and the West: The Making of an Image.* Edinburgh: Edinburgh University Press, 1960.

Davies, Hugh W. *Bernhard von Breydenbach and his Journey to the Holy Land, 1483–4: A Bibliography.* London, 1911.

Delaunay, Paul. "L'Aventureuse existence de Pierre Belon du Mans," *Revue du seizieme siècle,* 9–12 (1922–25).

Dioscorides. *The Greek Herbal of Dioscorides,* trans. J. Goodyer (1655), ed. R. T. Gunther. New York: Hafner, 1959.

Dodoens, Rembert. *Florum et coronariarum odoratarumque nonnullarum herbarum historia.* Antwerp, 1569.

——— *A nievve herball, or historie of plants,* trans. H. Lyte. London, 1578.

——— *Cruydt-Boeck van Rembertus Dodonaeus.* Leyden, 1608.

Durling, Richard J. "Conrad Gesner's *Liber amicorum* 1555-1565," *Gesnerus* 22 (1965), 134–159.

Ehrenberg, Richard. *Das Zeitalter der Fugger: Geldkapital und Creditverkehr im 16. Jahrhundert,* vol. I. Jena: G. Fischer, 1912.

Elton, G. R., ed. *The Reformation, 1520–1559.* New Cambridge Modern History, vol. II. Cambridge, Eng.: Cambridge University Press, 1958.

Encyclopedia of Islam. 4 vols. and supplement. Leyden, 1913–38. New edition ed. H. A. R. Gibbs, J. H. Kramers, E. Lévi-Provençal, and J. Schacht. Leiden: Brill, 1960–.

Fabri, Felix. *The Wanderings of Felix Fabri.* Library of the Palestine Pilgrims' Text Society, vols. VII–X. London, 1896–97.

Foerstemann, C. E. *Album Academiae vitebergensis ab a. Ch. MDII usque ad a. MDLX.* 3 vols. Leipzig and Halle am Saale, 1841–1905.

Friedensburg, Walter. *Geschichte der Universität Wittenberg.* Halle am Saale, 1917.

Germain, Alexandre. *La Renaissance à Montpellier: Étude historique d'après les documents originaux avec pièces justificatives inédites.* Montpellier, 1871.

Gouron, Marcel. *Matricule de l'université de Médecine de Montpellier (1503–99).* Geneva: Droz, 1957.

Greene, Edward Lee. *Landmarks of Botanical History. Part I: Prior to 1562* A.D. *Smithsonian Miscellaneous Collections,* vol. 54. Washington, 1909.

Gronovius, Johann F. *Flora orientalis sive recensio plantarum quas botanicorum coryphaeus Leonhardus Rauwolffus . . . collegit.* Leyden, 1755.

Guiaud, L. *Le procès de Guillaume Pellicier, évêque de Magluelone-Montpellier de 1527–1567.* Paris, 1907.

Haddad, E. N. "Political Parties in Syria and Palestine (Qaisî and Yemenî)," *Journal of the Palestine Oriental Society,* 1 (1921), 209–214.

Hakluyt, Richard. *The Principal Navigations Voyages Traffiques and Discoveries of the English Nation.* 10 vols. London: J. M Dent, 1927–28.

Haller, Alberto von. *Bibliotheca Botanica qua scripta ad rem herbariam facientia a rerum initiis recensentur.* 2 vols. Zurich, 1771–72.

Hammer, Joseph von. *Geschichte des Osmanischen Reiches,* vol. IV. Pest, 1829.

Hamy, E.-T. "Le père de la zoologie française: Pierre Gilles d'Albi," in *Revue des Pyrénées,* 12 (1900), 561–588.

Harff, Arnold von. *The Pilgrimage of Arnold von Harff, Knight,* trans. and ed. M. Letts. Hakluyt Society, ser. 2, vol. 94. London, 1946.

Heyd, Uriel. *Ottoman Documents on Palestine, 1552–1615.* Oxford: Clarendon Press, 1960.

Hitti, Philip K. *Lebanon in History from the Earliest Times to the Present.* London: Macmillan, 1957.

Hommel, Fritz. *Ethnologie und Geographie des alten Orients.* München: C. H. Beck, 1926.

Hortus sanitatis. Gart der Gesundheit. Mainz, 1485.

Hunger, F. W. T. "Charles de l'Escluse (Carolus Clusius), 1526–1609," *Janus,* 31 (1927), 139–151.

—— *Charles de l'Escluse, Carolus Clusius, Nederlandisch kruidkundige, 1526–1609.* 2 vols. 's Gravenhage, 1927–42.

—— "Dodonée comme botaniste," *Janus,* 21 (1917), 153–162.

Hurewitz, J. C. *Diplomacy in the Near and Middle East: A Documentary Record, 1535–1919,* vol. I. Princeton: Princeton University Press, 1956.

James, Montague Rhodes. *The Apocryphal New Testament.* Oxford: Clarendon Press, 1924.

Jenkinson, Anthony. *Early Voyages and Travels to Russia and Persia,* ed. E. D. Morgan and C. H. Coote. Hakluyt Society, vol. 72. London, 1886.

Kiechel, Samuel. *Die Reisen des Samuel Kiechel,* ed. K. D. Haszler. Bibliothek des Litterarischen Vereins in Stuttgart, vol. 86. Stuttgart, 1866.

Knolles, Richard. *The Generall Historie of the Turkes from the first beginning of that Nation to the rising of the Othoman Familie.* London, 1603.

Krafft, Hans U. *Ein deutscher Kaufmann des sechzehnten Jahrhunderts: Hans Ulrich Krafft's Denkwürdigkeiten,* ed. Adolf Cohn. Goettingen, 1862.

—— Reisen und Gefangenschaft Hans Ulrich Kraffts, ed. K. D. Haszler. Bibliothek des Litterarischen Vereins in Stuttgart, vol. 61. Stuttgart, 1861.

Lambert, S. W., Wiegand, W., and Ivins, W. M. Three Vesalian Essays to Accompany the Icones Anatomicae of 1934. New York: Macmillan, 1952.

Laufer, Berthold. Sino-Iranica; Chinese Contributions to the History of Civilization in Ancient Iran. Pub. 201, Anthropological Series, vol. XV, No. 3. Chicago: Field Museum of Natural History, 1919.

Leclerc, Lucien. Histoire de la médecine arabe. 2 vols. Paris, 1876.

Leersum, E. C. van. "Rembert Dodoens (29 June, 1517–10 March, 1585)," Janus, 21 (1917), 141–152.

Legré, Ludovic. La botanique en Provence au XVIᵉ siècle: Léonard Rauwolff, Jacques Raynaudet. Marseilles, 1900.

Le Strange, Guy. Baghdad during the Abbasid Caliphate. Oxford: Clarendon Press, 1924.

—— The Lands of the Eastern Caliphate: Mesopotamia, Persia, and Central Asia from the Moslem conquest to the time of Timur. Cambridge, Eng.: Cambridge University Press, 1930.

—— Palestine under the Moslems: A Description of Syria and the Holy Land from A.D. 650 to 1500. Boston, 1890.

Linschoten, John Huyghen van. The Voyage of John Huyghen van Linschoten to the East Indies, 2 vols., edited by A. C. Burnell and P. A. Tiele. Hakluyt Society, vols. 70–71. London, 1885.

Lint, J. G. de. "Les Portraits de Rembertus Dodonaeus," Janus, 21 (1917), 174–181.

Longrigg, S. H. Four Centuries of Modern Iraq. Oxford: Clarendon Press, 1925.

Luckenbill, D. D. Ancient Records of Assyria and Babylonia. 2 vols. Chicago: University of Chicago Press, 1926–27.

Lybyer, Albert Howe. The Government of the Ottoman Empire in the time of Suleiman the Magnificent. Cambridge, Mass.: Harvard University Press, 1913.

M. J. B. E. "Notice sur la vie et les ouvrages de Rauwolf," Annales des voyages de la géographie et de l'histoire, 13 (1811), 96–110.

Mattioli, P. A. Opera quae extant omnia. Basel, 1674.

Menckenius, J. B. Scriptores rerum Germanicarum praecipue Saxonicarum, vol. I. Leipzig, 1728.

Meyer, Ernst H. F. Geschichte der Botanik, vol. IV. Königsberg, 1857.

Michaud, Joseph F. Biographie universelle, ancienne et moderne. 85 vols. Paris, 1811–28.

Miall, L. C. The Early Naturalists, Their Lives and Works. London: Macmillan, 1912.

Mieli, Aldo. Gli scienziati italiani, vol. I. Rome: Casa Editrice Leonardo da Vinci 1923.

Minadoi, Giovanni T. Historia della guerra fra Turchi, et Persiani, descritta in Quattro libri. Rome, 1587. English edition trans. Abraham Hartwell. London, 1595.

Mingara, A. "List of the Turkish Governors and High Judges of Aleppo from the Ottoman Conquest to A.D. 1747," Bulletin of the John Rylands Library, 10 (1926), 515–523.

Monardes, Nicholas. Joyfull Newes out of the Newe Founde Worlde written in

Spanish by Nicholas Monardes physician of Seville and englished by John Frampton, Merchant anno *1577*. 2 vols. London: Constable, 1925.

Montaigne, Michel de. *The Diary of Montaigne's Journey to Italy in 1580 and 1581*, trans. E. J. Trechmann. London: L. and Virginia Woolf, 1929.

Morison, Robert. *Plantarum historiae universalis oxoniensis seu Herbarum distributio nova*. 3 vols. Oxford, 1715.

Moryson, Fynes. *An Itinerary containing his ten yeeres travell through the twelve Dominions of Germany, Bohmerland, Sweitzerland, Netherland, Denmarke, Poland, Italy, Turkey, France, England, Scotland and Ireland*. 4 vols. Glasgow: J. MacLehose 1907–08.

Niceron, R. P. *Mémoires pour servir à l'histoire des hommes illustres dans la république des lettres*. 43 vols. Paris, 1727–45.

Niebuhr, Carsten. *Reisenbeschreibung nach Arabien und anderen umliegenden Ländern*. 3 vols. Copenhagen, 1774–1837.

Nissen, Claus. *Die botanische Buchillustration: Geschichte und Bibliographie*. 2 vols. in one. Stuttgart: Hiersemann, 1951.

—— *Die illustrierten Vogelbücher: Geschichte und Bibliographie*. Stuttgart: Hiersemann, 1953.

Oaten, Edward F. *European Travellers in India during the fifteenth, sixteenth and seventeenth centuries*. London: K. Paul, Trench, Trübner, 1909.

Occo, Adolph. *A Facsimile of the First Edition of the Pharmacopoeia Augustana*. Madison, Wis.: University of Wisconsin Press, 1927.

Omont, H. "Inventaire de la bibliothèque de Guillaume Pelicier, évêque de Montpellier (1529–1568)," *Revue des Bibliothèques*, 1 (1891), 161–172.

Orta, Garcia da. *Colloquies on the Simples and Drugs of India*, trans. Sir Clements Markham. London: H. Sotheran, 1913.

Ortelius, Hieronymus. *Ortelius redivivus et continuatus oder der Ungarischen Kriegs-Emporungen historische beschreibung*. Frankfurt am Main, 1665.

Paré, Ambroise. *The Apologie and Treatise of Ambroise Paré*, ed. Geoffrey Keynes. Chicago: University of Chicago Press, 1952.

Penrose, Boies. *Travel and Discovery in the Renaissance, 1420–1620*. Cambridge, Mass.: Harvard University Press, 1952; paperback edition, New York: Atheneum, 1962.

Pinkerton, John. *A General Collection of the Best and Most Interesting Voyages and Travels in all Parts of the World*, vol. X. London, 1811.

Platter, Felix. *Thomas und Felix Platters und Theodor Agrippa d'Aubígnés Lebensbeschreibungen*, ed. Otto Fischer. München: M. Mörike, 1911.

—— *Beloved Son, Felix. A Journal of Felix Platter, a Medical Student in Montpellier in the Sixteenth Century*, trans. Seán Jennett. London: F. Muller, 1961.

Plukenet, Leonard. *Opera*, vol. II: *Almagestum botanicum sive phytographiae plukenetianae Onomasticon*. London, 1696.

—— *Almagestum botanicum Mantissa*. London, 1700 and 1769.

Purchas, Samuel. *Hakluytus Posthumus or Purchas His Pilgrimes*. 20 vols. Glasgow: J. MacLehose, 1905–07.

Pyrard, François. *The Voyage of François Pyrard of Laval to the East Indies, the Maldives, the Moluccas and Brazil*, trans. Albert Gray and H. C. P. Bell. Hakluyt Society, vol. 76. London, 1887.

Rashdall, Hastings. *The Universities of Europe in the Middle Ages.* 3 vols. London: Oxford University Press, 1958.

Ratzel, Friedrich. "L. Rauwolf aus Augsburg," *Biographische Blätter,* 1 (1895), 90–95.

Rauwolf, Leonhard. *Aigentliche beschreibung der Raisz so er vor diser zeit gegen Auffgang inn die Morgenländer . . . selbs volbracht.* Laugingen, 1583.

Ray, John. *Historiae plantarum tomus tertius qui est supplementum duorum praecedentium.* London, 1704.

—— *Philosophical letters between the late Mr. Ray and several of his ingenious correspondents, natives and foreigners.* London, 1718.

—— *Select Remains of the Learned John Ray, M.A. and F.R.S. with his Life by the late William Derham, D.C.* London, 1760.

—— *Stirpium Europaearum extra Britannias nascentium sylloge.* London, 1694.

—— *Travels through the Low-countries, Germany, Italy, and France, with curious observations, natural, topographical, moral, physiological, etc.,* vol. II. London, 1738.

Rinn, Hermann. *Augusta, 955–1955. Forschungen und Studien zur Kultur- und Wirtschaftgeschichte Augsburgs.* Augsburg: Verlag Hermann Rinn, 1955.

Robinson, E., and Smith, E. *Biblical Researches in Palestine, Mount Sinai and Arabia Petraea,* vol. III. London, 1841.

Röhricht, Reinhold. *Bibliotheca Geographica Palaestinae.* Berlin, 1890.

—— *Deutsche Pilgerreisen nach dem Heiligen Lande.* Innsbruck, 1900.

Roth, Friederich. "Zum Bankerott der Firma Melchior Manlich in Augsburg im Jahre 1574," *Zeitschrift des historischen Vereins für Schwaben und Neuburg,* 34 (1908), 160–164.

Rouillard, C. D. *The Turk in French History, Thought, and Literature, 1520–1660.* Paris: Boivin, 1938.

Russell, Alexander. *The Natural History of Aleppo and Parts Adjacent.* London, 1756. 2nd ed., 2 vols. London, 1794.

Ryley, J. Horton. *Ralph Fitch: England's Pioneer to India.* London, 1899.

Saint-Lager. "Histoire des herbiers," *Annales de la société botanique de Lyon,* 13 (1885), 1–120.

Sanderson, John. *The Travels of John Sanderson in the Levant, 1584–1603,* ed. Sir W. Foster. Hakluyt Society, ser. 2, vol. 67. London, 1931.

Sarton, George. *The Appreciation of Ancient and Medieval Science during the Renaissance (1450–1600).* Philadelphia: University of Pennsylvania Press, 1955.

—— *Six Wings. Men of Science in the Renaissance.* Bloomington, Ind.: University of Indiana Press, 1957.

Sauvaget, Jean. *Alep. Essai sur le développement d'une grande ville syrienne, des origines au milieu du XIXe siècle.* Paris: P. Geuthner, 1941.

Sayous, André-E. "Le commerce de Melchoir Manlich et Cie d'Augsbourg à Marseille et dans toute la Méditerranée entre 1571 et 1574," *Revue historique,* 176 (1935), 389–411.

Schramm, Albert. *Der Bilderschmuck der Frühdrucke,* vols. XIV, XV. Leipzig: K. W. Hiersemann, 1931–32.

Schuster, Julius. "Leonhart Rauwolff als Kämpfer gegen das Kurpfuschertum 1593," *Sudhoff's Archiv für Geschichte der Medizin,* 14 (1922), 125–126.

Schweigger, Salomon. *Gezweyte neue nutzliche und anmuthige Reisz-Beschreibung. Die Erste nach Constaninopel und Jerusalem.* Nürnberg, 1664.

Seide, J. "Doctors and Naturalists as Pilgrims and Travellers to the Holy Land," *Janus,* 48 (1959), 53–61.

Shorter Encyclopaedia of Islam, ed. H. A. R. Gibbs and J. H. Kramers. Ithaca, N.Y.: Cornell University Press, 1953.

Sirks, M. J. "L'herbier Flamand de Rembert Dodoens," *Janus,* 21 (1917), 182–204.

Sousa, Nasim. *The Capitulatory Regime of Turkey: Its History, Origin, and Nature.* Baltimore: Johns Hopkins Press, 1933.

Southern, R. W. *Western Views of Islam in the Middle Ages.* Cambridge, Mass.: Harvard University Press, 1962.

Sprengel, Kurt. *Geschichte der Botanik,* vol. I. Altenburg and Leipzig, 1817.

—— *Historia rei herbariae,* vol. I. Amsterdam, 1807.

Stannard, Jerry. "Dioscorides and Renaissance Materia Medica," *Analecta Medico-historica,* 1 (1966), 1–21.

—— "P. A. Mattioli and Some Renaissance Editions of Dioscorides," *Books and Libraries at the University of Kansas,* 4/1 (1966), 1–5.

Stetten, Paul von. *Geschichte der Heilige Römische Reichs freyen Stadt Augspurg.* 2 vols. Frankfurt and Leipzig, 1743–58.

Steinschneider, Moritz. *Die europäischen Uebersetzungen aus dem Arabischen bis Mitte des 17. Jahrhunderts,* vols. I and II. Graz: Akademische Druck- und Verlagsanstalt, 1956.

Strieder, Jakob. *Das Reiche Augsburg. Aufsätze Jakob Strieders zu Augsburg und süddeutschen Wirtschafsgeschichte des 15. und 16. Jahrhunderts,* ed. H. F. Deininger. München: Duncker und Humblot, 1938.

—— *Zur Genesis des modernen Kapitalismus.* Leipzig: Duncker und Humblot, 1904.

Stripling, George W. F. *The Ottoman Turks and the Arabs, 1511–1574.* Urbana, Ill.: University of Illinois Press, 1942.

Teixeira, Pedro. *The Travels of Pedro Teixeira,* trans. William F. Sinclair. Hakluyt Society, ser. 2, vol. 9. London, 1902.

Tenreiro, Antonio. *Itinerários da India a Portugal por terra,* ed. A. Baião in *Scriptores rerum lusitanarum,* ser. B., II. Coimbra: Impr. da Universidade, 1923.

Thou, Jacques Auguste de. *Historiarum sui temporis.* 5 vols. Avrelianae-Colonia Allobrogum, 1626–30.

Tritton, A. S. *Islam: Belief and Practices.* London: Hutchinson House, 1951.

Varthema, Ludovico di. *The Travels of Ludovico di Varthema in Egypt, Sinai, Arabia Deserta and Arabia Felix, in Persia, India, and Ethiopia, A.D. 1503–1508,* trans. J. W. Jones and G. B. Badger. Hakluyt Society, vol. 32. London, 1863.

Wadding, Luke. *Annales minorum seu trium ordinum a S. Francisco institutorum ab anno MDLXV usque ad annum MDLXXIV,* 3rd ed., vol. XX. Florence: Ad Claras Aquas, 1933.

Welser, Marcus. *Chronica der Weitberuempten Keyserlichen Freyen und desz H. Reichs Statt Augspurg in Schwaben,* trans. E. Werlich. Frankfurt am Main, 1595.

Wickersheimer, Ernest. *Dictionnaire biographique des Médecins en France au Moyen Age.* Paris: E. Droz, 1936.

Weisner, Joseph. "Leonhart Rauwolf als Altertumsforscher," *Sudhoff's Archiv für Geschichte der Medizin,* 43 (1959), 355–360.

Zorn, Wolfgang. *Augsburg: Geschichte einer deutschen Stadt.* Augsburg: H. Rinn, n.d.

NOTES

CHAPTER I. TRAVELERS IN THE LEVANT

1. See, for example, the literature discussed in Boies Penrose, *Travel and Discovery in the Renaissance, 1420–1620* (Cambridge, Mass., 1952; paperback ed., New York, 1962).

2. Douglas Carruthers, "The Great Desert Caravan Route, Aleppo to Basra," *Geographical Journal*, 52 (1918), 157–184.

3. Antonio Tenreiro, *Itinerários da Índia a Portugal por terra*, ed. A. Baião, in *Scriptores rerum lusitanarum*, ser. B. (Coimbra, 1923), II, 1–127.

4. The paucity of French works in this area is evident in Geoffroy Atkinson, *La littérature géographique française de la renaissance. Répertoire bibliographique* (Paris, 1927), and in his *Les nouveaux horizons de la renaissance française* (Paris, 1935). A short, anonymous sixteenth-century description of Aleppo in French is appended to Jean Chesneau, *Le voyage de Monsieur d'Aramon* (*Recueil de voyages et de documents pour servir à l'histoire de la géographie depuis le XIIIe jusqu'à la fin du XVIe siècle*) (Paris, 1887), VIII, 249–255.

5. English translations of Federici's account are found in Richard Hakluyt, *The Principal Navigations Voyages Traffiques and Discoveries of the English Nation*, (10 vols.; London, 1927–28), III, 198–269; and in Samuel Purchas, *Hakluytus Posthumus or Purchas His Pilgrimes* (20 vols.; Glasgow, 1905–07), X, 88–143. Balbi's account, *Viaggio dell' Indie orientali*, was published in Venice in 1590; English translation in Purchas, *Hakluytus*, X, 143–164.

6. Anthony Jenkinson, *Early Voyages and Travels to Russia and Persia*, ed. E. D. Morgan and C. H. Coote for the Hakluyt Society (2 vols.; London, 1886), I, 5; and Hakluyt, *Principal Navigations*, III, 57–61.

7. E. F. Oaten, *European Travellers in India during the fifteenth, sixteenth, and seventeenth centuries* (London, 1909), pp. 106–111; J. Horton Ryley, *Ralph Fitch: England's Pioneer to India* (London, 1899); Hakluyt, *Principal Navigations*, III, 271–315, 321–328; and Purchas, *Hakluytus*, VIII, 449–481; X, 165–204.

8. Wilfrid Blunt, *The Art of Botanical Illustration* (London, 1950), pp. 33–35; and Claus Nissen, *Die botanische Buchillustration* (2 vols.; Stuttgart, 1951), I, 28–31.

9. *Hortus sanitatis. Gart der Gesundheit* (Mainz, 1485), fols. 1–2. The translation is that found in Agnes Arber, *Herbals, Their Origin and Evolution* (Cambridge, Eng., 1938), pp. 24–25. See also S. W. Lambert, W. Wiegand, and W. M. Ivins, *Three Vesalian Essays to Accompany the Icones Anatomicae of 1934* (New York, 1952), pp. 53–54.

10. Blunt, *Botanical Illustration,* pp. 36–37. The woodcuts are reproduced in A. Schramm, *Der Bilderschmuck der Frühdrucke,* XIV (Leipzig, 1931).

11. The woodcuts are found in Schramm, *Der Bilderschmuck,* XV (Leipzig, 1932). See also L. C. Miall, *The Early Naturalists, Their Lives and Works* (London, 1912), p. 54; and Hugh W. Davies, *Bernhard von Breydenbach and his Journey to the Holy Land* (London, 1911). The canon was on his pilgrimage from April, 1483 to January, 1484.

12. Chesneau, *Le Voyage,* and C. D. Rouillard, *The Turk in French History, Thought, and Literature, 1520–1660* (Paris, 1938), pp. 195–196.

13. On Belon see Paul Delaunay, "L'Aventureuse existence de Pierre Belon du Mans," *Revue du seizième siècle,* 9–12 (1922–25), reprinted as a volume in Paris, 1926; Louis Crié, "Les voyages de P. Belon et l'Egypte au XVIᵉ siècle," *Revue scientifique,* 17 (1883), 197–203; George Sarton, *The Appreciation of Ancient and Medieval Science during the Renaissance* (Philadelphia, 1955), pp. 57–60; and R. P. Niceron, *Mémoires pour servir à l'histoire des hommes illustres dans la république des lettres* (43 vols.; Paris, 1727–45), XXIV, 36–45.

14. Pierre Belon, *Les observations de plusieurs singularitez et choses mémorables trouvées en Grèce, Asie, Judée, Egypte, Arabie et autres pays estranges, rédigées en trois livres* (Paris, 1555), p. 4ʳ.

15. In the sixteenth century the work was reprinted in Paris in 1554, 1555, and 1588; in Lyons in 1558 and 1568; and twice in Antwerp in 1555. A Latin translation by Charles de l'Ecluse (Clusius), the Flemish botanist, was published at Antwerp in 1589 and 1605.

16. The last item is also dealt with at some length in his *De arboribus Coniferis, resiniferis alliis quoque nonnullis sempiterna fronde virentibus, cum earundem iconibus ad vivum expressis* (Paris, 1553).

17. Claus Nissen, *Die illustrierten Vogelbücher: Geschichte und Bibliographie* (Stuttgart, 1953), pp. 163, 208.

18. Kurt Sprengel, *Historia rei herbariae* (Amsterdam, 1807), I, 377–379.

19. Saint-Lager, "Histoire des herbiers," in *Annales de la société botanique de Lyon,* 13 (1885), 70.

20. See especially E. T. Hamy, "Le père de la zoologie française: Pierre Gilles d'Albi," *Revue des Pyrénées,* 12 (1900), 561–588; Niceron, *Mémoires,* XXIII, 402–412; and Sarton, *Appreciation,* pp. 60–61.

21. His meticulous observations provoked the ridicule of Rabelais, *Gargantua et Pantagruel,* Bk. 5, chap. 31: "Entre iceux, j'y advisai, continue Pantagruel, Pierre Gilles, lequel tenoit un urinal en main, considerant en profonde contemplation l'urine de ses beaux poissons."

22. The full title is *Ex Aeliani historia per Petrum Gyllum latini facti itemque ex Porphyrio, Heliodoro, Oppiano, tum eodem Gyllio luculentis accessionibus aucti libri XVII De vi et natura animalium.* The work was reprinted at Lyons in 1535, 1562, and 1565.

23. Printed as *Elephanti descripto missa ad R. cardinalem Armaignacum ex urbe Berrhoea Syriaca* in the later editions of his *De vi et natura animalium.*

24. The letter was printed in the 1565 edition of *De vi et natura animalium.*

25. His explorations at Constantinople resulted in his *De topographia Constantinopoleos et de illius antiquitatibus, libri IV* (Lyons, 1561).

26. Niceron, *Mémoires,* XXIII, 74–83 and Joseph F. Michaud, *Biographie universelle, ancienne et moderne* (85 vols.; Paris, 1811–28), XLV, 386–388.

27. Niceron, *Mémoires*, XIII, 84–89 and Michaud, *Biographie universelle*, XIX, 110–11.

28. Ernst H. F. Meyer, *Geschichte der Botanik* (Königsberg, 1857), IV 403, remarked that he could not consider Guilandinus a "true naturalist." Matthias Lobelius, the Flemish botanist, saw papyrus for the first time at Pisa; see G. Sarton, *Six Wings: Men of Science in the Renaissance* (Bloomington, Ind., 1957), p. 148.

29. On Prospero Alpino, see Aldo Mieli, *Gli scienziati italiani*, I (Rome, 1923), 84–90; Arber, *Herbals*, p. 90; Michaud, *Biographie universelle*, I, 634–635; and Sarton, *Six Wings*, p. 148.

30. Later editions: Patavi, two editions in 1640; Leyden, 1735.

CHAPTER II. EARLY LIFE

1. For biographical data, see especially F. Ratzel's article in the *Allgemeine deutsche Biographie*, XXVII, 462–465; Michaud, *Biographie universelle*, XXXVII, 142–143; Franz Babinger, "Leonhard Rauwolf, ein Augsburger Botaniker und Orientreisender des sechzehnten Jahrhunderts," *Archiv für die Geschichte der Naturwissenschaften und der Technik* (Leipzig, 1913), IV, 148–161; Ludovic Legré, *La botanique en Provence au XVIe siècle: Leonard Rauwolff, Jacques Raynaudet* (Marseilles, 1900); F. Ratzel, "L. Rauwolf aus Augsburg," *Biographische Blätter*, I, Heft 1 (Berlin, 1895), 90–95; M.J.B.E., "Notice sur la vie et les ouvrages de Rauwolf," *Annales des voyages de la géographie et de l'histoire*, 13 (1811), 96–100; Johann Beckmann, *Litteratur der älteren Reisebeschreibungen* (2 vols.; Goettingen, 1807–09), I, 1–21; II, 170–173; Johann Fredericus Gronovius, *Flora orientalis* (Leyden, 1755); and Joseph Wiesner, "Leonhart Rauwolf als Altertumsforscher," *Sudhoff's Archiv für Geschichte der Medizin*, 43 (1959), 355–360.

2. Gronovius, *Flora orientalis*, p. iiiʳ. A famous master lute-maker of Augsburg, named Sixt Rauwolf, Senior, died in 1557; see Hermann Rinn, ed., *Augusta, 955–1955. Forschungen und Studien zur Kultur- und Wirtschaftsgeschichte* (Augsburg, 1955), p. 313.

3. Leonhard Rauwolf, *Aigentliche beschreibung der Raisz so er vor diser zeit gegen Auffgang inn die Morgenländer . . . selbs volbracht* (Laugingen, 1583), p. iiᵛ (hereafter cited as *Raisz*).

4. C. E. Foerstemann, *Album Academiae vitebergensis ab a. Ch. MDII usque ad a. MDLX* (3 vols.; Leipzig and Halle, 1841–1905), I, 324.

5. Meyer, *Geschichte der Botanik*, IV, 317–322, 402–404; Edward Lee Greene, *Landmarks of Botanical History*, vol. 54 of Smithsonian Miscellaneous Collections (Washington, 1909), pp. 270–314.

6. Foerstemann, *Album Academiae vitebergensis*, I, 247; *Allgemeine deutsche Biographie*, IV, 349–351.

7. Jules Camus, "Historique des premiers herbiers," *Malpighia*, 9 (1895), 310; Foerstemann, *Album Academiae vitebergensis*, I, 245; Marcel Gouron, *Matricule de l'université de médecine de Montpellier (1503–1599)* (Geneva, 1957), p. 150.

8. Walter Friedensburg, *Geschichte der Universität Wittenberg* (Halle a. S., 1917), pp. 259, 273.

9. On the history of the medical school at Montpellier, see Hastings Rashdall, *The Universities of Europe in the Middle Ages* (3 vols.; London, 1958), II,

116–128, 135–139; Alexandre Germain, *La Renaissance à Montpellier: Étude historique d'après les documents originaux avec pièces justificatives inédites* (Montpellier, 1871); Jean Astruc, *Mémoires pour servir à l'histoire de la faculté de médecine de Montpellier* (Paris, 1767); *Cartulaire de l'université de Montpellier* (2 vols.; Montpellier, 1890 and 1912); and Vern L. Bullough, "The Development of the Medical University at Montpellier to the end of the Fourteenth Century," *Bulletin of the History of Medicine*, 30 (1956), 508–523.

10. Rashdall, *Universities*, II 127–128; *Cartulaire*, I, 347–348; Bullough, "Development of the Medical University at Montpellier," p. 519. The reading of No. 8 is uncertain in the document as both Philaretus and Theophilus wrote books entitled *De pulsibus et urinis*. The text reads: *quoad duas primas seu cum Iohannicio de pulsibus et urinis Theophili*. Avicenna (ibn Sina, 980–1037) was a noted Arab physician and philosopher; Bartholomew the Englishman (Bartholomaeus Anglicus) an encyclopedist of the thirteenth century; Galen, a Greek physician of the second century A.D., long regarded as authoritative in medicine; Hippocrates, a Greek physician of the fifth and fourth centuries B.C.; Isaac Judaeus, Abu Jakub Ishak ben Soleiman el-Israeli, an Egyptian Jew of the ninth and tenth centuries; Johannitius, Hoein ibn Ishak (809–873), a Nestorian physician noted for his translations from Greek to Arabic; and Theophilus Protospatharius, a seventh-century Byzantine physician.

11. Germain, *La Renaissance à Montpellier*, pp. 2–17; *The Catholic Encyclopedia*, s.v. Pellissier; H. Omont, "Inventaire de la bibliothèque de Guillaume Pelicier, évêque de Montpellier (1529–1568)," *Revue des Bibliothèques*, 1 (1891), 161–172. The bishop is commemorated botanically by the *Linaria pelisseriana*.

12. Germain, *La Renaissance à Montpellier*, pp. 17–22.

13. *Ibid.*, p. 145.

14. Gouron, *Matricule*; Germain, *La Renaissance à Montpellier*, p. 97.

15. *Ibid.*, pp 42–43, 129.

16. *Ibid.*, pp. 49, 137.

17. Gouron, *Matricule*, p. 149, Legré, *La botanique en Provence*, p. 3 gives the full registration: *Ego Leonhartus Rauwolff Augustanus receptus sum in numerum studiosorum Medicinea Academiae Monspeliensis post factam solitam a doctoribus examinationem. Dedi me in fidem clarissimi viri D. Ant. Saporta atque illis debitam obedientiam praestaturum promitto. Scripsi anno 1560 die 22 Novembr.*

18. *Thomas und Felix Platters und Theodor Agippa d'Aubignés Lebensbeschreibungen*, ed. Otto Fischer (Munich, 1911), p. 209; Felix Platter, *Beloved Son, Felix. A Journal of Felix Platter, a Medical Student in Montpellier in the Sixteenth Century*, trans. Seán Jennett (London, 1961), p. 46; Gouron, *Matricule*, p. 126 (Nov. 4, 1552).

19. Ernest Wickersheimer, *Dictionnaire biographique des Médecins en France au Moyen Age* (Paris, 1936), pp. 529–530.

20. Astruc, *Mémoires*, p. 242.

21. Germain, *La Renaissance à Montpellier*, p. 124.

22. *Ibid.*, p. 138.

23. *Ibid.*, pp. 109–110. Besides these authors approved in 1550, the list of 1534 also contained the *Isagoge* of Johannitius, the *De Virtutibus naturalibus* of Batholomew the Englishman, and a collection of medical writings called *Articella*.

Mesue the Younger, Masawayk al-Maridini (d. 1015), was a Jacobite physician at the court of the caliph in Cairo; Rhazes, Muhammed ibn Zakariya al Razi (865–925), was a great Moslem physician. For the many Renaissance editions of all these classical and Arab authors see George Sarton, *Appreciation,* and Ludwig Choulant, *Handbuch der Bücherkunde für die ältere Medicin* (Leipzig, 1841).

24. Rashdall, *Universities,* II, 138. On the struggle between the Greek and Arabic traditions see Donald Campbell, "The Medical Curriculum of the universities of Europe in the sixteenth century, with special reference to the Arabist tradition," *Science, Medicine and History* (London, 1953), I, 357–367.

25. Sarton, *Appreciation,* pp. 69–78. See also Jerry Stannard, "Dioscorides and Renaissance Materia Medica," *Analecta Medico-historica,* 1 (1966), 1–21.

26. Sarton, *Appreciation,* pp. 75–76; Jerry Stannard, "P. A. Mattioli and Some Renaissance Editions of Dioscorides," *Books and Libraries at the University of Kansas,* 4/1 (1966), 1–5.

27. *Raisz,* p. 112 (75). Page references given in parentheses after a reference to those in Rauwolf's *Raisz* refer to the page(s) in the English translation by N. Staphorst in John Ray's *Travels through the Low-countries* (London, 1738), II. This is the translation I have used throughout.

28. Sarton, *Appreciation,* pp. 63–69.

29. *Ibid.,* pp. 78–86.

30. *Raisz,* pp. ii^r, 410 (287).

31. Sarton, *Appreciation,* pp. 34, 38, 66, 86. The *arnabo* of Paul is probably the *Curcuma Zeodoaria* Rosc.

32. Lucien Leclerc, *Histoire de la médecine arabe* (2 vols.; Paris, 1876), I, 466–477.

33. Sarton, *Appreciation,* pp. 39–45.

34. Moritz Steinschneider, *Die europäischen Uebersetzungen aus dem Arabischen bis Mitte des 17. Jahrhunderts* (2 vols. in one; Graz, 1956), I, 5.

35. Leclerc, *Médecine arabe,* I, 337–354.

36. On the translations and editions of Rhazes, see Sarton, *Appreciation,* p. 40; and Steinschneider, *Uebersetzungen,* I, 14, 25.

37. Leclerc, *Médecine arabe,* II, 152–156.

38. Steinschneider, *Uebersetzungen,* I, 76–77.

39. Rashdall, *Universities,* II, 136; *Cartulaire,* I, 344; Germain, *La Renaissance à Montpellier,* pp. 66–67, 136. Rabelais attended one of the dissections of 1530.

40. Germain, *La Renaissance à Montpellier,* pp. 67–68, 151–153.

41. *Thomas und Felix Platters,* pp. 216–217.

42. Germain, *La Renaissance à Montpellier,* p. 72.

43. *Thomas und Felix Platters,* p. 217.

44. Germain, *La Renaissance à Montpellier,* p. 136.

45. *Ibid.,* p. 145.

46. Astruc, *Mémoires,* pp. 236–239; Niceron, *Mémoires,* XXXIII, 306–322; Michaud, *Biographie universelle,* XXXVIII, 546–549.

47. *Raisz,* p. 9 (not trans.)

48. From the title page of Vol. I of Rauwolf's herbarium; Legré, *La botanique en Provence,* p. 10.

49. *Raisz,* pp. ii^v–iii^r. Martius matriculated at Montpellier on June 2, 1558; Gouron, *Matricule,* p. 143.

50. Legré, *La botanique en Provence*, p. 6. Jean Bauhin, a brother of the celebrated anatomist and naturalist Caspar Bauhin, matriculated at Montpellier on October 20, 1561; Gouron, *Matricule*, p. 154.

51. Sarton, *Six Wings*, p. 149; Camus, "Historique des premiers herbiers," 283-314.

52. *The Diary of Montaigne's Journey to Italy in 1580 and 1581*, trans. E. J. Trechmann (London, 1929), p. 18.

53. Legré, *La botanique en Provence*, pp. 28-53.

54. G. R. Elton, ed., *The Reformation, 1520-1559* (Cambridge, 1958), p. 218.

55. See Philippe Corbière, *Histoire de l'Église Réformée de Montpellier depuis son origine jusqu'à nos jours* (Montpellier and Paris, 1861), pp. 10-56, on Protestantism at Montpellier in the middle of the Sixteenth century.

56. *Thomas und Felix Platters*, pp. 221-224.

57. Corbière, *Histoire de l'Église Réformée*, pp. 48-54. Niceron, *Mémoires*, XXXIII, 315-316 reports that when Bishop Pellicier was sent to prison in 1552, Rondelet burned all the Protestant books in his own library.

58. *Catholic Encyclopedia*, s. v. Montpellier; L. Guiaud, *Le procès de Guillaume Pellicier, évêque de Magluelone-Montpellier de 1527-1567* (Paris, 1907).

59. On the University of Valence, see Rashdall, *Universities*, II, 201-203; *Catholic Encyclopedia*, s. v. Valence.

60. Heinrich Boos, *Thomas und Felix Platter* (Leipzig, 1878), pp. 201, 212.

61. Title page of vol. III of Rauwolf's herbarium; Legré, *La botanique en Provence*, pp. 7-9.

62. Rauwolf inscribed his name in Gesner's *Liber amicorum* on May 1, 1563 and stayed with the naturalist for a few days; Richard J. Durling, "Conrad Gesner's *Liber amicorum*, 1555-1565" *Gesnerus*, 22 (1965), 138 144, 155.

63. Babinger, "Leonhard Rauwolf," 151. In 1564 a total of 925 citizens of Augsburg died of the plague; Marcus Welser, *Chronica der Weitberuempten Keyserlichen Freyen und desz H. Reichs Statt Augspurg in Schwaben*, trans. E. Werlich (Frankfurt am Main, 1595), pt. 3, p. 113.

64. F. W. T. Hunger, *Charles de L'Escluse, Carolus Clusius, Nederlandsch kruidkundige, 1526-1609* (2 vols.; 's Gravenhage, 1927-43), I, 74. Legré, *La botanique en Provence*, pp. 18-20, 57, points out that in a number of cases Rauwolf's identifications were more accurate than those of Clusius.

65. Babinger, "Leonhard Rauwolf," 151.

66. *Ibid,;* Legré, *La botanique en Provence*, p. 58; M. J. B. E., "Notice sur la vie et les ouvrages de Rauwolf," 98.

CHAPTER III. AUGSBURG TO TRIPOLI

1. *Raisz*, p. 1 (1).

2. On the Manlich firm, see Jakob Strieder, *Das Reiche Augsburg. Aufsätze Jakob Strieders zu Augsburg und süddeutschen Wirtschaftsgeschichte des 15. und 16. Jahrhunderts*, ed. Heinz F. Deininger (München, 1938), pp. 101-109, 167-189; Jakob Strieder, *Zur Genesis des modernen Kapitalismus* (Leipzig, 1904), pp. 20-21, 193-196; André-E. Sayous, "Le commerce de Melchior Manlich et Cⁱᵉ d'Augsbourg à Marseille et dans toute la Méditerranée entre 1571 et 1574," in *Revue historique*, 176 (1935), 389-411; and Richard Ehrenberg, *Das Zeitalter*

der Fugger: Geldkapital und Creditverkehr in 16. Jahrhundert (Jena, 1912), I, 224–226.

3. *Raisz,* p. iii^v.

4. Described in *Raisz,* pp. 2–9 (2–6).

5. The autobiography of Krafft was published in the original Swabian dialect by K. D. Haszler as *Reisen und Gefangenschaft Hans Ulrich Kraffts,* vol. 61 of Bibliothek des Litterarischen Vereins in Stuttgart (1861). The version in modern German, edited by Adolf Cohn, *Ein deutscher Kaufmann des sechzehnten Jahrhunderts: Hans Ulrich Krafft's Denkwürdigkeiten* (Goettingen, 1862), is used throughout this work, cited hereafter as *Denkwürdigkeiten.*

6. Krafft, *Denkwürdigkeiten,* pp. 19–21. The Manlich ships averaged about 30 percent profit on their voyages (Strieder, *Das Reiche Augsburg,* pp. 180–189).

7. See Nasim Sousa, *The Capitulatory Regime of Turkey: Its History, Origin, and Nature* (Baltimore, 1933); pp. 54–68, 314–320; André Bruneau, *Traditions et politique de la France au Levant* (Paris, 1932), pp. 28–31; 371–376; J. C. Hurewitz, *Diplomacy in the Near and Middle East. A Documentary Record: 1535–1919* (Princeton, N.J., 1956), I, 1–5; and Ernest Charrière, *Négociations de la France dans le Levant* (4 vols.; Paris, 1848–60).

8. The fine Manlich house, purchased by Anton Manlich on October 5, 1571, was located on "la rue du port" and had earlier belonged to a famous naval captain (Sayous, "Le commerce de M. Manlich," 399).

9. *Raisz,* p. 9 (6). On Raynaudet, see Legré, *La botanique en Provence,* pp. 107–133.

10. Krafft, *Denkwürdigkeiten,* pp. 22–25.

11. *Ibid.,* pp. 25–26.

12. The voyage to Tripoli and the stop at Cyprus is described in *Raisz,* pp. 10–21 (7–14) and in Krafft, *Denkwürdigkeiten,* pp. 26–54.

13. Hakluyt, *Principal Navigations,* III, 26–27.

14. Laurence Aldersey, an English traveler, reported only seventeen inhabitants in 1581 (Hakluyt, *Principal Navigations,* III, 81). See also Samuel Kiechel, *Die Reisen des Samuel Kiechel,* ed. K. D. Haszler, vol. 86 of Bibliothek des Litterarischen Vereins in Stuttgart (1866), pp. 249–250.

15. Krafft, *Denkwürdigkeiten,* p. 47.

16. *Encyclopedia of Islam,* s. v. Tarabulus; and Guy Le Strange, *Palestine under the Moslems* (Boston, 1890), pp. 348–352.

17. Hakluyt, *Principal Navigations,* III, 321–322.

18. See also William Biddulph, in Purchas, *Hakluytus,* VIII, 255.

19. Kiechel, *Reisen,* pp. 251–256, 326–329.

20. Fynes Moryson, *An Itinerary containing his ten yeeres travell through the twelve Dominions of Germany, Bohmerland, Sweitzerland, Netherland, Denmarke, Poland, Italy, Turky, France, England, Scotland and Ireland* (4 vols.; Glasgow, 1907–08), II, 50–51.

21. John Sanderson, *The Travels of John Sanderson in the Levant, 1584–1603,* ed. Sir William Foster for the Hakluyt Society (London, 1931), pp. 5, 53.

22. Tripoli described in *Raisz,* pp. 21–39 (14–26); and in Krafft, *Denkwürdigkeiten,* pp. 51–54.

23. Le Strange, *Palestine,* p. 352.

24. Kiechel said a blue linen cloth was used for this purpose in the baths at Aleppo; *Reisen,* p. 268.

25. On December 12, 1573, Krafft was the guest of Elias, a Jew, who was the best of the three interpreters employed by the French at Tripoli (*Denkwürdigkeiten,* p. 99).

CHAPTER IV. ALEPPO

1. Tripoli to Aleppo, *Raisz,* pp. 64–68 (42–44). John Newberry traveled from Tripoli to Aleppo in January, 1580, and gave the following towns on his route: Draa, Ewsen, Mowa, Metteni, Sihi, Aman, Det, Marra, Ledeghe, Sarraket near Syrmin, Aleppo—a 15-day trip (Purchas, *Hakluytus,* VIII, 451).

2. Krafft, *Denkwürdigkeiten,* pp. 124–131. Krafft made the trip in four days.

3. Kiechel, *Reisen,* pp. 258, 272. In Hellenistic times, Hama was called Epiphania. Although besieged, the city was never taken by the crusaders; see *Encyclopedia of Islam,* s. v. Hama; and Le Strange, *Palestine,* pp. 357–360. John Eldred who made the trip from Tripoli to Aleppo in one week in 1583, described Hama as in ruins (Hakluyt, *Principal Navigations,* III, 322–323).

4. Kiechel, *Reisen,* pp. 272–273.

5. Hakluyt, *Principal Navigations,* III, 267.

6. *Encyclopedia of Islam,* s. v. Ma'arrah al-Nu'man. In Ottoman control since 1516, it had a fine new khan built in 1566–67. See also Le Strange, *Palestine,* pp. 495–496.

7. Krafft surprised the Italian and French merchants at Aleppo by riding into the city (May 13, 1574) on a horse led by a servant of a Turkish friend who had come with him from Tripoli (*Denkwürdigkeiten,* p. 131).

8. *Encyclopedia of Islam,* s. v. Halab.

9. Le Strange, *Palestine,* pp. 360–367.

10. *The Travels of Pedro Teixeira,* trans. and annotated by William F. Sinclair for the Hakluyt Society (London, 1902), pp. 114–115. Henry Lyte, the English translator of Rembert Dodoens' herbal, wrote of the "great town of Aleph, so called of the first letter of the Hebrew Alphabet, where as is a great resort and traffique of marchants" (*A nievve herball, or historie of plants* [London, 1578], p. 705).

11. Hakluyt, *Principal Navigations,* III, 199, 267 (Federici); 323 (Eldred); and Purchas, *Hakluytus,* VIII, 451–452 (Newberry).

12. Kiechel, *Reisen,* pp. 259–271, 462.

13. Teixeira, *Travels,* pp. 112–123.

14. The city of Aleppo, its trade, and its plants are described in *Raisz,* pp. 68–128 (45–85). Jean Sauvaget, the French historian of Aleppo, considered Rauwolf's account of Aleppo, "One of the best descriptions of the city which has been preserved, full of unpublished details and original observations" (*Alep. Essai sur le développement d'une grande ville syrienne, des origines au milieu du XIXᵉ siècle* [Paris, 1941], p. 48).

15. Eldred (1583) estimated the garrison at Aleppo at 400 to 500 Janissaries (Hakluyt, *Principal Navigations,* III, 323).

16. Fynes Moryson, the English traveler, was in Aleppo in June, 1596, and found the air so hot "as me thought I supped hot broth, when I drew it in" (*Itinerary,* II, 60).

17. Sauvaget, *Alep,* p. 217.

18. Johannes van Cotovico, *Itinerarium Hierosolymitanum et syriacum* (Antwerp, 1619), p. 409.

19. Purchas, *Hakluytus*, VIII, 261; and Sanderson, *Travels*, p. 167.

20. Teixeira, *Travels*, p. 114.

21. Purchas, *Hakluytus*, VIII, 276. Sanderson accused Biddulph of gross immorality and drunkenness (*Travels*, p. 56, n. 4, and p. 264).

22. *The Travels of Ludovico di Varthema in Egypt, Sinai, Arabia Deserta and Arabia Felix, in Persia, India, and Ethiopia, A.D. 1503-1508*, trans. J. W. Jones and G. P. Badger (London, 1863), p. 374.

23. *Joyfull Newes out of the Newe Founde Worlde written in Spanish by Nicholas Monardes physician of Seville and englished by John Frampton, Merchant anno 1577* (2 vols.; London, 1925), I, 28.

24. Garcia da Orta, *Colloquies on the Simples and Drugs of India*, trans. Sir Clements Markham (London, 1913), p. 379. He devoted the forty-seventh colloquy (pp. 378-389) to the root, giving recipes, and pointing out that Emperor Charles V took the root as medicine.

25. Hakluyt, *Principal Navigations*, III, 233; *The Voyage of John Huyghen van Linschoten to the East Indies*, ed. A. C. Burnell and P. A. Tiele for the Hakluyt Society (2 vols.; London, 1885), II, 107-112.

26. *The Voyage of François Pyrard of Laval to the East Indies, the Maldives, the Moluccas and Brazil*, trans. and ed. A. Gray and H. C. P. Bell (London, 1887-89), I, 182. Compare the Sanskrit *phirangaroga*, "disease of the Franks" (Berthold Laufer, *Sino-Iranica: Chinese Contributions to the History of Civilization in Ancient Iran* [Chicago, 1919], pp. 556).

27. *Ibid.*, pp. 547-551.

28. *The Greek Herbal of Dioscorides*, trans. John Goodyer (1655), ed. R. T. Gunther (New York, 1959), p. 233.

29. da Orta, *Colloquies*, pp. 390-392.

30. Hakluyt, *Principal Navigations*, III, 233.

31. *Raisz*, p. 94 (62).

32. *Ibid.*, pp. 94-95 (62-63).

33. Pierre Belon, *Les observations de plusieurs singularitez*, p. 228.

34. da Orta, *Colloquies*, p. 280.

35. *Raisz*, pp. 95-96 (63).

36. da Orta, *Colloquies*, pp. 362-366, 481.

37. Teixeira, *Travels*, pp. 229-231.

38. *The Apologie and Treatise of Ambroise Paré*, ed. Geoffrey Keynes (Chicago, 1952), pp. 197-200.

39. Teixeira, *Travels*, p. 230.

40. Paré, *Apologie*, p. 198.

41. Gronovius, the eighteenth-century botanist, identified this reed as *Donax arundinaceus* Pal-Beauv. (*Arundo donax* L.). The *Arundo donax*, however, is very common in the Near East and there was certainly no need to import such reeds from India. It was most probably the *Calamus rotang* L.

42. Not identified by Gronovius.

43. Krafft, *Denkwürdigkeiten*, pp. 158-160.

44. *Encyclopedia of Islam*, s.v. Kahwa.

45. Uriel Heyd, *Ottoman Documents on Palestine, 1552-1615* (Oxford, 1960), pp. 160-162.

46. *Raisz*, pp. 102–103 (68). Alexander Russell questions the identification of *Coffea arabica* with the *buncho* and *ban* of Avicenna (*The Natural History of Aleppo*, 2nd ed. [2 vols.; London, 1794], I, 372). Compare Avicenna, *Libri in re medica omnes* (Venice, 1564), II, chaps. 82, 91.

47. Purchas, *Hakluytus*, VIII, 266.

48. Teixeira, *Travels*, pp. 201, 62–63, 121.

49. See Appendix I.

CHAPTER V. ALEPPO TO RAQQA

1. According to Krafft, this Dutch jeweler knew a little Arabic (*Denkwürdigkeiten* p. 163). Travel preparations are described in *Raisz*, pp. 131–135 (87–90).

2. The trip from Aleppo to Bir is described in *Raisz*, pp. 135–144 (90–96).

3. William Barret, the first English consul at Aleppo, reported in 1584 that the charge for camels from Aleppo to Bir was 60 medines for each camel's load and 45 medines per mule (Hakluyt, *Principal Navigations*, III, 339). For near-contemporary and brief accounts of the passage from Aleppo to Bir, see Purchas, *Hakluytus*, VIII, 452 (Newberry) and 482 (Cartwright).

4. D. D. Luckenbill, *Ancient Records of Assyria and Babylonia* (2 vols.; Chicago, 1926–27), I, 559, 560, 601 *et passim;* *Encyclopedia of Islam*, s.v. Biredjik; and Le Strange, *Palestine*, p. 423.

5. Hakluyt, *Principal Navigations*, III, 199 (Federici); III, 282, 323 (Fitch); Purchas, *Hakluytus*, VIII, 452 (Newberry); and VIII, 484 (Cartwright).

6. Hakluyt, *Principal Navigations*, III, 324, 323.

7. Purchas, *Hakluytus*, VIII, 483–484.

8. Hakluyt, *Principal Nagivations*, III, 199–200 (Federici); III, 282 (Fitch); III, 339 (Barret); and III, 323 (Eldred).

9. *Ibid.*, III, 200 (Federici); III, 282, 323 (Fitch, Eldred); Purchas, *Hakluytus*, VIII, 452–454 (Newberry); VIII, 382–383 (Sherley); X, 143–145 (Balbi).

10. The large caravan of which Cartwright was a member in 1603 made the trip from Bir to Kara Amid in seven days (Purchas, *Hakluytus*, VIII, 484–485).

11. Barret noted the charge at Bir for four dishes of raisins and twenty pounds of soap as 35 medines and for meat for travelers as 200 medines (Hakluyt, *Principal Navigations*, III, 339).

12. The voyage downstream to Raqqa is described in *Raisz*, pp. 144–164 (96–109).

13. Federici commented that "Harquebuzes are very good weapons against them, for they stand greatly in feare of the shot" (Hakluyt, *Principal Navigations*, III, 200).

14. Guy Le Strange, *The Lands of the Eastern Caliphate* (Cambridge, Eng., 1930), p. 107, and *Palestine*, pp. 501–502. The "Castle of the Star" is called "Calatelnegiur" by Balbi (Purchas, *Hakluytus*, X, 143).

15. Imperial firmans of 1571 and 1577, addressed to the Beg of Safad, forbad the possession of muskets by anyone but Janissaries and holders of *timars* and *zi'amets*. The Bedouins especially were to be warned "not to use muskets contrary to the noble firman." In 1574, the Druzes were paying 15 to 20 gold pieces for muskets from gunrunners (Heyd, *Ottoman Documents*, pp. 80–81, 95–96).

16. Hakluyt, *Principal Navigations,* III, 200 (Federici); III, 283 (Fitch); III, 328 (Eldred); III, 340 (Barret); Purchas, *Hakluytus,* VIII, 269 (Biddulph); VIII, 383 (Sherley).

17. Undoubtedly Balis, the Roman Barbalissus, once the great river port for Syria and the center of many caravan routes (Le Strange, *Palestine,* p. 417, and *Eastern Caliphate,* p. 107).

18. Hakluyt, *Principal Navigations,* III, 323–324. In 1603, Cartwright, who did not go down the Euphrates, copied Eldred in this but added knives to the list (Purchas, *Hakluytus,* VIII, 483).

19. Kala'ah Ja'bar or Kala'ah Dushar. In A.D. 1104 the fortress was taken by the crusaders from Edessa, 100 miles to the north.

20. On Raqqa, see Le Strange, *Eastern Caliphate,* pp. 101–103, 124, and *Palestine,* p. 518.

21. Purchas, *Hakluytus,* VIII, 452 (Newberry); Hakluyt, *Principal Navigations,* III, 339 (Barret).

22. The stay at Raqqa is described in *Raisz,* pp. 164–174 (110–116).

23. Eldred wrote in 1583 that their "haire, apparell, and colour are altogether like to those vagabond Egyptians, which heretofore have gone about in England" (Hakluyt, *Principal Navigations,* III, 324).

CHAPTER VI. RAQQA TO BAGHDAD

1. Passage from Raqqa to Deir: *Raisz,* pp. 174–184 (117–124). Balbi gave the following names to the towns between Raqqa and Deir: Elamora, Aman, Avagia, Abulena, Casubi, Celibi, Castle Zelebe, and Elder (Deir), "anciently called the Port of the Chaine" (Purchas, *Hakluytus,* X, 143–144).

2. Josephus *Antiquities of the Jews* i. 12; Gen. 21:9–21; Ps. 83:6.

3. Matt 3:4. See also Isa. 7:15, "Butter and honey shall he eat." It is surprising that Rauwolf, well versed in biblical passages, did not refer to this verse.

4. Rauwolf cited Aristotle for the pelican, but identified the cormorants as a "kind of sea-eagle" (*Raisz,* p. 180 [120–121]).

5. Passage from Deir to 'Anah: *Raisz,* pp. 185–196 (124–132).

6. Newberry gave the following names to the villages along the banks of the river between Deir and 'Anah: Rab (west), Ashar (west), Subercan (east), and Manalle (west) (Purchas, *Hakluytus,* VIII, 453). Balbi gave the following names: Muachesir, Elpisara, Rahbi, Zoxosuldan, Siara, Gorur, Sora, Elersi, Anga, Chaime, Sema, Carpilchelbi, Fochelcurni, Edir, Rechtalmel, Zafara, Elcuxi, Elmesetana, and Castle Anna (*Ibid.,* X, 144).

7. Hakluyt, *Principal Navigations,* III, 324 (Eldred); III, 283 (Fitch); Purchas, *Hakluytus,* VIII, 270 (Biddulph).

8. *Raisz,* p. 193 (130) and fig. 27 (1583 ed.). Theophrastus did not use the word "Trionum" or describe this plant.

9. Luckenbill, *Ancient Records,* I, 409, 469.

10. Purchas, *Hakluytus,* VIII, 453. Barret gave the customs at 'Anah as ten medines per camel load (Hakluyt, *Principal Navigations,* III, 340).

11. Teixeira, *Travels,* pp. 81–89.

12. Passage from 'Anah to Felugia: *Raisz,* pp. 196–202 (132–136). Balbi named the following places enroute: Ile Anatelbes, Beggian Ile, Cabin, Sberie, Zovia, Giera, Germa, Benexi, Duletgi dit, Zibida, Urasa, Fuochelbera, Abusabur,

Aditi, Zezirnalus, Giuba, Nausa, Eit, Caragoul, and Felugia (Purchas, *Hakluytus,* X, 144–145).

13. Rauwolf equated one say with less than three "Batzen" in Germany. Barret gave the customs as two say or ten medines "per barke" (Hakluyt, *Principal Navigations,* III, 340). On Haditha, see *Encyclopedia of Islam,* s.v. Haditha.

14. Le Strange, *Eastern Caliphate,* p. 65.

15. Purchas, *Hakluytus,* X, 144–145 (Balbi); and Hakluyt, *Principal Navigations,* III, 327 (Eldred). See also Purchas, *Hakluytus,* VIII, 453 (Newberry); Hakluyt, *Principal Navigations,* III, 283 (Fitch); and III, 202–203 (Federici). Cartwright copied Eldred (Purchas, *Hakluytus,* VIII, 522).

16. The fact that the ruins of ancient Babylon were located about 50 miles below Felugia at Hillah was seldom recognized in the sixteenth century by Europeans. Garcia da Orta, the Portuguese botanist, saw this error and pointed it out in his work on Indian plants and drugs (*Colloquies,* p. 282).

17. Probably the ruins of the great arched Kantarah (bridge) Dimimma which crossed the Nahr (canal) 'Isa where this canal left the Euphrates near Ambar at the village of Dimimma, located just above Felugia (Le Strange, *Eastern Caliphate,* p. 66, and *Baghdad during the Abbasid Caliphate* [Oxford, 1929], pp. 50, 70).

18. Rauwolf does not mention the biblical association of "dragon" with the desolation of ruined Babylon; Jer. 51:37 and 50:39.

19. Le Strange, *Eastern Caliphate,* p. 67; *Encyclopedia of Islam,* s.v. 'Akarkuf; and Fritz Hommel, *Ethnologie und Geographie des alten Orients* (München, 1926), p. 344.

20. Hakluyt, *Principal Navigations,* III, 201–202.

21. *Ibid.,* III, 283 (Fitch) and III, 324–325 (Eldred). See also Sir Anthony Sherley (Purchas, *Hakluytus,* VIII, 385), and Cartwright (*ibid.,* 521), who as usual copied Eldred.

22. Hakluyt, *Principal Navigations,* III, 202.

23. Eldred (1583) could find no camels for hire at Felugia but secured 100 asses for the 18-hour trip to Baghdad (*ibid.,* III, 324).

24. Purchas, *Hakluytus,* X, 145.

25. Undoubtedly the course of the medieval Nahr Sasar, the great transverse canal that once carried the water of the Euphrates from a point ten miles above Felugia to the Tigris above Madain and below Baghdad (Le Strange, *Eastern Caliphate,* pp. 32, 35, 67).

CHAPTER VII. BAGHDAD

1. Le Strange, *Baghdad during the Abbasid Caliphate* (Oxford, 1924).

2. *Ibid.,* p. 344.

3. Hakluyt, *Principal Navigations,* III, 201 (Federici); 282–283 (Fitch); 325 (Eldred); and Purchas, *Hakluytus,* VIII, 454 (Newberry).

4. Purchas, *Hakluytus,* VIII, 385.

5. *Ibid.,* 520.

6. Teixeira, *Travels,* pp. 60–72.

7. Eldred reported that the ditch at the base of this wall could be flooded by opening a sluice and admitting water from the Tigris (Hakluyt, *Principal Navigations,* III, 325).

8. The mosque of the caliph, Jami-al-Kasr, was built in the first decade of the tenth century, partially burned in 1258, but Hulagu ordered it restored. The College of Mustansiriyah was completed in 1234. See Le Strange, *Baghdad,* pp. 252, 266–270.

9. Baghdad: *Raisz,* pp. 209–233 (142–159).

10. Rauwolf may have seen the inscription with the date 633 (A.D. 1236) on the great mosque of the palace restored by Caliph Mustansir (Le Strange, *Baghdad,* p. 269).

11. In 1185, Ibn Jabayr, the Spanish traveler, reported over 2,000 baths in medieval Baghdad and "in these the halls were so firmly plastered with bitumen, brought from Basrah, that the visitor imagined the walls to be lined with slabs of black marble" (*ibid.,* p. 335).

12. *Ibid.,* p. 269 and Carsten Niebuhr, *Reisebeschreibung nach Arabien und anderen umliegenden Ländern* (Copenhagen, 1778), II, 296. Because Rauwolf could not find anyone who could read the inscription, Babinger assumed that it was in ancient cuneiform (*"Leonhard Rauwolf,"* p. 153).

13. Hakluyt, *Principal Navigations,* III, 325.

14. *Ibid.*

15. On the passage to and from Basra and for the descriptions of this city, see Hakluyt, *Principal Navigations,* III, 202–204 (Federici, 1563); 283–284 (Fitch, 1583); 325–327 (Eldred, 1583); 329–331, 340 (Barret, 1584); Purchas, *Hakluytus,* VIII, 455–456 (Newberry, 1581); X, 145–146 (Balbi, 1580); Teixeira, *Travels,* pp. 25–33; and Le Strange, *Eastern Caliphate,* pp. 44–48.

16. G. W. F. Stripling, *The Ottoman Turks and the Arabs, 1511–1574* (Urbana, Ill., 1942), pp. 82–84.

17. *Raisz,* p. 215 (146).

18. *Ibid.,* p. 216 (147); Varthema, *Travels,* p. 126; Hakluyt, *Principal Navigations,* III, 205 (Federici).

19. Hakluyt, *Principal Navigations,* III, 212 (Federici); 285 (Fitch); 333–334 (Barret); and Teixeira, *Travels,* p. 29.

20. The alliance between the Portuguese and the Christians of Abyssinia as well as the use of this East African region as a base for the lucrative spice trade with India, led to repeated Turkish attacks and Turkish supported raids on the coastal areas of Abyssinia. After 1572 the Turks gained the entire seacoast here and briefly made it a province (Stripling, *Turks and Arabs,* pp. 96–98).

21. Music was never used in the Moslem mosque.

22. *Raisz,* pp. 222–224 (151–152). Rauwolf called the Shah Tahmasp Gamaël. Stripling, *Turks and Arabs,* p. 84, gives a similar incident in 1568 with the Persian forces under Prince Eklas Mirza, who escaped, however. S. H. Longrigg, *Four Centuries of Modern Iraq* (Oxford, 1925), p. 33, dismisses Rauwolf's mention of this attack as "half-understood divan-talk."

23. Krafft, *Denkwürdigkeiten,* p. 178.

24. Hakluyt, *Principal Navigations,* III, 203 (Federici); 284 (Fitch); and 326 (Eldred).

25. *Ibid.,* 265–267.

26. *Ibid.,* 327–328.

27. Teixeira (*Travels,* pp. 86–87) reported that on the desert-crossing it was customary to carry as food for the camels "sacks of barley meals, cotton seed, and other things, whereof are made for them a sort of roll, of the size and

shape of an ostrich egge, with which they are fed at night, in addition to what they get by browsing." The Portuguese traveler also said that the strongest camel could carry 600 pounds for nine to ten hours, "limping at every step."

CHAPTER VIII. BAGHDAD TO ALEPPO

1. In 1590, Fitch traveled by land to Mosul, Merdin, Orfa, Bir, and Aleppo (Hakluyt, *Principal Navigations,* III, 315).
2. Baghdad to Aleppo: *Raisz,* pp. 234–262 (159–178).
3. Rauwolf cited Eusebius (*ca.* 260–*ca.* 340) and Nicephorus Callistus, a Byzantine historian of the fourteenth century.
4. *Encyclopedia of Islam,* s.v. Kirkuk.
5. The Ptolemaic Gorgas is the Diala River which enters the Tigris River between Baghdad and the site of Ctesiphon. The Lesser Zab River is called the Caprus by Ptolemy.
6. Rauwolf does not refer to the last battle of Alexander the Great with Darius fought in 331 B.C. at Gaugamela, about fifty miles west of Arbela. Arbela served as headquarters for Darius before the battle.
7. The Great Zab River is called the Lycus by Ptolemy.
8. Probably the Ghazir Su, the ancient Buradis on whose banks Darius camped before the fatal battle of Gaugemela. Rauwolf incorrectly identified it with the Ptolemaic Lycus.
9. The traditional route led through Balad (Eski Mosul), Ba'aynatha, Barka'id, Adhramah, and Nisibin (Le Strange, *Eastern Caliphate,* pp. 99–100).
10. *Ibid.,* p. 45.
11. A *cha'ush* was a member of the important Corps of Pursuivants who were sent by the sultan as special commissioners for supervision, inspection, and investigation. In 1577, the arbitrary seizure of horses by the *cha'ush* and other officials led to the establishment of a series of relay stations on the road from Damascus to Cairo (Heyd, *Ottoman Documents,* pp. 117, 126–127).
12. On Urfa, see Le Strange, *Eastern Caliphate,* pp. 103–104.
13. Hakluyt, *Principal Navigations,* III, 315.
14. Purchas, *Hakluytus,* VIII, 484–485.
15. Apoc., Tob. 11.
16. On 'Ain Tab, the modern Gaziantep, see Le Strange, *Palestine,* pp. 386–387.
17. Friedrich Roth, "Zum Bankerott der Firma Melchior Manlich in Augsburg im Jahre 1574," *Zeitschrift des Historischen Vereins für Schwaben und Neuburg,* 34 (1908), 160–164; J. B. Menckenius (ed.), *Scriptores rerum Germanicarum praecipue Saxonicarum* (Leipzig, 1728), I, cols. 1939, 1946; and Marcus Welser, *Chronica der . . . Stadt Augspurg in Schwaben,* pt. 3, p. 134.
18. The horse, black and shiny, had been purchased earlier in Aleppo for 15 ducats, a small price for a horse that Krafft thought would bring 100 thaler in Germany (Krafft, *Denkwürdigkeiten,* p. 137).
19. *Ibid.,* pp. 5, 175.
20. See *Raisz,* pp. 263–67 (179–182), for this brief stay in Aleppo.

CHAPTER IX. MOUNT LEBANON

1. Tripoli: *Raisz*, pp. 267–272 (182–185).
2. Mt. Lebanon: *Raisz*, pp. 273–290 (186–197).
3. Krafft, *Denkwürdigkeiten*, p. 115.
4. Purchas, *Hakluytus*, VIII, 253.
5. Krafft, *Denkwürdigkeiten*, p. 117.
6. The first modern scientist to describe the cedars was Pierre Belon, who visited the celebrated grove in 1548 (*Les observations*, p. 153). Krafft counted 27 cedars with three of that number being dead (*Denkwürdigkeiten*, p. 118). Jerome Dandini, a special Jesuit delegate of the pope to the Maronites, counted 23 trees in 1595–96, while a companion saw only 21 (Dandini, "A Voyage to Mount Lebanon," in John Pinkerton, *A General Collection of the Best and Most Interesting Voyages and Travels in all Parts of the World* [London, 1811], X, 288–289). See also Philip K. Hitti, *Lebanon in History from the Earliest Times to the Present* (London, 1957), pp. 35–37.
7. Krafft, *Denkwürdigkeiten*, p. 99.
8. Kurt Sprengel, *Historia rei herbariae* (Amsterdam, 1807), I, 379. Kiechel was in Tripoli in the winter of 1587–88 and may be referring to Rauwolf's work when he wrote: "What else can be found on this mountain by way of the many fine fruit trees and useful herbs, it is necessary to consult the physicians or those who delight in the simples" (*Reisen*, p. 255).
9. Krafft, *Denkwürdigkeiten*, p. 209.
10. *Raisz*, pp. 290–295 (198–201).
11. Stripling, *Turks and Arabs*, pp. 66–67.
12. These ancient and hostile parties, the Yamanî and the Quisî, were political and not religious in character (F. N. Haddad, "Political Parties in Syria and Palestine," *Journal of the Palestine Oriental Society*, 1 [1921], 209–214).
13. Heyd, *Ottoman Documents*, pp. 79, 82, 94.
14. *Raisz*, pp. 302–303 (200).
15. Probably a reference to the execution of Emir Fakhr-Eddin I in 1544 by the Pasha Mustapha of Damascus. This was not instigated by the sultan, but an independent act of the pasha and was based on personal differences. Fakhr-Eddin's son, Korkmaz ibn Maʻn, the father of the more famous Fakhr-Eddin II (1590–1635), desired vengeance for the execution of his father. See Narcisse Bouron, *Les Druzes; histoire du Liban et de la montagne haouranaise* (Paris, 1930), pp. 108–109; and Joseph von Hammer, *Geschichte des Osmanischen Reiches* (Pest, 1829), IV, 139.
16. In 1585 the seizure by the Druzes of a treasure enroute from Cairo to Constantinople led to a disastrous war under the leadership of Ibrahim, the governor of Egypt. In this war, the Whites aided the Ottoman forces and Korkmaz ibn Maʻn was killed. See Hammer, *Geschichte des Osmanischen Reiches*, IV, 137–139; Giovanni T. Minadoi, *Historia della guarra fra Turchi, et Persiani, descritta in Quattro libri* (Rome, 1587), pp. 288–290; (*The History of the Warres betweene the Turkes and the Persians*, trans. Abraham Hartwell [London, 1595], pp. 290–292).
17. *Raisz*, pp. 270–271 (184–185); Krafft, *Denkwürdigkeiten*, pp. 200–201.
18. *Raisz*, p. 271 (185).

CHAPTER X. PILGRIMAGE TO JERUSALEM

1. The trip from Tripoli to Jaffa is described in *Raisz*, pp. 299–311 (203–211). For a brief survey of visits to Palestine by other naturalists, see J. Seide, "Doctors and Naturalists as Pilgrims and Travellers to the Holy Land," *Janus*, 48 (1959), 53–61.

2. These vessels received their name from Karamürsell, a town on the east shore of the Sea of Marmara and noted for its shipbuilding.

3. For similar views of the crusading and Christian origin of the Druzes, see George Sandys (1611) in Purchas, *Hakluytus*, VIII, 239–240; Henry Maundrell (1697) in Pinkerton, *General Collection*, X, 324; and Richard Pococke (1737) in Pinkerton, X, 480. The latter also reports an alternate tradition by which the Druzes were descendants of English crusaders. For Guillaume Postel's interest in the French (Druid) origin of the Druzes, see W. Bouwsma, *Concordia mundi: The Career and Thought of Guillaume Posel, 1510–1581* (Cambridge, Mass., 1957), pp. 143–144.

4. Burj el-Burajineh?

5. Mukaddasi, A Moslem geographer of the tenth century, wrote of those coastal towers in southern Palestine and the use of fire and smoke, in this case to assemble villagers to ransom Moslems from Greek ships (Guy Le Strange, *Palestine*, pp. 23–24).

6. Probably Ras el-'Ain (E. Robinson and E. Smith, *Biblical Researches in Palestine, Mount Sinai and Arabia Petraea* [London, 1841], III, 386–390).

7. Haifa, first taken in 1100 by Godfrey de Bouillon, was later dismantled by Saladin in 1177.

8. The Chateau Pelerin or *Castellum Peregrinorum* was taken from the Templars in 1187.

9. Caesarea of Palestine fell to the crusaders in 1101 and was retaken by the Moslems in 1265.

10. For a discussion of this commonly held view among Christian writers, see Norman Daniel, *Islam and the West: The Making of an Image* (Edinburgh, 1960), pp. 309–313.

11. The trip from Jaffa and the entry into Jerusalem is recorded in *Raisz*, pp. 311–332 (212–219).

12. Josephus, *The Jewish Wars*, ii.18, iii.9.

13. *The Wanderings of Felix Fabri*, trans. A. Stewart (London, 1896), VII, 224. Late in the sixteenth century it was impossible for European pilgrims to find Venetian ships sailing directly to Jaffa (Reinhold Röhricht, *Deutsche Pilgerreisen nach dem Heiligen Lande* [Innsbruck, 1900], p. 39).

14. According to the Turkish Cadastral Register, Christian pilgrims in the sixteenth century were to pay only eight aspers and Jews six aspers as a toll. The *beglerbeg* of Damascus, who had Jerusalem in his jurisdiction, was warned by the sultan in 1552 that "pilgrims must not be forced to pay more taxes than was customary in the past and is laid down in the Cadastral Register. The protection-fee is to be abolished altogether" (Heyd, *Ottoman Documents*, pp. 182–183).

15. Röhricht, *Deutsche Pilgerreisen*, p. 17.

16. Ramle had earlier been important as the capital of the Arab Jund of Filastin (Palestine) (Le Strange, *Palestine*, pp. 303–308). Saladin destroyed the city in 1187.

17. Laurence Aldersey, a Protestant English merchant, was to experience the same difficulties in 1581 (Hakluyt, *Principal Navigations*, III, 78).

18. Luke Wadding, *Annales minorum seu trium ordinum a S. Francisco institutorum ab anno MDLXV usque ad annum MDLXXIV*, 3rd ed. (Florence, 1933), XX, 426. Aldersey reported (1581) that in the monastery his group "lay, & dieted of free cost, we fared reasonable well, the bread and wine was excellent food, the chambers cleane, & all the meat well served in, with clean linnen" (Hakluyt, *Principal Navigations*, III, 78).

19. The area about Jerusalem, and especially the plain directly north of the city and thus just outside the city wall near the monastery, was a favorite burial place for the Moslems of all nations, for according to the Jewish (Joel 3:2) and Moslem traditions this area and the adjacent Valley of Jehoshaphat were to be the site of the resurrection and final judgment (Le Strange, *Palestine*, pp. 218–220). The warning about trespassing in cemeteries was one usually given pilgrims by the Father Guardian (Röhricht, *Deutsche Pilgerreisen*, p. 18).

20. The statements of Michael Servetus concerning the desolation of sixteenth-century Palestine brought severe criticism; see Roland H. Bainton, *Hunted Heretic: The Life and Death of Michael Servetus* (Boston, 1953), pp. 95–96, 184–185.

21. *Raisz*, pp. 333–346 (229–239).

22. The walls of Jerusalem had been destroyed and rebuilt several times in the crusading period. The walls which Rauwolf saw had been rebuilt by order of Sultan Suleiman in 1542.

23. William Biddulph in 1601 counted "thirteene Peeces of Brass-ordinance planted on the wall about the gate" (Purchas, *Hakluytus*, VIII, 300).

24. Although a firman of the sultan, dated September 27, 1552, ordered all monks and other Franks expelled from the vicinity of the mosque, the actual expulsion did not take place until 1561 (Heyd, *Ottoman Documents*, p. 178; George Sandys (1611) in Purchas, *Hakluytus*, VIII, 182 and 213).

25. In 1498, Arnold von Harff bribed a Mameluke and thus viewed the places; *The Pilgrimage of Arnold von Harff, Knight*, ed. and trans. by M. Letts (London, 1946), p. 193. Felix Faber (1483) visited the mosque secretly more than ten times when the gate was accidentally left unlocked by the Moslem custodian (*Wanderings*, VII, 304).

26. *Raisz*, pp. 346–357 (239–256).

27. From the distance, Rauwolf could not see that the mosque was badly in need of repair. Before he died in 1566, Sultan Suleiman had ordered "iron, steel, lead, copper, wood, and first-rate marble" to be collected in Jerusalem for the repair of the two mosques. The repairs were not made because, among other reasons, no artisans and skilled craftsmen were available in Jerusalem. See Heyd, *Ottoman Documents*, pp. 156–157, for the imperial firmans of 1576 and 1579.

28. Ten years earlier, in 1565, the sultan complained to the beg and the cadi of Jerusalem about the poor housekeeping and the filthy condition of the court and ordered remedial action (*ibid.*, pp. 152–154).

29. The intrepid von Harff bribed a Mameluke with four ducats and thus had a good look at the forbidden area and the buildings (*Pilgrimage*, pp. 208–211).

30. The Gate Beautiful of Acts 3:2.10 became the Golden Gate by changing ὡραία into *aurea*.

31. The Justinian edifice was destroyed by Chosroes II in A.D. 614.

32. See also Fabri, *Wanderings*, IX, 118. Von Harff described the vault as "a stable of the Sultan or the Mamelukes, with accomodations for some six hundred horses" (*Pilgrimage*, p. 210).

33. The visit to Mount Bethzeda is described in *Raisz*, pp. 372–375 (258–260).

34. The visit is described in *Raisz*, pp. 375–388 (260–269).

35. Probably few Christians paying the entrance fee knew that some of the money collected was paid as salary to Koran readers. By deliberate corruption of the words "Church of [the Resurrection]" the Turks called the building the "dung-heap" (kiyāma—kumāme) (Heyd, *Ottoman Documents*, pp. 182–183).

36. In 1601 John Sanderson paid nine zechins (sequins), those under the Greek patriarch paid four and one-half, and some less than this (Sanderson, *Travels*, p. 107).

37. *Raisz*, pp. 448–462 (309–315).

38. Rauwolf showed his knowledge of Scriptures and Josephus in pointing out that this could not be the tomb of Absalom (II Sam. 18:17 and Josephus *Antiquities* vii.10). Sanderson (1601) refers to the buildings as a tomb and mentions the throwing of stones (*Travels*, p. 105).

39. Rauwolf, citing Josephus *Antiquities* i.11, and the reports of pilgrims, seems to have accepted the story of the ever renewing pillar of salt that had once been Lot's wife. Von Harff searched unsuccessfully for six days but could not find this pillar (*Pilgrimage*, p. 224).

40. *Raisz*, pp. 448–462 (316–324).

41. Sandys (1611) reported the "absurd" tradition that this tree offered shade to Mary as she traveled between Bethlehem and Jerusalem (Purchas, *Hakluytus*, VIII, 204).

42. Pilgrims throughout the centuries have been consistent in their admiration of this edifice.

43. Felix Faber (1483) saw the figure of Jerome on the manger "distinctly . . . just as though it had been delicately painted" (*Wanderings*, VIII, 561). On the other hand, when the Protestant Sandys was shown the vein, he commented, "But surely they bee the eyes of Faith that must apprehend it; yet present they it in Picture" (Purchas, *Hakluytus*, VIII, 208).

44. The Herodium is today known as the Frank Mountain. See also Henry Maundrell in 1697 and R. Pococke in 1737 (Pinkerton, *Voyages and Travels*, X, 350, 438). These two travelers do not, however, associate these last crusaders with the origin of the Druzes. According to the tradition told them, the crusaders defended the stronghold for 40 years after the fall of Jerusalem.

45. The sceptical Sandys (1611) remarks: "Yet seemeth it strange unto me, that a Chariot should be able to passe those rocky and declining Mountaines, where almost a Horse can hardly keepe footing" (Purchas, *Hakluytus*, VIII, 210).

46. Rauwolf cites the imaginative *Proto-Evangelium of St. James* as his source. This second-century work was introduced to Europe in a Latin translation by

Guillaume Postel. For the story of Elizabeth and Joan see Montague Rhodes James, *The Apocryphal New Testament* (Oxford, 1924), p. 48.

47. Here Rauwolf gives as his source the "book of the Martyrs of the learned and reverend" Ludoviuc Rabus, *Historien der heyligen ausservoelten Gottes Zeugen, Bekennern und Martyrern* (Strassburg, 1552), two parts in one; part three (1555); part four (1556), or *Historien der Martyrer* (Strassburg, 1571).

48. The first Protestant to visit Jerusalem was Daniel Ecklin (1552–53) (Röhricht, *Deutsche Pilgerreisen*, p. 226). In 1581, Salomon Schweigger, a Lutheran pastor, visited the Holy Land and commented that while some came to see the land and people, he came to see the Sepulcher of Christ. His very brief description gives little information and lacks the character of a pilgrimage report (*Gezweyte neue nutzliche und anmuthige Reisz-Beschreibung . . . nach Constantinople und Jerusalem* [Nurnberg, 1664]).

49. Purchas, *Hakluytus*, VIII, 265.

50. *Ibid.*, 186.

51. *Raisz*, p. 449 (316–317). As told to Maundrell in 1697 and to Pococke in 1737, the Virgin Mary was responsible for the miracle (Pinkerton, *Voyages and Travels*, X, 349, 345).

52. Purchas, *Hakluytus*, VIII, 303. For other inconveniences, threats, and pressures for conversion see Röhricht, *Deutsche Pilgerreisen*, pp. 21, 69, nn. 265–267. In 1611 Sandys reported the murder of six Englishmen and the forcible conversion of another by the Franciscans (Purchas, *Hakluytus*, VIII, 213). In 1601, the Greek patriarch of Jerusalem told Sanderson of "foure other Englishmen, not long before seene to enter their [Franciscan] monasterie but never seene to come foorth" (Sanderson, *Travels*, p. 121).

53. In 1611, Sandys and his three companions "for eight dayes entertainment bestowed little lesse amonst them then an hundred Dollers; and yet they told us wee had hardly payed for what wee had eaten. A costly rate for a monastical diet" (Purchas, *Hakluytus*, VIII, 182).

54. Rauwolf's memory or his notes failed him when he recorded that he arrived back in Tripoli on October 1, 1575—or the date of his visit to the Church of the Holy Sepulcher, September 27, is wrong.

55. Tripoli to Augsburg: *Raisz*, pp. 463–480 (327–338).

56. John Locke (1553) reported a water-spout off Jaffa and described the sailors' use of a black-hafted knife and an incantation to destroy it (Hakluyt, *Principal Navigations*, III, 23–24).

CHAPTER XI. ISLAM

1. See Daniel, *Islam and the West*; and R. W. Southern, *Western Views of Islam in the Middle Ages* (Cambridge, Mass., 1962).

2. *Raisz*, pp. 357–358 (247).

3. Gen. 16:10–16; Josephus *Antiquities* i.12.

4. *Raisz*, pp. 356–357 (246).

5. *Ibid.*, pp. 358–364 (247–251).

6. Daniel, *Islam and the West*, pp. 209–210; *Shorter Encyclopedia of Islam*, ed. H. A. R. Gibbs and J. H. Kramers (Ithaca, N.Y., 1953), p. 114.

7. *Raisz*, pp. 364–365 (252–253).

8. *Ibid.*, pp. 366, 407 (253, 285).

9. *Ibid.*, p. 367 (254).

10. *Shorter Encyclopedia of Islam*, pp. 468–469, 578–579; *Raisz*, p. 368 (254–255).

11. *Shorter Encyclopedia of Islam*, p. 156. Rauwolf gave the Turkish names for the minor and major festivals as "Vleibairam" and "Chairbairam" (*Raisz*, pp. 368–369 [255]).

12. *Raisz*, pp. 352, 355 (242–243, 245).

13. *Ibid.*, pp. 353–355 (243–245); 398–401 (278–281); 403–405 (282–283).

14. *Shorter Encyclopedia of Islam*, pp. 579–583; A. S. Tritton, *Islam: Beliefs and Practices* (London, 1951), pp. 89–108.

15. *Raisz*, pp. 143–144 (95–96).

16. *Ibid.*, pp. 147–149 (99–101). Rauwolf also said that the dervishes made much use of opium (p. 126 [84]).

17. Probably Djamaliya, a Persian branch of the Suhrawardiya, a Baghdad order founded in the twelfth century (*Shorter Encyclopedia of Islam*, p. 575).

18. The *Qalandri* or *Kalandariya* who were strongly influenced by Indian rites (*ibid.*, p. 214).

19. *Raisz*, p. 150 (100).

20. *Ibid.*, pp. 150–152 (100–101).

21. *Shorter Encyclopedia of Islam*, pp. 94–95.

22. *Raisz*, pp. 295, 303 (201, 206).

23. *Ibid.*, pp. 295–296 (201–202). The marriage of fathers with their daughters is also reported by Minadoi, *The History of the Warres betweene the Turkes and the Persians*, p. 290. Richard Knolles wrote that the Druzes "make it lawful among them (most unlawfully) to marrie with their own daughters" *The Generall Historie of the Turkes from the first beginning of that Nation to the rising of the Othoman Familie* [London, 1603], p. 982).

24. *Raisz*, pp. 351–352, 357 (242–243, 246).

25. *Ibid.*, p. 352 (243); Daniel, *Islam and the West*, pp. 148–152, *et passim*.

26. *Raisz*, pp. 370–371 (256).

27. *Ibid.*, pp. 371–372 (256–257). The "two misfortunes that are not quite over," refers to Rev. 9:12.

CHAPTER XII. EASTERN CHRISTIANS AND JEWS

1. *Raisz*, pp. 394–398 (275–277), 406–408 (284–285).

2. The Greeks, Syrians, Georgians, Armenians, Nestorians, Jacobites, Abyssinians, Maronites, and Franciscans are described in *Raisz*, pp. 410–431 (288–303).

3. Aldersey (1581) reported five openings, "like the holes of Taverne doores in London" (Hakluyt, *Principal Navigations*, III, 79).

4. For the knighting of Lutherans in the Church, see Röhricht, *Deutsche Pilgerreisen*, pp. 234, 274. Rauwolf was severely criticized by the Jesuit Jakob Gretser for his lack of knowledge of the knighting ceremony (Beckmann, *Literatur*, I, 16).

5. *Raisz*, pp. 405–406 (283).

6. *Ibid.*, pp. 299, 324–327, 35 (204, 222–224, 23).

7. *Ibid.*, pp. 70–71 (46).

8. See Belon, *Les observations,* pp. 322^r–322^v.
9. *Raisz,* pp. 408–410 (285–287).

CHAPTER XIII. GOVERNMENT AND SOCIETY

1. See especially Albert H. Lybyer, *The Government of the Ottoman Empire in the Time of Suleiman the Magnificent* (Cambridge, Mass., 1913).
2. Rauwolf's discussion of Turkish government and customs can be found in *Raisz,* pp. 40–53 (26–35), 77–92 (51–61), 110 (73).
3. On the short duration of governorships and judgeships, see A. Mingara, "List of Turkish Governors and High Judges of Aleppo from the Ottoman Conquest to A.D. 1747," *Bulletin of the John Rylands Library,* 10 (1926), 515–523.
4. Heyd, *Ottoman Documents,* pp. 13–31, *et passim.*
5. Krafft, *Denkwürdigkeiten,* p. 107.
6. Tamerlane captured the sultan.

CHAPTER XIV. LATER LIFE

1. Babinger, "Leonhard Rauwolf," p. 154. The 1613 edition of the *Pharmacopoeia Augustana,* a work originally published by Adolph Occo III, contains a formula, *Conserva Hederae terrestris,* contributed by Rauwolf and recommended as a drug for plague victims (*A Facsimile of the First Edition of the Pharmacopoeia Augustana,* with introductory essay by Theodor Husemann [Madison, Wis., 1927], p. xxx).
2. F. W. T. Hunger, *Clusius,* II, 73.
3. *Ibid.,* 122.
4. *Raisz,* pp. 286–287 (195).
5. Robert Morison, *Plantarum historiae universalis oxoniensis seu Herbarum distributio nova* (Oxford, 1715), II, pt. 3, p. 317.
6. Legré, *La botanique en Provence,* p. 101.
7. J. Camerarius, *Hortus medicus et philsoophicus* (Frankfurt am Main, 1588), p. 67 and fig. 16.
8. Krafft, *Denkwürdigkeiten,* pp. 353–428.
9. Krafft, *Denkwürdigkeiten,* pp. 436–437, 443. On June 29, 1581, Krafft did receive 200 kronen as final settlement from the trustees of the Manlich firm (*ibid.,* p. 444).
10. F. W. T. Hunger, *Clusius,* II, 122–124.
11. Besides the elaborate biography by Hunger, see the brief article by the same author in *Janus,* 31 (1927), 139–51; see also R. P. Niceron, *Mémoires,* XXX (Paris, 1734), 38–48; and *Biographie nationale de Belgique,* V, 383–404.
12. Legré, *La botanique en Provence,* pp. 100–101.
13. Dodoens, see *Biographie nationale de Belgique,* VI, 85–112; the articles by E. C. Van Leersum, E. W. T. Hunger, M. A. van Andel, J. G. de Lint, and M. J. Sirks in *Janus,* 21 (1917), 141–204; and Niceron, *Mémoires,* XXXIV (Paris, 1736), 41–47.
14. *Raisz,* p. 114 (76); R. Dodoens, *Florum, et coronariarum odoratarumque nonnullarum herbarum historia* (Antwerp, 1569), pp. 164–166.
15. *Raisz,* p. 285 (194).

16. On Lobelius, see the article by E. Morren in *Biographie nationale de Belgique*, V, 452–465, and G. Sarton, *Six Wings*, pp. 145–146.

17. Pliny *Natural History* xxv. 4.8, 5.9, 10.29.

18. See Blunt, *The Art of Botanical Illustration*, chaps. i–v; Arber, *Herbals, Their Origins and Evolution;* and Claus Nissen, *Die botanische Buchillustration.*

19. Legré, *La botanique en Provence,* p. 101.

20. Alberto von Haller, *Bibliotheca Botanica* (2 vols.; Zurich, 1771–72), I, 361. Saint-Lager, repeating the error of Melchior Adam, *Vitae germaronum medicorum* (Frankfurt am Main, 1705) p. 110, cited a Latin translation, *Hodoeporicum sive itinerarium Orientis,* as being *très rare* and having an appendix entitled *Histoire des plantes du Lyonnais* ("Histoire des herbiers," p. 71).

21. Camerarius, *Hortus medicus,* p. 19.

22. Johann Bauhin, *Historia plantarum universalis* (3 vols.; Ebroduni, 1650–51), I, i, 150; ii, 209; iii, 278, 279, 348; iv, 422; viii, 198, 200, 219, 220, 221; III, xxvii, 148. Johann Bauhin (1541–1613) entered Montpellier on October 20, 1561, a year later than Rauwolf.

23. E.g., Leonard Plukenet, *Almagestum botanicum* (London, 1696 and 1769) pp. 50, 76, 141; John Ray, "Stirpium Orientalium rariorum catalogi tres" and "Stirpium Aegyptiacorum Catalogus" in *Stirpium Europaearum extra Britannias nascentium sylloge* (London, 1694). Rauwolf's book appeared in the list of 29 authors used in Caspar Bauhin's edition of Mattioli's *Opera* (Basel, 1674).

24. E.g., J. Bauhin, *Historia plantarum universalis,* III, xxvi, 163; Plukenet, *Almagestum,* pp. 16, 140, 337; Plukenet, *Almagestum botanicum Mantissa* (London, 1700 and 1769), p. 91; and Robert Morison, *Plantarum historiae,* I, 610.

25. For a description of the four volumes, see Legré, *La botanique en Provence,* pp. 9–11, 16; and Saint-Lager "L'Histoire des herbiers," pp. 72–73. The latter is in error in his statement that the fourth volume contained 338 plants, that number being the species of plants named by Rauwolf in his travel book and enumerated by Gronovius.

26. See Babinger, "Leonhard Rauwolf," pp. 159–160; and Legré, *La botanique en Provence,* pp. 88–91. There is a fifth volume, mentioned by Beckmann, *Litteratur der älteren Reisebeschreibungen,* I, 11, and M. J. B. E., "Notice sur la vie . . . Rauwolf," p. 103, but this is not Rauwolf's. It is different from the other four (Legré, *La botanique en Provence,* pp. 95–97).

27. Camerarius, *Hortus medicus,* pp. 141, 159.

28. Legré, *La botanique en Provence,* p. 100.

29. Krafft, *Denkwürdigkeiten,* p. 209.

30. Babinger, "Leonhard Rauwolf," p. 159, and Beckmann, *Litteratur der älteren Reisebeschreibungen,* I, 11.

31. Breyn, *Plantarum exoticarum Centuria prima,* p. 82 as cited by Legré, *La botanique en Provence,* p. 90, and Gronovius, *Flora orientalis,* p. v.

32. Morison, *Plantarum historiae,* III, 84, 319, 617; Plukenet, *Almagestum,* pp. 50, 76, 141; John Ray, *Historiae plantarum tomus tertius* (London, 1704), II, 636; *Philosophical letters between the late Mr. Ray and several of his ingenious correspondents, natives and foreigners* (London, 1718), p. 266. See also *Select Remains of the Learned John Ray,* ed. W. Derham (London, 1760), pp. 70–71, for details regarding the decision to make the English translation of Rauwolf's book, which was published in 1693.

33. *Raisz,* p. 346 (238).

34. Wolfgang Zorn, *Augsburg: Geschichte einer deutschen Stadt* (Augsburg, n.d.), p. 202; Paul von Stetten, *Geschichte der Heilige Römische Reichs freyen Stadt Augspurg* (2 vols.; Frankfurt and Leipzig, 1743–58), I, 659–683.

35. Stetten, *Geschichte Augspurg,* I, 705; Ratzel, "L. Rauwolf," p. 92.

36. As Clusius was in Linz on August 28, 1588, he may have visited Rauwolf (Hunger, *Clusius,* I, 168). On June 21, 1593, Rauwolf and four other physicians addressed a request to the authorities that quack Jewish physicians should be forbidden to practice medicine (Julius Schuster, "Leonhart Rauwolff als Kämpfer gegen das Kurpfuschertum 1593," *Sudhoff's Archiv für Geschichte der Medizin,* 14 (1922), 125–126).

37. On the battle of Hatvan, the withdrawal to Waitzen, and the death of Rauwolf, see Hieronymous Ortelius, *Ortelius redivivus et continuatus oder der Ungarischen Kriegs-Emporungen historische beschreibung* (Frankfurt am Main, 1665), pp. 198–200; Jacques Auguste de Thou, *Historiarum sui temporis* (5 vols.; Avrelianae-Colonia Allobrogum, 1626–30), V, 640–641; and Babinger, "Leonhard Rauwolf," pp. 155–157.

INDEX

HARVARD MONOGRAPHS IN THE HISTORY OF SCIENCE